Credit Modelling: Advanced Topics

Credit Modelling: Advanced Topics

by Terry Benzschawel

Published by Risk Books, a Division of Incisive Media Investments Ltd

Incisive Media
Haymarket House
28-29 Haymarket
London SW1Y 4RX
Tel: +44(0) 20 7316 9000
E-mail: books@incisivemedia.com
Sites: www.riskbooks.com
    www.incisivemedia.com

ISBN 978-1-78272-259-5

British Library Cataloguing in Publication Data
A catalogue record for this book is available from the British Library

Publisher: Nick Carver
Commissioning Editor: Sarah Hastings
Managing Editor: Lewis O'Sullivan
Designer: Lisa Ling

Copy-edited by Laurie Donaldson
Typeset by Tricolour Design

Printed and bound in the UK by Berforts Group

Contents

Abbreviations

ABBI	Asian Broad Bond index
ACF	Autocorrelation function
ADF	Augmented Dickey–Fuller
AR	Accuracy ratio
ASF	Available stable funding
AUC	Area under the curve
BAB	Build America Bond
BHC	Bank holding company
BIC	Bayesian information criterion
BIG	Broad Investment Grade
C&R	Cut-and-rotate
CAP	Cumulative accuracy profile
CAPM	Capital asset pricing model
CCA	Contingent claims analysis
CCF	Cross-correlation function
CD	Certificate of deposit
CDF	Cumulative density function
CDO	Collateralised debt obligation
CDS	Credit default swap
CLO	Collateralised loan obligation
Coco	Contingent conversion
CPDC	Citigroup Pension Discount Curve
CPLI	Citi's Pension Liability index
CRP	Constant risk premium
DTM	Decision tree model
ECDF	Empirical cumulative density function

ECR	Euromoney's Country Risk
EDF	Expected default frequency
EMH	Efficient markets hypothesis
ETF	Exchange-traded fund
ETN	Exchange-traded note
FCI	Financial Conditions Index
FDIC	Federal Deposit Insurance Corporation
Garch	Generalised autoregressive conditional heteroscedasticity
GO	General obligation
GTB	Gradient tree boosting
HPD	Hybrid probability of default
HT	Hampden-Turner
IMF	International Monetary Fund
IMM	International Monetary Market
ISM	Institute of Supply Management
LCR	Liquidity coverage ratio
LEI	Leading Economic Index (LEI)
LG	Linear regression
LGD	Loss given default
LOWESS	Locally weighted scatterplot smoothing
MKI	Market-implied
MLE	Maximum likelihood estimation
MSE	Mean squared error
MV	Minimum variance
NAICS	North American Industry Classification System
NAV	Net asset value
NDS	Non-default spread
NSFR	Net stable funding ratio
OCC	Office of the Comptroller of the Currency
OIS	Overnight indexed swap

OLS	Ordinary least squares
OOB	Out-of-bag
OTC	Over-the-counter
P&L	Profit and loss
PCA	Principal components analysis
QE	Quantitative easing
RMS	Root mean squared
ROA	Return on assets
ROC	Receiver operating characteristic
ROE	Return on equity
RSF	Required stable funding
RuBI	Rule-based investment
RV	Recovery value
SIC	Standard industry code
SLRI	Systemic liquidity risk index
SNL	Savings and loans
STLFSI	St. Louis Federal Reserve Bank's Financial Stress Index
TIS	Transition-probability inferred spreads
TMCR	Text Mining Credit Risk
TRUP	Trust-preferred security
VaR	Value-at-risk
VAR	Vector autoregressive
VIX	Volatility Index

About the Author

Terry Benzschawel is a managing director in Citigroup's institutional clients business and heads their Credit Trading Analysis group, which develops and implements quantitative tools and strategies for credit market trading and risk management for clients and in-house applications. His financial career began in 1988, and has centered on modelling the default risk and relative value of cash and synthetic debt of consumers, sovereign nations, municipalities and corporations. Terry worked initially in Chase Manhattan Bank's North American Finance Group, before moving to Citibank's Credit Card Division, and then to Salomon Brothers Fixed Income Arbitrage Group. In 1998, he joined Citi's institutional clients business, alternating between quant and strategy roles while focusing on model-based trading, corporate debt, structured products, credit derivatives and credit portfolio optimisation. In addition to writing the first edition of *Credit Risk Modelling* in 2012, Terry contributed to *Credit Derivatives*, also published by Risk Books.

Preface

This book is my second on the topic of credit modelling. The first being, *Credit Risk Modelling: Facts, Theory and Applications* (also published by Risk Books), which contained research that was conducted over a 14-year period from 1998 to 2012. That initial volume reflected my personal journey from laboratory scientist to financial modeller, capturing the process of the development of my understanding of credit risk up to that time. The present work, consisting of research conducted since 2012, describes applications and observations made possible by many of the insights gained from those initial studies. The volume and quality of the analysis in this book reflects the fact that, since 2012, I have had the opportunity to work with many talented and productive individuals both in Citi's Institutional Clients Group and at several major universities. The contributions of those co-workers, as described in the acknowledgments, are critical to the research reported in this book.

Although this book builds upon the framework presented in my earlier one, it contains little duplication of material. I have written the book to be self-contained and, like its predecessor, to appeal to a wide audience. Some of the chapters, such as the initial ones on credit models, are designed for those wishing to become acquainted with the methods used for estimating default probabilities and to provide my perspective on the future of credit modelling. The later chapters on the credit risk premium and on beating credit indexes should appeal to readers with a range of credit market experience. The chapters towards the end of this book on hedging the credit risk premium, simulation methods, and liquidity are designed to appeal to more experienced practitioners. Additional to the chapters, I have also provided extensive references for those individuals interested in more detailed study.

The book begins with a discussion of the history of credit modelling leading up to the various types of default models that are in use today. That discussion is presented from a practitioner's viewpoint, emphasising the advantages and disadvantages of each model. This is followed by Chapter 2 with a discussion of unsolved problems in credit modelling, and the different types of techniques that might prove useful for their solution. These include examples that build upon traditional methods along with more novel approaches afforded by expert systems and "big data" techniques. The next two chapters deal with models to predict market-wide annual default rates and individual firm recovery values in default, respectively. As regards predicting default rates, it is demonstrated that knowledge of expected defaults and current market conditions provides valuable information regarding subsequent market moves. Chapter 4 presents determinants of firms' recovery values in default and the development of a model to capture those effects. Although default models abound, there have been very few models proposed for recovery value in default and Chapter 4 is an attempt to help fill this void.

Chapters 5–7 deal with the credit risk premium. In those sections, I describe the relationship between the yield necessary to account for loss of cash flows in default and the larger remainder of the yield spread to Treasuries, which I call the risk premium. Chapter 5 describes in detail the theory and supporting results that underlie the credit risk premium in the US corporate bond market, whereas Chapters 6 and 7 apply those methods to credit default swaps (CDS) and municipal bonds, respectively. In addition, those chapters introduce the concept of "embedded leverage" in financial assets. I demonstrate how to measure the yield value of embedded leverage in corporate bond, CDS, and municipal bond markets.

The remainder of the book presents a variety of applications beginning with Chapter 8 on predicting bank defaults. That chapter presents an adaptive walk-forward model for predicting bank defaults at one- to five-year horizons. Of particular interest is the analysis of variables that are important for predicting bank defaults as they vary with time horizon. Chapter 9, on beating credit benchmarks echoes work from my earlier book, but presents updated performance analysis of the cut-and-rotate strategy since 2012, as well as its application to a number of other markets.

Chapter 10, on hedging the credit risk premium, builds on the discussions from Chapters 5-7. In this chapter, I show how CDS index products can be used to hedge corporate bonds' exposures to changes in the credit risk premium. Furthermore, it demonstrates how one might construct portfolios that track corporate bond returns using synthetic instruments. The next chapter on managing pension fund liabilities builds on Chapters 9 and 11. In this chapter, I show that one can outperform pension liability benchmarks using the cut-and-rotate strategy and that one can create synthetic portfolios to match pension fund liabilities based on the credit risk premium.

Chapter 12 presents a method for estimating value-at-risk (VaR) in corporate bond portfolios using simulation methods. This application provides an alternative to the currently popular, copula model. That simulation method, while computationally intensive, simulates future patterns of default rates, ratings transitions and credit spreads. It represented the efforts of many individuals over several years.

The final chapter in the book deals with systemic liquidity risk. It begins with a description of illiquidity spirals such as occurred in the credit crisis of 2007-08. That is followed by a discussion of Basel III standardised measures of liquidity; the liquidity coverage ratio (LCR) and net stable funding ratio (NSFR). The chapter proceeds to discuss systemic liquidity and bank exposure during the crisis and the effectiveness of the Basel III requirements for preventing subsequent liquidity crises. Next, proposed measures of liquidity are presented. These include the Systemic Liquidity Risk Index (SLRI) and the Market Liquidity Index (CLX), along with a discussion of their advantages and disadvantages. The final section of the chapter describes an early warning system based on the CLX.

I thank you for purchasing this book and I hope that the intellectual rewards prove adequate compensation for your time and expense.

Terry Benzschawel
December 2016

Acknowledgements

This second book on credit modelling presents original research generated over several years. During that time, I had the privilege of working with many talented individuals, both at my employers and at a number of major universities. Although many of the contributions by my collaborators can be inferred from their listings in the references section at the end of the book, I make them explicit here.

First, I wish to express special thanks to Yong Su, whose contributions can be found throughout this book, particularly in Chapters 3, 4, 5, 6, 9 and 12. Special thanks also go to Andrew Assing, Jiacui Li, Cedric Lommaert and Xing Xin for their work on the credit risk premium and bank models. Other colleagues whose work has contributed to the projects in this book are:

Martin Bernstein	Chen-Yen Lee	Glen McDermott
Alper Corlu	Jacqueline Linden	Jure Skarbot
Eliot Deutsch	Jia Liu	Lei Wang
Brent Hawker	Cedric Lommaert	Tuohua Wu
Alexei Kroujiline	Lorenzo Lorilla	Wanling Xu

I also wish to add my thanks to students in the Masters of Financial Engineering programmes at the Universities of California at Berkeley and Los Angeles, and their respective programme heads, Linda Kreitzman and Sandra Buchan. For many years, I have worked with over a dozen groups of students from those programmes, and several of the projects have contributed to results presented in this book. Those contributions and their participants are:

❑ Chapter 7: Risk and relative value in the municipal bond market – Wontai Cho, Jaewoo Jung, Bing Leng, Preeda Ratanasoponchai and Maoqi Wang.
❑ Chapter 9: Model for sovereign default and relative value –

Saran Ananth, Dahai Cao, Wing Sum Cheng, Weijian Chuah, George Diaconu, Mayank Gupta, Rahul Gupta, Darren Ho, Amarnath Jha, Seung Ju Lee, Hang Li, Paolo Miranda, Kaname Nakagawa, Jorge Silva, Arsheep Singh, Abay Srivastava, Li Sun and Jue Wang.

❏ Chapter 11: Equity and debt markets – Brad Lookabaugh, Ugo Passaniti, Jean Santini and William Summer.
❏ Chapter 13: Simulating combined spread and default moves – Mingye Chen, Zhuo Chen, Geng Cheng, Paul Ponmattam, Sahil Puri, Biswaranjan Sahu, Jae-Sang Shim, Heng Su, Dishen Wang and Luping Yang.

As in my previous book on credit modelling, I cannot overemphasise my gratitude to Moody's Investors Service and Standard & Poor's. Those firms have served as collectors and repositories for nearly a century of data on credit ratings, defaults and recovery values. Those data provide the empirical basis for our understanding of credit risk. Furthermore, the agencies generously share their data with the public. In a similar vein, I am grateful to Salomon Brothers, then Salomon Smith-Barney, and ultimately Citigroup, my employers over the past 26 years, for collecting and preserving the unique set of monthly data on credit spreads from all major issuers since 1985. Without access to those, and other supporting data, much of the work in this book would not have been possible. Furthermore, those data have provided the empirical basis for many of the insights that have shaped my work over the years. I also thank the many supervisors and managers I have had for their patience in allowing me to pursue problems whose value was only realisable in the longer term: a rare privilege in the world of securities trading, where the focus tends to be on the short term.

As any author knows, the demands of writing a technical book require the patience and support of those persons closest to us. Thus, I thank my partner, Halle Becker, and Maya Henkin for their love and support throughout this project, along with Charlotte for the joy that they add to my life on a daily basis.

Finally, I would like to thank Risk Books for the opportunity to publish this work and, in particular, to Sarah Hastings and Lewis O'Sullivan for editorial and production assistance.

Part I

HISTORY AND MAJOR THEMES

Credit Models Past and Present

The extension of credit is a display of faith in the future. It involves the exchange of a liquid asset (such as cash) for a documented promise of repayment at a later date. Instruments of credit typically consist of loans, bonds, charge account balances with commercial firms and, latterly, credit default swaps (CDS) and other more complicated financial obligations.[1] A feature of credit instruments is that their expected return profiles are negatively skewed, owing mainly to potential losses from default. That is, one takes on the risk of a low likelihood of a large loss for a more likely steady stream of smaller returns. This chapter will present an historical description of methods developed to analyse the default risk of credit obligors. This first chapter will trace the origins of credit analysis from the fundamental analysis of government bond risk up to the popular structural and risk-neutral default models. The second chapter will discuss some existing and future directions for default modelling, including expert systems and "big data" techniques. Although most historically successful forms of credit analysis continue to play various roles in financial markets, modern requirements for daily quantitative estimates of default probabilities for credit trading and risk management have fuelled the demand by broker–dealers and investment firms for mathematical-based risk-neutral and structural credit models.

Having been involved in the development and application of quantitative methods for estimating credit risk for over two decades, I have witnessed the evolution of modelling of default risk moving from fundamental analysis, agency ratings and regression-based models to become dominated by structural and reduced form models in their various forms. I have also seen the evaluation of default model accuracy change from anecdotal descriptions of predictive successes to quantitative measures using methods derived from statistical decision theory. In that regard, it is important to note that default prediction is a statistical problem: one rarely knows with certainty if an obligor will default prior to the actual non-payment of an obligation. Given the inherent uncertainty in the default process, it appears that after several decades of refinements, modern modelling approaches are reaching limits in their abilities to accurately predict default at time horizons of a year or more.[2] That fact, along with the scarcity of useful frameworks for estimating the default risk of sovereign nations, municipalities, financial firms and private companies, is fuelling demand for new classes of credit models. We are beginning to see the development and deployment of "expert consensus" and "big data" methods to fill that demand, and examples of such approaches will be described in Chapter 2.

Much of the discussion in this book will concern the application of quantitative techniques for estimating credit risk and relative value. However, it is important to acknowledge that no existing credit model can serve as an adequate substitute for human analysis in making investment decisions. In fact, as I often suggest to clients, a fundamental evaluation of a credit investment is the last step in the credit vetting process, a process that should also involve analysis using quantitative techniques. That view is captured by a couple of quotations that express my perspective on quantitative approaches to credit modelling (and modelling in general): "All models are wrong, some models are useful" (Box, 1976); and "In the land of the blind, the one-eyed man is king" (Erasmus, 1500). The essence of these quotes is that no model is adequate to capture the complexity of reality, but being ahead of the competition can be profitable. That perspective has served me well in the development and applications of credit models to problems in credit risk and valuation.

ORIGINS OF THE BOND MARKET AND EARLY CREDIT ANALYSIS

The development of credit analysis is closely linked to the evolution of financial markets. The creation of modern financial assets is generally attributed to the Dutch who, in 1609, invented common stock to finance the Dutch East India Company. The Dutch also established the first version of a central bank at that time (Neal, 1990). By the 1600s, the Dutch already had a government bond market for decades, and soon thereafter had all the major components of a modern financial system. In 1688, the British invited William of Orange, the Dutch leader, to be their king and he brought experienced Dutch financiers to England. The Bank of England was subsequently established in 1694, and the UK went on to have the first industrial revolution and to lead the world economy in the 18th and 19th centuries (Dickson, 1967).

A century later, Alexander Hamilton, the first US Secretary of the Treasury (1789–95), worked to establish a modern financial system modelled on the Dutch, UK and French precedents. Thus, by 1795 the US, essentially a bankrupt country before 1789, had strong public finances, a stable dollar, a banking system, a central bank, and bond and stock markets in several cities. Just as the British had succeeded the Dutch in economic and financial leadership, within a century the US went on to displace the UK as the world's pre-eminent national economy.

For much of the four century history of modern capital markets there were few questions regarding credit quality as most bond investing was in the public or sovereign debt of nations, and governments and investors trusted the willingness and ability of countries and municipalities to honour their commitments. In fact, up until the 19th century, only the Dutch, the UK and the US – countries with representative governments – issued significant amounts of sovereign debt.

The development of the railroads in the 1800s fuelled the demand for capital in the US. However, even before the advent of the railroads in the 1820s, the US had developed the competitive corporation to a greater extent than any other country. Early on, this demand for capital could be met with bank credit and stock issues. However, after 1850 railroad corporations grew larger and expanded into territories where obtaining financing from local banks and investors proved difficult. The solution to that problem was the development of a huge market, both domestic and international, for the bonded debt of US railroad corporations. Along with this came the demand for information on the investment quality of those firms.

Figure 1.1 Precursors to the bond rating agency that represents a fusion of functions performed by these institutions prior to the 1900s

Credit reporting agencies	Financial press	Investment bankers
• Letters of recommendation from a known source sufficed until the 1830s	• Rail roads were America's first big business	• Bankers who underwrote the deals put their reputations (and capital) on the line in all deals
• Lewis Tappan founded the Mercantile Agency in 1841 that sold information to subscribers (became Dunn & Bradstreet in 1859)-by 1900, over one million subscribers	• The *American Railroad Journal* began In 1832 and Henry Poor became its editor In 1849	• The banker was an insider, insisting that companies disclose relevant information, even insisting on being on their boards of directors
• John Bradstreet founded a similar firm in Cincinnati and published the first commercial rating book in 1851	• After the Civil War, Poor and his son published *Poor's Manual of the Railroads of the US*, the recognised authority on rail roads	• International contacts for capital depended on the bankers reputation (eg, JP Morgan, Kuhn Loeb & Co, Goldman Sachs)
• Merged with Dunn in 1933 to become Dunn & Bradstreet and acquired by Moody's in 1962	• The Poor company entered the rating business in 1915 and merged with Standard Statistics In 1941 to form Standard & Poor's (S&P), later acquired by McGraw Hill publishers	• Resentment rose over bankers access to inside information, rather than banker dominance of corporations

The credit rating agency

Although sovereign debt had been trading for centuries, it was not until 1909 that John Moody devised a scale for rating the credit quality of risky obligors, in this case the railroads. By that time, the railroad bond market was a half-century old and the sovereign bond market had been operating for centuries. Thus, both the sovereign and corporate bond markets were able to operate without the benefit of agency ratings. How was this possible? Sylla (2002) argues that three important US developments combined to lead to the emergence of the bond rating agency innovated by Moody. These are the credit reporting (but not rating) agency, the specialised financial press and the investment banker. The development of each of these institutions is summarised in Figure 1.1. The agency started by Moody in 1909 represents a fusion of the function of those three institutions that preceded it.

CREDIT, CREDIT RISK, AND CREDIT MODELS

Model-based approaches for estimating credit risk and relative value share some common, if implicit, assumptions and also have some common objectives. First, it is assumed that useful estimates of obligors' likelihoods of default can be derived from information in financial statements, analysts' reports, news services and market prices. In addition, that usefulness implies that changes in agency credit ratings tend to lag market perceptions of changing credit quality, thereby fuelling demand for alternative approaches to estimating default risk. Some models imply further that idiosyncratic changes in credit quality from equity-based models and expert systems can often predict moves in bond yields. Finally, default probabilities, in conjunction with estimates of recovery values in default, and bond prices and volatilities are useful determinants of the "fair values" of risky bonds.[3]

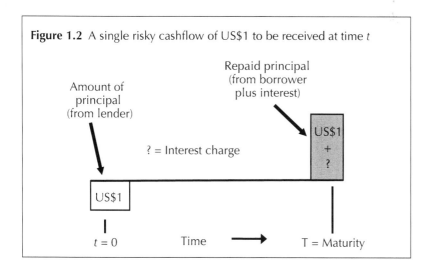

Figure 1.2 A single risky cashflow of US$1 to be received at time *t*

Amount of principal (from lender)

Repaid principal (from borrower plus interest)

US$1 + ?

? = Interest charge

US$1

t = 0   Time   T = Maturity

Let us define credit as the provision of access to liquid assets today in return for a promise of repayment in the future. Typically, credit is thought of as the debt that one party owes another. In a credit transaction there is usually a lender, the provider of credit, and the borrower, also called the obligor or debtor. Most common instruments of credit, particularly with maturities greater than one year, are coupon-bearing instruments called bonds and loans. The simplest debt instrument is one without coupons, called a zero-coupon or discount bond. A diagram of the cashflows from the lender to the borrower of a zero-coupon bond appears in Figure 1.2. The fundamental question in credit analysis is "How much should an investor charge the obligor for lending money to be repaid at a future date?"

Credit risk involves several types of risk, but what separates credit risk from interest rate risk is the potential that an obligor may not make the coupon payments and may fail to pay back the principal. The main risk thought to be associated with credit is default risk.[4] When such a credit event occurs, the due date for repayment of principal is usually accelerated to the date of non-payment and all future coupons are forfeited.[5] The lender has a claim on the borrower's assets for the principal and accrued interest up to that time. Although there is room for legal disagreement about what constitutes default on a financial asset, there is general agreement that it involves several types of credit event (Moody's, 2010). These are:

❏ a missed, delayed payment of interest and/or principal;
❏ bankruptcy, administration, legal receivership or other legal block to the timely payment of interest and/or principal; or
❏ a distressed exchange whereby the issuer offers debt holders a security that amounts to a diminished financial obligation, and the exchange has the apparent purpose of helping the borrower avoid default.

In default, lenders rarely receive the full value of principal and interest, and those claims have levels of priority depending on whether the debt is secured, senior or subordinated.[6] In addition, the recovery value, or more specifically the loss given default (LGD) also depends on the firm's industry sector, economic conditions, geography and other factors.[7] Finally, there is market risk associated with credit investments owing to the fact that the value of a credit instrument may change prior to maturity. Market risk results from changes in interest rates, changes in market liquidity and the credit risk premium. The credit risk premium, which will be described in detail in subsequent chapters, reflects interplay between the willingness of lenders to lend and borrowers' demands for credit.

HISTORICAL DEFAULT RATES AND RECOVERY VALUES

Credit rating agencies have been tracking corporate defaults for nearly a century, and have also documented cumulative default rates over time. To provide a historical perspective on the cyclicality of corporate defaults, Figure 1.3 displays average annual default rates since 1920 for firms with speculative grade ratings, (ie, rated below Baa3; see Table 1.1 for the credit rating scale) as reported by Moody's (Emery *et al*, 2008; Moody's, 2013). The table reveals that default rates are far from uniform, displaying large spikes and clusters in times of economic stress and periods of little or no default. Also, rarely is a very high default year followed by a very low one; default rates tend to change gradually. Finally, the figure shows that we have emerged from another cycle of high default rates.

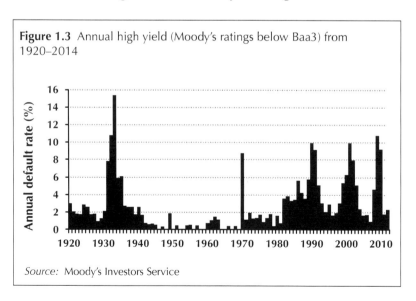

Figure 1.3 Annual high yield (Moody's ratings below Baa3) from 1920–2014

Source: Moody's Investors Service

Other aspects of annual default rates are worth noting, as illustrated by the frequency distribution of annual default rates presented in Figure 1.4. First, the distribution of default rates is not normally distributed (ie, not Gaussian): it is highly skewed toward higher values. Although the average annual default rate is 2.8%, rates near that value occur only in about 10% of the years. In fact, for most years the annual high-yield default rate is between 0% and 1%. Historical annual default rates for individual ratings categories (not shown) are also skewed. Thus, although one often hears reference to average historical default rates, historical averages are clearly not appropriate measures of their central tendency.

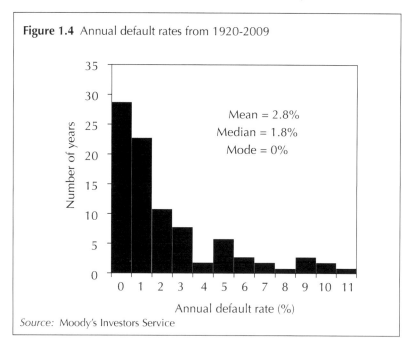

Figure 1.4 Annual default rates from 1920-2009

Mean = 2.8%
Median = 1.8%
Mode = 0%

Source: Moody's Investors Service

Although measuring and modelling the default rates on risky debt has a long history, the amount recovered in default has received much less attention. This is surprising in that the recovery value in default plays an equal part with default probability in losses from default on risky assets. Since the expected loss given default, EL, depends on both default and recovery. That is:

$$EL = PD * (1 - RV)$$

(1.1)

where *PD* is the probability of default and *RV* is the recovery value in default. Despite the fact that expected loss depends on both recovery value and default probability, when estimating portfolio losses, managers commonly will assign *PDs* based on a model, but assume a constant *RV*. The major credit rating agencies have already started to report statistics on recovery values in default, with subsequent research increasing greatly our understanding of recovery value and our ability to construct predictive models.[8]

The earliest reported calculations of historical bond prices just after default averaged roughly 40% of face value (Hickman, 1958; Altman and Nammacher, 1984; Altman and Kishore, 1996). Consequently, those early studies provide the basis for the oft-used constant value of 40% recovery of face value by market practitioners. However, the top panel of Figure 1.5 reveals the wide range of recovery values observed for defaulted firms. Moreover, the shape of the distribution of recovery rates is highly skewed, and even bimodal. Also, it appears that neither the mean recovery rate of 40% nor the median of 34.5% are very good predictors of the recovery rate for any single case, and that the most common amount recovered in default is about 20%.

Figure 1.6 shows that the amount recovered in default depends on other factors as well. These include the seniority of the debt in the firm's capital structure, its industry sector and agency rating prior to default. The interdependencies of all these factors and the relative lack of historical data on recoveries have made it difficult to generate accurate estimates of recovery value in default. Thus, despite the crucial role of recovery value on expected losses in default, very few well-tested models of recovery value have been proposed.[9] The issues regarding recovery value are presented herein to illustrate an existing problem for which newer types of model, such as crowd sourcing and big data, offer potential for greatly improving our ability to accurately estimate expected losses on credit portfolios.

Figure 1.5 Top: frequency distribution of recovery rates for bonds and loans, Moody's (1970–2003); middle: annual default rates (bars) and recovery rates (circles; inverted axis); bottom: scatterplot of annual recoveries versus defaults

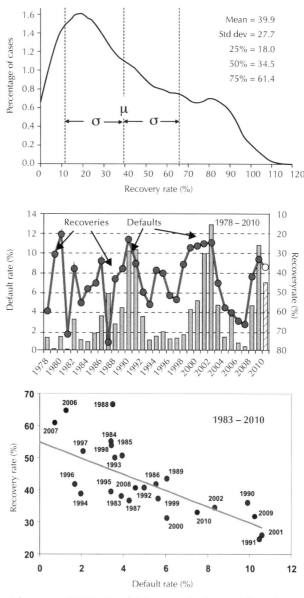

Source: Schuermann (2005); Moody's Investors Service; and the author

Figure 1.6 Dependence of recovery value in default on seniority (top), industry sector (middle) and agency rating prior to default (bottom)

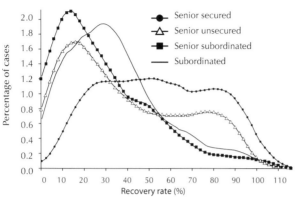

Sector name	SIC code (# digit)	SIC code (2 digit)	Average (%)	Std. dev. (%)	Count
Agriculture / mining	0199-1499	01-14	53	26	107
Construction	1500-1799	15-17	47	27	110
Food / tobacco / clothing	2000-2299	20-22	53	31	106
Clothes / wood / furniture	2300-2599	23-25	43	27	65
Paper / printing	2600-2799	26-27	38	27	150
Chemicals / Rubber	2800-3099	28-30	44	30	136
Leather /stone / metal	3100-3499	31-34	44	30	156
Machinery / electronics	3500-3699	35-36	45	30	134
Transportation equipment	3700-3799	37	40	31	127
Manufacturing (misc.)	3800-3999	38-39	40	29	55
Land transportation	4000-4499	40-44	44	22	54
Transport / pipelines (other)	4500-4799	45-47	33	19	224
Communications	4800-4899	48	37	30	371
Utilities	4900-4999	49	58	33	229
Wholesale trade	5000-5199	50-51	42	33	89
Retail trade	5200-5999	52-59	49	29	266
Depository financial	6000-6099	60	33	30	144
Nondepository financial	6100-6199	61	63	27	150
Securities / broker dealer	6200-6299	62	9	2	294
Insurance / real estate	9600-6799	63-67	39	29	149
Travel / entertainment services	7000-7999	70-79	53	29	211
Services (misc.)	8000-8799	80-87	62	22	431

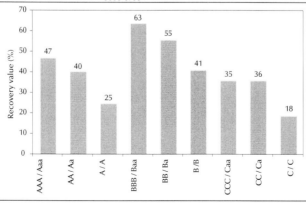

CREDIT RISK MODELS

Appendix 1.1 presents a graphical summary of the classes of credit risk models developed prior to 2010, including fundamental analysis, agency ratings and financial ratios. These also include models, such as Altman's (1968) Z-score and other statistical models, Merton-type structural models as developed by Moody's/KMV (Kealhofer and Kurbat, 2001), risk-neutral models (Hull and White, 1995) and the Sobehart–Keenan statistical/structural (hybrid) model (Sobehart and Keenan (2002, 2003).

Origins: Fundamental analysis, agency ratings and financial ratios

In this first section, however, we consider the origins of quantitative credit analysis as embodied in fundamental analysis, including agency ratings, and the initial applications of financial ratios to default risk.

Fundamental credit analysis

Fundamental credit analysts examine in detail a firm's balance sheet and income statement, and evaluate its management, position within its industry, and future prospects. On that basis, they form opinions regarding whether a firm's credit is improving, deteriorating or stable, and possibly if its debt is rich, cheap or priced fairly. For example, financial analysts typically consider a firm's past records of:

❏ assets;
❏ earnings;
❏ sales;
❏ products;
❏ management; and
❏ market positioning.

From that, they predict future trends in those indicators and their implications for firms' success or failure. They may even make qualitative judgements about a firm's default risk relative to other firms, and whether or not that firm's assets are fairly priced.

Fundamental analysis is a well-established and critical aspect of investment strategy, and continues to be so. However, despite its usefulness, fundamental analysis has many limitations. Table 1.1 lists some advantages and disadvantages of fundamental credit analysis. An advantage of fundamental analysis is that it can provide an in-depth monitoring of a firm's activities as well as a detailed assessment of its management. Analysts are also forward-looking in that they attempt to project the prospects of the firm in the context of its industry and the economic environment. Fundamental analysis is particularly useful for avoiding credit spread "blow-ups" and for early identification of firms' financial problems. Furthermore, analysts can identify potential event risk, such as leveraged buy-outs, equity buy-backs and mergers, events that are often challenging for model-based approaches.

Table 1.1 Advantages and limitations of fundamental analysis

Advantages	Disadvantages
❑ Close and in-depth monitoring of firm's activities	❑ Only single analyst's opinion
	❑ Difficult to quantify
❑ Useful for avoiding "blow-ups" and defaults	❑ Intermittent, incomplete and inconsistent coverage of universe of firms
❑ Can identify potential "event risk" (LBO, equity buybacks, etc)	❑ Don't always respond to market movements and events
❑ Forward-looking	❑ Analysts are expensive

Nevertheless, different analysts' views on a firm's prospects can often diverge. Also, even at the same advisory company, a new analyst's opinion of a given firm's prospects may differ from that of their predecessor. In particular, analysts' views can be difficult to quantify; they rarely specify a probability of default or a spread value of richness or cheapness, tending to limit their analyses to qualitative assessments. Fundamental analysts also do not provide an opinion every day, so it is not always clear that one has their latest opinion and an analyst may not respond in a timely way to market moves or events. Also, coverage of a firm may be intermittent – an analyst may leave and coverage of a firm or industry may be suspended. In fact, there is necessarily incomplete coverage of the large number of firms issuing debt, and tracking an analyst's performance can be difficult. Finally, analysts are "expensive", particularly relative to model-based approaches.

The rating agencies
Credit agencies began analysing firm default risk in the 19th century. As listed in Figure 1.1, Lewis Tappan founded the Mercantile Agency in 1941 and the forerunner of Dunn & Bradstreet was organised in Cincinnati, Ohio, in 1849 to provide investors with independent credit investigations based on fundamental analysis. At that time, information of firms' credit quality was particularly scarce, and firms found that they could issue debt more cheaply if their firms had been reviewed by a respected credit agency. Still, it was not until 1909 that John Moody developed the credit rating scale, which he first applied to characterise the relative riskiness of railroad bonds (see Figure 1.7).

Moody's credit rating scale appears along with those of its major competitor, Standard & Poor's (S&P), in Figure 1.8.[10] The major features of the rating scales are well-known: credits rated AAA/Aaa by S&P/Moody's are of the highest quality, and bonds in all categories down through BBB–/Baa3 are called "investment grade" as they have very little near-term risk of default. Typically, investors in investment-grade bonds are concerned with either liability management or collecting steady income from coupons, while monitoring their exposure to mark-to-market risk from changes in credit spreads. Bonds rated below BBB–/Baa3 are called "speculative grade" or "high-yield" bonds. High-yield bonds are typically held in different investment funds than investment-grade bonds, and traded by different individuals within the same investment firms. Also, high-yield bond investors typically seek higher yields, speculating on price appreciation and on decreases in firms' default risk over time.

Figure 1.7 John Moody in 1956; he invented the credit rating scale in 1909

Source: The New York Times (Redux Photos)

Bonds' initial agency credit ratings appear to order well their long-term default risk. For example, Figure 1.8 shows cumulative default rates by year as a function of initial agency rating on linear and logarithmic default axes. The graphs indicate clearly that bonds in each lower rating category (see Table 1.2 for the ordering) have subsequently higher cumulative default rates across the entire 30-year time period. Also, the logarithmic plot shows a very regular vertical spacing of cumulative default curves by rating category. Note, in Figure 1.8 that after about seven to ten years, curves for all rating categories are parallel. That is, marginal default rates settle in, but at rates that are higher for each successively lower-rated category.

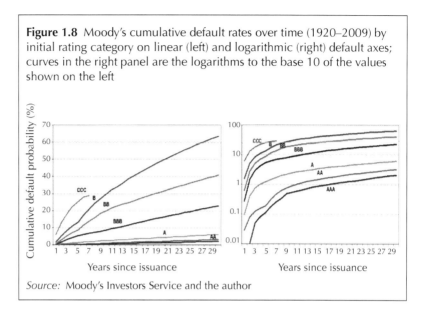

Figure 1.8 Moody's cumulative default rates over time (1920–2009) by initial rating category on linear (left) and logarithmic (right) default axes; curves in the right panel are the logarithms to the base 10 of the values shown on the left

Source: Moody's Investors Service and the author

The pattern of yield spreads by maturity for each agency rating category also indicates, at least on average, that there is general agreement between agency ratings and investors' perceptions of credit risk. To demonstrate this, consider first the top left panel of Figure 1.9, which displays a typical bond with promised annual coupons, c, paid at semi-annual intervals and a bullet payment at maturity. The equation at the lower left in Figure 1.9 specifies how the yield on a bond is determined as the single annual discount rate, y, which serves to equate the sum of the discounted cash-flows to the current market price. That equation can be used to derive the curves in the plot at the right in Figure 1.9. That graph displays, for each letter rating category, average yield curves as a function of maturity fit to US Treasury bonds and corporate bonds in Citi's Broad Investment Grade (BIG) and High Yield indexes.[11] The lowest yields are for US Treasury bonds (UST), which serve as a benchmark for comparison with the riskier corporate bonds, whose average yield curves are higher for all rating categories and at all maturities. In particular, as one moves down the credit quality scale (ie, as agency ratings get lower), magnitudes of yields at each maturity are monotonically related to credit risk: the lower the agency rating the higher the yield. Finally, note that for almost all risk categories, the yield curves are upward sloping: they increase with maturity. However, for the riskiest bonds (ie, the ones rated triple-C) the curve is inverted, with yields for bonds having short maturities higher than longer maturity ones. In fact, this pattern, while not always present, is typical and generally assumed to indicate that the marginal risk of high-default obligors is perceived to decrease over time.[12]

Figure 1.9 Left: cashflows from a typical semi-annual fixed coupon bond and the formula for its yield; right: par yield curves by agency credit rating

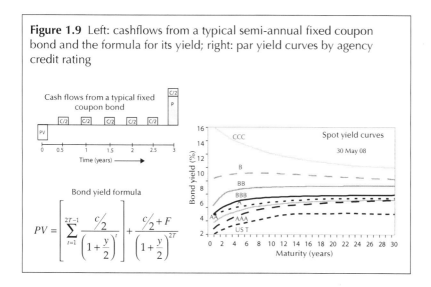

The credit risk of a bond is typically quoted in terms of yield spread – that is, the increment in yield over the yield of a Treasury bond of similar maturity (or the term structure of credit spreads) required to match the market price of a bond with a given coupon. The bond's spread serves to isolate the price of its credit risk and is typically quoted in basis points (where 1bp is $1/100$ of 1%) of yield increment relative to Treasuries (or some other reference, such as the London Interbank Borrowing Rate, Libor). The left panel of Figure 1.10 illustrates the credit spreads of hypothetical triple-A corporate bonds of various maturities as the differences in yields between those bonds and US Treasuries of similar maturities. The concept of a credit spread has become an important measure for describing the relative riskiness of bonds.

Table 1.2 Credit rating scales from Standard & Poor's and Moody's; credit quality descriptions, average yield spreads to Treasuries, and market segmentation are also shown

Number code	S&P / Fitch	Moody's	Yield book	From	To	Avg	Interpretation	Class
0			a4	0	0	0	Risk-free	Investment grade
1	AAA	Aaa	a3	0	0.03	0.03	Highest quality	
2	AA+	Aa1	a2+	0.03	0.05	0.04	High quality	
3	AA	Aa2	a2	0.05	0.06	0.06		
4	AA-	Aa3	a2-	0.06	0.08	0.07		
5	A+	A1	a1+	0.08	0.10	0.09	Strong payment capacity	
6	A	A2	a1	0.10	0.16	0.13		
7	A-	A3	a1-	0.16	0.23	0.19		
8	BBB+	Baa1	b3+	0.23	0.37	0.28	Adequate payment capacity	
9	BBB	Baa2	b3	0.37	0.61	0.50		
10	BBB-	Baa3	b3-	0.61	0.84	0.73		
11	BB+	Ba1	b2-	0.84	1.1	0.96	Likely to fulfill obligations; ongoing uncertainty	High yield
12	BB	Ba2	b2	1.1	1.3	1.2		
13	BB-	Ba3	b2-	1.3	1.6	1.4		
14	B+	B1	b1+	1.6	2.1	1.8	High risk obligations	
15	B	B2	b1	2.1	2.8	2.4		
16	B-	B3	b1+	2.8	3.4	3.2		
17	CCC+		c3+	3.4	4.0	3.7	Current vulnerability to default	
18	CCC	Caa	c3	4.0	6.3	4.2		
19	CCC-		c3-	6.3	14	9.4		
20	CC	Ca	c2	14	31	21	In bankruptcy or default, or exhibits other shortcomings	Distress
21	C	C	c1	31	67	45		
22	D	D	d	67	100	100		

Figure 1.10 Top: yield curves for US Treasuries and for single-A corporate bonds; middle: formula for calculating yield spreads to Treasuries; bottom: yield spreads to Treasuries by rating

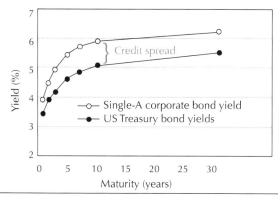

The present value, PV, of a bond with maturity, T for:

US Treasuries
$$PV = \left[\sum_{t=1}^{2T-1} \frac{C/2}{\left(1 + \frac{r_t}{2}\right)^t} \right] + \frac{C/2 + 100}{\left(1 + \frac{r_T}{2}\right)^{2T}}$$

Corporates
$$PV = \left[\sum_{t=1}^{2T-1} \frac{C/2}{\left(1 + \frac{r_t + s}{2}\right)^t} \right] + \frac{C/2 + 100}{\left(1 + \frac{r_T + s}{2}\right)^{2T}}$$

Credit spread

Where PV is the price of bond with coupons (c), r_T is the term structure of US Treasury spot yields at 0.5 intervals, and s is the yield spread of the bond to US Treasuries.

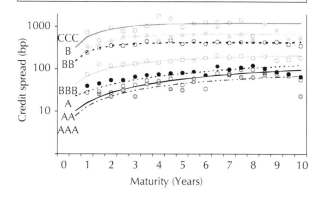

The middle panel of Figure 1.10 presents formulas for computing US Treasury yields at 0.5-year maturities from their cashflows and market prices, and how those yields are used in the formula for calculating bond spreads to Treasuries. Applying that formula to the cashflows of corporate bonds in Citi's BIG and High Yield indexes on August 1, 2011, generated the points in the right panel of Figure 1.10. The curves fit to credit spreads by maturity for each letter rating category are generated using a modified Nelson–Siegel (1987) procedure. As for the absolute yields in Figure 1.9, yield spreads to Treasuries increase with decreasing credit quality. However, unlike the inverted yield curve for triple-C-rated bonds, the spread curve for triple-Cs in Figure 1.10 is upward sloping.[13]

Having demonstrated some positive features of agency ratings, there are also some well-documented limitations. Consider first the top panel of Figure 1.11. The differences between spreads of over 2,500 downgraded bonds and over 2,000 upgraded bonds were tracked to the average spreads of their future rating categories before and after the ratings changes. The figure shows average differences for upgrades and downgrades separately. For upgrades, spreads start to tighten two to three years prior to the upgrade, arriving at the average spread during the month of the upgrade. For downgrades, spreads start to widen only nine months prior to the downgrade, but are also at the spread of the target rating category at the month of the downgrade.

The middle and bottom panels of Figure 1.11 show results of a study by McDermott, Scarabot and Kroujiline (2003, 2004), who constructed portfolios each year from 1994 to 2002 using identical construction rules as regards agency ratings distributions, maturities and industry sectors, but different selection rules.

❏ Random: Select bonds at random as long as they satisfy the rules (ie, the benchmark).
❏ Greedy: Select the highest-yielding bonds first.
❏ Conservative: Select the bonds with the lowest expected PDs from Moody's KMV (Vasicek, 1995) model first.

Figure 1.11 Limitations of agency ratings; top: average credit spreads are at agency rating means in month of change; middle and bottom: 500 annual identically rated portfolios constructed using different rules have different average default rates per portfolio

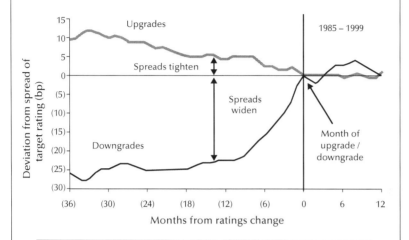

Portfolio construction rules:

1. 100 credits
2. Uniform ratings from single-A to single-B
3. Average rating: Triple-B-
4. Maturities from 4 to 12 years
5. Sector / Issuer maximum: 20% / 2%

Random: Pick bonds at random
Greedy: Select highest yielding bonds first
Conservative: Select bonds with lowest expected PDs from the KMV model first

Defaults per portfolio

	Random	Greedy	Conservative
1994	0.00	0.00	0.00
1995	0.00	0.00	0.00
1996	0.00	0.00	0.00
1997	0.25	1.47	0.00
1998	0.11	0.40	0.00
1999	0.75	3.26	0.00
2000	0.70	0.22	0.00
2001	0.46	1.67	0.00
2002	2.68	4.82	0.00
Mean	0.57	1.32	0.00

Source: Benzschawel and Adler (2002)

Multiple portfolios of 100 corporate bonds were selected each year from the bonds in Citi's BIG and High Yield indexes. The bottom panel of Figure 1.11 shows the average number of defaults per portfolio by year and the overall average. Note that according to agency criteria, all of those portfolios should be equally risky. Clearly, that is not the case. Selecting based on yield as in the "greedy" method produced over twice the number of defaults per portfolio as the "random" method. Conversely, the "conservative" method, picking safe credits according to the KMV model (described below), avoided all defaults, thereby also demonstrating its ability to outperform agency ratings at predicting default risk (or safety in this case).

The rating agencies: Summary of pros and cons
The development of agency credit rating scales has proven critical to the expansion and function of modern credit markets over the last century. Some positive features of agency ratings appear in the left column of Table 1.3, with limitations presented in the right column. For example, the agencies have developed consistent rating methodologies, they cover a wide range of corporate, municipal and sovereign issuers, and they have collected and shared publicly their detailed data on bond defaults since the 1920s. Furthermore, agency ratings have proven useful, at least on average, as indicators of credit risk and relative value. Nevertheless, as listed in the right portion of Table 1.3, agencies are slow to react to credit events – on average, the market recognises changes in credit quality months, and even years, prior to ratings changes. That is, typically, changes in agency ratings trail changes in credit spreads. Also, although the rating agencies have long histories and present average default rates by year and credit quality, Figures 1.3 and 1.4 illustrate that default rates are highly dependent on the credit cycle, and rarely are they at their mean values. Finally, subscriptions to agency ratings are expensive and, as will be shown below, inferior to other types of models in ordering bonds by default risk.

Table 1.3 Advantages and limitations of agency ratings

Advantages	Disadvantages
❏ Ratings by Moody's, S&P and Fitch are reliable and generally correct when made	❏ Agencies are slow to react to credit events
	❏ Reluctant to change a rating, often erring on the conservative side
❏ The agencies cover a wide spectrum of debt issuers	
	❏ subscriptions are expensive
❏ Provide accurate long-term rankings of default probabilities	❏ Ratings changes tend to trail changes in credit spreads
	❏ Use of average historical defaults ignores effects of the credit cycle on default rates
❏ Agreement, on average, between market spreads and rating	
	❏ Other models perform better at predicting defaults

Despite the limitations of agency ratings, it is difficult to overstate their importance for the development of the financial markets, not only in the US, but globally. One would be hard-pressed to identify a major corporate or sovereign bond issuer that has found it unnecessary to have an agency credit rating. Furthermore, agency credit ratings have been written into legislation, loan agreements, pension targets and fund indentures. Although the rating agencies have been criticised as being slow to react to credit changes and to have overstepped their expertise as regards the rating of structured credit products, no other credit scoring system has had comparable acceptance over such an extended period. In fact, the agency rating is arguably the most successful credit model in existence today.

Financial ratio analysis
The first reference to ratio analysis can be traced to Euclid in 300 BC (Heath, 1956), who described its benefits and properties. How-

ever, the application of ratio analysis in finance originated much later, its origins being traced to the late 19th century.[14] A financial ratio (or accounting ratio) is a quotient of two numbers where both numbers are taken from an enterprise's financial statements. The earliest reference to a financial ratio is the "quick ratio" (attributed to Rosendale, 1908), but Horrigan (1968) claims that James Cannon, a pioneer of financial statement analysis, was using 10 different ratios as early as 1905, while Foulke (1961) suggests that the current ratio may have emerged as early as 1891.[15] In any case, the use of financial ratios for credit analysis developed rapidly with the introduction of first ratio criterion for risk, the "2:1 current ratio", along with inter-firm comparisons and relative ratio criteria. Despite this, few analysts used financial ratios prior to World War I and those who did were inclined to use only the current ratio. The passage of the federal income tax code in 1913 and establishment of the Federal Reserve System in 1914 increased demand for financial statements and improvement in their analysis. Wall (1919) responded to this need with his now classic study of seven different financial ratios for 981 firms, stratified by industry and location.

The rapid development of different ratios took place during the 1920s,[16] a proliferation that continued until the 1960s. There are many financial ratios now linked to financial risk, and several of the most widely used ratios are listed in Figure 1.12. Although quantitative, financial ratios are typically viewed as part of fundamental analysis as, until relatively recently, their relationship to default was not explicitly specified. Fisher (1959) and Beaver (1966) were the first to attempt to systematically evaluate the relationship between financial ratios and corporate failure, and they identified many of the ratios that are viewed as important today. In fact, that effort by Beaver can be said to have provided the bridge between the classical and modern periods in credit risk analysis.

Figure 1.12 Popular financial ratios

- **Quick Ratio (Liquid Ratio):**
  The ability of a company to use its cash or quick assets to extinguish or retire its current liabilities immediately

  $$\text{Quick ratio} = \frac{\text{Cash} + \text{Marketable securities} + \text{Accounts receivable}}{\text{Current liabilities}}$$

- **Return on Equity (ROE):**
  The rate of return on the ownership interest of the common stock

  $$\text{Return on equity} = \frac{\text{Net income}}{\text{Average shareholders equity}}$$

- **Debt Ratio (Leverage):**
  The percentage of a company's assets that are provided via debt

  $$\text{Debt ratio} = \frac{\text{Total debt}}{\text{Total assets}}$$

- **Operating Margin (Profitability):**
  The ratio of operating divided by net sales

  $$\text{Operating margin} = \frac{\text{Operating income}}{\text{Net sales}}$$

THE MODERN ERA: QUANTITATIVE DEFAULT MODELS

The modern era in credit modelling can arguably be traced back to the development of statistical models based on financial ratios. In particular, those models generate probabilistic estimates of future default risk based on historical relationships observed between measurable characteristics of firms and their past payment performance. Along with those probabilistic default estimates, a characteristic feature of the modern period is the application of techniques from statistical decision theory for assessing the accuracy of models at predicting defaults.

Statistical default models
Altman's Z-score model

The first, and most notable, of the early statistical models is Altman's (1968) Z-score. Altman, shown in the top panel of Figure 1.13, derived his Z-score model by performing a discriminant analysis between defaulting and non-defaulting firms using five financial ratios calculated from data in their financial statements. The ratios chosen for analysis that appear in the right portion of Figure 1.17 were those that had been highlighted by Fischer (1959) and Beaver (1966). Also, the values needed to calculate those ratios were available from the financial statements of publicly traded firms. In fact, Beaver had already demonstrated that ratio analysis could be useful for discriminating defaulters from non-defaulters, but had not combined them into a predictive model. To build the Z-score model, Altman assembled financial information from 66 manufacturing firms, half of which had defaulted within a year of reporting those financials while the other 33 did not. The resulting discriminant function appears underneath the photo of Altman in Figure 1.13, with the lower portion of the figure showing the five financial ratios and the Z = 2.6 cut-off between bankrupt and non-bankrupt firms reported by Altman. These values of Z were mapped to historical one-year default rates to produce the first quantitative estimates of firms' default probabilities.

Not only was the Z-score model an immediate success, it has continued to be useful over time, even as its particular applications have evolved. Importantly, the model gives probabilistic estimates of default probabilities. Although the Z-score was widely used for estimating default probabilities for individual firms in the several decades following its development, its relative usefulness for that purpose has declined due to several factors. First, the model is backward-looking – that is, the financial ratios in Figure 1.13 are already at least a month or two old when reported, and firms' financial prospects may have changed since their publication. Furthermore, firms' financial reports are updated quarterly at best, and some information only annually. This is too infrequent for modern credit investors, who now more typically rely on structural and risk-neutral models (described below) for assessing individual firm risk. Those latter models, incorporating market information, are inherently forward-looking and can produce updated estimates of default daily.

Figure 1.13 Top: Edward Altman, creator of the Z-score model, the first to estimate actual default probabilities; bottom: Altman's (1968) Z-score model for predicting corporate default

$$Z = .012X_1 + .014X_2 + .033X_3 + .006X_4 + .999X_5$$

X_1 = Working capital / total assets

X_2 = Retained earnings / total assets

X_3 = Earning before interest and taxes / total assets

X_4 = Market value of equity / book value of debt

X_5 = Sales / total assets

Z = Overall index

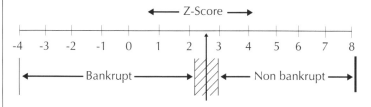

Source: Incisive Media (with permission)

The success of the Z-score spawned an entire class of statistical approaches to predicting default risk. These include ordinary least squares models, probit and logit models, along with non-linear models and others based on neural networks (Odom and Sharda, 1990), decision trees (Bozsik, 2012), genetic algorithms (Marose, 1990; Marose, Rothenberg and Sankaran, 1992) and Bayesian inference (Kazemi and Mosleh, 2012), to name a few. Although some of these models have proven useful for understanding certain aspects of default, none have displaced Altman's Z-score. Often, investors have found these models too difficult to interpret in terms of their relation to actual properties of firms, and tend to view the more complicated statistical models as "black boxes", often lacking economic intuition, prone to over-fitting the data, and too computationally intensive and complex. Thus, none has achieved the acceptance or longevity that has been accorded the Z-score model and its offshoots.

Adaptive non-linear regression
Statistical approaches to modelling default have become more sophisticated since the development of the Z-score model. As described in detail in this section, more recent statistical models use adaptive non-linear modelling techniques to predict defaults and evaluate model performance using methodology derived from statistical decision theory. An example of such an application can be found in Campbell. Hilscher and Szilagyi (2008). The logistic regression function (see middle panel of Figure 1.14) is commonly used to transform model input variables when the values of the inputs are non-linearly related to the desired output. The adaptive method is so called because it deploys a walk-forward construction method to compute a new model by selecting input variables each year from a set of candidates, while adding the data from the previous year to the development sample. We illustrate the non-linear adaptive modelling approach using the model developed by Benzschawel, Li and Lee (2013) in Figure 1.14 as it embodies the non-linear adaptive approach, along with step-wise variable selection, and evaluates performance using cumulative accuracy profile (CAP) curves.

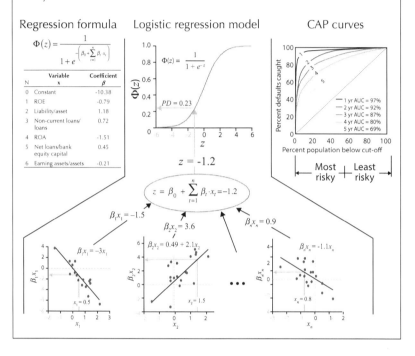

Figure 1.14 Non-linear adaptive regression model: left: regression formula and variable inputs for 2013 model; middle: non-linear regression showing how normalised input variables are passed through a non-linear transform before output; right: cumulative accuracy profiles illustrating model performance at predicting defaults at one- to five-year horizons

The major features of the bank default model are presented in Figure 1.14. The equation in the upper left panel of the figure specifies the model, whose variable inputs are shown just below it. The variables shown were chosen via step-wise variable selection from a set of 20 candidate financial ratios, with all input variables transformed into standard normal distributions testing as inputs to each annual model. Model construction begins with only the logistic function:

$$PD = \frac{1}{1 + e^{-(\alpha_i + \beta_i x_i)}} \tag{1.2}$$

For each candidate input variable, values of α_i and β_i are selected that best predict default on the development sample. The variable

29

with the greatest predictive power with respect to default is chosen as the first input variable.[17] After selection of the first variable, the process is repeated to select a second variable, and so on until model performance ceases to improve. Once all the variables for the model are selected, the value of the constant β_0 and coefficients $\beta_i (i = 1,\dots, n)$ for each of the variables are refit to minimise the error in the logistic regression. The variables and their values of β for the 2013 one-year model appear on the left in Figure 1.14.

Benzschawel *et al* constructed an annual series bank model using all available US bank data from 1992 to 2012. Their procedure is typical of improvements in model development that have occurred over several decades. One, now standard, component of model development is to ensure no look-forward bias in model construction and to measure performance out-of-sample. This can be accomplished using a walk-forward procedure as illustrated in Figure 1.15. For example, data from the years 1992 to 1999 were used to construct the first annual model. That model was then used to score all non-defaulting banks existing at the beginning of 2000, and its accuracy in predicting defaults in 2000 was determined. That procedure was repeated annually until 2012. In addition, each year a series of five models were built, each predicting default at a different annual horizon for one to five years.

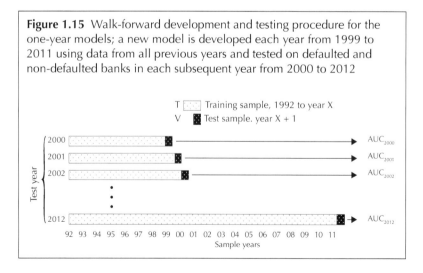

Figure 1.15 Walk-forward development and testing procedure for the one-year models; a new model is developed each year from 1999 to 2011 using data from all previous years and tested on defaulted and non-defaulted banks in each subsequent year from 2000 to 2012

Out-of-sample performance of the five annual bank models at default prediction was evaluated at horizons of one to five years, respectively, for each year from 2002 to 2012. The model has proven superior to agency ratings at predicting defaults at all horizons (see below). In addition, Benzschawel and Lommaert (2014) present a detailed analysis of the factors contributing to default risk over the credit cycle, and how those factors change in importance when predicting default over different time horizons. Before describing those results further, it is useful to examine methods for evaluating the relative accuracy of default models. These methods will be used throughout the remainder of this chapter for comparing default model performance.

Analysing model performance: Cap curves

Although several studies have related financial ratios to corporate distress (Fischer, 1966; Beaver, 1966), powerful quantitative methods for evaluating model performance at predicting default have only been applied in the past 20 years. Quantifying default model performance can be challenging as only a very small fraction of existing firms default in any year, and many firms with very high risk may not default. Furthermore, default is typically not known with certainty before the actual event. Thus, evaluating model performance must necessarily rely upon probabilistic comparisons. Along with the development of more sophisticated default models in the 1990s came the application of more rigorous methods for evaluating model performance at predicting defaults. Most notable of these improvements is the application of CAP curves from statistical decision theory.[18] The earliest reports of using CAP curves to evaluate the predictive power of default models are those of Sobehart, Keenan and Stein (1999) and Kealhofer and Kurbat (2001). A detailed treatment of the history and application of statistical decision theory to financial model validation appears in Stein (2007). I describe the construction of CAP curves briefly here as they will be used frequently in the following sections.

Figure 1.16 demonstrates how CAP curves are constructed from both agency ratings and model-derived default probabilities (PDs) for a hypothetical example of 100 firms. The first step in the process, shown at the left, involves ordering firm risk (either by agency ratings or PDs) from highest to lowest, typically at the beginning of each year.

At the end of the year, each firm's risk score is associated with a "D" or "N" depending on whether it defaulted or did not default, respectively. The middle panel shows how the ranked scores and associated outcomes (D or N) are used to construct the CAP curve. Consider the dashes between ranks 10 and 11 in the left portion of Figure 1.16 that divide the upper 10% and remaining 90% of the riskiest firms by agency rating and the PD model. Assume that, of the 100 firms, there are 15 total defaults. Then, in the top 10%, the agency ratings capture five of the 15 or 33% of the defaulters. This is the value of the lower bar at 10% on the x-axis of the CAP curve in the middle panel of Figure 1.16. Similarly, the PD model captures eight of the 15 defaults, or 53% of the defaulters in the top 10%, the higher bar at 10% population cut-off.

Figure 1.16 Demonstration of how distributions of defaulted and non-defaulted firms ranked by risk from agency ratings and a PD model are used to calculate CAP curves

Firms ranks by risk

Rank	Rating	D or N	PD (%)	D or N
0	CCC	D	4.1	D
1	CCC	D	3.9	D
2	CC	N	3.7	D
3	C	D	3.5	D
4	C	N	3.2	N
5	B-	N	3.0	D
6	B-	D	2.9	D
7	B	N	2.6	N
8	B	D	2.4	N
9	B+	N	2.2	D
10	B+	N	2.1	D
11	BB-	D	2.0	N
12	BB-	N	1.7	D
• • •				
88	A+	N	0.92	N
89	A+	N	0.88	N
90	AA-	D	0.57	D
91	AA-	N	0.42	N
92	AA	N	0.30	N
93	AA	N	0.12	N
94	AA	D	0.10	N
95	AA+	N	0.09	N
96	AA+	N	0.07	N
97	AA+	N	0.05	N
98	AAA	N	0.03	N
99	AAA	N	0.02	N
100	AAA	N	0.01	N

Highest / Risk / Lowest — Riskiest 10%

Cumulative accuracy profile curve

To plot CAP Curves:

1. Rank all defaulted firms by both EDF and by agency credit rating
2. For each decile in each ranked population calculate the percentage of the total of defaulted firms in or above that value
3. Plot that value for each model to be tested (eg, PD model versus agency ratings)

Model PDs vs agency ratings

Defaults below cut-off (%): 100, 90, 80, 70, 60, 50, 40, 30, 20, 10, 0
Chance line
■ PD model   □ Rating
10 20 30 40 50 60 70 80 90 100
Population below cut-off (%)

Distributions of defaults and non-defaults

The CAP curve analysis summerasis how well a model serves to separate distributions of defaulters and non-defaulters on the dimension of riskiness (the x-axis)

Agency ratings

AAA AA A BBB BB B CCC D

Relative frequency
Predicted default probability
0   0.5   1   10

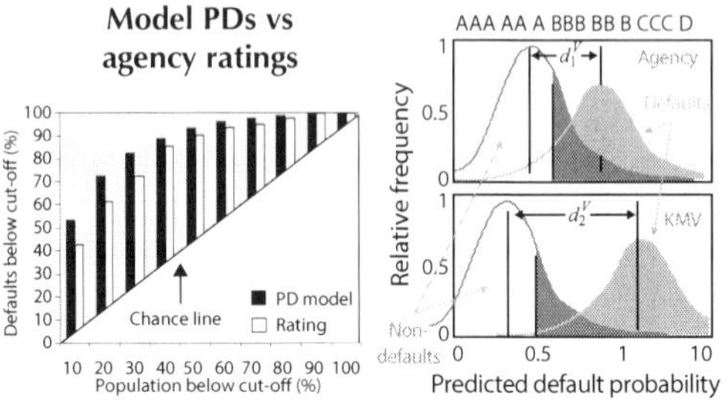

The other bars of the curve are constructed similarly, as the criterion is expanded at 10-percentile intervals on the ranked risk dimension. The CAP curve reveals that, for all percentiles, the PD model outperforms the hypothetical agency ratings. Finally, note that a model assigning risk scores at chance would catch 10% of the defaulters in the top 10%, 20% in the top 20% and so on. This "chance line" is the diagonal line in the figure, and is indicative of no ability to sort defaulters from non-defaulters. Hence, the area above the chance line is a measure of the relative classification ability of the model.

The right portion of Figure 1.16 shows how the CAP curve summarises the discriminatory power of a given model. Frequency distributions can be constructed from the ranked scores and their associated outcomes (D or N). These plots show separately how the scores for the defaulters and non-defaulters are distributed by risk score (ie, the x-axis). The greater the separation between the distributions of defaulters and non-defaulters is indicative of a model with better accuracy. CAP curve analysis has become standard procedure in evaluating credit models, and we will see several examples of their use below.

Bank model performance

Having described construction of CAP curves, we are now in a position to analyse the performance of the Benzschawel, Li and Lee (2013) bank default model. The right panel of Figure 1.14 shows CAP curves that summarise the accuracy of the bank models to predict defaults at one- to five-year horizons over the period 1999–2012. The curves show how discriminatory power decreases with time horizon, being nearly perfect at one year, but still demonstrating a good deal of discriminatory power at predicting default five years out. A useful measure of predictive power from CAP analysis is the area under the curve (AUC), which is the percentage of the area under each CAP curve, and these are inset in the figure.

For comparison with agency ratings, Figure 1.17 presents CAP curves from agency ratings and the bank model for one- to four-year horizons. The top row shows results for Bank Holding Companies and the bottom row is for Savings and Loans. Clearly, both the bank default model and Kroll agency ratings order banks' risk at better than chance levels, even out to four years. It is also evident that predictive accuracy for both models decreases as the year of prediction gets farther out in time. Visual comparison of the CAP curves in Figure 1.17 indicates that for all horizons, the adaptive non-linear bank model outperforms Kroll agency ratings. Although performance decreases for both models as the time horizon increases from two to four years, decreases are greater for Kroll ratings than for Citi's bank model.

To demonstrate the richness of the adaptive non-linear modelling approach, Table 1.4 from Benzschawel and Lommaert (2014) presents a quantitative analysis of the variable contributions by time horizon of prediction. The left-hand table shows the likelihood of each variable being selected for the one- to five-year default models in each year over the period from 2000 to 2012. The table on the right displays the average order of selection if the variable was included in the model at the listed horizons. Consider first the probabilities of variable selection. Although return on equity (ROE) and the ratio of liabilities to assets are included in all one-year models, their contributions drop off rapidly at two-to-five years. Also, performance on earning assets (earning assets to assets) is important at one- and two-year horizons, but is not included in three- and four-year models, with only moderate contributions to five-year models.

The most consistently important variable is the percentage of non-current loans, included in all annual models from one to three years, and dropping off to 69% at four years and 15% at five years. For two-to four-year horizons, the yield on earning assets and net loans to bank equity capital become important, while having less influence in the one- and five-year models. In fact, the five-year models appear to have the most diversity of variable contributions with no model in more than 54% of annual models. Finally, net interest margin appears relatively unimportant, except at the five-year horizon, with the ratio of non-current loans to loan loss allowance only included in a small fraction of models at one- and three-year horizons.

The bank model is presented to illustrate the high predictive power of the adaptive non-linear modelling approach, a modern extension of the statistical approach that originated with Altman's Z-score. In addition, the analysis demonstrates the richness of information yielded by the model regarding the determinants of default over time horizon and credit cycle provided by the dynamic

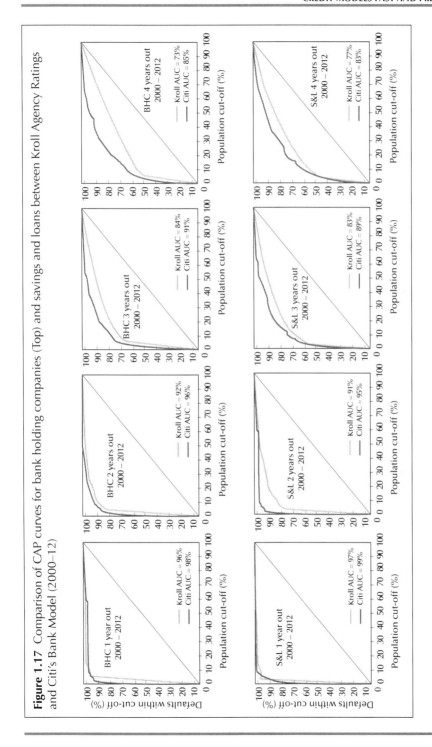

Figure 1.17 Comparison of CAP curves for bank holding companies (Top) and savings and loans between Kroll Agency Ratings and Citi's Bank Model (2000–12)

variable selection method. Despite these advantages, the adaptive linear model can be difficult to implement as it requires highly standardised financial information, which may not be available for all other types of firm.[19] In addition, the high degree of predictive power and analytical richness of the adaptive non-linear approach comes at the cost of much greater mathematical and computational complexity. It also requires annual assembly of updated data and new model construction for one- to five-year models. Thus, the approach is not suitable for all applications.

Reduced form models: Risk-neutral default probabilities

Many default models were proposed between Altman's Z-score in the late 1960s and the mid-1990s. However, for various reasons, none proved satisfactory for use by broker–dealers for hedging their credit exposure. First, there was little out-of-sample testing of the models' abilities to predict defaults. This lack of testing was partially the result of researchers' lack of access to data on individual defaults, and the fact that methods from statistical decision theory had not yet been applied to default models. There were also difficulties and limitations associated with access to data necessary for input to models in a trading setting. Finally, early evidence suggested problems with default predictions from the Merton structural model (discussed below in the section on structural models).

To meet the need for an easy-to-apply, simple to understand and general framework for measuring credit risk, the risk-neutral pricing framework was applied to credit risk in the form of the reduced form model. Reduced form credit models generate default probabilities directly from market credit spreads without any assumptions regarding the source or causes of obligors' credit risk premiums. In that sense, reduced form models represent another type of statistical approach to measuring default risk. It is unlikely that a liquid credit derivatives market would have emerged without the availability of reduced form credit models. Applications of risk-neutral pricing theory to credit can be traced to several sources, including Hull and White (1995), Jarrow and Turnbull (1995), Perry (1995) and Duffie and Singleton (1999), and this approach has given rise to a large body of research since then.

Risk-neutral pricing theory specifies that the present value of a

Table 1.4 Probabilities of variable selection by model horizon (left) and average order of inclusion if selected at given horizon (right) for annual models over the period 2000–12

Variables	Probability of selection					Average order if selected				
	1y	2y	3y	4y	5y	1y	2y	3y	4y	5y
ROE	100%	92%	15%	0%	0%	1.0	2.7	4.5	-	-
Liabilities/assets	100%	23%	31%	31%	23%	2.1	5.7	3.0	4.0	4.3
Non-current loans/loans	92%	100%	100%	69%	15%	3.9	1.1	2.1	2.4	8.0
Net operation income/assets	92%	0%	69%	69%	8%	4.9	-	3.9	2.7	2.0
Earning assets/assets	85%	85%	0%	0%	31%	3.5	4.3	-	-	1.0
Yield on earning asset	46%	85%	92%	77%	54%	5.8	4.2	4.3	2.3	2.6
ROA	23%	0%	0%	8%	8%	4.0	-	-	6.0	2.0
Assets	23%	23%	23%	15%	46%	5.7	5.7	5.7	4.0	4.0
Non current loans/loan loss allowance	15%	0%	8%	0%	0%	5.0	-	11.0	-	-
Net loans/bank equity capital	0%	100%	100%	31%	23%	-	3.6	1.8	3.0	2.7
Annual default rate	0%	23%	23%	31%	31%	-	5.3	2.0	2.0	2.5
Assets 90 days past due/30 – 89 days past due	0%	31%	23%	23%	23%	-	5.8	6.0	1.3	3.0
Net interest income/earning assets	0%	15%	15%	8%	23%	-	8.0	9.0	8.0	6.7
Net interest margin	0%	0%	8%	8%	38%	-	-	10.0	7.0	3.6

set of cashflows is equivalent to their expected likelihoods of receipt discounted from the time of their receipt by the corresponding risk-free rates of return. Consider again Figure 1.2, which depicts a single default-risky cashflow to be received one year from now. We begin by noting that one can view a one-period bond as a portfolio of two securities:

❑ one that pays US$1 at time T if the issuer does not default; and
❑ one that pays an amount R if default occurs before maturity T.

Also, one can express the present value PV of that single cashflow of US$1 at time T as:

$$PV = e^{(-yT)}$$

(1.3)

Let the probability of non-payment (ie, default) of the US$1 cashflow be p_T and its recovery value in default be R. Then, within risk-neutral pricing theory, the expected value of the US$1 to be received at time T is the probability-weighted sum of receiving the US$1 or the recovery value. That is:

$$E[T] = \left\{ \left[(1 - p_T) * 1 \right] + p_T R \right\}$$

(1.4)

Furthermore, given the price-yield formula in Equation 1.3 and the expected cashflows in Equation 1.3, one can express the discount yield y on the US$1 resulting from the fraction p_T of times one expects to only receive the recovery value R as the sum of the risk-free yield r plus a yield spread s such that:

$$e^{-T(r+s)} = e^{-rT} \left\{ \left[(1 - p_T) * 1 \right] + p_T R \right\}$$

(1.5)

By taking the natural logarithms of both sides and rearranging, we can write:

$$s = -\frac{1}{T} \ln \left[1 - \left(p_T * LGD \right) \right]$$

(1.6)

where LGD is the expected loss given default such that $LGD = 1 - R$.

An example of how risk-neutral pricing can be applied to solve for a default rate, the risk-neutral default rate, for a one-period risky bond is depicted in the top panel of Figure 1.18. Assume that the bond is priced at par (ie, its price is 100), and that the:

❑ maturity is one year from the present;
❑ bond has an 8% coupon;
❑ recovery value in default is 50% of par; and
❑ the one-year risk-free rate is 6%.

One can calculate the risk-neutral default probability, p_T^Q using the following:[20]

$$100 = \frac{1}{1.06}\{[(1 - p_1^Q) * 108] + (p_1^Q * 50)\} \qquad (1.7)$$

Solving for p_1^Q in Equation 1.7 gives a risk-neutral default rate of 3.5%. Note that while Equations 1.3–1.7 are useful for illustrating the concepts behind the risk-neutral model, they do not illustrate formal richness of the approach, one that appeals to many academics and practitioners. To provide a sample of that formalism, a brief explanation of the risk-neutral model in continuous time is presented in Appendix 1.2.

More generally, one can calculate the compounded rate of return on a risk-free asset over a time interval t as e^{rt} and the rate of return on a risky asset as $e^{(r+s)t}$. Assuming for the moment that the recovery value is zero, the risk-neutral default probability can be calculated as $(1 - p_T^Q)e^{(r+s)t}$, and can be written as:

$$(1 - p_T^Q)e^{(r+s)t} = e^{rt} \qquad (1.8)$$

and solving for p_T^Q gives:

$$p_t^Q = 1 - e^{st} \qquad (1.9)$$

Figure 1.18 Top: representation of a one-period par bond within the risk-neutral framework; bottom: bond yields, spreads and risk-neutral default rates

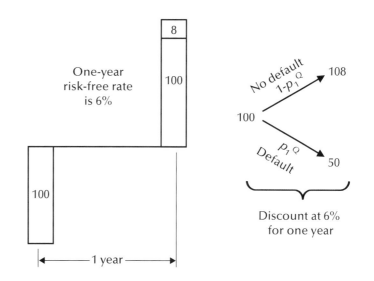

One-year
risk-free rate
is 6%

Time to maturity (t)	Risk-free spot rate (r)	Corp bond yield (y)	Credit spread (s)	Cum risk-neutral default prob	Annual risk-neutral default prob
0.5	3.57%	3.67%	0.10%	0.083%	0.083%
1.0	3.70%	3.82%	0.12%	0.200%	0.117%
1.5	3.81%	3.94%	0.13%	0.325%	0.125%
2.0	3.95%	4.10%	0.15%	0.499%	0.175%
2.5	4.06%	4.22%	0.16%	0.665%	0.166%
3.0	4.16%	4.32%	0.16%	0.798%	0.133%
3.5	4.24%	4.44%	0.20%	1.163%	0.365%
4.0	4.33%	4.53%	0.20%	1.328%	0.165%
4.5	4.42%	4.64%	0.22%	1.642%	0.314%
5.0	4.45%	4.67%	0.22%	1.823%	0.181%

Equation 1.9 can be used to calculate risk-neutral default probabilities from credit spreads on bonds. However, Equation 1.8 must be modified to include another term to account for the usual non-zero recovery value of bonds in default as:

$$\left(1 - p_t^Q\right)e^{(r+s)t} + Rp_t^Q e^{(r+s)t} = e^{rt} \tag{1.10}$$

and:

$$p_t^Q = \frac{\left(1 - e^{(-st)}\right)}{(1 - R)} \tag{1.11}$$

Equation 1.11 can be used to determine risk-neutral default probabilities for an entire corporate yield curve. Consider the hypothetical yield curve for a corporate firm in the third column of the bottom portion of Figure 1.18. The time to maturity and the spot rates from the US Treasury yield curve are shown in columns one and two, respectively. The credit spreads in column four are simply differences between the corporate and Treasury yield curves. Using Equation 1.11 and an assumed recovery rate of 40%, risk-neutral default probabilities were calculated at 0.5-year intervals up to the five-year point on the curve. As an illustration, the five-year cumulative default rate for the curve in Figure 1.18 is calculated as:

$$p_t^Q = \frac{1 - e^{-0.0022*5}}{1 - 0.4} = 1.823\% \tag{1.12}$$

Despite the wide use of the reduced form approach, comprehensive studies of the probabilities of default inferred from these models have been sparse or very limited in scope.[21] To demonstrate how the formulas in Equations 1.10 and 1.11 are employed in practice, Figure 1.19 shows how risk-neutral default curves by ratings are generated from par bond yield curves for June 8, 2009, and assuming an average recovery rate of 40%.

Figure 1.19 Deriving risk-neutral default probabilities from corporate bond yield curves

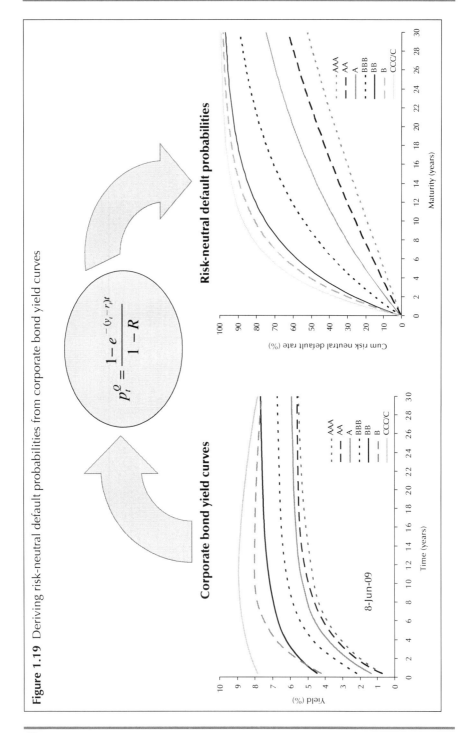

One reason for the success of reduced form credit models is that they only require information about the securities' nominal cashflows, their yields and risk-free interest rates. That is, one only needs bonds' market prices and assumed recovery rates to calculate risk-neutral PDs in a consistent manner for all credits. Unfortunately, default rates implied by the risk-neutral models are much higher than even the highest historical default rates. Consider, for example, Figure 1.20, which presents risk-neutral default rates on June 8, 2009 (top) with average historical default rates (bottom). Clearly, the risk-neutral default rates are much larger than their physical counterparts. One-year risk-neutral default rates for all triple-B rated and high-yield credits are greater than the actual cyclically high default rate of 12% in 2009. The vertical line spanning the figures connects 10-year historical and risk-neutral default rates for triple-B credits, and serves to highlight the contrast between the 8% cumulative historical rate and its corresponding 52% risk-neutral value. In fact, 10-year cumulative default rates are over 70% for the entire set of high-yield credits, much higher than those ever observed historically. The overestimation of actual default probabilities poses problems for using the reduced form model for estimating default probabilities. The reasons for the consistent overestimation of physical default probabilities by risk-neutral measures will be made evident in the context of the discussion on the credit risk premium.

It is difficult to overstate the importance of the risk-neutral framework for our understanding of credit, the development of the credit markets and for quantitative financial modelling in general. Still, there are limitations to this approach for understanding and quantifying credit risk. The overestimation of default probabilities has already been discussed. In addition, although reduced form models appear to make few assumptions about physical default, they require the assumption of a recovery value to infer PDs or hazard rates. It is not clear why, in principle, default probabilities could not be fixed at historical rates and recovery values varied to adjust expected cashflows such that their discounted values match market prices. In fact, it might be argued that there is more extensive information on physical defaults and better default models than exist for recovery values in default. The reduced form approach has also been criticised as providing investors with few insights regarding the factors that influence credit risk, nor any guidance about the relative values of various credits. Also, the notion of a hazard rate that is a jump to default that underlies most applications is suspect, particularly for high-quality credits.[22] That is, default is not a surprise for the firm and often not for investors either. Finally, hazard rates are typically calculated from bond or CDS spreads.

Several authors have attempted to account for the overestimation of physical default rates by risk-neutral methods (eg, Bonn, 2000; Gray and Malone, 2008).[23] The calculation of the "physical" or actual probability of default is outside the contingent claims analysis (CCA) or "Merton" model (discussed in the next section), but it can be combined with an equilibrium model of underlying expected returns to produce estimates of expected returns. However, those frameworks require viewing the entire credit risk premium as an actual default, as depicted in Figure 1.21. This has resulted in problems in valuation and hedging of CDS (Benzschawel and Corlu, 2010). Duan, Sun and Wang (2012) also proposed a model that incorporates financial and economic variables in an intensity-based framework, whose outputs are calibrated to physical probabilities of default. Although it may prove useful for predicting defaults and for analysing factors underlying corporate failure, it will be less helpful for the hedging purposes that provided the initial motivation for the intensity-based framework.

Finally, accurate valuation of assets that depend on non-default credit state transitions is particularly problematic within the risk-neutral framework. This is because, when adjusting historical ratings transitions to risk-neutral ones, overstatement of default risk requires one to transfer probabilities from non-default credit states to the default state to account for the larger than physical risk-neutral default rates. This leaves other non-default transitions at a deficit, which can be important when valuing embedded options in bonds or loans. Thus, the risk-neutral framework is problematic when valuing corporate loans with credit-state-dependent optionality, calculations of value-at-risk for credit portfolios or for evaluating firm risk for regulatory purposes.

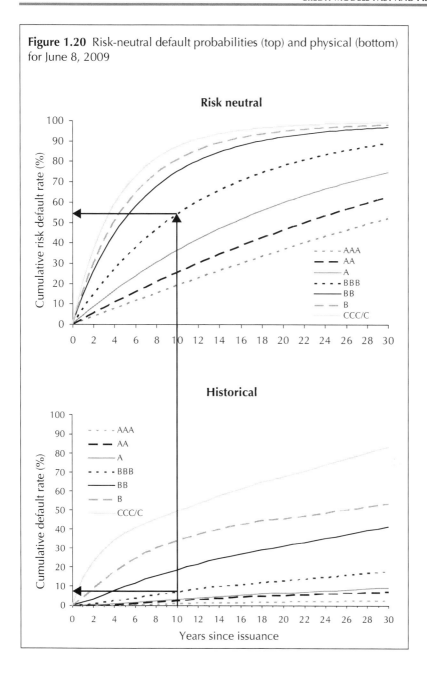

Figure 1.20 Risk-neutral default probabilities (top) and physical (bottom) for June 8, 2009

Figure 1.21 Bohn's (2000) model of physical and risk-neutral default

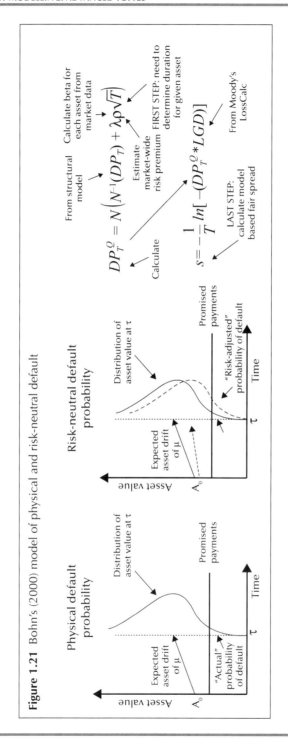

The Merton model: The equity–debt relationship

Decades before development of the risk-neutral framework, Robert Merton (1973, 1974) formalised the suggestion of Black and Scholes (1973) that a firm's equity and debt resembled contingent claims on the firm's assets and liabilities. For example, the relationship between a firm's equity and debt within the Merton theory is depicted in Figure 1.22. The left portion of the figure shows that the assets of the firm consist of its equity and its debt. The equity holders of the firm are viewed as having a call option on its assets, whereby those investors share in the profitability of the firm. Conversely, the debt holders of a firm are long a risk-free asset, having loaned the firm money at the risk-free rate, and are short a put that they sold to the equity holders in exchange for the premium over the risk-free rate. The strike price of the call and put is the face value of the firm's outstanding debt, which can be determined from the firm's balance sheet. The market value of the firm's assets can be inferred from its stock price and shares outstanding, and asset volatility from equity price volatility. The importance of the Merton formulation is that, if correct, a firm's equity and debt can be valued using the Black–Scholes option pricing formula.

Figure 1.22 Relationship between a firm's equity and debt in the Merton structure

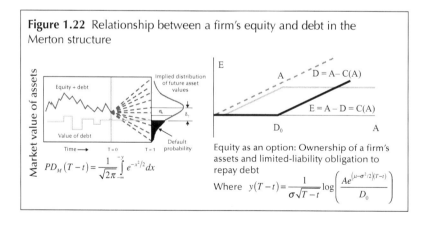

Figure 1.23 shows major features of the Merton model whose inputs come from the equity markets and firms' financial statements. The three main drivers of firm value are shown in the left panel. These are the market value of assets (ie, the equity plus the debt),

labelled V_A in the right panel, asset volatility σ_A and the level of the debt K. These values are used to calculate the distance-to-default, DD, over a given time horizon T. That is, the distance-to-default is calculated as:

$$DD = \frac{V_A - K}{\left(V_A * \sigma_A\right)\sqrt{T}}$$

(1.13)

where the numerator measures the magnitude that the business value exceeds the level of the debt, and the denominator measures investors' uncertainty regarding the future value of the firm.

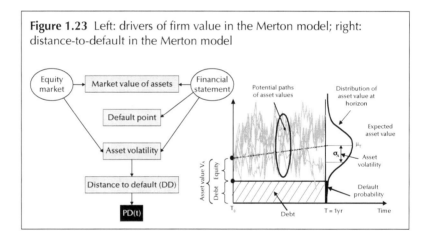

Figure 1.23 Left: drivers of firm value in the Merton model; right: distance-to-default in the Merton model

Problems with the Merton model

Before describing successful implementations in the Merton structural model framework, we consider some issues concerning the validity of the assumptions underlying the model. First, the original Merton model formulation comes directly from the Black–Scholes option pricing model, placing it on a firm foundation within financial theory (the Merton formulation is presented in Appendix 1.3). Accordingly, if the assumptions underlying the Merton formulation are correct, one ought to be able to use the Black–Scholes option pricing formula to determine a firm's probability of default and the "fair" yield spread to Treasuries (or price) of its bonds from the firm's equity price and balance sheet information. For several reasons, including lack of data and difficulty in its acquisition, it was not until the 1980s that Jones, Mason and Rosenfeld (1984) found that the Black–Scholes Merton model formulation consistently underestimated by large amounts the yield spreads over Treasuries observed in the market. This failure to predict credit spreads resulted in minimal use of the Merton model for assessing or hedging credit exposure, particularly by traders, much of which continues to this day. Nevertheless, the work of Jones *et al* spurred many attempts in academia to adapt the Merton model to account for credit spreads. Examples include the addition of uncertainty to the default boundary and estimates of firms' assets (Geske, 1979; Finger *et al*, 2002), and adding correlations among Treasury yields and credit risk (Longstaff and Schwarz, 1995).[24] Other adaptations include jumps in the value of assets, bond indenture provisions, taxes, bankruptcy costs, stochastic volatility and interest rates.[25]

In addition to the empirical problems, there are issues regarding the application of contingent claims analysis to value corporate liabilities. These relate to: (i) the unobservable character of the market value of firms' assets; (ii) the relatively illiquid nature of firms' liabilities; and (iii) the unrealistic dynamics of borrowing and lending implied by the model.[26] With respect to the market value of unobservable assets implied from equity prices, even fully informed equity prices are marginal prices, and therefore primarily reflect marginal supply and demand conditions rather than the value of the aggregate capital stock of the firm. Also, with respect to the Merton model's characterisation of firms' debt, the liabilities of most institutions do not possess the same characteristics as the securities for which many of the contingent claims models were first developed. That is, the issuance of debt is not associated with any *bona fide* hedging activity that would tend to result in a high volume of incremental rebalancing trades. This is important since the ideal hedge portfolio concept, which underlies the options pricing equation, requires an infinitesimal hedging/trading environment as a precondition.

Figure 1.24 Top: the leverage clock; bottom: debt risk premium from the CDS index minus the equity risk premium from the S&P 500

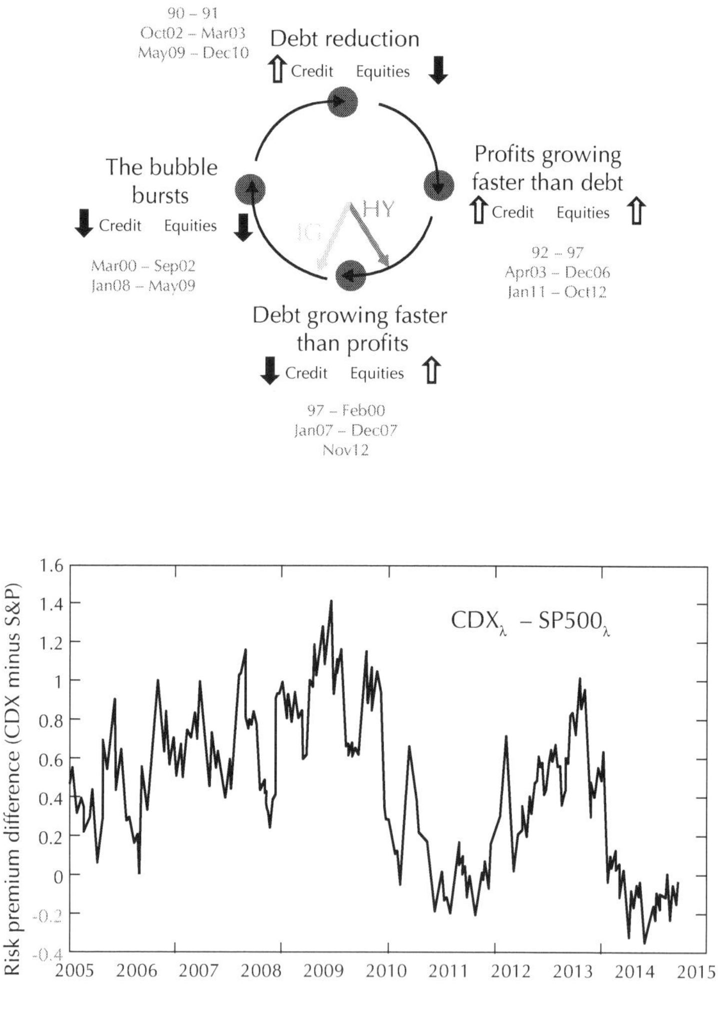

90 – 91
Oct02 – Mar03
May09 – Dec10

Debt reduction
⇑ Credit   Equities ⬇

The bubble bursts
⬇ Credit   Equities ⬇

Mar00 – Sep02
Jan08 – May09

Profits growing faster than debt
⇑ Credit   Equities ⇑

92 – 97
Apr03 – Dec06
Jan11 – Oct12

HY
IG

Debt growing faster than profits
⬇ Credit   Equities ⇑

97 – Feb00
Jan07 – Dec07
Nov12

$CDX_\lambda - SP500_\lambda$

Risk premium difference (CDX minus S&P)

Source: (top panel) Adapted from King (2012)

Another problem is that the Merton framework specifies a tight linkage between the risk premiums in the equity and debt markets, and Fridson (1999) suggests that those risk premiums frequently diverge. For example, as shown in the stylised leverage clock in the top panel of Figure 1.24, the equity and debt risk premiums are positively correlated in only two parts of the credit cycle. That is, both markets rally when profits are growing faster than debt, and they sell off together when the level of debt to profits cannot sustain existing debt and equity prices. In the other parts of the cycle, equity and debt prices move inversely. When firms are deleveraging after a debt and equity downturn, their debt rallies, but earnings are insufficient to raise equity prices. Also, amid an equity rally, debt tends to grow faster than profits, leading to an increase in the credit risk premium.

The hypothesised divergence between equity and debt risk premiums was documented by Benzschawel *et al* (2014), who measured daily equity and debt risk premiums from 2005 to mid-2014. The differences they reported between the daily debt premium for the CDX.NA.IG debt index and that of the S&P 500 equity index appear in the bottom panel of Figure 1.24. Clearly, although there are patterns of short-term deviations among equity and debt risk premiums, those deviations are superimposed on a lower frequency cyclical pattern of differences in their risk premiums. Furthermore, as will be shown below, these relations have implications for default probabilities generated using the Merton model formulation.

The Moody's/KMV model

Despite difficulties with the Merton framework, Kealhofer, McQuown and Vasicek developed a modified version of Merton's structural model, called the KMV model, to measure default risk (Vasicek, 1995), and formed the KMV Company in 1988 to market the model. KMV abandoned the use of the Merton framework for estimating credit spreads, and focused on its ability to predict defaults. Also, instead of using the total liabilities of the firm, TL, as the default boundary K, KMV set the boundary equal to the firm's current liabilities CL (debt due in less than one year) plus one-half its long-term debt, LTD, where $LTD = TL - CL$ (Kealhofer, 1999). That is:

$$K = CL + \frac{LTD}{2}$$

(1.14)

Of particular importance is that KMV abandoned the tight linkage between options theory and default, choosing to leave that relationship unspecified. Instead, they opted for an empirical approach, whereby they derived the historical relationship between firms' distances-to-default in Equation 1.13 and their subsequent likelihoods of default over time intervals of one to five years.[27] A demonstration of that mapping for one-year default probabilities appears in Figure 1.25. The figure shows how a given distance-to-default expressed in standard deviation units, in this case 3.7σ, corresponds to a given one-year default probability, 1.0% in the example. Thus, for a given distance-to-default from Equation 1.13, the KMV model can assign a historically derived probability of default, called the expected default frequency (EDF), at annual horizons of one to five years.

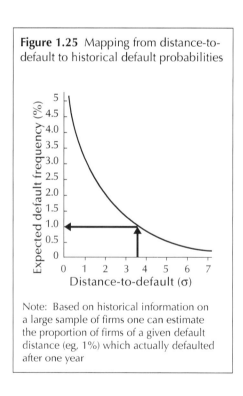

Figure 1.25 Mapping from distance-to-default to historical default probabilities

Note: Based on historical information on a large sample of firms one can estimate the proportion of firms of a given default distance (eg, 1%) which actually defaulted after one year

Significantly, Kealhofer and Kurbat (2001) used CAP curve analysis to demonstrate the superiority of the KMV model to agency ratings at predicting corporate defaults. In fact, the performance of the KMV model relative to agency ratings is that presented in the illustration of CAP curve analysis in Figure 1.16. The KMV model has had a great deal of commercial success and continues to be widely used for investment and risk management purposes. However, that success has come at the cost of abandoning the strict linkage to the theoretically elegant Merton and Black–Scholes formulation (in reality, no known successful implementation of the Merton framework follows that original formulation explicitly). Despite the success of the KMV model, it has failed to displace the risk-neutral model as the method preferred by broker–dealers for managing the risk of credit derivative positions.

Hybrid structural/statistical models

The issues with the Merton model described above have become central to the debate over quantitative risk assessment models, particularly regarding the completeness of the Merton formulation for estimating firms' default probabilities and valuing their liabilities. For example, Stein (2000) found that adding firms' return on assets to the Merton model could increase its discriminatory power between defaults and non-defaults. Acknowledging that firms' equity and debt premiums diverge over the credit cycle, and allowing for the possible relevance of additional variables related to the firm's debt capacity, is the essence of the hybrid modelling approach. That is, the hybrid approach blends a variant of the Merton model to capture firms' asset valuations, while adding a set of variables selected to assess firms' borrowing capacities. Deviations of the hybrid approach from the standard Merton model concern three main issues:

1. the impact of divergence of equity and debt markets on estimates of firms' default probabilities;
2. the role of firms' debt capacities; and
3. the concept of the default point.

A detailed theoretical treatment of each of these issues and the implications for their inclusion in a hybrid Merton statistical model

appears in Sobehart and Keenan (2003). Thus, we address those issues only briefly below. That discussion will be followed by a definition and evaluation of a hybrid statistical model.

Note that in the Merton model and KMV's implementation there
is no specification regarding firms' abilities to restructure their liabilities when under financial stress. In practice, however, if the firm
has borrowing capacity it can reduce the amount currently due by
rolling over its debt, thereby reducing its probability of default in
the short term. In fact, several extensions of the Merton model have
relaxed this limitation, introducing variable liabilities (Colin-Dufresne and Goldstein, 2001), multiple liabilities with different time
horizons (Geske, 1979; Longstaff and Schwartz, 1995), continuous
rollover of debt (Leland, 1999), stochastic assets (Huang and Kong,
2003), stochastic liabilities and default boundary (Finger *et al*, 2002;
Hsu, Saa-Requejo and Santa Clara, 2010), and stochastic macroeconomic variables (Li, 2013), to name a few.[28]

The relationship between an obligor and its lending institutions
is another factor to consider in estimating its likelihood of default.
Obligors having large exposures to its lenders create incentives for
lenders to roll over debt under times of stress. Also, lenders can extend
additional credit based on their estimation of the borrower's capacity
to service that debt. These factors are related to key accounting
information such as the borrower's profitability, liquidity and capital
structure, as well as information on the business environment and
the borrower's competitiveness. Additional variables in hybrid
models are intended to capture these factors. In fact, Duffie *et al*
(2009) introduced the idea of frailty to capture the effects of these risk
factors on expected defaults under times of stress.

Thus, despite the success of the KMV model, the considerations
above suggest that adding relevant variables to structural models
of default risk might improve the model's performance at predicting defaults. Working on this assumption, Sobehart *et al* (2000) proposed a hybrid approach called the HPD model that incorporates
the Merton model framework along with financial variables related
to firms' size, profitability and cashflow.[29] The model, described in
detail by Sobehart and Keenan (2002, 2003), appears in Figure 1.26
and a formal description of the model appears in Appendix 1.4.

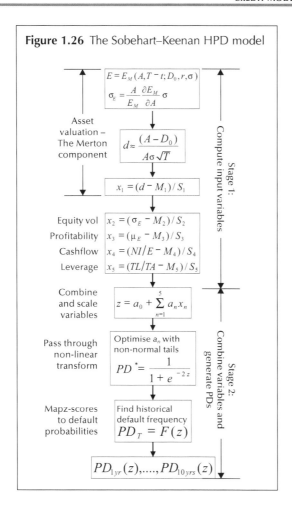

Figure 1.26 The Sobehart–Keenan HPD model

To begin, Sobehart and Keenan selected a set of market and accounting variables to describe the value of the firm's assets and its borrowing capacity. They retained much of the Merton model formulation and variables required for the asset valuation portion of the model. Variables that account for firms' borrowing capacity were selected from those available in the market or firms' financial statements by a trial-and-error process, placing emphasis in those variables that were available for the widest number of firms. The selected variables are:

- ❏ the firm's market value of equity, E;
- ❏ 12-month volatility of the firm's equity price, σ_E;
- ❏ the firm's 12-month return on equity, μ_E;
- ❏ book value of total assets, TA;
- ❏ the book value of current liabilities, CL;
- ❏ the book value of total liabilities TL; and
- ❏ net income, NI.

The default boundary of the firm, D_0 in Figure 1.26 is calculated according to the method introduced by Kealhofer (1999) in Equation 1.14, where D_0 equals short-term liabilities plus one-half long-term debt.[30] To capture the asset valuation of the firm, Sobehart and Keenan also used KMV's variation of the Merton model formulation in Equation 1.13, whereby the distance-to-default, d, corresponding to Merton's δ_T in Equation A.1.3.3, is defined as:

$$d = \frac{(A - D_0)}{A\sigma\sqrt{T}}$$

(1.15)

where A corresponds to Merton's VA, and D is K, respectively, and T is the time horizon, typically one or five years.

To capture a firm's borrowing capacity, Sobehart and Keenan chose a linear combination of the following variables:

- ❏ 12-month equity volatility, σ_E;
- ❏ 12-month equity return relative to the S&P 500 index: $\mu_E - \mu_{S\&P500}$;
- ❏ profitability ratio: net income to equity, NI/E; and
- ❏ book value of leverage TL/TA.

The purpose of these variables is to penalise volatile, highly leveraged and/or unprofitable companies, thereby reducing their borrowing capacity.

Figure 1.26 shows the two general stages of the HPD model. The first stage involves assembling and transforming the input variables as preparation for the second stage, which computes firms' estimated PDs. Having defined the quantities for input, the inputs to the model are used to generate five variables, $x_1, \ldots, x_5$ where the first variable is the distance-to-default and the others characterise the firm's equity volatility, its profitability, cashflow and size. In particular, Figure 1.26 and Appendix 1.4 show that each of the variables, including distance-to-default, is normalised with respect to their means and standard deviations calculated from non-defaulting firms in the development sample.

The second state of the model first combines the variables $x_1, \ldots, x_5$ linearly to generate a single quantity, z, which characterises the risk of the firm as:

$$z = a_0 + \sum_{n=1}^{5} a_n x_n$$

(1.16)

which is identical in form to Altman's Z-score. As the x_i variables are normalised with respect to the non-defaulted firms in the sample, the variable z measures the deviation of firms' credit quality from the historical average of healthy firms. Finally, Sobehart and Keenan use the following functional form to approximate firms' probabilities of default, PD:

$$PD \approx \frac{1}{1 + e^{-2z}}$$

(1.17)

Sobehart and his colleagues have tracked the relative predictive power of the HPD and KMV models between 2000 and 2011, and a summary of those analyses from Sobehart (2013) appears in Figure 1.27. The CAP curve at the left in Figure 1.27 is a composite of results from annual analysis from 2000–11 based on over 800 firm defaults and 50,000 non-default observations. At the beginning of each year, both models were presented with the same sample of firms that defaulted during the subsequent 12 months along with non-defaulting firms in that year.[31] The CAP curve demonstrates that, for all population percentile criteria, the HPD model isolates more defaulters in the sample than KMV. For example, the vertical line in the CAP curve illustrates model accuracy for the 10% of the population ranked riskiest (ie, largest PDs) by both models. In that 10%, KMV captures about 57% of the defaulters in that sample, performing well above chance (ie, 10%).[32] Nevertheless, HPD is performing even better, capturing roughly 65% of the defaulting firms in their riskiest top 10%.

The right panel of Figure 1.27 lists accuracy ratios (ARs) by year for the HPD and KMV models, along with numbers of defaulting and non-defaulting firms. The HPD model has higher ARs than KMV for 10 of the 12 years tested. Also, when HPD underperforms KMV as in 2010 and 2011, its ARs lag by only 1% and those years were among those with the lowest defaults over the period. Finally, as shown in Figure 1.27, the average annual AR for the HPD model is 81%, as opposed to the 75% average annual AR for the KMV model.

Implications of equity–debt risk premium divergence for credit models

Practitioners familiar with the KMV model will likely have noticed how swings in equity market values move predicted default probabilities, which are not necessarily followed by changes in firms' overall default probabilities. For example, the top left and right panels of Figure 1.28 present analysis from Sobehart (2005) on one-year EDFs from Moody's/KMV model on December 31, 2002, for 4,997 US firms.[33, 34] Based on the EDFs assigned by the KMV model to those firms, one would have expected an overall default rate of 8.7% in 2003, but only 84 of those firms defaulted, a 1.7% rate. Furthermore, a rough estimate of the default rate for high-yield firms in the sample is 20%, but Moody's Investors Service (Ou, Chiu and Metz, 2012) reports a 5.3% default rate for high-yield firms in 2003. These types of results underlie the often-voiced and apparently accurate criticism that Merton models, as embodied in the KMV formulation, generate too many "false positive" default signals.

The results in Figure 1.28 are also useful for illustrating the importance of the normalisation of the variables in the HPD model (see Appendix 1.4) for minimising the effect of equity and debt risk premium divergence on model PDs.[35] Consider scores assigned by the HPD model to those same defaulting (lower left) and non-defaulting firms (lower right) at the end of 2002. A comparison of the distributions of defaulters between KMV and HPD (ie, the left panels) would seem to indicate better performance of the KMV model – the defaulters appear have higher default probabilities.[36] However, when one considers the distributions of the non-defaulters in the right-hand panels, one observes a huge number of non-defaulters to which KMV assigns high default probabilities. In contrast, the HPD model maintains very low estimates of default

Figure 1.27 Left: CAP curves for HPD and KMV models (2000–11); right: sample statistics by year and corresponding accuracy ratios for HPD and KMV models

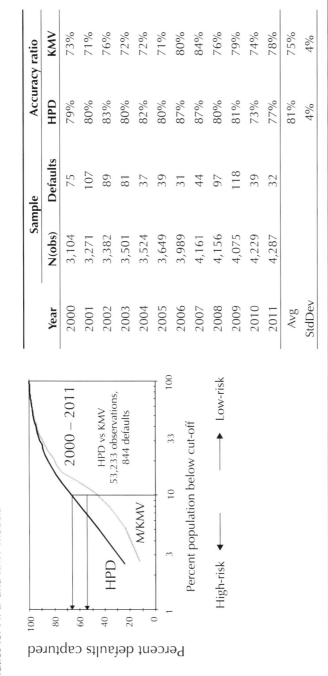

Year	Sample		Accuracy ratio	
	N(obs)	Defaults	HPD	KMV
2000	3,104	75	79%	73%
2001	3,271	107	80%	71%
2002	3,382	89	83%	76%
2003	3,501	81	80%	72%
2004	3,524	37	82%	72%
2005	3,649	39	80%	71%
2006	3,989	31	87%	80%
2007	4,161	44	87%	84%
2008	4,156	97	80%	76%
2009	4,075	118	81%	79%
2010	4,229	39	73%	74%
2011	4,287	32	77%	78%
Avg			81%	75%
StdDev			4%	4%

probabilities for the non-defaulting firms amid the huge equity sell-off in late 2002, but with the subsequent only average realised defaults in 2003. In fact, regardless of population criterion, KMV excludes more non-defaulters for each defaulter excluded by the HPD model. For example, if one sets their investment criterion for PD values $< = \ln(3)$ (ie, default greater than 20%), the ratio of non-defaulters excluded to defaulters detected is the following.

❑ KMV – 1400 non-defaulters: 70 defaulters, or 20:1.
❑ HPD – 450 non-defaulters: 50 defaulters, or 9:1.

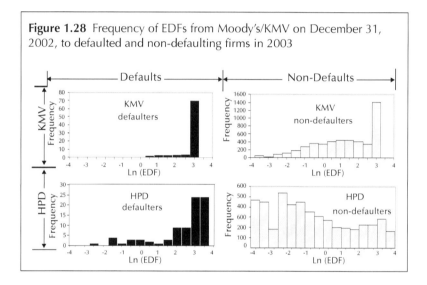

Figure 1.28 Frequency of EDFs from Moody's/KMV on December 31, 2002, to defaulted and non-defaulting firms in 2003

Structural and hybrid models: Advantages and limitations

Although structural and hybrid credit models have proven superior to agency ratings at predicting defaults, they too have limitations. Before discussing innovations in credit modelling in the next chapter, we consider briefly the advantages and disadvantages of the structural and hybrid structural/statistical approach, particularly as regards gaps in our ability to predict defaults for the range of risky asset classes. A summary of those features appears in Table 1.5, and they are described briefly below.

Table 1.5 Advantages and limitations of structural and statistical models

Advantages	Disadvantages

❏ Strong financial/economic foundation rooted in option pricing theory
  - Implies ability to model actual credit spreads from model inputs
	❏ Implied credit spreads from option pricing theory are smaller than observed spreads
	  - Actual default rates need to be calibrated to historical data

❏ Directly verifiable inputs from market and balance sheet information
  - Available from all firms with publicly-traded equity
	❏ Can be "fooled" by equity friendly – bond unfriendly actions
	  - Leveraged "buy-outs" cause equity rally, but bond sell-off
	  - Equity buybacks

❏ Models are "forward-looking" they incorporate information from the equity market
  - Changes in firms' equity tend to lead changes in bond spreads
  - Able to predict risk and cheap credits for relative value trading
	❏ Cannot score firms without tradable equity or public financials. This excludes
	  - Sovereigns
	  - Municipalities
	  - Private Firms

❏ Demonstrated superiority over agency ratings at predicting default	❏ Do not work well estimating default for banks and other financial firms

Consider first some positive features of the structural and hybrid models as embodied in the KMV and HPD models, respectively. The basic concept of equity and debt as options on the firms' assets is deeply rooted in financial theory. Also, the inputs to the models are available from public information and are directly verifiable. Importantly, these models are forward-looking, incorporating information from the equity market whose investors are presumably evaluating firms' future prospects. In particular, structural and hybrid models have been demonstrated to be useful for predicting ratings changes and superior to agency ratings at predicting defaults. In addition, although not the subject of this chapter, the KMV and HPD models have proven useful for predicting changes in credit spreads (Li, Zhang and Crossin, 2012; Benzschawel *et al*, 2014b).[37]

While structural and hybrid models have proven extremely useful, they have some common limitations. First of all, to be successful, both types of model had to abandon their strict linkage to the theoretical foundations of the Merton/Black–Scholes framework. Although that break has proven advantageous in practice, it leaves unexplained the relationship between defaults and credit spreads. In addition, Merton-based models can be "fooled" by equity investor-friendly, bond holder-unfriendly events such as leveraged buy-outs and equity buy-backs. Both types of events cause equities to rally and bonds to sell off, leaving bonds looking erroneously cheap. Structural models do not do well at estimating default probabilities for banks or firms with both a manufacturing and a financial arm, such as the major car manufacturers. These firms appear highly leveraged relative to most non-financial firms, leading to overly high estimates of default probabilities. Also, unlike non-financial companies, financial institutions such as banks and brokerage firms tend to fail rapidly, often due to a lack of confidence, making it impossible to fund their liabilities.

The most general problem with the equity-based structural and hybrid models is that they cannot estimate PDs for obligors without tradable equity. Thus, the structural framework cannot be applied to the risk of sovereign debt, municipalities or private firms. Although Gray, Merton and Bodie (2007) have attempted to expand the Merton contingent claims framework to estimate sovereign risk, that model requires extensive and critical user-defined estimates of macroscopic conditions and linkages between private and public sector debt. Thus, the model, while of particular interest for macro-economic analysis, has not yet found widespread use for estimating likelihoods of default for trading and risk management purposes. In the following chapter, we will consider several more classes of models that, although still in their infancy, hold promise for predicting defaults for countries, municipalities and private firms, and perhaps improve on modelling default for publicly traded firms.

CONCLUSION

This chapter has presented a short history of quantitative approaches to credit risk modelling from a practical point of view, concentrating on default prediction. It began by describing the origin of credit modelling along with the debt markets, and explored various innovations such as statistical, reduced form, structural and hybrid structural–statistical models. The discussion highlighted the advantages and disadvantages of each approach. A major theme that emerged from historical analysis of credit modelling was that older successful models typically do not become extinct even though they give way to more accurate and/or timely models. That is, for each type of innovation – from financial ratios to agency ratings and even Altman's Z-score – there remain a range of applications for which the level of accuracy of those models is sufficient. The survival of less powerful approaches results from the fact that nearly every innovation in credit modelling has come at the expense of increasing requirements for input data, enhancements in computational power and greater theoretical complexity. Furthermore, although those innovations have enabled greater accuracy at predicting defaults and credit relative value, that information is not required for all investor applications. This leads one to suspect that existing models will continue to be used in the future, albeit likely in more restricted domains. There remains ample room for the development of models to handle the tougher credit modelling problems such as predicting default for private firms, municipalities, sovereigns and along with limitations of existing models of default for public corporations. Finally, none of these models can so far substitute for human judgement, which remains as the last step in the analytical credit analysis process, particularly as it involves investment decisions.

APPENDIX 1.1 CREDIT RISK MODELS PRE-2010

All existing popular default models have their advantages and limitations, but none has proved satisfactory for all asset classes and applications. Figure A.1.1 presents examples of the major types of credit models in use. Fundamental analysis remains popular and, at least for the foreseeable future, will likely remain the final step in investors' decision-making. Statistical approaches to estimating default risk continue to be used, particularly for modelling private firms, banks and sovereign risk. The risk-neutral modelling framework is the dominant method for measuring and hedging risk by broker–dealers in credit products. Structural and hybrid structural/statistical models remain popular, being particularly suited for estimating credit relative value owing to their dependence on daily equity data, which appears to provide advance signals of credit spread moves.

Figure A1.1 Examples of popular approaches to estimating credit risk

Fundamental analysis

- Analyse firms' assets, earnings, sales, products, management and market position

Advantages:

- Close and in depth monitoring of firms' activities
- Useful for avoiding "blowups" and defaults
- Can identify potential "event risk" (LBO, equity buybacks, etc)
- Forward-looking

Disadvantages:

- Only single analyst's opinion
- Difficult to quantify default
- Intermittent inconsistent coverage of universe of firms
- Don't always respond to market moves and events
- Analysts are expensive

- No current model that can substitute totally for fundamental analysis.

Statistical and risk-neutral approaches

Statistical models

Altman's Z-score and adaptive logistic regression models are examples of statistical models

$$Z = .012X_1 + .014X_2 + .033X_3 + .006X_4 + .999X_5$$

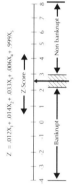

Enhancements or the Altman approach are non-linear adaptive models, where variables are updated annually based on predictive power

$$PD = \frac{1}{1 + \exp(\sum \beta_i.x_i)} \left.\begin{array}{l} \\ \\ \end{array}\right\} \begin{array}{l} \text{Non-linear} \\ \text{PD function} \end{array}$$

Risk-neutral PDs

Representation of a one-period bond under risk-neutral measure

No default $1-p_1^Q$ 108

100

Default p_1^Q 50

Discount at 6% for 1 year

The bond is at par (100); its price is the present value of the expected payoff and p_1^Q is calculated as:

$$100 = \frac{1}{1.06}[(1-p_1^Q) \times 108 + (p_1^Q \times 50)]$$

Figure A1.1 (*Continued*)

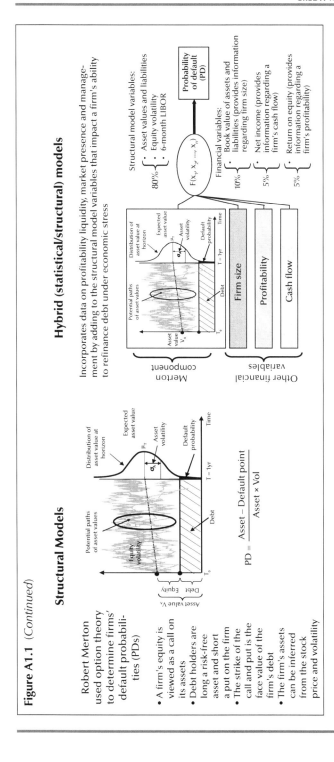

Structural Models

Robert Merton used option theory to determine firms' default probabilities (PDs)

- A firm's equity is viewed as a call on its assets
- Debt holders are long a risk-free asset and short a put on the firm
- The strike of the call and put is the face value of the firm's debt
- The firm's assets can be inferred from the stock price and volatility

Potential paths of asset values

Distribution of asset value at horizon

Expected asset value

μ_T

Asset volatility

σ_t

Equity volatility

Default probability

$T = 1yr$

Time

Debt

Asset value V_A

Debt / Equity

$$PD = \frac{Asset - Default\ point}{Asset \times Vol}$$

Hybrid (statistical/structural) models

Incorporates data on profitability liquidity, market presence and management by adding to the structural model variables that impact a firm's ability to refinance debt under economic stress

Merton component

Potential paths of asset values

Distribution of asset value at horizon

Expected asset value

μ_T

Asset volatility

σ_t

Default probability

$T = 1yr$

Time

Debt

Asset value V_A

T_0

Other financial variables

Firm size

Profitability

Cash flow

Structural model variables:
- Asset values and liabilities
- Equity volatility
- 6-month LIBOR

80%

$F(x_1, x_2, ..., x_n)$

Financial variables:

10%
- Book value of assets and liabilities (provides information regarding firm size)

5%
- Net income (provides information regarding a firm's cash flow)

5%
- Return on equity (provides information regarding a firm's profitability)

Probability of default (PD)

65

CREDIT MODELLING: ADVANCED TOPICS

APPENDIX 1.2 THE REDUCED FORM MODEL IN CONTINUOUS TIME

To highlight the elegant formalism that underlies risk-neutral pricing theory, the framework presented in Equations 1.3–1.7 is reiterated in this appendix, but using continuous time mathematics. For example, consider again the one-period bond in Figure 1.2. As in the figure, let $v(0)$ be the bond's present value of 100, τ be the time of default, and T and R as defined previously. Then, the present value can be expressed as:

$$v(0) = E_0^T \left[e^{-\int_0^T r dt} 1_{\tau > T} \right] + E_0^T \left[e^{-\int_0^T r dt} R_{\tau \leq T} \right]$$

(A.1.2.1)

where e is the base of the natural logarithm ($e = 2.71828...$) and E_0^T is the expectation of each quantity between time 0 and T. Jarrow and Turnbull (1995) introduced the now conventional method of modelling the default process as a Poisson event[38] where the risk-neutral cumulative probability of default to time t, p_t^Q is given as:

$$p_t^Q = 1 - e^{-\int_0^t r dt}$$

(A.1.2.2)

where γ is an instantaneous jump-to-default or hazard rate. Given the market-implied risk neutral default rate of 3.5%, solving for the default intensity using Equation A.1.2.2 gives $\gamma = \ln(0.965) = 0.36$.[39]

APPENDIX 1.3 THE MERTON MODEL FORMULATION

Merton's formalism comes directly from Black–Scholes: the debt of a firm is an investment in a risk-free bond plus a put sold to the equity holders of the firm at par. Merton linked the firm's equity value, V_E and equity volatility, σ_E, to the otherwise unobservable asset value, V_A, and asset volatility, σ_A via the relations:

$$V_E = V_A N(\delta_T + \sigma_A \sqrt{T}) - e^{rt} KN(\delta_T)$$

(A.1.3.1)

and:

$$\sigma_E = \frac{V_A}{V_E} N(\delta_T = \sigma_A \sqrt{T}) \sigma_A$$

(A.1.3.2)

where $N(.)$ is the function specifying the normal distribution. Once V_A and V_E are known, the distance-to-default, and hence the value of the put option (ie, the credit spread of the debt to US Treasuries) can be calculated using the Black–Scholes formula as:

$$\delta_T = \frac{log\left(\dfrac{V_A}{K}\right) + (r - \dfrac{1}{2}\sigma_A^2)T}{\sigma_A \sqrt{T}}$$

(A.1.3.3)

Although the calculation of the distance-to-default δ_T is relatively straightforward, each stage of the parameter estimation process of the inputs to Equations A.1.3.1–A.1.3.3 has generated its own body of academic research in response to observations regarding the oversimplification of Merton's original formulation for valuing firm's debt.

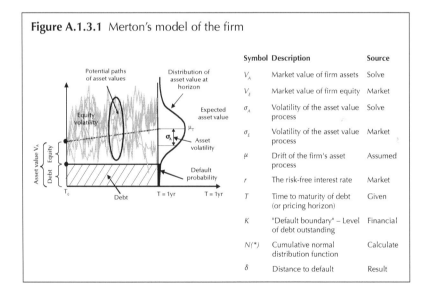

Figure A.1.3.1 Merton's model of the firm

Symbol	Description	Source
V_A	Market value of firm assets	Solve
V_E	Market value of firm equity	Market
σ_A	Volatility of the asset value process	Solve
σ_E	Volatility of the asset value process	Market
μ	Drift of the firm's asset process	Assumed
r	The risk-free interest rate	Market
T	Time to maturity of debt (or pricing horizon)	Given
K	"Default boundary" – Level of debt outstanding	Financial
$N(*)$	Cumulative normal distribution function	Calculate
δ	Distance to default	Result

APPENDIX 1.4   THE SOBEHART–KEENAN HPD MODEL

Figure A.1.4.1 The Sobehart–Keenan HPD model

HPD model variables
The variables required for the distance-to-default component are taken from Merton, with those for size, profitability and cashflow identified by trial-and-error, with emphasis on those offering the widest coverage of firms. The selected variables are:

❑ the firm's market value of equity, $\nu(E)$;
❑ 12-month stock volatility $\sigma(E)$;
❑ 12-month stock return $\omega(E)$;
❑ Book value of total assets, TA;
❑ Book value of current liabilities, CL;
❑ Book value of total liabilities TL; and
❑ Net income, NI.

The total liabilities of the firm required by the model are defined as $D = CL + LTD/2$. The long-term debt is: $LTD = TL - CL$. The distance-to-default, variable x(1), is calculated as shown at the right as:

$$\delta = \frac{(A - D)}{A\sigma\sqrt{T}}$$

where A is the asset value calculated as described below. The impact of size, profitability and cashflow is described as a linear combination of:

  x(2) 12-month stock volatility $\sigma(E)$;
  x(3) 12-month stock return relative to the S&P 500, $\omega(E)$;
  x(4) Profitability: net income/equity market value, NI/E;
  x(5) Book value of leverage, TL/TA.

As inputs to the model, the variables, x(1), . . . , x(5) are all normalised (ie, Z-scores) relative to the population of healthy firms. This is an important feature of the model.

Estimating firm asset value and volatility
Firms' assets and volatility are unobservable, but are solved using Merton's method of inverting the following equations

$$E = E_M(A, T, D, r, \sigma)$$

$$\sigma_E = \frac{A}{E_M} \frac{\partial E_M}{\partial A} \sigma$$

Figure A.1.4.1 (*Continued*)

where E is the observed value of equity and $E_M(A,T,D,r,\sigma)$ is the equity value implied by Merton's formula for a European call option of strike D with expiry T and r is the risk-free rate. The volatility of equity $\sigma(E)$ is the firm's asset volatility, σ, adjusted by firm leverage.

The variables, $x(1), \ldots, x(5)$ are weighted and summed as

$$z = a_0 + \sum_{n=1}^{5} a_n x_n$$

with $a(0), \ldots, a(n)$ obtained by maximum likelihood adjusted for the assumed fat-tailed distribution of default probabilities to obtain value of p^* as

$$p^* = \frac{1}{1 + e^{-2z}}$$

Finally, to provide default probability estimates that match historical default experience, the model score, z, is mapped to the observed default frequencies for time horizons up to 10 years.

Stages of processing in the HPD model

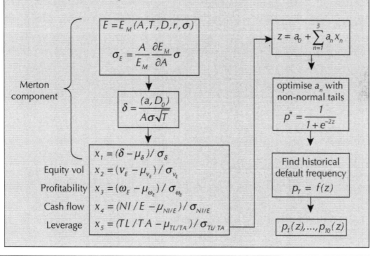

4   These include structured credit products such as collateralised loan obligations (CLOs), single-tranche collateralised debt obligations (CDOs), credit options, and even counterparty credit risk.

5   For example, the "best" available credit models all capture roughly 60–70% of firms that will default within the next year within the top 10% of the firms that they rank as the riskiest.

6   Evidence for these claims is presented below.

7   In fact, although default risk plays a major role in what drives credit spreads, market risk is likely a greater factor in most changes in the value of credit instruments – see the discussion on the credit risk premium in Chapter 2.

8   Also, there are typically provisions of cross-default, whereby failure to make a specified payment on one obligation triggers defaults on the firm's other debt instruments, even if no payment from those are due at that time.

9   The position of a given type of debt in the firm's capital structure has legal implications in recovery via the absolute priority rule (Eberhart, Moore and Rosenfelt, 1990). However, despite legal priority, in practice the strict priority rule is violated routinely. Despite this, the effect of priority on amount recovered in default has been confirmed (Altman and Eberhart, 1994; Fridson and Garman, 1997). An excellent discussion of the role of seniority in recovery value in default can be found in Schuermann (2005).

10   The likelihood of default has been much more well-documented and received greater attention from modellers than LGD, but its importance in risk and relative value is coming to be widely recognised, particularly with changes in the regulatory environment such as Basel. Although recovery models are not the subject of this chapter, extensive treatments can be found in Benzschawel (2012) and Benzschawel and Su (2013), as well as in Chapter 3.

11   For example, see Verde (2003); Varma and Cantor (2004); Vazza, Aurora and Miller (2007); and Emery, Ou and Tennant (2010).

12   These include Moody's LossCalc (Dwyer and Korablev, 2008), S&P's Ratings Direct (Standard and Poor's, 2008) and Citi's E-3 Ensemble Model (Benzschawel and Su, 2013).

13   It is difficult to overemphasise the contribution to the development of the credit markets and to credit modelling efforts of the agency rating scale. Not only did it allow quantification of judgements on firms' credit qualities, thereby aiding issuers and investors, but it enabled historical tracking of defaults and credit spreads by ratings for use by subsequent generations of credit modellers (including myself).

14   Citigroup Index Group (2013) describes the criteria for inclusion of bonds in the corporate indexes.

15   That is, if a risky obligor with default probability $p_{0,1}$ survives one year, the one-year probability between years one and two, $p_{1,2} < p_{0,1}$. However, see Berd, Mashal and Wang (2004) for an alternative interpretation.

16   In fact, the spread curve for triple-C rated bonds has become inverted again, and that for double-B bonds is flat (Lee, Su and Benzschawel, 2014).

17   See Horrigan (1968) for a detailed history of the development of ratio analysis. Also, Brown (1955) provides an even more detailed description of the early history of financial ratio analysis.

18   The quick ratio is a measure of a firm's liquid assets relative to its current liabilities.

19   In fact, Lincoln (1925) had already discussed and illustrated 40 different financial ratios.

20   We chose the Bayesian information criterion (BIC) developed by Schwartz (1978) as our measure of predictive power. The BIC measures how well the model fits the data, but also imposes a penalty for having too many variables, thereby guarding against over-fitting the data. A detailed description of model construction can be found in Benzschawel, Li and Lee (2013).

21   Receiver operating characteristic (ROC) curves, the precursor to CAP curves, and its analysis were originally described by Green and Swets (1966) and Egan (1975) to quantify the detection of signals in noise. The relationship between ROC and CAP curves is described in Sobehart, Keenan and Stein (2000).

22   In the case of the bank model, all of the data are posted on the Federal Deposit Insurance Corporation's website and so are in standardised form and easily sourced for model calibration.

23   The superscript Q is used to denote the fact that default probabilities are determined under the risk-neutral measure.

24   See, for example, Chava and Jarrow (2002) and Janossi, Jarrow and Yildrim (2003).

25   In fact, an examination of calculations of risk-neutral default probabilities reveal them to be simply logarithmic transformations of spreads modified by expected recovery values in default.

26   Bielecki and Rutkowski (2002) describe various extensions of reduced for models.

27   Many of these modifications are discussed in Anderson and Sundaresan (2000).

28   See, for example, Black and Cox (1976); Kim, Ramaswamy and Sunderasan (1993); Longstaff and Schwartz (1995); Levin and van Deventer (1997); Wei and Guo (1997); Briys and Varenne (1997); Leland (1999); Schwartz and Moon (2000); Kao (2000) and references therein.

29   A detailed description of these issues appears in Benzschawel (2013), so are described only briefly herein.

30   KMV made several other modifications of the Merton framework, including bounding default probabilities between 0.02% (best) and 20% (worst), and adjusting asset volatilities for certain types of industrial firms. A detailed description of the KMV model can be found in Crosbie and Bohn (2001). The KMV corporation was sold to Moody's Investors Service in 2002 for US$210 million, and the company was renamed Moody's/KMV.

31   See Huang (2010) for a description various extensions of credit risk structural models.

32   HPD stands for "hybrid probability of default", as the model is a combination of the Merton and statistical modelling approaches.

33   Sobehart and Keenan explored other combinations of current liabilities and long-term debt, finding only small changes in the performance of the model given their available dataset.

34   Note that the HPD model was last recalibrated in 2000, so all results for the HPD model are out-of-sample. Most results are also out-of-sample for the KMV model, but after being acquired by Moody's in 2004 the model was recalibrated in 2008, and its performance appears to have improved relative to HPD since then, although default rates have also been low since 2008.

35   Note that the value of 57% at the 10% criterion is very similar to that presented by Kealhofer and Kurbat (2001) that appears in Figure 1.16.

36   A more detailed explanation of this study appears in Benzschawel (2012).

37   Some may recall the situation in the debt and equity markets near the end of 2002. The telecom bubble in the equity markets had burst, capped by the large and high profile defaults by WorldCom and Enron. The massive sell-off in the equity markets led to high estimates of one-year PDs for 2003 from the KMV model as illustrated in Figure 1.28. However, by that time firms' balance sheets had begun to improve, and the high-yield default rate dropped to 5.3% in 2003.

38   Recall that the input variables to the HPD model are all Z-scores calculated relative to their means and standard deviations in the development sample.

39   Note that the x-axes in the figures are in natural logarithms of PDs. This is because the logarithms of PDs are linearly related to agency rating categories. Also, note that the natural logarithm of 20 is 3.

40   In fact, KMV and HPD models have proven extremely useful for predicting spread market moves and have given rise to many well-documented successful trading strategies.

41   The Poisson distribution expresses the probability of the occurrence of a given number of independent events whose average of occurrence per unit time is known to occur in a

fixed period of time. The distribution usually describes processes for which the number of expected events is small given the time interval of interest. Give an expected number of occurrences in the interval is λ, then the probability that there are exactly k occurrences (k being a non-negative integer, k = 0, 1, 2, ...) is equal to:

$$f(k,\lambda) = \frac{\lambda^k e^{-\lambda}}{k!}$$

where e is the base of the natural logarithm ($e = 2.71828...$), k is the number of occurrences of an event – the probability of which is given by the function $f(k,\lambda)$! (pronounced k-factorial) is the product of all numbers from 1 to k (ie, 1 times 2 times,..., times k) and λ is a positive real number equal to the expected number of occurrences during the given interval. For instance, if the events occur on average four times per year, and one is interested in the probability of an event occurring k times in a 10 year period, one would use a Poisson distribution as the model with $\lambda = 10 \times 4 = 40$. The Poisson distribution usually describes well systems with a large number of possible events each of which is rare, such as the defaults by risky firms.

42 Where the letters *ln* are conventional notation for the natural logarithm; the one having a base of *e*.

2

Credit Models: Looking to the Future

The previous chapter presented an historical overview of credit models that have gained wide acceptance among practitioners. As discussed, although successful in their various domains, each of those models has limitations. Furthermore, there have been markets for which no satisfactory default risk models have been proposed. These include models for private firms, sovereigns and municipalities. In this chapter, I will describe several approaches that might help to either improve existing methods for estimating firm default risk or offer promise for estimating default risk for previously underserved obligors.

The chapter will begin with consideration of the market-implied default model, based on the measurement of the daily credit risk premium. To the extent that the risk premium, as described below, can be measured in a market, it holds the promise of providing unbiased estimates of default probabilities for any obligor with a short history of market prices. These include private firms, sovereigns and municipalities. This is followed by a discussion of an expert system for measuring sovereign default called the Euromoney credit score, which can be combined with measures of default from structural models and historical default probabilities to provide estimates of default probabilities for sovereign bond issuers. The final section of the chapter concerns a "big data" model for predicting default for corporate firms: the Thomson Reuters StarMine model. The StarMine model takes natural language inputs from various sources and filters, and combines these to estimate default probabilities for corporate bond issuers.

THE MARKET-IMPLIED DEFAULT MODEL

As mentioned, the lack of a framework for predicting defaults for countries, municipalities and private firms has led to the need for development of other classes of models. This section will describe the development of a market-implied default model (MKI) that is an amalgamation of the structural model, the risk-neutral model discussed in Chapter 1 along with the capital asset pricing theory (CAPM). The foundation of the model relies on the assumption that one can separate the yield spread over Treasuries into two components: the compensation for not receiving the cashflows due to default and the remainder, the credit risk premium, resulting from exposure to the volatility of credit spreads. Since an understanding of the credit risk premium is a critical feature of the MKI model, we describe it in detail in the next section, followed by a description of how that risk premium is used in the MKI model.

The credit risk premium

Although the early work of Jones, Mason and Rosenfeld (1984) established firmly that Merton's structural model underestimates the spread values of risky debt, only relatively recently have market participants begun to unravel the components that underlie the spread compensation for investing in default-risky assets. Elton *et al* (2001) first documented the role of the credit risk premium in corporate bond spreads.[1] Using the logic embedded in the risk-neutral pricing equation:

$$e^{-T(r+s)} = e^{-rT} \left\{ [(1 - p_T) * 1] + p_T R \right\} \tag{2.1}$$

Elton *et al* used historical default rates for double-A rated corporate bonds, their durations and an assumed recovery value of 40%, as input into Equation 2.1. Their calculations revealed that only a small fraction of the yield spread over Treasuries could be attributed to not receiving the cashflows because of default. Some other factor, since termed the "credit spread puzzle" (Amato and Remolona, 2003; Driessen, 2003), and later the credit risk premium, is the major determinant of credit spreads, while Turnbull (2005) argues that the relationship between default and credit spreads is a major unsolved issue in credit modelling.

Benzschawel (2012) confirmed the results of Elton *et al* in a more systematic analysis of the credit risk premium for corporate bonds, providing estimates by agency rating category, results which are summarised in Figure 2.1. The table lists average cumulative 4.5-year default probabilities by rating category from the Sobehart and Keenan (2002) HPD model for corporate bonds in Citi's BIG and High Yield Indexes over the period 1994–2010.[2] 4.5-year cumulative default rates were used as they correspond roughly to the average duration of the bonds in those indexes. The figure also shows average monthly spreads, s, by rating category over the 17-year period, along with the spread compensation for default s_d, calculated using:

$$s = -\frac{1}{T}\ln\left[1-\left(p_T * LGD\right)\right]$$

(2.2)

Equation 2.2 is a rearrangement of Equation 2.1, with inputs of average PDs, 4.5-year duration and a 40% recovery value in default. The last column of the table presents differences by rating category between average spreads and spread due to default, the non-default spread or risk premium, designated as s_λ. For all rating categories, magnitudes of, s_λ are over twice that of s_d, with that ratio increasing for less risky credits, for which the risk premium accounts for nearly the entire credit spread to US Treasuries.

The right portion of Figure 2.1 presents graphically by rating category the average values of the default spread s_d (dark area), while the lighter area represents average values of the credit risk premium, s_λ. The value of s_d can be viewed as the spread necessary to compensate investors for the expected loss of cashflows due to default. That is, an investor who receives a yield spread to US Treasuries equal to s_d receives only an amount equal to the expected return from an equivalent-duration US Treasury security. For this reason, s_d could be called a "rock bottom spread". The average value of the credit risk premium, s_λ, ranges from 69bp for triple-A rated bonds to 727bp for triple-C rated ones, but is at least five-to-10 times larger than the average compensation for default regardless of rating category.

Figure 2.1 Average credit spreads due to default and non-default spreads by agency rating category (1994–2010)

S&P Credit Rating	4.5 Year Implied PD	Average Spread (bp)	Spread Due to Default (bp)	Non-Default Spread (bp)
AAA	0.3%	70	1	69
AA+	0.3%	87	4	82
AA	0.4%	88	5	83
AA–	0.5%	104	6	98
A+	0.6%	113	8	105
A	0.7%	122	9	112
A–	0.9%	137	11	126
BBB+	1.0%	160	14	146
BBB	1.3%	178	17	161
BBB–	1.6%	223	21	201
BB+	1.9%	126	25	301
BB	2.3%	166	10	336
BB–	2.7%	383	36	347
B+	3.8%	438	51	386
B	5.7%	511	77	433
B–	8.2%	588	113	476
CCC+	11 .8%	891	164	727

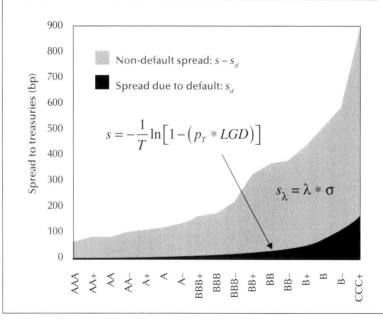

Non-default spread: $s - s_d$

Spread due to default: s_d

$$s = -\frac{1}{T}\ln\left[1 - \left(p_T * LGD\right)\right]$$

$$s_\lambda = \lambda * \sigma$$

Although Figure 2.1 shows average values of the risk premium, default rates vary over the credit cycle, as do credit spreads. Perhaps by determining the relationship between credit spreads and default rates, one could make inferences as to PDs from current values of credit spreads, or vice versa. Then, applying this knowledge to individual credits, one could determine what differences in bonds' credit spreads imply regarding their probabilities of default or how changes in default probabilities impact bonds' credit spreads. Unfortunately, this has not proven satisfactory, as illustrated in Figure 2.2, which displays annual average high-yield credit spreads against the comparable default rates over the period 1986–2009. That is, even though overall spread levels and defaults are correlated ($R^2 = 0.77$), that relationship is not sufficiently strong to be useful for the accurate prediction of overall spread levels, much less credit spreads by rating category or for individual firms. The dashed lines in Figure 2.2 show that errors can be large. For example, in 2008, the average spread was 912bp but the default rate was only 4.37%, as opposed to the predicted value of 9.7%. The divergence between factors controlling default and credit spreads was also noted by Colin-Dufresne, Goldstein and Martin (2001), who find that changes in spreads are highly correlated among issuers but are unrelated to macroeconomic or financial variables that influence default.

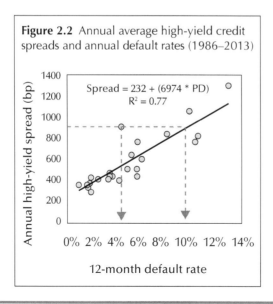

Figure 2.2 Annual average high-yield credit spreads and annual default rates (1986–2013)

A key to understanding the credit risk premium comes from observations of historical credit spreads by rating categories over time. The top panel of Figure 2.3 shows monthly average yield spreads to US Treasuries by rating category. Clearly, spread values vary widely over the credit cycle. However, when plotted on logarithmic axes, as in the bottom panel of Figure 2.3, one sees that credit spreads by rating seem to move in tandem at a constant ratio across rating categories. This suggests that while default rates and the credit risk premium may not be perfectly correlated, spread moves for default-risky credits, regardless of rating, are all related by changes in a single common factor.

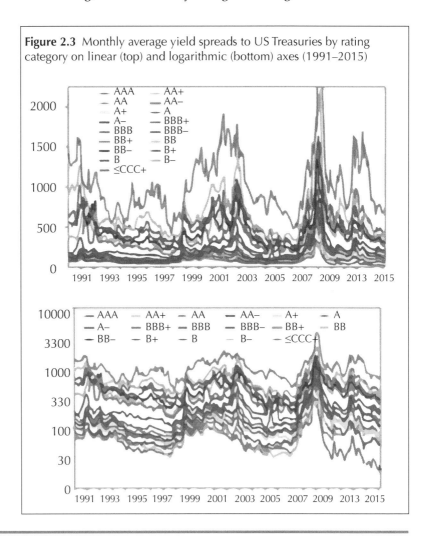

Figure 2.3 Monthly average yield spreads to US Treasuries by rating category on linear (top) and logarithmic (bottom) axes (1991–2015)

Benzschawel and Assing (2012) provide insight into the factor controlling the non-default spread, s_d, from examination of the volatility of average credit spreads over time. For example, the connected white dots in the first panel of Figure 2.4 (below) show that average monthly spread volatility as a function of rating category is a straight line when plotted on a logarithmic spread axis. Furthermore, the volatility-to-spread ratio (grey points referenced to right axis) is a constant of roughly 0.3 for all rating categories. Importantly, this implies that the market charges the same average spread per unit of volatility. Finally, we find the volatility of the rolling spread-to-volatility ratio (the black triangles) is also constant across rating categories.

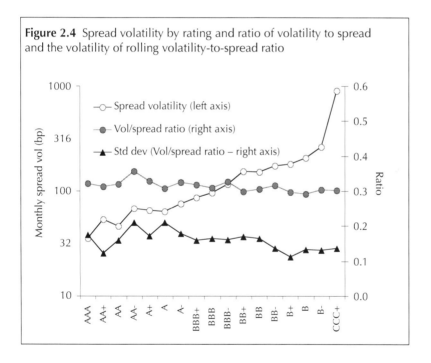

Figure 2.4 Spread volatility by rating and ratio of volatility to spread and the volatility of rolling volatility-to-spread ratio

Figure 2.4 (*Continued*) Top: Merton-type structural model used to estimate default probabilities to compute default spreads s_d; bottom: non-default spreads by volatility for the calibration universe using HPD PDs

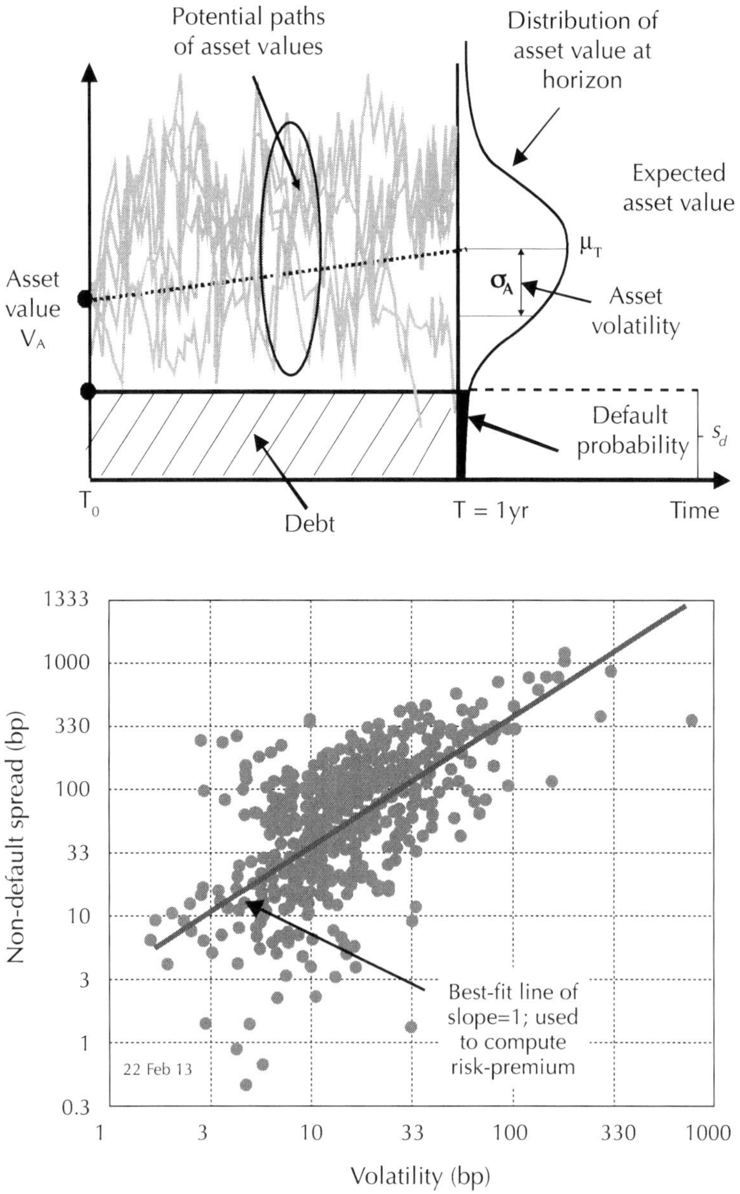

The results in the first panel of Figure 2.4 suggest that the credit risk premium might be related to spread volatility. To test this, Benzschawel and Assing first computed values of default spread, s_d, for bonds in Citi's BIG and High Yield Indexes using the HPD model. As shown in the middle panel of Figure 2.4, one can think of p_T in the structural framework of Merton (1974) as the likelihood that a given firm is insolvent at time T. Then, given a firm's p_T (from HPD), its duration and an assumed value for LGD (in this case 60%), one can use Equation 2.2 to determine the spread values of default for its bonds. By subtracting the value of s_d from the bond's overall spread, s, one can determine the value of the non-default spread, s_λ. That is, we model the bonds spread as $s = s_d + s_\lambda$. The resulting values of s_λ for the bonds in our sample appear on a logarithmic scale as a function of log spread duration volatility in the bottom panel of Figure 2.4. If, as required by our working hypothesis, the market charges by the same amount on average per unit of volatility regardless of its source, then the relationship between non-default spread and spread volatility should have a slope of 1.0 in log–log coordinates. In fact, the solid line in the bottom panel of Figure 2.4 with a slope of 1.0 fits the points well. Note that all points on the line have the same ratio of spread to volatility, and we call this ratio λ and designate $\lambda\sigma = s_\lambda$ as the value of the daily risk premium for a given bond.[3]

Historical analyses of plots of non-default spreads versus volatility as in Figure 2.4 indicate that, at least to a first approximation, lines of slope equal to 1.0 fit the data well. Accordingly, we can compute historical values of the daily ratio of spread-to-volatility (ie, λ). The resulting values of λ appear in Figure 2.5. Average spreads and spread volatilities are also shown. The left panel of Figure 2.5 displays daily values of λ since 1999, whereas the right panel shows λ from June 2014 to June 2015. The dashed line in each plot is the average value of λ, which is 4.8bp per unit of spread volatility.

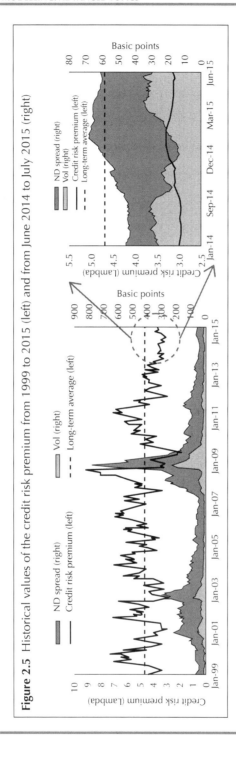

Figure 2.5 Historical values of the credit risk premium from 1999 to 2015 (left) and from June 2014 to July 2015 (right)

To summarise, to derive the credit risk premium, we first decompose bonds' credit spreads into the compensation for default s_d and into compensation for spread volatility s_λ, where:

$$s_d = -\frac{1}{T}\ln\left[1-\left(p_T \cdot LGD\right)\right] \text{ and } s_\lambda = \lambda_t\sigma$$

(2.3)

where T is the duration of the bond, p_T is the cumulative default probability to time T, LGD is the expected loss in default, σ is the spread volatility and σ_t is the price of spread volatility on day t (ie, the Sharpe ratio), and λ_t is the same for all credits. Putting those two expressions together, we can express the overall yield spread to US Treasuries on day t as:

$$s = \lambda_t\sigma - \frac{1}{T}\ln\left[1 - p_T \cdot LGD\right]$$

(2.4)

Thus, the model of spreads represented in Equation 2.4 requires physical probabilities of default (PDs) from the structural model, risk-neutral theory to convert PDs to spreads and the Sharpe ratio from the capital asset pricing model (CAPM) to estimate the daily spread value of volatility, λ_t.

Estimating obligor PDs

Thus far, I have described a framework for interpreting the relationship between credit spreads, default, recovery and spread volatility; however, the objective is to estimate firms' default probabilities, p_T. That is, even if one has bond spreads and volatilities, and a reasonable assumption for LGD (eg, 1–RV = 60%), one still requires an estimate of the current market price of risk at time t (ie, λ_t). To provide daily estimates of λ_t, we use one-year PDs from the HPD model for the commercial and industrial firms in Citi's investment-grade and high-yield bond indexes to construct plots like that in the bottom panel of Figure 2.4. Once we have λ_t, we plot firms' one-year spreads and spread volatilities as in the first panel of Figure 2.6 and fit those points with a quadratic function as shown in the figure.[4] Having inferred that day's value of λ_t, we can estimate a firm's p_1 using a recent history of their credit spreads. The bond's current spread and spread volatility are used to infer fair spreads and volatilities at the intersection of the line perpendicular to the bond's spread and volatility, and the best-fit line in the first panel of Figure 2.6. For example, assume that the value of $\lambda_t = 4.7bp/vol$ and that a bond has a volatility of 10bp and spread of 20bp (the black dot in Figure 2.6). That point would be referred to the point 7bp volatility and 29bp spread as shown by the arrow. If one assumes an LGD of 60%, the obligor would have a one-year market-implied default probability from Equation 2.2 of 1.6bp, or 0.016%.

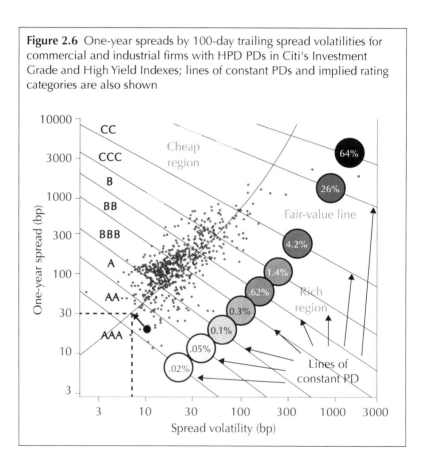

Figure 2.6 One-year spreads by 100-day trailing spread volatilities for commercial and industrial firms with HPD PDs in Citi's Investment Grade and High Yield Indexes; lines of constant PDs and implied rating categories are also shown

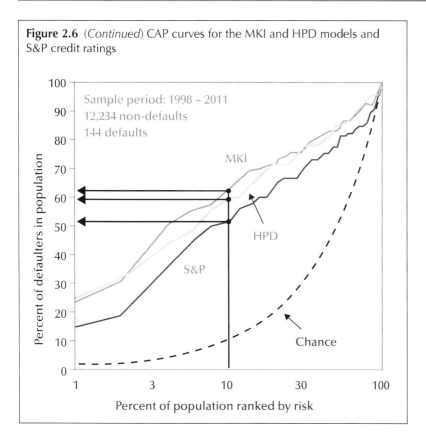

Figure 2.6 (*Continued*) CAP curves for the MKI and HPD models and S&P credit ratings

The second panel of Figure 2.6 displays CAP curves for HPD and MKI models along with S&P agency ratings on the same set of 144 defaults and over 12,000 non-defaults over the period from 1998 to 2011.[5] Although the sample size of defaulters is relatively small, the CAP curves indicate that the MKI model performs similarly to HPD at predicting defaults, and both outperform agency ratings. The similarity of accuracy of HPD and MKI is not surprising since PDs from the HPD model are used to determine the risk premium and the spread versus volatility curve.

More generally, once λ_t is determined one can calculate a market-implied PD for any obligor from its recent series of credit spreads. For example, the top panel of Figure 2.7 illustrates how the MKI model can be used to generate PD estimates for sovereigns that cannot be generated by structural models. The graph displays time se-

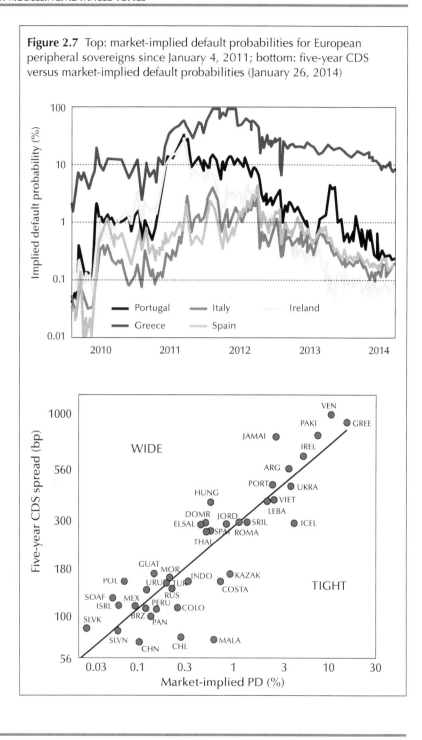

Figure 2.7 Top: market-implied default probabilities for European peripheral sovereigns since January 4, 2011; bottom: five-year CDS versus market-implied default probabilities (January 26, 2014)

ries of PDs for peripheral European sovereigns that span the most critical part of the European credit crisis of 2011–13. It also shows how, after PDs spiked in early 2012, they have decreased steadily since then. The bottom panel of Figure 2.7 (from Benzschawel *et al*, 2011) shows how PDs generated from sovereign bond data by the MKI model can be used to identify rich and cheap five-year CDS. That is, sovereigns' five-year CDS premiums versus logarithms of PDs are fit well by a straight line. CDS plotting above the line might be viewed as cheap, with those below the line as rich.

The market-implied approach is relatively new, but interesting and unique applications have already been demonstrated. For example, the CDX index (CDX.NA.IG) can be an effective hedge for the credit risk premium (Benzschawel and Su, 2014a), predicted default rates can be used to forecast the credit risk premium (Benzschawel and Su, 2014b) and that the MKI framework can be used to estimate the bail-in probabilities for banks contingent conversion (Co-co) bonds (Benzschawel *et al*, 2014a). As described above, the MKI model has already proven useful for tracking sovereign risk, and we are currently applying that model to measure the risk premium in the municipal bond market and estimate MKI PDs for municipal bonds (Benzschawel and Su, 2015).

THE FUTURE: EXPERT SYSTEMS AND BIG DATA MODELS
Although the statistical, structural and hybrid models of Chapter 1 have had a good deal of success at predicting defaults at one-year horizons for commercial and industrial firms (and perhaps banks), predictive models of default with similar accuracy remain to be developed for private firms, sovereign issuers and municipalities. Most of those frameworks are not well-suited for those problems or remain untested in those domains.[6] Furthermore, predicting default is inherently a probabilistic endeavour. Given the convergence of accuracies of existing models at predicting default, it seems likely that we are reaching an asymptote in our ability to predict corporate firm defaults at the one-year horizon from publicly available financial and market information. This fact, and our lack of models for sovereign and municipal defaults, has prompted the search for models that embed other sources of information such as news stories, analyst reports and expert opinions as input to predictive

models of default. We examine examples of such approaches in the remainder of this chapter.

We now consider classes of models that are expected to play an important role in credit modelling in the future. Although these models are in their infancy, they are sufficiently detailed to allow testing of their predictive power, albeit over relatively restricted timeframes. One of the classes is referred to as an expert system, consensus model or sophisticated crowd-sourcing model. This approach involves soliciting views from "experts" on various aspects of obligor creditworthiness on a regular basis. An example of an expert system is the Euromoney Country Risk (ECR) scorecard-based model (Mortimer, 2013). The other class is "big data" models, as embodied in Thomson Reuters StarMine model (Roser, Bonne and Smith-Hill, 2013), that incorporate information from news services, published research, conference call transcripts and company filings to generate daily estimates of obligor default risk. To illustrate these approaches and their potential for addressing unsolved issues in credit modelling, the Euromoney and Thomson Reuters models are described briefly below, along with some preliminary tests of their abilities to predict credit changes.

ECR score

Although models for estimating physical default probabilities (PDs) for corporate borrowers abound, estimating physical PDs for sovereign issuers within existing frameworks has proven problematic. Although agency ratings for sovereign debt issues are useful for some applications, their use has several shortcomings. Also, macroeconomic models, while also useful for some applications, rarely generate default probabilities, are backward-looking, or otherwise require user-estimated inputs of future economic performance. However, a novel approach to sovereign default risk was introduced by Euromoney in 2011. Their ECR score embeds experts' estimates on political, economic and structural risk into a standard framework to generate a country risk score (ECR score) that varies from 100 (no default risk) to 0 (default). The ECR score does not generate an estimate of physical default *per se*, but Benzschawel, Lee and Li (2013) have demonstrated how ECR scores can be converted to default probabilities using average defaults by rating category from the Sobehart–Keenan HPD model or from defaults by rating from the market-implied PD model. Before describing the ECR-HPD model and tests of that framework at predicting ratings changes and changes in CDS spreads, the methodology underlying the ECR score will be briefly described.

The ECR scorecard

The ECR scorecard is presented in the first panel of Figure 2.8.[7] The ECR scores are opinions of over 400 experts worldwide on two main dimensions: country risks and qualitative factors, with each contributing 70% and 30%, respectively, to the total score. The top three sections of the scorecard show country score categories, each consisting of expert scores on 15 variables relating to economic, political and structural factors. The country scores consist of 30% contributions from economic factors and political factors, and a 10% contribution from structural factors. The items in each factor are as follows.

❑ Economic assessments: Participants rate each country from 0–10 across five sub-factors, each weighted 6%, for a maximum score of 30%. Categories of economic risk are bank stability/risk, GNP outlook, unemployment rate, government finances and monetary policy/currency stability.

❑ Political risk: Participants rate countries from 0–10 across six sub-factors, each weighted 5%, for a maximum score of 30%. The political risk categories are corruption, government non-payments/non-repatriation, government stability, information access/transparency, institutional risk, and regulatory and policy environment.

❑ Structural risk: Participants rate countries from 0–10 across four sub-factors, each weighted 2.5%, for a maximum score of 10%. The categories are demographics, hard infrastructure, labour market/industrial relations and soft infrastructure.

Figure 2.8 The ECR scorecard for sovereign issuers

The ECR scorecard

	Weights	Sub wght
Economic factors	30%	
Sub-factors	Bank stability	6.00%
	Economic – GNP outlook	6.00%
	Employment / unemployment	6.00%
	Government finances	6.00%
	Monetary / Currency stability	6.00%
Political factors	30%	
Sub-factors	Corruption	5.00%
	Govt non-Payment / non-repatriation	5.00%
	Government stability	5.00%
	Information access / transparency	5.00%
	Institutional risk	5.00%
	Regulatory policy & environment	5.00%
Structural factors	10%	
Sub-factors	Demographics	2.50%
	Hard infrastructure	2.50%
	Soft infrastructure	2.50%
	Labour market industrial relations	2.50%
Other Inputs		
Access to capital	10%	
Credit ratings	10%	
Debt indicators	10%	
Access to capital:	A survey of the "Head of debt syndicate" at major global banks on ease of raising capital	
Credit ratings:	Credit ratings from the major rating agencies	
Debt indicators:	World bank / IMF debt indicator statistics	

Figure 2.8 (*Continued*) How the ECR system works: a panel of experts (top left) inputs views via scorecards (top right) that are aggregated into country scores and summaries (bottom right) to create a set of country scores and risk rankings (bottom left)

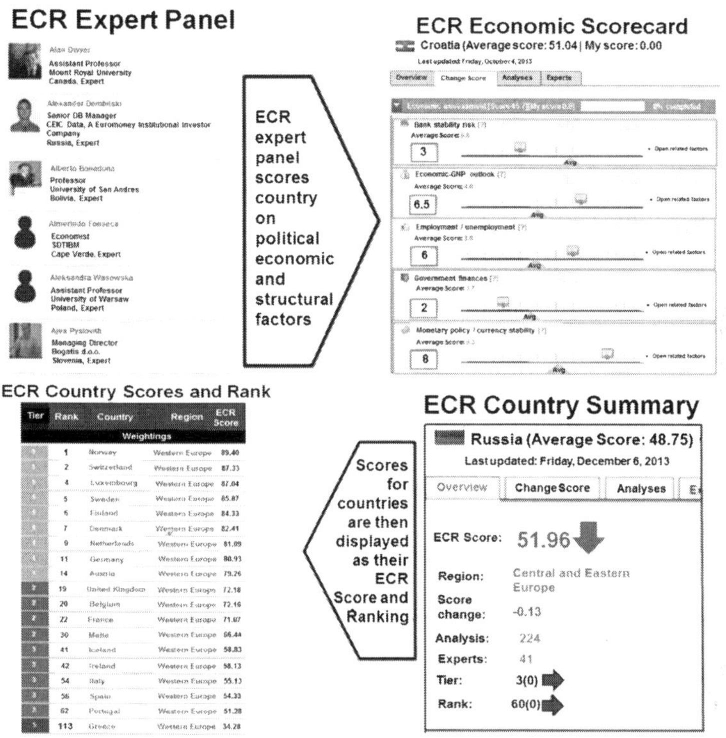

The remaining 30% contribution is from three qualitative factors (labelled "other inputs" in Figure 2.8): overall credit ratings,[8] debt indicators and access to capital, with each contributing 10% to the ECR score. The scores on all of the factors are averaged across experts and average scores are summed to produce a composite ECR score. The ECR score can have a value from 100 to 0, with 100 being nearly devoid of any risk, and 0 being completely exposed to every risk (at or near default).

A diagram of the ECR rating system appears in the bottom panel of Figure 2.8. The first stage, the assembling of "experts" is depicted in the top left panel. The experts are domiciled globally not just in major financial centres, and their occupations span the financial industry, government and academia. This diversification of expert backgrounds is intentional, as Euromoney wishes to capture a broad survey of sentiment rather than only one sector of interest. In addition, the backgrounds of the experts and the countries to which they contribute their views are also available.

The experts input their views on each sub-factor into the ECR system using a method shown at the top right of the bottom panel in Figure 2.8. Items in each major category are scored using sliders to set ratings on scales of 10 (best) to 0 (worst). Then, for a given country, scores from the experts assigned to that country are aggregated to produce a country report. An example of that report for Russia in December 2013 appears in the lower right portion of Figure 2.8. That report contains the overall county rating, in this example an ECR score of 51.96, along with changes in ECR score, country rank and information on the number of expert opinions. In addition, the summary provides information on ratings for each of the factors (economic, political and structural) and their momentum, as well as their rating, access to capital and debt indicators.

The output of the ECR system is a table of country scores and rankings as shown in the lower left part of Figure 2.8. A sample of a more detailed report by country appears in Table 2.1, which presents ECR scores and ratings on each of the six factors for the top-ranked portion of the 186 country sovereign universe. As mentioned, the ECR score ranges from 100 to 0, with Norway having the highest ECR score of 91.17 (on December 1, 2011). The sum of the sub-factor ratings contributing to each of the three country factor scores are normalised to provide a score on each factor in the range from 100 to 0. The three qualitative factors are expressed on a scale of 10 to 1.

Table 2.1 Sample of highest ECR composite scores, category scores and qualitative scores (December 2011)

11-Dec								
Rank	Country	ECR score	Economic risk 30'(100)	Political risk 30'(100)	Structural risk 10'(100)	Debt indicators 10'(100)	Credit ratings 10'(100)	Access to capital 10'(100)
1	Norway	91.17	88.17	92.36	82.13	8.88	10.00	10.00
2	Singapore	88.51	79.25	87.94	84.69	10.00	10.00	9.88
3	Switzerland	88.40	82.92	88.42	86.08	8.39	10.00	10.00
4	Luxembourg	87.84	79.88	91.85	83.75	8.76	10.00	9.00
5	Denmark	85.36	73.11	90.71	83.72	8.10	10.00	9.75
6	Finland	85.10	75.36	89.09	78.48	7.92	10.00	10.00
7	Sweden	85.08	78.83	90.15	82.35	8.24	10.00	7.88
8	Netherlands	84.71	75.93	86.79	78.29	8.02	10.00	10.00
9	Canada	84.70	77.40	88.37	77.95	7.24	10.00	9.88
10	Hong Kong	83.68	79.33	82.18	80.11	8.23	9.58	9.00

ECR scores to PDs

Although useful for a relative ranking of country risk, the ECR does not provide an estimate of likelihood of default (ie, PDs) *per se*, and is therefore of limited use for quantifying expected losses on sovereign credit portfolios. For this reason, Benzschawel, Lee and Li (2013) devised a method for linking ECR scores with PDs from the Sobehart–Keenan HPD model using agency credit ratings as a bridge. As mentioned, the HPD model cannot generate PDs for sovereigns because countries do not have tradable equity. However, one can construct a map between HPD model ECR scores as illustrated in Figure 2.9.

The first step in mapping ECR scores to default probabilities is to determine a correspondence between the ECR scores on a given day and rating categories. For example, the left panel of Figure 2.9 shows the mapping between credit ratings and ECR scores for August 1, 2013. That map is constructed by determining the number of triple-A rated sovereigns in the sample and that same number of sovereigns with the highest ECR scores. Assume that number is 10. Given the upper bound on the ECR scores is 100, we need only establish the lower bound. This is given by the average ECR score for the 10th and 11th ranked countries, which in this example is a score of 81. We proceed similarly down the rating categories scale until we get to single-C rated credits. We set the boundary between single-C and default at the average of the ECR score of the lowest single-C sovereign and 0.

Next, as illustrated in the middle panels of Figure 2.9, we determine similar correspondences between HPD model PDs and agency ratings and HPD PDs and ECR scores, using agency ratings as the bridge. The right panel of Figure 2.10 combines results of the middle panel into a three-way map between agency ratings, default probabilities from the HPD model and ECR scores.[9]

ECR/HPD model performance

Benzschawel, Lee and Li (2013) examined if changes in ECR scores would anticipate sovereigns' upgrades and downgrades by credit rating agencies.[10] To that end, we acquired monthly agency credit ratings for the 143 sovereigns in the ECR scoring system over the sample period from December 2011 to August

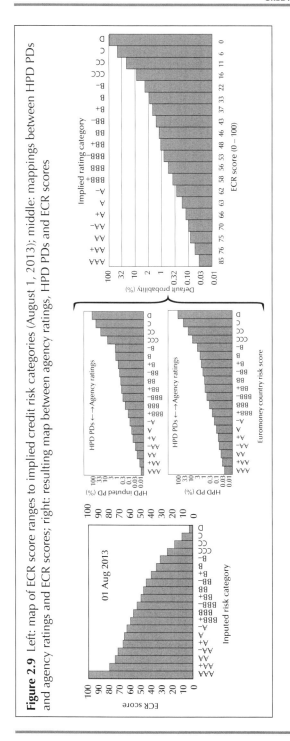

Figure 2.9 Left: map of ECR score ranges to implied credit risk categories (August 1, 2013); middle: mappings between HPD PDs and agency ratings and ECR scores; right: resulting map between agency ratings, HPD PDs and ECR scores

2013.[11] The sample contained 44 upgrades and 69 downgrades. For each month preceding the sovereign upgrade/downgrade, we computed the difference between that sovereign's ECR score and the average ECR score of that country's target rating category. The left panel of Figure 2.10 displays the differences in ECR scores for the upgrades (dark grey circles) and downgrades (light grey circles) in months relative to that of the upgrade and downgrade (0 on the x-axis).[12] The ECR model scores lead agency ratings changes: average ECR scores for upgrades increase prior to the upgrade and scores for downgrades decrease. Furthermore, in the month of the ratings change, the average sovereign ECR scores for both upgrades and downgrades are at the averages of their target rating categories.[13]

Benzschawel, Lee and Li (2013) also simulated long/short sovereign credit default swaps (CDS) trades based on ECR scores similar to that devised for long/short investment-grade corporate CDS trades based on the HPD model (Benzschawel and Lee, 2012). The middle panel of Figure 2.10 plots five-year CDS spreads versus ECR scores for sovereigns in Citi's World Government Bond Index (Citigroup Index, 2012). Corresponding ECR-based inferred PDs from the HPD model, denoted PDs, are plotted on the top axis. A regression line is fit to five-year CDS spreads versus ECR scores (and/or) PDs, which is defined as the "fair value" line. Although points deviate from the line, a linear function provides a good functional form for the relationship between ECR scores or PDs and CDS premiums. As regards value, CDS spreads that plot above regression line (ie, fair value) in Figure 2.10 are inferred to be cheap, offering investors above average compensation for their credit risk. Conversely, sovereign CDS spreads below the line are rich. Lines of +/–0.5σ are chosen to define sell/buy boundaries for short/long CDS trades. In each month, we simulate a long/short CDS trade by:

❑ eliminating from the trade the 10% of the credits with the largest PDS;
❑ selling protection on all the CDS above; and
❑ buying credit protection on sovereign CDS below the given criterion (eg, between –0.5σ or, for other studies, a fixed number of CDS).

Figure 2.10 Left: time series of average ECR scores for upgraded (N = 44)/downgraded (N = 69) sovereigns relative to average scores of their target rating categories in months relative to the ratings change; middle: five-year WGBI sovereign CDS premiums versus ECR scores and ECR-HPD PDs, illustrating "cheap" and "rich" CDS defined by +/-0.5σ from the "fair value" regression; right: cumulative P&L for long/short trades and long-only benchmark with three-month holding periods

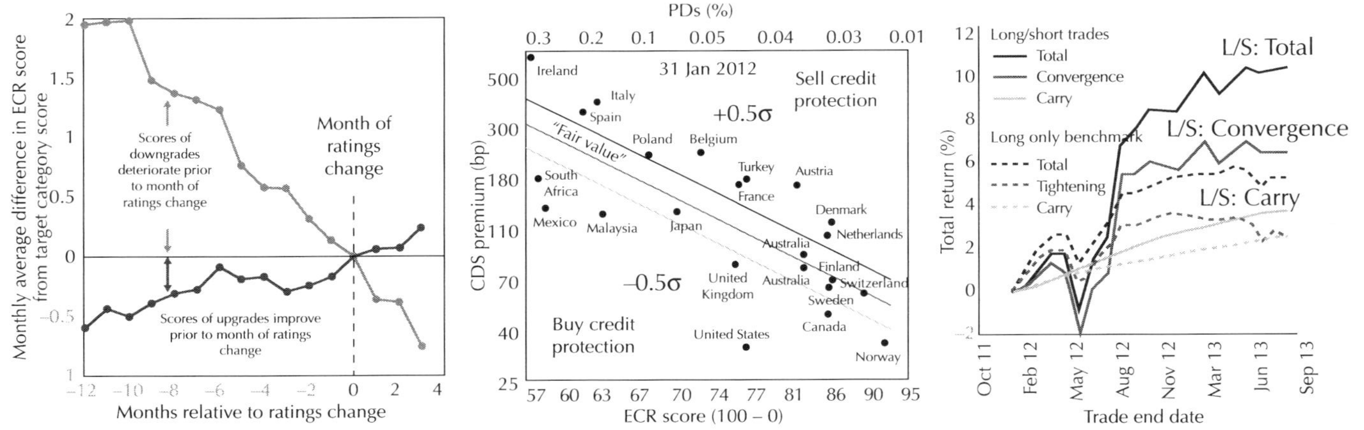

The right panel of Figure 2.10 presents cumulative P&L from the monthly series of simulated three-month long/short sovereign CDS trades (solid lines) and the benchmark (ie, just sell protection) long-only strategy (dashed lines). P&L is broken out by total P&L (black lines), carry (dark grey) and convergence (light grey), where convergence for the long-only strategy is from spread tightening only. Consider first the total P&L. The long-only benchmark portfolio is profitable, generating roughly 6.5% from December 2011 to August 2013. However, total P&L from the long/short CDS trades is almost double the long-only, topping 10% over the period. Both long/short and long-only CDS trades produce consistent positive carry as indicated by the light grey line and light grey dashes, respectively. For the long-only strategy, the 2.2% return from carry comes from premiums on the 30% of CDS nearest to fair value. In comparison, positive carry from the three-month long/short CDS trades is 4.0% over the period, reflecting the difference between premiums received from selling protection on cheap CDS over those paid for protection on rich CDS. P&L from convergence is just over 6% for long/short strategy (the dark grey line), topping the 2% spread tightening for the long-only strategy (the dark grey dashes).[14]

Clearly, the ECR model with inferred PDs from the HPD model holds promise for providing investors with a forward-looking model for sovereign credit risk and relative value. A major limitation of the model is the relatively short history of ECR scores available for backtesting the model: the model history does not include a negative part of the credit cycle. Still, no other model is known to have demonstrated similar success at predicting ratings downgrades and CDS spread convergence. Also, preliminary testing indicates that ECR scores may prove useful as predictors of foreign currency moves for non-G10 sovereigns. The ECR framework has also been criticised for having arbitrary scorecard weights. However, Benzschawel, Lee and Li (2013) have shown that those weights can be optimised adaptively to predict market data and ratings changes. Thus, a fixed weight standardised scorecard is an advantage in terms of consistency of rater's judgements and, by subsequent optimisation, allowing analysis of changing determinants of global sovereign default risk.

Finally, although useful for modelling sovereign risk, the crowd-sourcing model approach as embodied in the ECR score is more difficult to apply to corporate or municipal default risk. That is, unlike the manageable 194 countries scored by the Euromoney model, there are over 30,000 corporations globally and over 100,000 municipal issuers in the US on which scores would need to be solicited. However, models for a subset of those firms (banks for example) may be a more manageable application for the consensus approach. Another new approach that holds promise for estimating default risk for corporations and municipalities is the "big data" approach described in the next section.

Big data: The Thomson Reuters TMCR model

In this section, we consider a model that employs "big data" methodology to predict likelihoods of default for corporate firms. Thomson Reuters' StarMine Text Mining Credit Risk (TMCR) model described by Roser, Bonne and Smith-Hill (2013) is the first commercially available credit risk model to measure corporate default risk by quantitatively analysing text. More importantly, as shown below, Roser *et al* present evidence of the predictive power of the TMCR model.

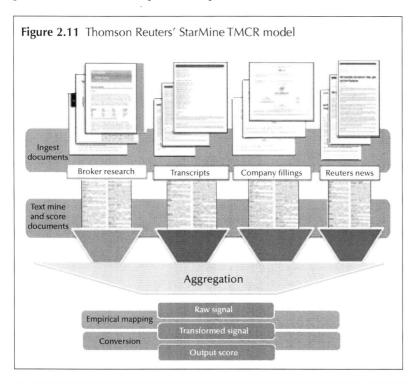

Figure 2.11 Thomson Reuters' StarMine TMCR model

The StarMine TMCR, depicted in Figure 2.11, assesses the default risk of publicly traded companies by systematically evaluating the language in Reuters News, StreetEvents conference call transcripts, corporate filings (10-K, 10-Q and 8-K), and research documents from over 600 participating brokers. The TMCR model scores over 25,000 companies daily. StarMine TMCR creates a ranked component score for each of the four document sources and combines the component scores to provide an overall rating of company credit risk. The overall score is available as a letter grade, probability of default and a rank from 1 to 100.

At the core of the TMCR model is a "bag of words" (Salton and McGill, 1983) text mining algorithm. This algorithm breaks a document into its constituent words and phrases, and establishes relationships between the frequencies of these words and phrases and a known training variable, such as empirical default probability. Development of the StarMine TMCR consisted of extensive research to determine unique dictionaries of language for each document source within the context of financial analysis that are useful for robustly assessing the credit risk of a company. In developing the dictionaries, StarMine analysed the text in millions of individual documents across more than 10 years of history to identify which words and phrases have the strongest and most robust relationship to company credit risk. StarMine TMCR calculates the frequency of the dictionary words and phrases for each document, and then uses a learning algorithm to calculate an overall score for the document from these frequencies. From that analysis, StarMine creates a ranked component score from each of the four document sources on the four dimensions of interest, as shown in the left panel of Figure 2.12.

❑ Income: Income statement related.
❑ Structural: Balance-sheet and debt structure related.
❑ Legal: Legal obligations and terms.
❑ External: Terms related to external and market factors.

The category outputs are not used in the calculation of the overall TMCR score, but are designed to provide insight into the language that drives the TMCR score. The left panel of Figure 2.12 indicates that each TMCR component contains a different combination of language relating to the four relevant dimensions.

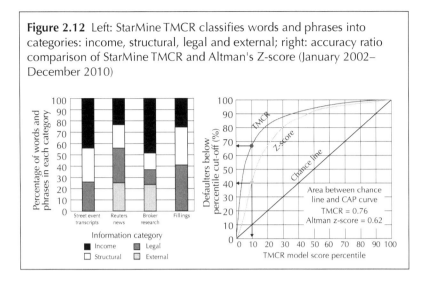

Figure 2.12 Left: StarMine TMCR classifies words and phrases into categories: income, structural, legal and external; right: accuracy ratio comparison of StarMine TMCR and Altman's Z-score (January 2002–December 2010)

Roser, Bonne and Smith-Hill (2013) present CAP curves and accuracy ratios for the TMCR score and Altman's Z-score model (Altman, 1968) for all years from 2002 to 2010, and these are reproduced in the right panel of Figure 2.12. The figure indicates that StarMine TMCR performs significantly better than the Z-score, capturing 68% of default events in the bottom 10% (most risky) of model scores versus 40% for the Z-score. Although the samples differ somewhat, the TMCR model's CAP curve is roughly equivalent to that of the HPD model in Chapter 1 and superior to that of the KMV model. Given the additional complexity of the data mining approach to predicting default, it is somewhat disappointing that, at least for a one-year horizon, default predictions from TMCR are roughly equivalent to the previously best models. The similarity of model performances is consistent with the idea that, at least for one year out and the inherent uncertainty of default, default prediction models based on publicly available information are approaching an asymptote in accuracy. However, the TMCR model may still prove superior as an indicator of relative value, but that remains untested.

The performance of the TMCR model at predicting corporate defaults suggests that its application to municipal and sovereign defaults may prove useful. As mentioned above, there are few models of default for sovereign debt and none for municipalities. In fact, the municipal default problem is particularly well-suited for data mining approaches due to the large number (ie, over 100,000) of municipalities and the lack of competing models.

Big data: Potential uses and challenges

The big data approach holds the potential to solve several outstanding problems in credit modelling. The problems of municipal and sovereign defaults have already been mentioned. Other potential problems include estimating recovery value in default, which remains a difficult problem and is important for expected losses and relative value. In addition, the data mining approach holds particular promise for shorter-term predictions of index and asset relative value, but remains relatively untested for those purposes. For example, the ability to predict the next day's closing CDS index prices or market opening prices after a night of new information would be particularly useful. Also, applying data mining to firm-specific information for over- and underweighting various bonds over short intervals is another potential application.

Table 2.2 Data mining: Potential uses and challenges

Potential Uses	Challenges
❏ Timeliness of the data can provide an information advantage	❏ Not yet clear how to best use the data
❏ Potential to provide first movers with a key differentiator from the slower-to-adopt competitors	❏ Developing an appropriate front-end to extract and analyse the data is critical
❏ Sentiment data can be leveraged as proxy measures for data that is currently not available to improve our analysis (eg, private firms)	❏ Text analysis in the financial sector has only recently transitioned from high frequency and event-based trading
❏ There may be a subset of data ("low hanging fruit") that can be leveraged quickly and add immediate value	❏ Not just about trading on sentiment (positive or negative)
❏ Forecasting the short- to medium-term returns remain elusive and pioneering this area will be a significant competitive advantage	❏ News volume, timing and market absorption of news needs to be understood and varies across securities and asset classes
	❏ Determinants of returns and relationship to sentiment data need to be determined

Table 2.2 presents some of the potential uses and challenges of data mining approaches to credit. Consider first some potential uses of sentiment data. Big data can provide an information advantage as it goes beyond traditional fundamental analysis. It also offers potential for creation of indexes based on traditional structured data (eg, macro and market data). The application of sentiment modelling can provide first-movers with a competitive advantage over slower-to-adopt competitors. It also holds promise for determining proxy measures for data that is not available (eg, financial information from private firms). There may be data that can be leveraged quickly and add immediate value.

Despite the potential of big data and sentiment models, there remain challenges to its application to credit modelling. Effective use of sentiment data requires new ways of thinking, hypothesis creation and relevant data. There are technical challenges as well – for instance, the dataset is massive, involving storage and retrieval, handling and display. These involve knowledge of how the data is to be used and how to integrate it within existing applications. Also, technologists need to be engaged in dialogue with data analysts and quants to develop effective models. There are also problems to be solved with respect to prediction of default, recovery and market movements.

CONCLUSION

This chapter has presented an overview of potential future directions in credit model development. These included the market-implied default model, the Euromoney Credit Risk score and the Thomson Reuters StarMine model. As with most innovations in credit modelling, these newer approaches come at the expense of increasing requirements for input data, enhancements in computational power and greater theoretical complexity. One can foresee the trend for consensus models and big data sentiment models playing a greater role in the very near future, and even to help solve some of the tougher credit modelling problems described above.

APPENDIX 2.1   NEXT GENERATION CREDIT MODELS

The next generation of credit models will incorporate information and techniques from existing models, but will also take advantage of advances in communication and technology. These include estimating the risk premium in various markets and backing out the default probability as in the market-implied PD model. Also, consensus models such as the ECR scorecard are offering investors advance notice of ratings changes for global sovereign issuers and advance signals in credit spread moves. Finally, big data and sentiment models offer promise for attacking unsolved problems in credit risk, such as recovery value in default, estimating municipal default probabilities and short-term moves in credit spreads. Examples of these models appear in Figure A.2.1.

Figure A.2.1 Next generation of default models

Market-implied PD model

Uses structural models to estimate the daily risk premium and uses spreads and volatilities to infer default probabilities

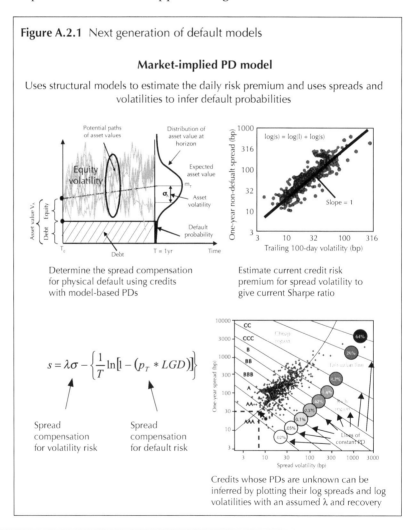

Determine the spread compensation for physical default using credits with model-based PDs

Estimate current credit risk premium for spread volatility to give current Sharpe ratio

$$s = \lambda\sigma - \left\{\frac{1}{T}\ln\left[1 - \left(p_T * LGD\right)\right]\right\}$$

Spread compensation for volatility risk

Spread compensation for default risk

Credits whose PDs are unknown can be inferred by plotting their log spreads and log volatilities with an assumed λ and recovery

Figure A.2.1 (*Continued*)

Crowd sourcing / Expert systems

Launched in March 2011, the Euromoney Country Risk score is a consensus of a network of 400 economic & political experts

- Experts score countries for 15 variables that contribute to country risk
- The consensus scores of these variables are combined with credit ratings, debt indicators & access to capital to determine the ECR score

The ECR scorecard

	Weights	Sub wght
Economic factors	30%	
Sub-factors	Bank stability	6.00%
	Economic – GNP outlook	6.00%
	Employment / unemployment	6.00%
	Government finances	6.00%
	Monetary / Currency stability	6.00%
Political factors	30%	
Sub-factors	Corruption	5.00%
	Govt non-Payment / non-repatriation	5.00%
	Government stability	5.00%
	Information access / transparency	5.00%
	Institutional risk	5.00%
	Regulatory policy & environment	5.00%
Structural factors	10%	
Sub-factors	Demographics	2.50%
	Hard infrastructure	2.50%
	Soft infrastructure	2.50%
	Labour market industrial relations	2.50%
Other Inputs		
Access to capital	10%	
Credit ratings	10%	
Debt indicators	10%	

Figure A.2.1 (*Continued*)

Big data – sentiment models

Market sentiment models "scrub" data from numerous sources, analyse that data using sophisticated algorithms and output estimates of PDs.

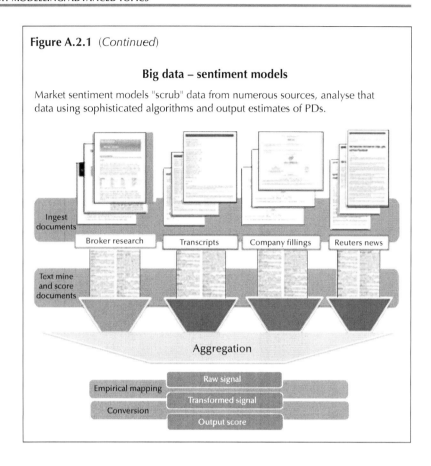

1   It may also contain a premium for liquidity/illiquidity. For now, we use the term "credit risk premium" to refer to the entire spread compensation over and above that necessary for the present value of expected cashflows to equal that of an equal-duration US Treasury security.

2   See Citigroup Index (2013) for descriptions of Citigroup's BIG index and High Yield index.

3   For simplicity, we presented a simplified description of how the points in the right panel of Figure 2.4 were determined. In fact, as described in Benzschawel and Lee (2011), we use a Nelson–Siegel (1987) procedure to determine one-year equivalent spreads (ie, $T = 1$) for all firms in our sample, and these are the values that appear in Figure 2.4. Also, we compute spread volatility on the trailing 100 daily spread values, but impose an exponential decay with a half-life of three months (ie, 66 days) on trailing spread values.

4   A quadratic function has a term with, and exponent of, two such as $s = a_0 + a_1\sigma + a_2\sigma^2$.

5   The sample size was limited to firms for which we had scores from both HPD and KMV models at the beginning of each year, as well as credit ratings from Standard and Poor's.

6   In fact, several statistical models for sovereign defaults have been proposed (Altman and Rijken, 2011), but these remain largely untested, require user-determined inputs, and/or

are difficult to implement (Gray, Merton and Bodie, 2007).

7 A more detailed description of the ECR methodology can be found in Benzschawel, Lee and Li (2013).

8 The credit rating is a composite of the average of ratings from Fitch, Moody's and Standard and Poor's converted to numerical scales and normalised to the range between 10 (highest) and 0 (default).

9 We have since determined that the mapping of PDs using the sovereign PDs from the market-implied model (Benzschawel and Assing, 2012) provides more intuitive estimates of physical PDs than the corporate scale from the HPD model. In either case, the procedure is that described herein.

10 We thank students in the University of California at Berkeley's Masters of Financial Engineering programme for carrying out this research under our direction: Saran Ananth, Dahai Cao, George Diaconu, Weijian Chuah, Wing Sum Cheng, Mayank Gupta, Rahul Gupta, Darren Ho, Amarnath Jha, Seung Ju Lee, Hang Li, Paolo Miranda, Kaname Nakagawa, Jorge Silva, Arsheep Singh, Abay Srivastava and Jue Wang.

11 A rating change could be triggered by any of the major rating agencies: S&P, Moody's or Fitch. To avoid double-counting for sovereigns having similar ratings changes in subsequent months, we kept only the scores related to the first ratings change.

12 Note that because the various upgrades and downgrades took place over different periods in the 19-month ECR score sample, their histories do not overlap completely on the graph in Figure 2.10.

13 For a detailed description of the results of the ECR–HPD model, see Benzschawel, Lee and Li (2013).

14 For a long-only portfolio, over the long run one would expect little P&L from spread tightening as CDS premiums should fluctuate around their average value. The fact cumulative P&L from spread tightening on the long only trades is 2% (roughly equal to the carry) is indicative of the rally in sovereign CDS spreads over the relatively small sample period available for testing.

3

Predicting Annual Default Rates and Implications for Market Prices

Forecasts of future corporate default rates are useful for estimating value-at-risk on credit portfolios, and for evaluating the attractiveness of credit market investments. In this chapter, we will describe a macroeconomic model developed by Yong Su and myself (Benzschawel and Su, 2014) to predict annual one-year high-yield defaults. That model builds upon on earlier work by Hampden-Turner (2009), which predicts monthly default rates using four predictors with various lags:

❑ Libor three-month/10-year slope;
❑ US Lending Survey;
❑ US funding gap; and
❑ GDP quarter-over-quarter (QoQ) growth.

The existing model is based on a rigorous analysis of variable lags as they affect predictions of default and a logistic transformation of predicted default rates. Also, the model is developed with strict attention to avoiding "look-forward" biases, so predictions of annual default rates are all out-of-sample. Finally, changes in predicted default rates from the model, but not current default rates, are shown to be predictive of future changes in credit spreads.

Rating agencies typically calculate the current annual default rate as the percentage of high-yield firms that have defaulted over the past 12 months. For example, Moody's Investors Service publishes monthly trailing high-yield default rates calculated as the ratio of the number of firms rated below Baa/BBB that have defaulted during the trailing 12-month period to the total number of non-defaulted firms rated below Baa at the beginning of that period.[1] Since the universe of rated firms differs among the various rating agencies, it is not surprising that rating agencies typically report different trailing annual default rates. For example, Table 3.1 displays annual default rates from Standard & Poor's (Vazza and Kraemer, 2013) and Moody's (Ou *et al*, 2013) for all firms (left columns) and for high-yield firms only (right columns). Although default rates reported by Standard & Poor's appear to be slightly higher than those from Moody's, they tend to rise and fall in tandem. This is illustrated graphically in Figure 3.1, which displays the speculative annual default rates reported by S&P (dark bars) and Moody's (light bars).

Table 3.1 Annual default rates from Standard & Poor's and Moody's

Year	All firms		High yield	
	S&P	Moody's	S&P	Moody's
1981	0.1	0.2	0.6	0.7
1982	1.2	0.7	4.4	2.3
1983	0.8	0.5	2.9	1.8
1984	0.9	0.5	3.3	1.7
1985	1.1	0.4	4.3	1.4
1986	1.7	0.9	5.7	2.8
1987	1.0	0.6	2.8	1.6
1988	1.4	0.8	3.8	1.9
1989	1.7	1.4	4.7	3.3
1990	2.7	2.3	8.1	6.3
1991	3.3	2.0	11.1	6.0
1992	1.5	0.8	6.1	2.7

1993	0.6	0.6	2.5	2.0
1994	0.6	0.3	2.1	1.0
1995	1.0	0.5	3.5	1.6
1996	0.5	0.2	1.8	0.6
1997	0.6	0.3	2.0	0.9
1998	1.3	0.8	3.7	2.0
1999	2.1	1.5	5.6	3.5
2000	2.5	2.2	6.2	5.0
2001	3.8	3.4	9.8	8.4
2002	3.5	2.3	9.3	5.8
2003	1.9	1.2	5.0	3.2
2004	0.8	0.4	2.0	1.2
2005	0.6	0.3	1.5	0.8
2006	0.5	0.3	1.1	0.8
2007	0.4	0.2	0.9	0.5
2008	1.8	1.5	3.6	3.0
2009	4.1	3.7	9.6	8.3
2010	1.2	0.7	2.9	1.6
2011	0.8	0.5	1.7	1.2
2012	1.1	0.7	2.5	1.5
Average	1.5	1.0	4.2	2.7
Median	1.1	0.7	3.6	1.9
Max	4.1	3.7	11.1	8.4
Min	0.1	0.2	0.6	0.5

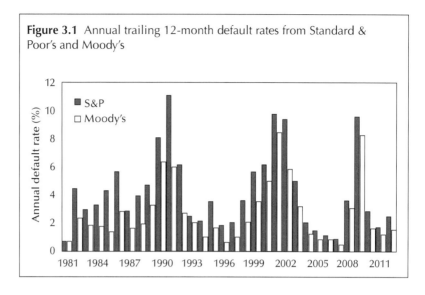

Figure 3.1 Annual trailing 12-month default rates from Standard & Poor's and Moody's

Although trailing default rates are of some interest to investors, projections of future default rates are even more relevant for performance of corporate markets, particularly those in high yield. Moreover, expected default rates are of interest to lenders, risk managers and other counterparties to credit-based transactions. In this chapter, the goal is to describe a model that we have developed to generate accurate forecasts of monthly default rates for the next 12 months, and to demonstrate their usefulness for making investment decisions.

There have been several approaches to modelling future default rates. Most begin with the observation of the current 12-month trailing default rate. One approach to projecting the default rate for the next 12 months is to generate stochastic future default rates using a model that relies on mean-reverting properties calibrated to the historical properties of historical default rates (Benzschawel, Lee and Li, 2012). The key assumption of this type of model is that default rates follow certain stochastic process and therefore the time-series record of actual default rates is a sample path generated by that process. Although this approach can be useful for simulation purposes, it constrains one to use mean default rates as expected levels of future default rates. To derive a statistical model with predictive power, others have adopted an alternative approach that incorporates econometric factors leading default. Examples include linear models detailed in Fons (1991), Helwege and Kleiman (1996), Jonsson and Fridson (1996). These authors have identified macroeconomic variables of explanatory power whose effectiveness is evaluated by calculating root mean squared errors between predicted and obtained default rates. An alternative model, proposed by Keenan, Sobehart and Hamilton (1999), incorporates the effect on default rates of changes in the universe of issuers, both in terms of their credit ratings and the time since they first came to market (the "ageing effect"). Their model also captures macroeconomic conditions as measured by the industrial production index and interest rate variables. Finally, Hampden-Turner (2009) has developed statistical models to predict future default rates from one to 12 months using least-squares regression and vector autoregressive models.

Unfortunately, most existing models that show good performance, including the Hampden-Turner (HT) model, are validated in-sample. However, we find most studies do not evaluate out-of-sample forecasts over a suitably long period (eg, cover an entire credit cycle), and it remains unclear how well these models perform, especially in periods of high-default rates. This chapter first presents the Hampden-Turner model, pointing out its advantages and limitations, then, building upon the HT framework, a statistical approach is applied to address that model's limitations while also reporting out-of-sample validation on the enhanced model. Finally, it demonstrates how an accurate model of default prediction can provide useful information regarding the attractiveness of investment in high-yield corporate debt.

THE HAMPDEN-TURNER DEFAULT MODEL

Since the proposed model takes its starting point from the Hampden-Turner formulation, the HT model is described briefly in this section. In general, the HT default model fits and predicts monthly default rates using lagged versions of the following four predictors.

1. *LIB*or slope (designated as *LIB*): This is the yield spread between 10-year and three-month Libor rates divided by the term difference between 10 years and three months (ie, 10.0–0.25).[2]
2. The US Lending Survey (denoted *LS*): The US Federal Reserve

sends lending surveys quarterly to gather opinions from banks' senior loan officers on bank lending practices. The survey estimates the net percentage of domestic banks tightening standards for commercial and industrial loans to large and middle-market firms. Banks tighten loan standards when financial conditions are deteriorating or are expected to worsen, thus leading to tougher environments for high-yield credits and higher default rates.

3. The US funding gap (denoted FG): FG is the macroeconomic equivalent of final free cashflow. It is the net cashflow a company receives (or requires) after capital expenditures, dividend payments, mergers and acquisitions, and net equity issuance. FG is typically negative in a bull market, indicating that corporations need to increase financing, and positive in a bear market, as consolidation occurs and spending is reduced.

4. GDP QoQ growth (designated as GDP): GDP is the market value of all officially recognised final goods and services produced within a country in a year. GDP growth is indicative of strong economic conditions, portending good corporate performance, and vice versa.

Of the four input variables, only LIB is collected monthly, while the other inputs are available quarterly. The HT model uses a simple linear interpolation to generate monthly values for variables LS, FG and GDP to be paired with monthly values of LIB between their quarterly updates. For example, to interpolate the value of GDP for a given prediction month t one month after the last GDP update at t–1, we use GDP_{t-1} and the corresponding value of GDP_{t-2} that will be reported next. That is:

$$GDP_t = \frac{GDP_{t+2} - GDP_{t-1}}{3} + GDP_{t-1}$$

(3.1)

Similarly:

$$GDP_{t+1} = GDP_{t+2} - \frac{GDP_{t+2} - GDP_{t-1}}{3}$$

(3.2)

Due to the linear interpolation, calculation of monthly data at time t requires data ahead at time t+2. As a result, the predictor values at time t can only be used to precdict default rates later than $t+1$ or $t+2$ unless it is the month of a GDP report (or other quarterly variables). In practice, this is not a problem as the model includes only monthly predictors with lags longer than two months.

HT's first default model fits a lagged regression using ordinary least squares (OLS) to predict monthly default rates, which for month t we denoted as Γ_t, so that:

$$\Gamma_t = \beta_0 + \beta_1 \cdot LIB_{t-24} + \beta_2 \cdot LS_{t-12} + \beta_3 \cdot FG_{t-12} + \beta_4 \cdot GDP_{t-12}$$

(3.3)

Hampden-Turner reports that the US Lending Survey is the most important predictor, leading the default rate by about 10–12 months. For example, Figure 3.2 plots historical normalised (ie, converted to Z-scores) values of the US Lending Survey and monthly default rates from Moody's since late 1997. Clearly, the US Lending Survey data not only lead default rates, but appear to predict their normalised magnitudes well.

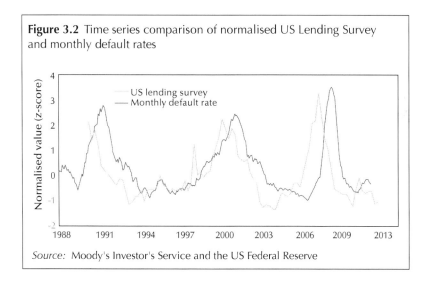

Figure 3.2 Time series comparison of normalised US Lending Survey and monthly default rates

Source: Moody's Investor's Service and the US Federal Reserve

In practice, each January the HT model generates 12 successive out-of-sample monthly default rates based on available data to the previous December. Each default rate for months $i = 1, \dots .12$ is calculated as:

$$\hat{\Gamma}_{t+1} = \hat{\beta}_0 + \hat{\beta}_1 \cdot LIB_{t+i-24} + \hat{\beta}_2 \cdot LS_{t+i-12} + \hat{\beta}_3 \cdot FG_{t+i-12} + \hat{\beta}_4 \cdot GDP_{t+i-12}$$

(3.4)

Figure 3.3 illustrates how the HT model is used in practice. That is, the figure shows that the model is trained on data up to the end of 2011, and then generates monthly predictions of trailing 12-month default rates for 2012 (the dashed line in Figure 3.3).

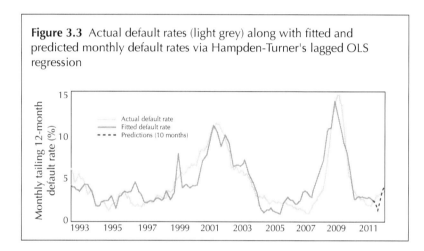

Figure 3.3 Actual default rates (light grey) along with fitted and predicted monthly default rates via Hampden-Turner's lagged OLS regression

Hampden-Turner proposed a second model to predict annual defaul rates in which a vector autoregressive (VAR) method is used to derive coefficients on the four variables above as well as on the lagged default rate. That is, VAR is used to derive the coefficients for each montly prediction of Γ_t:

$$\Gamma_t = \alpha_1 \cdot \Gamma_{t-8} + \alpha_2 \cdot \Gamma_{t-12} + \alpha_3 \cdot \Gamma_{t-24} + \alpha_4 \cdot \Gamma_{t-48} +$$
$$\beta_1 \cdot LIB_{t-4} + \beta_2 \cdot LIB_{t-8} + \beta_3 \cdot LIB_{t-12} + \beta_4 \cdot LIB_{t-24} +$$
$$\gamma_1 \cdot LS_{t-4} + \gamma_2 \cdot LS_{t-8} + \gamma_3 \cdot LS_{t-12} + \gamma_4 \cdot LS_{t-24} +$$
$$\delta_1 \cdot FG_{t-4} + \delta_2 \cdot FG_{t-8} + \delta_3 \cdot FG_{t-12} + \delta_4 \cdot FG_{t-24} +$$
$$\phi_1 \cdot GDP_{t-4} + \phi_2 \cdot GDP_{t-8} + \phi_3 \cdot GDP_{t-12} + \phi_4 \cdot GDP_{t-24} + \omega$$

(3.5)

Since the longest lag is for default rates 49 months prior, the first month of prediction requires 49 months of previous default rates (ie, $t \geq 49$). Unlike the lagged linear regression, the minimum lag in the *VAR* formula is four months. Therefore, in order to generate 12 out-of-sample predictions of $\hat{r}$, one requires predictions of *LIB*, *LS*, *FG* as well as *GDP* at least for months five through 12. HT proposes to fit a VAR model to each of these time series. For example, $\widehat{LIB}_{t+i}$ $(1 \leq i \leq 4)$ can be predicted by fitting the following *VAR* up to time t:

$$
\begin{aligned}
LIB_t = {} & a_1 \cdot DR_{t-8} + a_2 \cdot DR_{t-12} + a_3 \cdot DR_{t-24} + a_4 \cdot DR_{t-48} + \\
& b_1 \cdot LIB_{t-4} + b_2 \cdot LIB_{t-8} + b_3 \cdot LIB_{t-12} + b_4 \cdot LIB_{t-24} + \\
& c_1 \cdot LS_{t-4} + c_2 \cdot LS_{t-8} + c_3 \cdot LS_{t-12} + c_4 \cdot LS_{t-24} + \\
& d_1 \cdot FG_{t-4} + d_2 \cdot FG_{t-8} + d_3 \cdot FG_{t-12} + d_4 \cdot FG_{t-24} + \\
& e_1 \cdot GDP_{t-4} + e_2 \cdot GDP_{t-8} + e_3 \cdot GDP_{t-12} + e_4 \cdot GDP_{t-24} + f
\end{aligned}
$$

$$(3.6)$$

Then, to predict $LIB_{t+j} (5 \leq j \leq 12)$, HT treats $\widehat{LIB}_{t+i}$ $(1 \leq i \leq 4)$ as already observed data and applies the VAR formula in Equation 3.6 iteratively to generate estimates of *LIB* for months five to 12. Otherwise, the general training procedure for the VAR model is similar to that for the OLS predictions in Figure 3.3, for which the model is trained up to the end of each year and used to predict trailing 12-month default rates for each month in the following year. The resulting estimated trailing 12-month default rates from the VAR model and actual default rates appear in Figure 3.4.

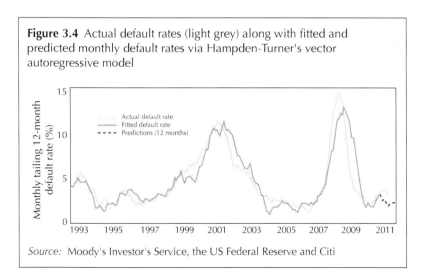

Figure 3.4 Actual default rates (light grey) along with fitted and predicted monthly default rates via Hampden-Turner's vector autoregressive model

Source: Moody's Investor's Service, the US Federal Reserve and Citi

ISSUES WITH THE HAMPDEN-TURNER OLS AND VAR MODELS

There are two statistical issues related with the linear and VAR regression models as implemented in the Hampden-Turner model. First, we find that both models may give rise to negative values for default rate predictions. In addition, we observed that although the VAR model performs well fitting default data in sample, it exhibited poor out-of-sample prediction performance. For example, Figure 3.5 shows actual default rates from 1996 to 2013 and out-of-sample predictions from the VAR model (left panel) and the OLS regression (right panel). Neither the VAR or the OLS model capture the actual annual rates well and both models predict negative annual default rates in year 2006. Also, comparison of out-of-sample performance in Figure 3.5 shows that the simple lagged regression performs better than the VAR model at predicting annual default rates.

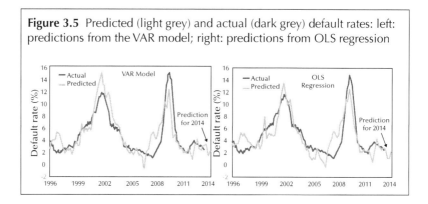

Figure 3.5 Predicted (light grey) and actual (dark grey) default rates: left: predictions from the VAR model; right: predictions from OLS regression

Another issue with the HT models involves lag selection. As discussed, if the minimum lag is less than 12 months, one cannot make 12 monthly out-of-sample default rate predictions from the available data. This motivated Hampden-Turner to build the VAR model for each predictor so that smaller lags can be used in the formula. For the simple lagged linear regression, small lags become a limitation of the model. For example, Hampden-Turner used the cross-correlation function (CCF) to determine the lag for the OLS model. As shown in the left panel of Figure 3.6, the estimated cross-correlation between LS and DR peaks around a lag of 10 to12 months. Hence, choosing a lag of 12 months for LS is convenient and reasonable – we can produce a total of 12 predictions, and we do not lose much predictive power (with respect to, say, a lag of 10 or 11). Picking lags for predictive variables can be difficult due to instability in their lagged relationships to future default rates.

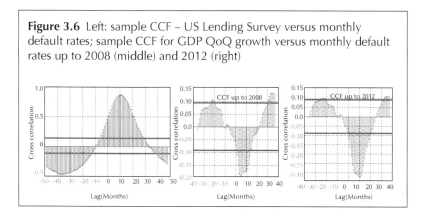

Figure 3.6 Left: sample CCF – US Lending Survey versus monthly default rates; sample CCF for GDP QoQ growth versus monthly default rates up to 2008 (middle) and 2012 (right)

Although picking the lag for the Lending Survey when predicting default was straightforward, Hampden-Turner claims that, for the other predictors, picking the lag is "not always this easy". For example, the middle and right panels of Figure 3.6 show CCFs for GDP quarter-on-quarter (QoQ) growth versus the monthly default rates using data up to 2008 and 2012, respectively. The CCFs in those panels peak at very different lags (ie, four months and 10 months), suggesting that using a fixed lag for all the periods may not be appropriate. In addition, both panels show that a lag of 12 months for the GDP is not the optimal choice, apart from its ability to make 12 monthly predictions. Thus, for the lagged linear regression, we must choose between the optimal lag and one that can make a sufficient number of predictions. On the other hand, the VAR model does not fully address the problem of lag selection. In fact, the VAR model involves considerably more lags that are arbitrarily selected, and how to carry out the selection procedure for the main model as well as for all the predictors is not obvious. In the following sections, we propose a quick fix to the lag selection dilemma along with a discussion of more advanced methods for its estimation.

LAGGED REGRESSION MODEL HT 2.0

We propose alternative methods to address the issues raised in the previous section regarding the HT models. First, we opt not to use the VAR model owing to: (i) its propensity to overfit the data; and (ii) the fact that it uses predicted results as model inputs, which may degrade accuracy of predictions (we also need to check that all the predictor time series are stationary, see Appendix 3.1 for a discussion of this). In addition, to ensure that the predicted default rates are not less than zero, we adopt a simple logistic transformation on the default rates. That is, instead of regressing default rates on the other four predictors, we transform them first via the logit function:

$$\widetilde{DR} = logit(DR\%) = \log \frac{DR\%}{1-DR\%} \tag{3.7}$$

Thus, the simple lagged regression is converted to:

$$\widetilde{DR}_t = \tilde{\beta}_0 + \tilde{\beta}_1 \cdot LIB_{t-24} + \tilde{\beta}_2 \cdot LS_{t-12} + \tilde{\beta}_3 \cdot FG_{t-12} + \tilde{\beta}_4 \cdot GDP_{t-12}. \tag{3.8}$$

Figure 3.7 Predicted and observed default rates from lagged regression with logistic transformation of default rates (left panel) and lagged lasso regression (right panel)

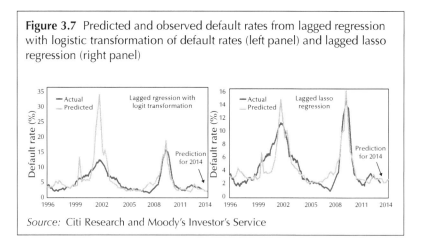

Source: Citi Research and Moody's Investor's Service

To get predictions for the original default rate, we can use the inverse logit transformation $DR = (100 \cdot e^{\widetilde{DR}}/(e^{\widetilde{DR}} +1)$, which is confined to the range (0,100). However, because of the exponential term in Equation 3.8, the predictions from the model are not satisfactory when the underlying regression becomes unstable. For example, the left panel of Figure 3.7 shows out-of-sample annual default rate predictions from 1996 to 2013 for the lagged regression with logistic transformation of default rates. Although all predictions are now greater than zero, the model has large errors in estimating default rates, particularly in the period 2001–02.

To improve model performance, we impose a lasso $\mathcal{L}_1$ penalty on the lagged logit-transformed regression so that the regression coefficients $\tilde{\beta}_1$, $\tilde{\beta}_2$, $\tilde{\beta}_3$ and $\tilde{\beta}_4$ in Equation 3.8 do not become overly large[3] (details of the lasso $\mathcal{L}_1$ penalty appear in Appendix 3.2). Note that the coefficients in Equation 3.8 are determined by finding:

$$\hat{\beta} = \text{argmin}_\beta \sum_{t=25}^{T} \left(\widetilde{DR}_t - \tilde{\beta}_0 - \tilde{\beta}_1 \cdot LIB_{t-24} - \cdots - \tilde{\beta}_4 \cdot GDP_{t-12} \right)^2 \quad (3.9)$$

The lasso finds the fitted coefficients by:

$$\hat{\beta}^{LASSO} = \text{argmin}_\beta \left\{ \frac{1}{2} \sum_{t=25}^{T} \left(\widetilde{DR}_t - \tilde{\beta}_0 - \tilde{\beta}_1 \cdot LIB_{t-24} - \cdots - \tilde{\beta}_4 \cdot GDP_{t-12} \right)^2 \right.$$
$$\left. + \lambda \left(\left| \tilde{\beta}_1 \right| + \left| \tilde{\beta}_2 \right| + \left| \tilde{\beta}_3 \right| + \left| \tilde{\beta}_4 \right| \right) \right\} \quad (3.10)$$

To address the issue of instability in lagged variable relationships, we first obtain the best lag from the trailing dataset and run the transformed regression with Lasso penalty as in Equation 3.10 until we cannot make further out-of-sample predictions. Then we re-run Equation 3.8 with minimum lag at 12 months to get the rest of the monthly default predictions. For example, say the lag selected for GDP is seven months. We use the seven-month lag to make the first seven predictions. Then we switch to a 12-month lag to make the next five predictions. The improvement in out-of-sample results is evident in the right panel of Figure 3.7, which shows the predicted default rates using the lagged lasso regression. We call our lagged lasso regression model HT 2.0 as an extension of the original Hampden-Turner model.

SELECTING LAGS

In the previous sections, we have used the absolute peak in CCF to choose the lags for the input variables in the regressions. One striking feature of these CCF plots in Figure 3.6 is that the estimated CCFs seem to be highly persistent. That is, there are numerous lags that cluster around the peak value, making it difficult, and perhaps even misleading, to choose the best lag relationship on that basis. The cause of this clustering is typically attributed to the autocorrelation structure in individual series. Here we used the "pre-whitening" technique introduced by Jenkins and Watts (1968) to clarify the lagged relationships.[4] See Appendix 3.3 for the "systems approach" (Chatfield, 2004) we use that is based on pre-whitening.

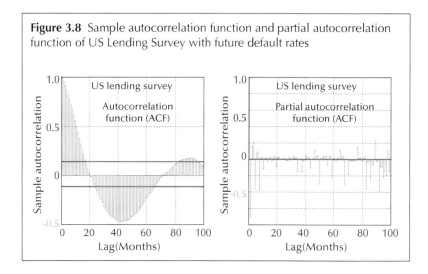

Figure 3.8 Sample autocorrelation function and partial autocorrelation function of US Lending Survey with future default rates

For example, to study the lagged relationship between monthly default rates and US Lending Survey data up to end-2012, we first plot the sample autocorrelation function (ACF) and partial autocorrelation function (PACF) of the US Lending Survey time series as shown in Figure 3.8. The ACF plot in the left panel displays a damped sine–cosine pattern and PACF cut-off before lag 10, indicative of an autoregressive process, $AR(p)$, with complex roots. By using the Bayesian information criterion (BIC)[5] as the model selection criterion, we choose the maximum lag $p = 8$ and arrive at an $AR(8)$ model that only includes lags at one and eight months. If we denote

B as the backshift operator (ie, $BX_t = X_{t-1}$), the estimated model can be written as:

$$(1 - 1.055B + 0.0914B^8)(LS_t - \mu)w_t \qquad (3.11)$$

Pre-whitened LS_t is just the residual w_t from the $AR(8)$ model. The top panels of Figure 3.9 confirm that the residual time series w_t does not show large deviations from the standard normal distribution.

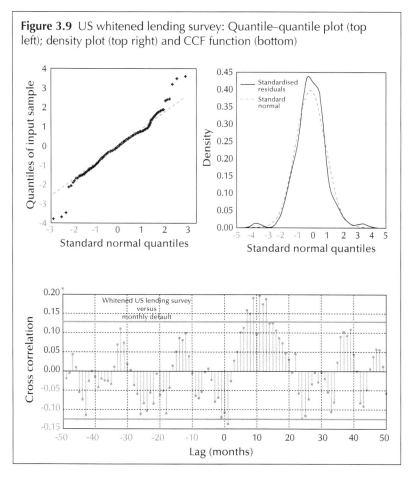

Figure 3.9 US whitened lending survey: Quantile–quantile plot (top left); density plot (top right) and CCF function (bottom)

Next, we filter the monthly default rate DR_t using the same $AR(8)$ model for LS_t, and obtain:

$$(1 - 1.055B + 0.0914B^8)DR_t = d_t \qquad (3.12)$$

Finally, in the bottom panel of Figure 3.9 we plot the sample CCF of d_t versus w_t, which differs dramatically from the CCF shown in Figure 3.6. We conclude that lags of LS_t at lags of nine, 11, 12 and 13 should be tried as predictors of DR_t and selected via BIC. Interestingly, lag 10 no longer appears to be significant in the new CCF plot. Figure 3.9 also shows why the VAR model for LS may be overfitting by including previous lags of DR; after all, LS is leading DR.

WHY PREDICT THE DEFAULT RATE?

One may question the utility of developing a model to predict the overall corporate default rate. After all, the rating agencies publish forecasts of default rates on at least an annual basis. The main reason for building this model to predict default is to test the ability of monthly out-of-sample forecasts of annual default rates to signal price moves in the corporate credit markets. In fact, the results of tests of that ability will be presented in this section. In addition, to implement the model, monthly estimates of default rates are required as inputs to another stochastic model of credit cycle-dependent rating transitions developed by Benzschawel, Lee and Li (2012) and presented in Chapter 12. Finally, it is desirable to gain insight into the factors that underlie overall default rates, and developing models to forecast default rates is one way to improve that understanding.

To illustrate the use of the HT 2.0 model to predict high-yield credit spreads, consider Figure 3.10. The figure displays annual changes in average high-yield corporate bond spreads versus either the trailing 12-month default rate (left panel), called the current default rate, or the predicted default rate (right panel). That is, monthly changes in average high-yield corporate bond spreads over the subsequent 12 months are plotted versus either the trailing or predicted 12-month default rate. These are the points on the graphs in the left and right panels of Figure 3.10, respectively. The predicted default rate has an $R^2 = 0.64$ over the period from January 1995 to June 2013, whereas the current default rate has an $R^2 = 0.13$.

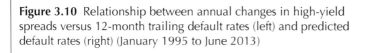

Figure 3.10 Relationship between annual changes in high-yield spreads versus 12-month trailing default rates (left) and predicted default rates (right) (January 1995 to June 2013)

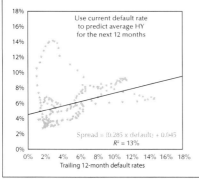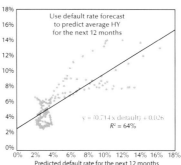

Figure 3.11 Top: average high-yield corporate bond spreads; bottom: ratios of high-yield spreads to predicted default rates (1995–2013)

Despite the advantage of predicted default rates over trailing default rates for estimating changes in high-yield spreads over the next year, neither predictor is satisfactory. In fact, a more relavent question for potential investors in high-yield bonds is: "How much yield will I receive for taking on a given level of default risk?" For example, even if default rates are relatively high, an investor may be well-compensated by outsized yield spreads to Treasuries (eg, think 2009). Conversely, if spreads are tight, defaults may be low and investors may still earn attractive returns owing to few defaults. Consider the historical series of average high-yield corporate bond spreads in the top panel of Figure 3.11. Clearly, spread levels vary widely over the cycle. However, the absolute level of spreads does not indicate whether investment in high yield is attractive nor provide reliable signals regarding the future direction of spread moves. A large determinant of those returns depends on the expected default rate over the investment horizon.

To determine if the ratio of high-yield spreads to default provides useful information to investors, consider the ratios of average high-yield spreads to predicted default rates from the HT 2.0 model since 1995 that appear in the lower panel of Figure 3.12.[6] The assumption is that the ratio of the current high-yield spread to the predicted default rate is indicative of the attractiveness of high-yield returns. Consider first the left-hand panels of Figure 3.12. The upper panel shows one-year changes in high-yield spreads as a function of ratios of the current high-yield average spreads to trailing 12-month default rates. In that plot, the light grey circles represent changes in spreads when the spread-to-default ratios are below average, with the dark grey squares plotting changes when the ratios are above average. Points are determined monthly, with the vertical grey line showing the average spread-to-default ratio over the period from 1995 to 2013. The scatterplot reveals that ratios using the current trailing 12-month default rate have little ability to forecast changes in high-yield spreads one year later. This is confirmed in the bar chart in the lower left-hand panel, which presents probabilities of spreads widening or tightening if the ratio of high-yield spreads to trailing default rates are above average or below average, respectively. That is, probabilities of spreads widening or tightening are independent of the ratio of high-yield spread to current default rate (ie, probabilities are roughly 50% for all ratios), falling at (or near) the dashed chance performance line.

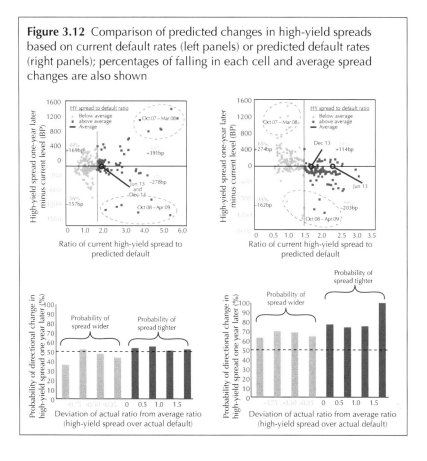

Figure 3.12 Comparison of predicted changes in high-yield spreads based on current default rates (left panels) or predicted default rates (right panels); percentages of falling in each cell and average spread changes are also shown

In contrast to the results using ratios of spreads to trailing default rates, the panels on the right in Figure 3.12 demonstrate that ratios of spreads-to-default using predicted 12-month default rates are strongly related to one-year changes in high-yield spreads. That is, when ratios of high-yield spreads to predicted default rates were above average, high-yield spreads one year later were tighter 85% of the time. When ratios were below average, spreads were wider 65% of the time. The histogram of percentages of spread widening or tightening as a function of the spread-to-default ratio in the lower right panel of Figure 3.12 confirms the above-chance performance over the entire range of ratios. The figure also reveals that the size of the ratio has little effect on directional accuracy, except if the ratio is above or below zero. In particular, notice how the directional changes in spreads reverse from widening to tighening on either side of the average spread-to-predicted default ratio. Finally, note that when there are "errors" in the signal from the spread-default ratio (ie, spreads tightening when ratios are below average, and vice versa), average "losses" are smaller than average gains when "correct". For example, when the spread-to-default ratio is above average, the average spread tightening is 203bp, whereas when spreads rise, they rise only by 114bp on average. In fact, given the spread-to-predicted default ratio in December 2013 indicated by the circle in upper right panel of Figure 3.12, the expected spread tightening by December 2014 is:

$$[84\% \times (-203bp)] + [16\% \times (+114bp)] = -152bp$$

Similarly, if the ratio of high-yield spreads to predicted default is less than average, then historical analysis suggests that the average high-yield spread will widen by:

$$[65\% \times (+247bp)] + [15\% \times (-162bp)] = +121bp$$

The results presented in Figure 3.12 are intended to demonstrate the usefulness of modelling predicted default rates.

PREDICTED DEFAULT RATES AND OTHER MARKETS
One can apply the same methods as applied to high-yield spreads to predict changes in other equity and credit derivatives markets. That is, the left panel of Figure 3.13 presents changes values of the S&P 500 equity futures contact (SPX) and ratios of its current value to the one-year predicted default rates. Results are similar to that for high yield. That is, above average values of the SPX to predicted defaults predict positive SPX returns over 90% of the time, whereas low ratios of the SPX to predicted default portend negative one-year equity returns. We see similar effects of current values to predicted default for investment-grade corporate bonds, and both investment-grade and high-yield CDX indexes.

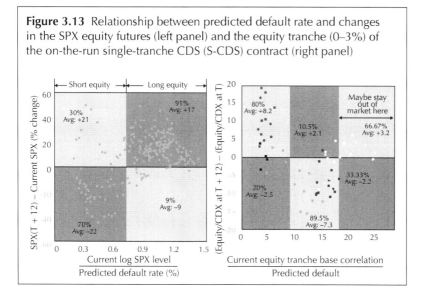

Figure 3.13 Relationship between predicted default rate and changes in the SPX equity futures (left panel) and the equity tranche (0–3%) of the on-the-run single-tranche CDS (S-CDS) contract (right panel)

Finally, consider the right panel of Figure 3.13, which displays ratios for values of the base correlation of the equity tranche (0–3%) of the five-year on-the-run single-tranche CDS (S-CDS) to the one-year predicted default rates. In general, low values of based correlation to predicted default tend to signal widening of 0–3% tranche spreads, while higher ratios signal spread tightening. However, at extremely high ratios of base correlation to predicted default rates, 0–3% tranche spreads tend to widen.

CONCLUSION

This chapter presented a model for predicting 12-month default rates and examined its performance in out-of-sample testing since 1994. The default forecasting model is called HT 2.0, as it is an extension of the model first described by Hampden-Turner (2009). HT 2.0 takes market prices and economic indicators as inputs and generates monthly default rate predictions for the next 12 months. The chapter began by providing some perspective on historical default rates, including a brief discussion of previous attempts to forecast corporate default rates. This was followed by a detailed description of the original Hampden-Turner model, along with some limitations of that model. These limitations include the possibility of generating negative default rates and the fact that, when the model is used to generate out-of-sample predictions, it has relatively poor performance. To overcome the shortcomings of the original HT model, the HT 2.0 model deploys a logistic transformation on predicted default rates to avoid negative values, imposes a penalty for large regression coefficients and uses statistical "pre-whitening" to improve estimates of optimal lags for the input variables. This was followed by a demonstration of the improvement offered by using the HT 2.0 model in out-of-sample predictions of historical default rates. Finally, to demonstrate the usefulness of having an accurate estimation of future default rates, forecasts of future default probabilities, but not current default rates, were shown to assist the prediction of subsequent changes in high-yield credit spreads.

APPENDIX 3.1 A CAUTIONARY TALE

To perform time series regressions, it is crucial to determine whether or not the series under consideration are stationary over time.[7] That is, regressing non-stationary series on non-stationary series may lead to spuriously significant regressions. To test if a time series is stationary, we can use the augmented Dickey–Fuller (ADF) test.

If one has identified a time series input to be non-stationary, care is suggested as regards including such series as a predictor. Some type of transformation should be applied to make the series more stationary. For example, the raw GDP time series may have an upward trend over the long run, so it is better to use, say, the quarterly GDP growth instead. In fact, this is the approach that was taken in the default prediction model of this chapter. One could also apply transformations such as first-order difference (for example, the monthly change in a predictor variable), or de-trending a series to avoid predictions that appear to fit well in-sample but will have low predictive power in practice.

APPENDIX 3.2 LASSO $\mathcal{L}_1$ PENALTY

Linear regression with $\mathcal{L}_1$ penalty: An introduction to the lasso

For a linear regression model with dependent variable y_i ($i = 1, \ldots, N$), input variables x_{ij} ($j = 1, \ldots, p$) and coefficients $\beta_0, \beta_1, \ldots, \beta_p$, the OLS estimate of $\beta_0, \beta_1, \ldots, \beta_p$ is given by:

$$\hat{\beta}^{OLS} = \text{argmin}_\beta \sum_{i=1}^{N}(y_i - \beta_0 - \sum_{j=1}^{p} x_{ij}\beta_j)^2 \qquad \text{(A.3.2.1)}$$

Although the fitted coefficients of the OLS regression are unbiased, they may suffer from ill-posed conditions and complicated correlation structure among variables. In addition, if one's focus is on time-series regression, the fitted coefficients may be unstable over time, leading to unintuitive changes in the fitted values over different training periods. Modern regularisation techniques such as the lasso ($\mathcal{L}_1$) attempt to overcome these problems by seeking a sparse solution by inclusion of a $\mathcal{L}_1$ penalty for the coefficients:

$$\hat{\beta}^{lasso} = \text{argmin}_\beta \sum_{i=1}^{N}(y_i - \beta_0 - \sum_{j=1}^{p} x_{ij}\beta_j)^2,$$

subject to $\sum_{j=1}^{p}|\beta_j| \leq t.$ (A.3.2.2)

Rewriting Equation A.3.3.2 in an equivalent Lagrangian form, we have:

$$\hat{\beta}^{lasso} = \text{argmin}_\beta \left\{ \begin{array}{c} \frac{1}{2} \sum_{i=1}^{N}\left(y_i - \beta_0 - \sum_{j=1}^{p} x_{ij}\beta_j\right)^2 \\ +\lambda \sum_{j=1}^{p} |\beta_j| \end{array} \right\}$$ (A.3.2.3)

Since the $\mathcal{L}_1$ constraint makes the solution to the optimisation problem non-linear in y_i, no closed-form solution exists. However, one can use quadratic programming to compute the lasso solution, and efficient algorithms are developed to generate the entire path of solutions with varying λ (Hastie, Tibshirani and Friedman, 2008).

Note that t or λ, the so-called shrinkage parameter, plays an important role in controlling the size of the fitted coefficients. For example, if t is sufficiently large, the penalty almost has no effect and the lasso estimate is essentially the OLS estimate. On the other hand, if t is relatively small, then some of the coefficients would be shrunk towards 0. In the extreme case when $t = 0$, all the coefficients will be shrunk to 0 in the optimisation routine.

As lasso tends to shrink many coefficients to 0, it automatically performs variable selection.

APPENDIX 3.3   PRE-WHITENING

Spurious correlation and pre-whitening for lagged regression

To identify the lags in a lagged time-series regression, a common approach is to examine the plot of the CCF between the response time series Y_t and input series X_t. Unfortunately, the CCF between Y_t and X_t may be influenced by the autocorrelation structure of these two series. That is, significant cross-correlation between two unrelated time series may be observed as an artifact of strong autocorrelation in both series. To avoid reading a spurious relationship between the two time series, one can deploy a "pre-whitening" strategy as outlined in the following steps:

1. Determine a time-series model for the X variable. For example, for stationary X_t with mean 0, fit an ($ARMA(p,q)$ model to X_t

$$X_t = \sum_{i=1}^{p} \varphi_i X_{t-i} + w_t + \sum_{j=1}^{q} \theta_j w_{t-j} \qquad \text{(A.3.3.1)}$$

where w_t is a white noise series (ie, independent and identically distributed random series with mean 0 and finite variance). Alternatively, one can simplify the above formulation by the backshift operator B as:

$$\varphi(B)X_t = \theta(B)w_t \qquad \text{(A.3.3.2)}$$

where $\varphi(B)$ and $\theta(B)$ are polynomials in B In other words, one can "whiten" the original series X_t by applying the filter $\varphi(B)/\theta(B)$:

$$\frac{\varphi(B)}{\theta(B)} X_t = w_t \qquad \text{(A.3.3.3)}$$

The fitted autoregressive moving average model (ARMA) parameters then lead to the residual $\widetilde{w}_t$:

$$\frac{\widehat{\varphi}(B)}{\widehat{\theta}(B)} X_t = \widetilde{w}_t \qquad \text{(A.3.3.4)}$$

One can check the normality assumption by a quantile–quantile plot on the residuals. It is not crucial, and often not practical, to find the exact time series model for X, but filtering X to an approximate white noise series is necessary.

2. Since Y and X are assumed to have a lagged linear relationship, one filters the Y variable similarly by the estimated whitening filter from the first step. That is:

$$\frac{\widehat{\varphi}(B)}{\widehat{\theta}(B)} Y_t = \tilde{d}_t$$

(A.3.3.5)

Note that, in practice, it is easier to filter Y by AR coefficients only (ie, $\theta(B) = 1$), so for convenience we may want to check if fitting X with an AR process suffices during the first step.

3. Examine the CCF plot $\tilde{w}_t$ and $\tilde{d}_t$, and identify possible lags for the lagged relationship between Y and X.

---

4   High-yield firms are those rated below Baa by Moody's and BBB– by Standard & Poor's, with investment-grade firms having higher ratings by each agency. These are also called "speculative-grade" firms.

5   Note that the Hampden-Turner (2009) documentation claims to use the number of high-yield issuers to the total number of issuers, but the actual implementation used the Libor slope instead.

6   The lasso method is one example of a regularisation method designed to prevent over-fitting by penalising extreme parameter values. Regularisation introduces a second factor, λ in Equation 3.10, which shrinks regression coefficients. For a technical discussion of the lasso method, see Tibshirani (1996) and Appendix 3.2.

7   The term "pre-whitening" is used in the construction of lagged regressions to minimise the effects of co-movements in the x- and y-variables in the lag analysis on the CCF.

8   The BIC, developed by Schwartz (1978), measures the variance reduction provided by the addition of each variable to the model. In addition, it imposes a penalty for having too many variables, thereby guarding against over-fitting the data.

9   The units for default in the numerator of the ratio in Figure 3.12 are in percentages. For the high-yield spread in the denominator, we use the spread in basis points. For example, for a predicted default rate of 2.3% and a current high-yield spread of 230bp, we calculate the ratio as $\left(\frac{2.3\%}{100\%}\right)\Big/\left(\frac{230bp}{10,000bp}\right) = 1$.

10   For example, the most salient condition for stationarity is that the mean of the series does not change over time. For example, an upward or downward drift in the series would imply non-stationarity. There are other considerations as well.

11   The Dickey–Fuller test (Dickey and Fuller, 1979) is used to determine whether a unit root is present in an autoregressive model.

4

An Ensemble Model for Recovery Value in Default

Although models for estimating firms' probabilities of default (PD) abound, there are very few models for estimating recovery values in default.[1] This is surprising as recovery values in default vary widely and expected losses in default depend equally on recovery value and likelihood of default. In an attempt to address this problem, Benzschawel and Li (2013) acquired Moody's default and recovery value database, and used the data to develop a decision tree model (DTM) for recovery value in default. They demonstrated that the DTM performed better than using industry averages at predicting recovery values on defaulted bonds. Nevertheless, it was suspected that applying more sophisticated statistical techniques could enhance model performance. To that end, Benzschawel and Su (2013) developed an ensemble system that combines linear regression with state-of-the-art machine learning algorithms that are based on regression trees (ie, random forests, RFs, and gradient tree boosting, GTB). Those models and their performance will be the subject of this chapter.

The chapter begins with a brief description of the Benzschawel–Li DTM, along with discussion of its advantages and limitations. This is followed by a look at the normalisation of recovery values in default and other aspects of data preparation, including the handling of missing values and the "walk-forward" model validation precursors for the E-3 model. Next, a description of random forests and gradient tree boosting methods is provided, followed by a brief description of the linear regression models and their combination in the E-3 ensemble.

THE DECISION TREE AND ENSEMBLE MODELS

Figure 4.1 Decision tree model for recovery value in default

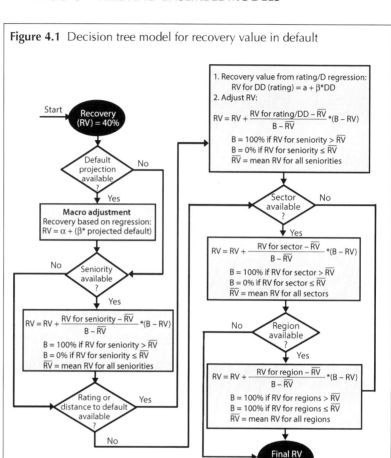

Source: Benzschawel, Haroon and Wu (2011)

Benzschawel, Haroon and Wu, (2011) and Benzschawel and Li (2013) described the construction and testing of a DTM to predict bonds' recovery values in default. The model, shown in Figure 4.1, embeds information on the overall default rate (macro environment), seniority in the capital structure, credit risk, industry sector and geographical jurisdiction as they affect recovery values generated from a decision tree framework. We have demonstrated how the DTM performs at predicting recovery value in out-of-sample testing for the period 1991–2011. For example, the left and right panels of Figure 4.2 display frequency distributions of errors using a constant recovery rate of 40% and those from the DTM, respectively. Analyses of those distributions show clearly the reduction in errors over average values provided by the DTM. These and other results (not reproduced here) suggest that the DTM is useful for estimating recovery values in default.

Figure 4.2 Frequency distributions of errors in estimating recovery values from defaulted firms in Moody's dataset using a constant value of 40% (left) or values from Citi's DTM (right)

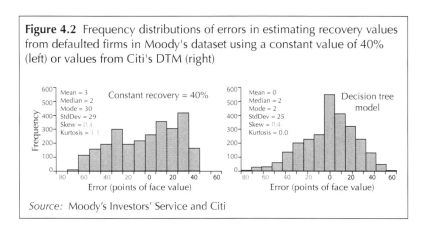

Source: Moody's Investors' Service and Citi

Despite the success of the DTM, we suspected that the model could be improved upon for several reasons. First, the decision tree structure uses a sequential estimation scheme that is inefficient in capturing non-linearities or interactions among input variables. In fact, the decision tree structure for modelling recovery was chosen because our earliest models of recovery value were developed using only average statistics on the dimensions represented. That is, prior to acquiring Moody's recovery value database, we did not have sufficient data on individual firms to develop a firm-level model. Since preliminary testing of a regression model on the individual firm data somewhat surprisingly provided little performance enhancement, we decided not to abandon the DTM framework. Still, there was reason to suspect that more sophisticated statistical techniques, combined with careful input variable preprocessing, might reveal additional information from data not captured by the decision tree framework – and, in turn, might lead to more stable predictive models as well as better predictive accuracy.

Random forests and gradient tree boosting

The RF and GTB help to capture non-linearity and interactions among input variables, while walk-forward linear regression (LG) avoids over-fitting the data. As demonstrated below, the E-3 model improves the stability of model predictions relative to the DTM, while achieving significant improvement in out-of-sample predictions of recovery value in default over the testing period from 1991 to 2011. For example, the E-3 model reduced the out-of-sample mean squared error (MSE) in predicting recovery values by two-thirds to 626, compared with 911 when using a constant value of 40%. Also, the correlation between predicted and actual recoveries is 55%, as opposed to –14% when the predictions are calculated based on historical averages. Finally, by imputing values within issuers as well as using a proximity measure from the RF algorithm, we are able to address the problem of missing input data when applying the model.

Figure 4.3 displays the three stages of our ensemble modelling framework. Each component in each stage will be described in detail in subsequent sections. Our goal is to predict recovery values in year $t + 1$ based on an expanding training window from 1982 to year t for values of t ranging from 1990 to 2010. The model can be adjusted easily for prediction windows of less than one year – for example, predicting recoveries at the next month or next quarter. Also, we do not predict recoveries for loans.

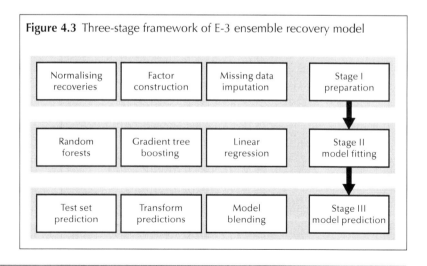

Figure 4.3 Three-stage framework of E-3 ensemble recovery model

Recovery values are expressed typically as percentages of face value[2] – that is, they range between 0% and 100%. The left panel of Figure 4.4 shows the distribution of recovery values from 1982 to 2011, while the right panel shows the number of recovery values by year. Note that recovery values are not normally distributed about their average value. The bounded nature of recoveries and their non-Gaussian distribution make it undesirable to fit a linear regression model directly, because, for example, predicted recoveries may lie well outside the range of observed values. To address this problem, we adopt a Box–Cox type transformation (Box and Cox, 1964) that normalises random variables with any given distributions.[3] The same statistical technique is used in Moody's LossCalc v1 and v2 models for recovery value (Gupton and Stein, 2002; 2005).

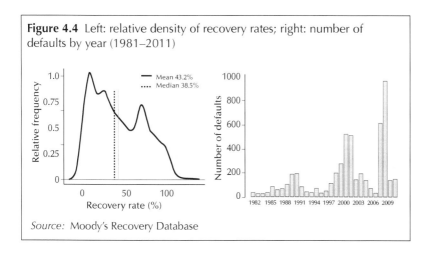

Figure 4.4 Left: relative density of recovery rates; right: number of defaults by year (1981–2011)

Source: Moody's Recovery Database

Assume a random variable x has a continuous cumulative distribution function (CDF) F. Then $\tilde{x} = \Phi^{-1}\{F(x)\}$ is normally distributed, where Φ denotes the CDF for standard normal distribution and Φ^{-1} denotes the inverse CDF. This is because[4]:

$$P(\tilde{x} \leq a) = P(\Phi^{-1}\{F(x)\} \leq a).$$
$$= P(F(x) \leq \Phi(a))$$
$$= F\{F^{-1}(\Phi(a))\} = \Phi(a). \tag{4.1}$$

Figure 4.5 Top: empirical cumulative distribution of recovery values; bottom: cumulative distribution of standard normal values historical values of the credit risk premium, λ since 1999

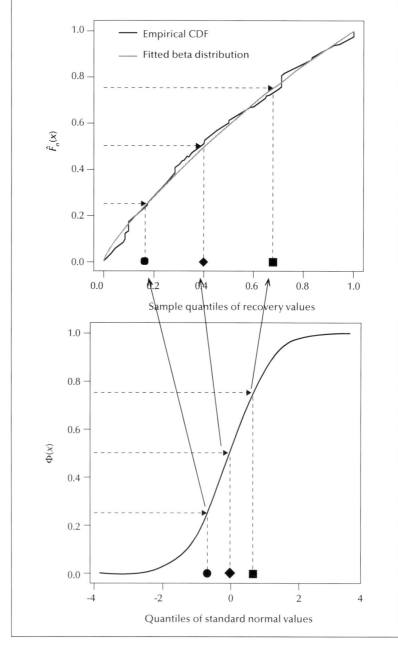

After normalisation, x with only support on the interval $[0,1]$ will be converted to $\tilde{x}$ with support on the real line $(-\infty,+\infty)$.

Application of the transformation in Equation 4.1 requires specifying F for all recovery values r. A natural parametric approximation of F for recovery values is the beta distribution $\beta(\alpha, \beta)$, as it is bounded by 0 and 1. The beta distribution is determined by two shape parameters, α and β. To fit recovery values in the training data up to time t, we use the method of moments to estimate $\hat{\alpha}_t$ and $\hat{\beta}_t$ for the beta distribution and subsequently transform r into $\tilde{r} = \Phi^{-1}\{B(r; \hat{\alpha}_t, \hat{\beta}_t)\}$. A description of the method of moments estimation procedure appears in Appendix 4.1.

The cumulative density function (CDF) fit to the beta distribution appears in the top panel of Figure 4.5, revealing the close match between that CDF and the empirical CDF of actual recovery values. The lower panel of Figure 4.5 shows the S-shaped CDF of the normal distribution and the mapping of the beta-distributed variables onto standard normal variables. Thus, instead of building predictive models for r *per se*, the normalised value of $\tilde{r}$ serves as the dependent variable for our model. Then, from the predicted values of $\tilde{r}$ one can back out the predicted values of r by reversing the transformation. For example, the solid dots in the lower panel of Figure 4.5 corresponding to the first quartile, median and third quartile) illustrate the one-to-one mapping between the normal CDF and the beta CDF in the upper and lower panels, respectively. Finally, since we use sets of training data over an expanding temporal window, $\hat{\alpha}_t$ and $\hat{\beta}_t$ are recalibrated for each training dataset.

Additional and modified variables

As indicated above, Citi's original DTM uses five predictive variables: one-year trailing default rate; seniority (position in the capital structure); jurisdiction (country in which the debt is issued); and the firm's agency credit rating and industry sector. To improve the predictive power of our recovery model, we added variables such as the debt class (available from Moody's ultimate recovery dataset), the trailing mean recovery by industry sectors (normalised according to Equation 4.1 above) and the change in Leading Economic Index (LEI). We also reclassify countries and sectors into various groups. The following sub-sections describe these new variables in detail.

Debt class variable

Table 4.1 displays debt classifications and frequencies of defaulted debt in Moody's database. The classifications are:

- ❑ REG – regular bond or debenture;
- ❑ BCF – bank credit facility;
- ❑ LTPD – long-term public debt;
- ❑ BL – bank loan;
- ❑ CON – conversion/exchange bond/debenture;
- ❑ EQT – equipment trust; and
- ❑ Other.

Table 4.1 Categories of debt class and frequencies in Moody's database

Debt Class:	REG	BCF	LTPD	BL	CON	EQT	Other
Frequency:	62.4%	11.2%	8.7%	5.8%	5.0%	3.4%	3.5%

Source: Moody's Investors Service and Citi

62% of the debt is classified as "REG", indicating this is a regular bond or debenture. However, knowing the exact debt class apart from regular cases may prove beneficial. For instance, if the debt class indicates a first mortgage bond (under category "Other"), in default we expect the bond to receive higher recovery because it is backed by mortgages.

Sector coding

For the DTM, we classified industry sectors based on their standard industry codes (SICs) as shown in Table 4.2. Then, for each sector we calculated average recovery rates for use in testing the model. However, for our E-3 model we use a combination of North American Industry Classification System (NAICS) codes (first three digits) and Moody's Broad Industry Sector codes. Our intent is to have a more specific coding for industrial companies (by using NAICS) and a more specific coding for banking and financial sectors (by using Moody's coding). The revised sector mapping for the ensemble model is shown in Table 4.3.

Table 4.2 Sector coding for Citi's DTM

Sector name	SIC code (4 digit)	Average %
Agriculture / mining	0199-1499	53
Construction	1500-1799	47
Food / tobacco / clothing	2000-2299	53
Clothes / wood / furniture	2300-2599	43
Paper / printing	2600-2799	38
Chemicals / rubber	2600-3099	44
Leather / stone / metal	3100-3499	44
Machinery / electronics	3500-3199	45
Transportation equipment	3700-3799	40
Manufacturing (misc)	3800-3999	40
Land transportation	4000-4499	44
Transport / pipelines (other)	4500-4799	33
Communications	4800-4899	37
Utilities	4900-4999	58
Wholesale trade	5000-5199	42
Retail trade	5200-5999	49
Depository financial	6000-6099	33
Non-depository financial	6100.6199	63
Securities / Broker–dealer	6200-6299	9
Insurance / real estate	6300-6799	39
Travel / entertainment services	7000-7999	53
Services (misc)	8000-8799	62

Table 4.3 Revised sector mapping for E-3 model

Sector name	NAICS	MDY_IND_BRD_CD	New code
Banking	522	BANKING	1001
Finance	522	FINANCE / SOVEREIGN	1002
Securities	523	SECURITIES	1003
Insurance	522/524	INSURANCE	1004
Thrifts	522	THRIFTS	1005
Real estate finance	525	REAL ESTATE FINANCE	1006
Other non-bank	522/525	OTHER NON-BANK	1007
Real estate / rental & leasing	53 X	INDUSTRIAL / TRANSPORTATION	1101
Transportation	48X	TRANSPORTATION	1201
Utility	22X	PUBLIC UTILITY	1301
Other industrial	522	INDUSTRIAL / SOVEREIGN	1401
Manufacturing	31, 32, 33X	INDUSTRIAL	1402
Wholesale trade	42X	INDUSTRIAL	1403
Retail trade	44X, 45X	INDUSTRIAL	1404
Agriculture / mining / construction	11, 21, 23X	INDUSTRIAL	1405
Service (misc)	51, 54, 56, 62, 71, 72X	INDUSTRIAL	1406
Public administration	92X	INDUSTRIAL	1407

Although most categories in the SIC-based sector code in Table 4.2 contain over 100 cases, standard deviations from average recovery rates within categories are large. Moreover, to strike a balance between errors in estimating sector averages and variance, we decided to reduce the number of sectors. A more general coding system will have less variance among sector averages since the historical average calculated on each sector will be close to the average on all sectors. However, such a coding system will also have larger bias as it ignores sub-sectors that are substantially different in a broad sector. On the other hand, a more specific coding system will have smaller bias but much larger variance since many of the specific sectors do not have enough sample data and may not display consistent larger or smaller recovery values.

Trailing sector mean recovery
Having defined industry sectors in accordance with Table 4.3, for each year of testing t (from 1991 to 2011), we determine the average recovery rate for that sector according to the following rule: If the given sector in question has observations prior to year t, use the historical average recovery rate for this sector; otherwise, if the sector type is unknown or has not appeared before t, use a constant 40% as the mean recovery value.

We have adopted this method to capture the variability in recovery rates for different sectors over time. Having determined the average sector recovery rates for year t, we subtract the trailing mean recovery of all sectors from that value to control for systemic shocks to all sectors, leaving the idiosyncratic sector recovery value adjustment. For example, Figure 4.6 displays deviations from overall trailing average recovery rates of utility and industrial companies. The mean recoveries of industrial companies have been relatively stable over time. However, utility companies have enjoyed consistently higher than average recoveries over time.

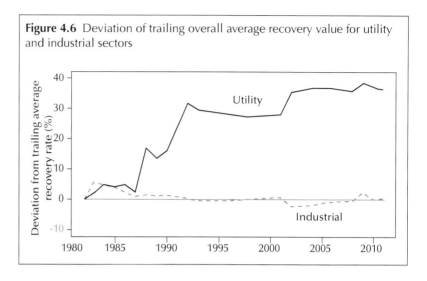

Figure 4.6 Deviation of trailing overall average recovery value for utility and industrial sectors

Adding leading economic indicators

In Citi's original DTM, the effect of business cycle on recovery rates was modelled by adjusting for the negative relationship between historical annual (high-yield) default rates and recovery rates (Altman *et al*, 2005). That relationship is illustrated in Figure 4.6. By using the annual default projection from the HT 2.0 model (see Chapter 3), one can adjust the recovery predictions accordingly. However, this operation is inappropriate for out-of-sample testing as that relationship was only evident after the year 2000. Furthermore, even if the look-back relationship in Figure 4.7 were used, one would have to use the projected one-year default rates as input to that function. Since the trailing default rate does not add to the predictive power of the model and the dataset did not include predicted default rates prior to 1995, the annual change in the Conference Board's Leading Economic Indicators (ΔLEI) was chosen as a proxy for the macroeconomic environment. As shown in Figure 4.8, although ΔLEI does not perfectly lead recovery experience, it does have some predictive power. Finally, although annual default rates and recoveries are strongly negatively correlated as is evident from their time series in Figure 4.8, this relationship is highly variable over time.

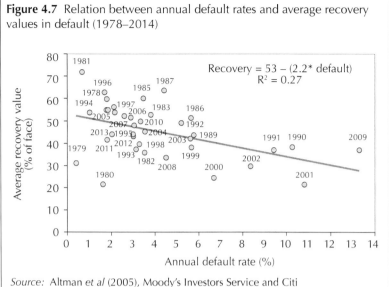

Figure 4.7 Relation between annual default rates and average recovery values in default (1978–2014)

Recovery = 53 – (2.2* default)
$R^2 = 0.27$

Source: Altman *et al* (2005), Moody's Investors Service and Citi

Figure 4.8 Standardised values of annual changes in leading economic indicators (ΔLEI) versus normalised mean recovery and standardised annual default rates

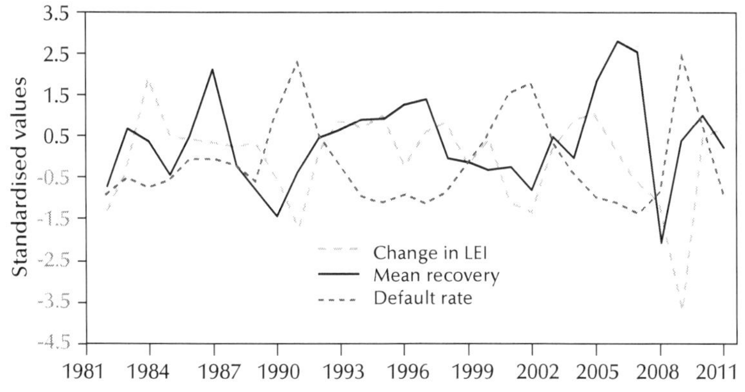

Change in LEI
Mean recovery
Default rate

Geographical jurisdiction (zones) leading

When developing the model, it became clear that country of jurisdiction, as a categorical variable, has very weak predictive power on its own.[5] Also, as shown in Figure 4.9, average recoveries for most countries over the entire period from 1985 to 2011 have very few observations. In particular, this presents a problem for out-of-sample testing for which it was necessary to use norms determined from recovery values obtained prior to the year of testing. In fact, note that 87% of the recovery data in Figure 4.9 is from issues subject to US law (as are most defaults in the data sample). As a result, the data are insufficient for training algorithms to capture consistent and meaningful predictive relationships. Before more data is collected on these countries, it was decided to group countries into different zones, based on their legal differences, total number of observations and geological proximity. This resulted in the construction of six zones: US; Canada; UK; Europe (excluding UK); Asia (including Australia and New Zealand); Central/Latin America and all other emerging markets.

Figure 4.9 Average recovery value by geographical jurisdiction (1985–2011); the number of observations in each jurisdiction are also shown

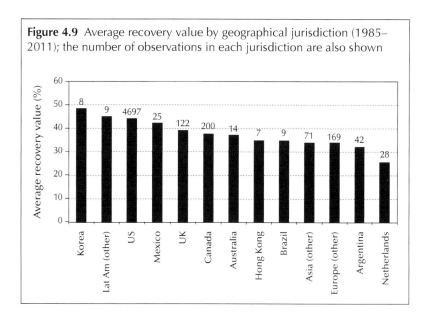

Some additional details and comments

Although the type of collateral underlying secured debt would seem important for recovery value in default, that information is only available for a very small number of observations. As this information is usually difficult to obtain and is absent in most of our training dataset, this variable was not included. Finally, although in testing it appears that including the default type increases the accuracy of predictions, it is unfortunately not possible to know the default type *a priori*.[6] In fact, attempts were made to predict default type for the observations in the test set based on the training data, but predictions from models using those estimated default types were inferior to models that did not include those values.

Walk-forward testing

The models described below were all evaluated using out-of-sample "walk-forward" testing similar to that used for testing the Moody's LossCalc v2.0 model by Gupton and Stein (2002) and Citi's DTM by Benzschawel and Li (2013). The walk-forward method, shown in Figure 4.10, is designed to test models in a manner in which the models would be used in practice. Briefly, the walk-forward procedure in Figure 4.10 is as follows.

1. Begin with the first year of testing (in this case, 1991).
2. Use data from all the previous years of the sample (eg, 1982–90) to establish norms for industry leading economic indicators, sector, seniority, credit quality and geography.
3. Generate model recovery values for all bonds in the following year (eg, 1991) using the previously established norms. Note that, using the walk-forward method, these are out-of-time and out-of-sample tests.
4. Save the estimated recovery values for use in the overall validation, but also compare errors between predicted and obtained recovery values from the model and using a constant 40% average recovery value.
5. Prepare to test predictions for the following year by updating the previous norms from the previous year by adding the data of the tested year.
6. Repeat steps 2 to 5 for all subsequent years through 2011, adding each tested year's data to refine the model norms before testing the following year.

Once the data has been collected for all years, they can be analysed by year or in aggregate to infer performance relative to using historical averages or other benchmarks.

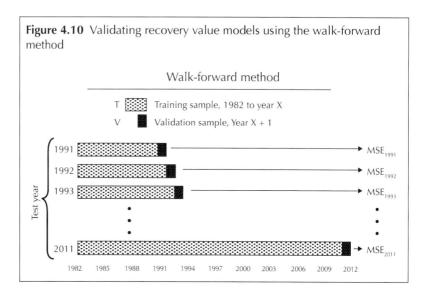

Figure 4.10 Validating recovery value models using the walk-forward method

FROM SINGLE TREE TO RANDOM FOREST AND GRADIENT TREE BOOSTING

Using the walk-forward model validation procedure, the original DTM has been shown to work well in most of the testing periods. However, in some years, predictions from the DTM have significantly underperformed or only marginally improved upon predictions made using constant recoveries (40%) or historical averages. For example, Figure 4.11 shows out-of-sample root mean squared (RMS) errors in predicting recovery rates from the DTM relative to those for historical averages. The circles highlight years in which the model underperforms or offers little predictive benefit relative to using historical averages. Still, overall predictions from the DTM outperform historical averages, and the model can be easily implemented and interpreted. However, we suspected that incorporating advances in tree-based models might improve model stability while increasing prediction accuracy. To that end, we deployed two tree-based learning algorithms that are included in the E-3 model: random forests and gradient tree boosting. The next sub-sections will present brief descriptions of the RF and GTB models. Detailed descriptions of those algorithms appear in Appendix 4.2 and 4.3, and the ensemble model is presented in the next section.

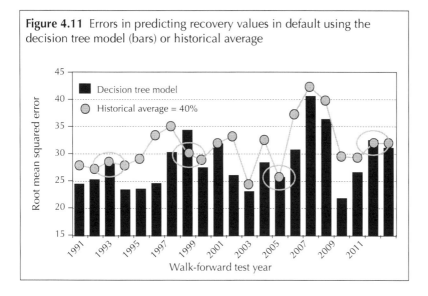

Figure 4.11 Errors in predicting recovery values in default using the decision tree model (bars) or historical average

Random forests

The RF method developed by Breiman (1996, 2001) has enjoyed tremendous success when embedded in modern machine-learning (predictive) algorithms. The RF algorithm has great accuracy, is highly efficient and can handle a large number of variables without the necessity of removing variables with little or no predictive power. Moreover, the algorithm does not over-fit and is robust with respect to noisy data. As the name aptly suggests, a random forest consists of an ensemble of many classification or regression trees, which are called base learners. The term "bagging" refers to the process of combining classifications from randomly generated training sets in the RF algorithm. Before discussing RFs, consider a single regression tree, which is a non-parametric approach to fit high-dimensional data. Regression trees are popular because they can model complex interaction structures, are robust to outliers and can accommodate missing data.

Figure 4.12 presents an example of a simple regression tree to predict the recovery value in default. In the example, there are three binary splits at nodes N_1, N_2 and N_3, and four terminal nodes that assign recovery values. The three splits correspond to the variables geographical zone, seniority and sector, respectively. Consider, for example, how the tree would generate a recovery value for a senior unsecured bond issued by a financial company domiciled in the US. At the first node, N_1, the decision tree branches to the left because the issuer is in the US. At node N_2, the tree branches to the right as the bond is not secured, and finally, at node N_3, the tree branches to the left and assigns the value of 30% at that terminal node.

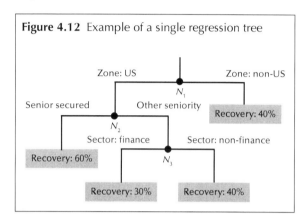

Figure 4.12 Example of a single regression tree

In practice, the regression tree fits the training data using a greedy algorithm that searches for the best variable value to split the sample as regards the decision variable, in this case recovery value. To do this, the algorithm samples possible splits at each node until some stopping criteria are met. At a given node N, x_i denotes the i-th variable and s_i is the value of the best split in x_i that locally minimises the sum of squared errors in all divided regions.[7] Then, the best split for the tree at node N is given by the variable split pair (x_i, s_i) that minimises the sum of squared errors on each side of the node. Given the dual objective of avoiding over-fitting the data while capturing the relevant structure, a large regression tree can be pruned using cost–complexity pruning techniques (see Hastie, Tibshirani and Friedman, 2009) designed to optimise the balance between tree size and its predictive power.

Although the regression tree can be implemented quickly and interpreted easily, it often suffers from high variance as a small change in the training data which can lead to dramatic changes in optimal splits, sometimes resulting in unintuitive tree structures. This high variability is reflected in the relative instability of tree-based algorithms, and consequently a compromise in out-of-sample accuracy.

The RF is designed to address the problem of instability in nodes of a single regression tree. The method is based on the statistical learning idea of bagging. In the initial step, one draws B samples with replacement from the original training data to model p input variables. A regression tree is then constructed for each of the B bootstrap samples. However, unlike the single regression tree that finds the best values to split the variables at each node, the RF selects at random a subset m of the p candidate variables and then chooses the best splits among these variables. As a rule of thumb, $m = [p/3]$ is approximately one-third of the total number of input variables in the model. An attractive feature of RFs is that it requires very little tuning (see Appendix 4.2). That is, increasing the number of trees B in the forest typically does not over-fit the data. Finally, after all the B trees are grown, the prediction for the new data is calculated as the average of all the predictions made by the trees in the forest. This procedure is depicted in Figure 4.13.[8]

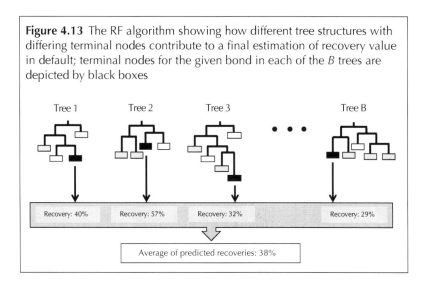

Figure 4.13 The RF algorithm showing how different tree structures with differing terminal nodes contribute to a final estimation of recovery value in default; terminal nodes for the given bond in each of the B trees are depicted by black boxes

It may not be obvious how the splits based on random sets of variables in the forest work to improve performance. That is, each bootstrap sample splits only on a subset m of the p variables. Thus, the splits on each of the m variables will likely be sub-optimal compared with those same splits based on the entire set of p variables. To understand how this method improves performance is to appreciate that bagging serves to reduce the variance of the single tree algorithm by averaging many noisy, but relatively unbiased, models. By randomising the optimal splits, RF constructs a large number of uncorrelated trees, and averaging their predictions reduces the variance of noisy individual trees (boosting, on the other hand, reduces bias instead of variance, and this will be considered in the next section).

Gradient tree boosting

Along with RFs, GTB is another remedy for the instability of a single regression tree. The gradient tree is based on the idea of "boosting" (Friedman, 2001), whose goal is to derive a function F such that the error in using $F(x)$ to predict r (the recovery values in default) on the training data is minimised with respect to some error function L. That is:

$$F^* = \operatorname{argmin}_F \sum_{i=1}^{N} L\left[r_i, F(x_i)\right]$$

(4.2)

However, finding F^* among the infinite number of possible functions is not feasible.[9] Instead, one seeks to approximate the function F^* by the function $\hat{F}_M(x)$, which is a weighted sum of base learners $\hat{f}_m(x)$ so that $\hat{F}_m(x) = \sum_{m=1}^{M} \lambda_m f_m(x) + c$. In a GTB algorithm, these base learners $\hat{f}_m(x)$ are individual regression trees fitted iteratively to the training data, and their weights λ_m are also determined sequentially.

The iterative procedure of GTB is illustrated in Figure 4.14. The algorithm begins by selecting a constant weak learner such as $c = \hat{F}_0(x)$ – for example, the average of all recovery rates in the training data – as our initial approximation.[10] Next, we calculate the residuals z_1 (called pseudo residuals, which will be explained later) not yet fully explained by the current constant predictor, and fit a regression tree $\hat{f}_1(x)$ to these residuals with covariates x_i. We then choose the weight λ_1 (called the gradient descent step size) so that adding the new tree $\hat{f}_1(x)$ to the current predictor best reduces the loss:

$$\lambda_1 = \operatorname{argmin} \sum_{i=1}^{N} L\left\{r_i \hat{F}_0(x_i) + \lambda f_1(x_i)\right\}$$

(4.3)

Note that the best approximation can now be updated by $\hat{F}_1(x) = \hat{F}_0(x) + \lambda_1 \hat{f}_1(x)$. In the proceeding iterative step m $(1 \leq m \leq M)$, we calculate the new residuals z_m fit a regression tree $\hat{f}_m(x)$, find λ_m and update $\hat{F}_m(x) = \hat{F}_{m-1}(x) + \lambda_m \hat{f}_m(x)$.

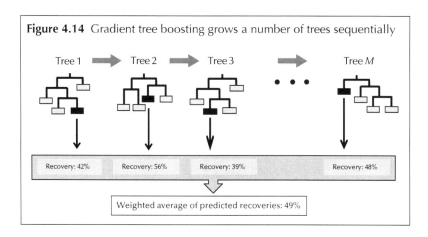

Figure 4.14 Gradient tree boosting grows a number of trees sequentially

Finally, consider the method of calculating the pseudo residuals at each step $z_m = (z_{1m}, \ldots z_{Nm})$. If the sole objective is to minimise the loss on the training data, one can apply a steepest descent rule whereby one updates $\hat{F}_m(x) = \hat{F}_{m-1}(x) + \lambda_m g_m$, where g_m is only defined at the training data points x_i by $g_{im} = -[\partial L(r_i, \hat{F}_{m-1}(x_i) / (\hat{F}_{m-1}(x_i)]$. However, in order to generalise $\hat{F}_m(x)$ to new data not necessarily contained in the training data, we set:

$$z_{im} = -\left[\frac{\partial L\left(r_i, \hat{F}_{m-1}(x_i)\right)}{\partial \hat{F}_{m-1}(x_i)} \right], 1 \leq i \leq N$$

(4.4)

and at each step m, a regression tree $\hat{f}_m(x)$ is fit, whose predictions are as close to the negative gradient in Equation 4.4 as possible on the training data. The gradient tree algorithm requires several tuning parameters such as the number of tress to boost as well as the complexity of each individual tree. These aspects of the algorithm will be discussed in Appendix 4.3.

Linear regression model

To complete the ensemble of models, we add a linear regression generated using the same variables as the RF and GTB models. The general form of the linear regression model is:

$$r = \beta_0 + \beta_1 x_1 + \cdots + \beta_n x_n + \varepsilon \tag{4.5}$$

where the coefficients of β_i $(i = 1, \ldots, n)$ are estimated by the ordinary least squares (OLS) method.[11] Since several of the input variables are categorical (debt type, ratings, etc), dummy variables are used for representing those levels in the model. For example, if there are six different geographical zones (say, A to F), we include only the following five dummy variables to avoid perfect co-linearity:

$$\beta_{ZONE, B} \cdot 1(zone = B) + \beta_{ZONE,C} \cdot 1(zone = C) + \cdots + \beta_{ZONE,F} \cdot 1(zone = F) \tag{4.6}$$

The reason we do not need the indicator 1 (zone = A) is because:

$$1(zone = A) = 1 - \sum_{i=B}^{F} 1(zone = i) \tag{4.7}$$

The linear regression model was then fit based on the same training sets for the RF and GTB. The model's performance at prediction was evaluated each year from 1991 to 2011 using the walk-forward testing method.

Treatment of missing data

In this section, the handling of missing data is discussed. Table 4.4 lists the percentage of missing items by variable in the model development sample. As is evident from Table 4.4, information on seniority, country and debt class is available for nearly all firms. However, industry sector is unknown for nearly 5% of defaults, and over one-fifth of the recovery rate sample has either missing ratings or is not rated. Figure 4.15 indicates that, although there is a tendency for fewer missing ratings in the more recent years of the sample, there are significant numbers of unavailable ratings across all years. This issue was not a problem when constructing the original DTM, since if a rating was not available the model skipped the recovery adjustment at that stage of the tree and moved on to the next.

Table 4.4 Proportion of missing data by variable in the development sample

	Missing
Seniority	0.6%
Industry	4.5%
Country	0%
Rating	21.2%
Debt class	0%

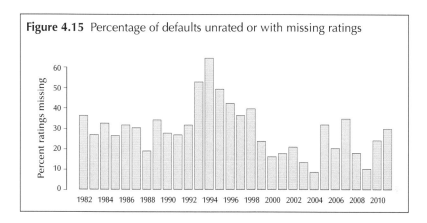

Figure 4.15 Percentage of defaults unrated or with missing ratings

One way to deal with missing data in the training sample is to disregard them as in our original DTM. However, ignoring missing data in the training set has the potential to cause biased estimates of recovery value and increase estimation errors if firms with missing data have systematic differences from others with data. Also, given the limitations of our relatively small sample size, it is preferable to use as much data as is possible. Since it is undesirable to reduce the sample size by dropping observations with missing variables, an alternative is to use all the data, but to treat the missing values as a separate category. However, results of the analysis presented in Figure 4.16 suggest that adding an indicator variable for missing ratings would provide little advantage. That is, annual recovery rates for data with and without rating information reveal little systematic difference (the top panel of Figure 4.16). Furthermore, the empirical cumulative density functions (ECDFs) of the recovery values for observations with and without ratings (bottomn panel of Figure 4.16) are similar. In fact, the two-sample Kolmogorov–Smirnov test (see Appendix 4.1) fails to reject the hypothesis (at the 5% confidence level) that those data come from the same distribution. Since the recovery rates for firms with and without ratings are similar, adding an indicator variable for rating, the most common missing variable, adds little predictive value.

An alternative approach is to impute values for the missing variables from data with non-missing variables. A popular choice considers imputation with sample mean (in the case of a continuous variable) or sample mode (in the case of a categorical variable) based on all non-missing values of that variable. More advanced methods involve random or iterative imputations.

To deal with missing data in the training sample, an iterative imputation method was introduced in the random forests. First missing values were filled in the training data by mean or mode, and fit with an initial forest. The fit produces an N by N proximity matrix for all N data points, in which the entry in the i-th row and j-th column is determined by the proportion of trees in the forest that observed data i and j, go into the same terminal node. Based on the proximity matrix, if the k-th continuous variable in data i is missing, its value is imputed by averaging over non-missing variables in the other data weighted by the proximity between data i and these other data. Similarly, if the k-th categorical variable is missing, its fill is calculated using the most frequent categories (ie, the modes) in non-missing data weighted by proximities. Then, another forest is fit and one recalculates the proximities and the fills. This process is repeat iterated five times to obtain the final imputed values.

Imputation of missing variables using RFs is reasonable as it automatically considers the relationship between variables. For example, consider an extreme case where most of a set of first mortgage bonds is rated single-A. If we have a new first mortgage bond without a rating, it makes more sense to fill its rating as single-A instead of filling the most frequent rating of all available data, which might be different, say single-B.

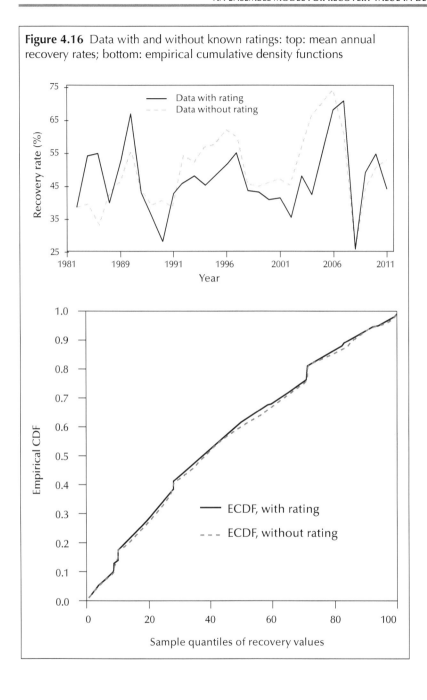

Figure 4.16 Data with and without known ratings: top: mean annual recovery rates; bottom: empirical cumulative density functions

Missing data: Two-step imputation process for unknown ratings

Roughly half of the missing ratings occur for issuers with multiple debt issues outstanding. Therefore, as step 1 one can impute these missing ratings by looking at identical or similar debt issues by the same issuer in each year. However, if no information is available from other debt issued by the same firm, one can proceed to step 2, in which RF is applied to impute missing data from the whole training dataset. Step 1 of the missing ratings imputation (performed on the entire dataset for unrated bonds) is summarised in Figure 4.17 (note that for bonds in the training sample with missing variables other than rating, such as industry and seniority, the proximity measure is used to impute their values).

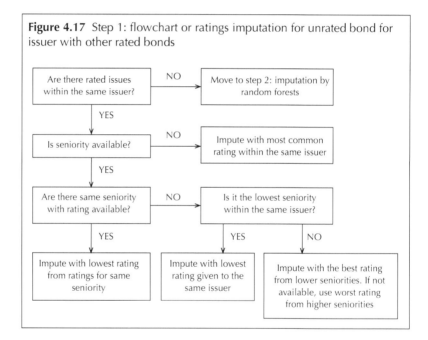

Figure 4.17 Step 1: flowchart or ratings imputation for unrated bond for issuer with other rated bonds

Missing data in the test set: Simple imputation

After fitting the RF and GTB models as described above using data up through year t, recovery rates for defaults in year $t + 1$ in the dataset are generated. As for the training sample, the test data may contain missing values. In this case, we use the most frequent level of the categorical factor in the training data to impute the missing value. The test set may also contain new levels of categorical factors (for example, a new debt type that is has not yet been encountered in our training set). We use the most frequent value as a substitute for that variable.[12]

THE ENSEMBLE METHOD AND ITS APPLICATION TO RECOVERY PREDICTION

An important innovation in predictive modelling is the idea that good learning algorithms can be combined in an ensemble to achieve even better predictive power. For example, the winning prediction model of the famous US$1 million Netflix Grand Prize is a blend of numerous prediction algorithms designed by multiple teams (see Bell, Koren and Volinsky, 2008). In earlier sections, it was shown how RF and GTB can be regarded as ensembles of regression trees. In fact, this idea of using an ensemble of inputs is common to human decision-making: if you have a panel of experts, would you want to listen to the majority of the experts, or would you just rely on a single expert? The ensemble approach works because the combination of independent models with uncorrelated errors serves to reduce aggregate errors. Admittedly, the improvement in performance with the ensemble approach comes at the expense of increasing model complexity. Nevertheless, with currently available computing power and a variety of available modelling techniques, this increase in complexity is manageable. Furthermore, as demonstrated below, the improvement in performance of the ensemble model at modelling recovery value more than compensates for its increased complexity.

The ensemble model for recovery value: E-3

We have included RF, GTB and linear regression models (based on the transformed data) in the final ensemble model, called E-3 for the three components. Predictions from each model carry an equal weight of one-third (the "committee method"). That is, predictions from the E-3 model are generated from equal contributions of recovery estimates from each of the constituent models as given by:

$$\hat{r}_{\text{Ensemble}} = \frac{1}{3}\left(\hat{r}_{\text{RF}} + \hat{r}_{\text{GTB}} + \hat{r}_{\text{LG}}\right)$$

(4.8)

Comparisons of the performance of the ensemble model relative to each of its constituents and over each the constant of its constituent is displayed in Figure 4.18. Average annual correlations appear in the top table and graph, and average annual mean squared errors appear in the bottom. Although the correlation of annual E-3 ensemble estimates with recovery values is highest, that advantage is slight, with all models having correlations of just over 40%. We also examined MSEs in estimating recovery values for the various models as well as for a constant value of 40%. The MSEs for each testing year are calculated as:

$$MSE = \frac{\sum (\hat{r}_i - r_i)^2}{n}$$

(4.9)

where $\hat{r}_i$ is the value output by the model for bond i and r_i is the actual value recovered in default.

The real value of the E-3 ensemble is evident in the reduction of MSEs, as shown in the bottom table and graph in Figure 4.18. First, consider the MSE for the constant 40% recovery value whose annual MSEs are indicated by the black dashes in the graph. As is evident from the graph, the constant 40% estimate has the highest average MSE of all models at 999, with all other models in the ensemble having only about 75% of that value on average. Although each of the models in the ensemble significantly reduces errors over the constant 40% value, the E-3 model again performs better than any individual constituent.

Variable contributions to recovery predictions

A detailed description of the procedure for assessing the importance of variables in each model and in the E-3 ensemble appears in Appendix 4.4. The relative contributions by year for each of the models in the E-3 ensemble are presented graphically in Figure 4.19. Each panel shows by model year the proportion of contributions to predictions for debt class, ΔLEI, trailing average recovery rate, agency rating prior to default, geographical jurisdiction, industry sector and seniority. Visual inspection is sufficient to conclude that seniority in the capital structure and industry sector are most important in all models, getting approximately 50% of the contributions to each model's predictions.

Figure 4.18 Comparisons of predicted and actual recoveries for the ensemble model and each constituent model by test year; top: correlations; bottom: mean squared errors

	Random forests	Gradient	Linear regression	Ensemble E-3
Average correlation	0.43	0.44	0.43	0.45
Standard deviation	0.20	0.18	0.18	0.19

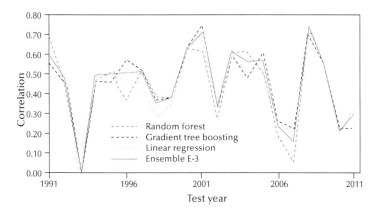

	Random forests	Gradient boosting	Linear regression	Ensemble E-3	Constant 40%
Average MSE	767	749	782	742	999
Standard deviation	294	253	301	284	296

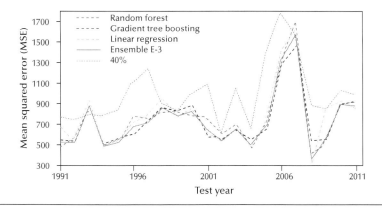

Figure 4.19 Relative contributions of variables in each model of the E-3 ensemble

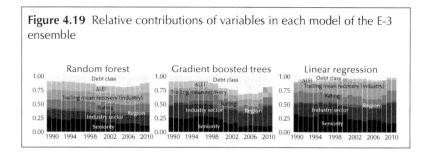

Table 4.5 Variable contributions to each component model of the ensemble; top: relative contributions; bottom: ranked contributions

	Debt class	ΔLEI	Industry trailing mean	Rating	Region	Industry sector	Seniority
Random forests	16.6%	14.7%	17.0%	15.2%	3.5%	14.9%	18.1%
Gradient boosting	19.5%	11.4%	9.6%	13.6%	3.2%	24.1%	18.6%
Linear regression	6.1%	4.4%	23.0%	15.8%	2.3%	22.9%	25.5%

	Seniority	Industry sector	Industry trailing mean	Debt class	Rating	ΔLEI	Region
Random forests	1	5	2	3	4	6	7
Gradient boosting	3	1	6	2	4	5	7
Linear regression	1	3	2	5	4	6	7
Average rank	1.7	3.0	3.3	3.3	4.0	5.7	7

A quantitative analysis of the relative importance of each of the seven input variables appears in the tables in Table 4.5. The percentage of each variable's contribution within each model is presented in the table at the top and the ranked contributions of the variables in each model are shown in the lower table. As expected from the graphs in Figure 4.19, seniority is consistently the most important determinant of recovery value. Seniority accounts for roughly 20% of the contribution across models, being ranked first in the random forests and linear regression model and second in the gradient boosting model. Industry sector is also an important contributor, averaging just about 20% across models, and just slightly less predictive than seniority. Debt class, industry trailing mean and credit rating are also important contributors to recovery value predictions, capturing about 12–15% of the predictive power across models. The change in leading economic indicators, our proxy for the credit cycle, contributes roughly 10% to predictions, with geographical region having the smallest contribution of about 3%.

Model validation

This section presents results of out-of-sample testing of the E-3 model. Consider first the results in Table 4.6, which displays correlations between actual recovery values in default and recoveries estimated from the E-3 model, the DTM or using a constant rate of 40% over the period from 1991 to 2011. The correlation between the actual and predicted recoveries is highest for the ensemble model, E-3, at 55%, followed by the DTM, which had a 31% correlation. Meanwhile, using historical averages was slightly negatively correlated with actual recovery values at –15%.

Table 4.6 Correlations of predicted and actual recovery values in default for the E-3, the DTM and historical averages by sector

	Ensemble model	Decision tree	Historical average
Correlation	0.55	0.31	–0.15

Figure 4.20 displays frequency distributions of errors in estimating recovery values for the ensemble model, decision tree and constant recovery model, from left to right, respectively. Note that the scales on the frequency axis (the y-axes in the plots) are identical, revealing the advantage of the E-3 model over the other two. That is, the error frequency distribution results are consistent with the correlation results in Table 4.6; the errors for the E-3 model are more frequently near zero than for the DTM, which in turn has a much tighter distribution of errors than using average values.

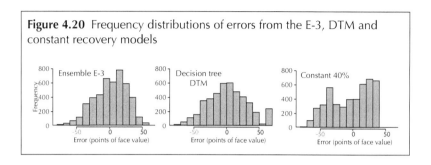

Figure 4.20 Frequency distributions of errors from the E-3, DTM and constant recovery models

The advantage of the E-3 model over the DTM and constant recovery assumption models is quantified in Figure 4.21. The left panel of the figure displays summary statistics of the error distributions that appear in Figure 4.20, serving to demonstrate the reduction in errors relative to the decision tree and constant recovery value assumptions. That is, the E-3 model has a reduction in the dispersion of errors around the mean of 16% relative to the decision tree and constant recovery models. The kernel density distributions of the errors for the models are superimposed in the right panel of Figure 4.21, and show again that errors from the DTM and 40% constant recovery assumption are both more widely dispersed than those from the E-3 model.

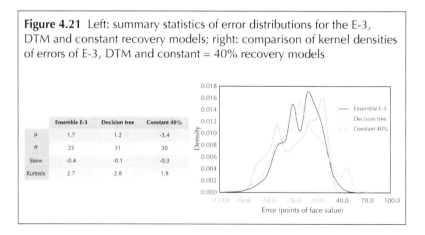

Figure 4.21 Left: summary statistics of error distributions for the E-3, DTM and constant recovery models; right: comparison of kernel densities of errors of E-3, DTM and constant = 40% recovery models

	Ensemble E-3	Decision tree	Constant 40%
μ	1.7	1.2	-3.4
σ	25	31	30
Skew	-0.4	-0.1	-0.3
Kurtosis	2.7	2.8	1.9

To assess further the overall predictive power of the E-3 model relative to statistical averages, we measured overall and annual MSEs in prediction for the E-3 model and MSEs for average values and tables of averages by seniority. The results by year appear in Figure 4.22. Of the 21 years of out-of-sample walk-forward testing, the E-3 model outperformed historical averages in all years except 1993 and 2007 and, in those years, the underperformance was relatively small. Also, the overall out-of-sample MSE for the E-3 model is 626, as compared with the 911 for historical average of 40% and 923 for the table of historical averages.

Figure 4.22 Annual RMS errors for out-of-sample testing of the E-3 model, historical averages by sector or a constant 40%

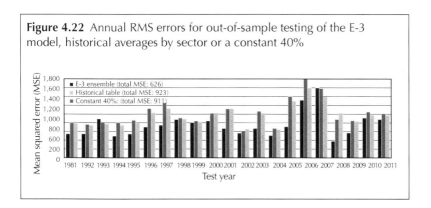

The final set of tests included examining the consistency of predicted and obtained recovery values, and the relative hit-to-false alarm ratios of the E-3, DTM and constant recovery models for the period 1991–2011. The left panel of Figure 4.23 displays the relationship between average predictions of ranked 5% subsets of the model with the actual values of recoveries in that sample. That is, predictions from the E-3 model were ranked according to magnitude on the 0–100% scale and average predictions of each of 20 successive five-percentile buckets was compared with the average recoveries in that bucket. The fact that the points in the graph are well fit by the predicted diagonal line ($R^2 = 0.89$) indicates that higher predicted recoveries are associated with higher actual recoveries.

Figure 4.23 Reliability of model forecasts. Left: Average recovery values in successive 5% bins of ranked predictions for the E-3 model; Right: ROC curves from E-3, the decision tree and constant recovery models showing proportion of "hits" (greater-than-average recovery values) as a function of "false alarms" predicted values greater-than-average recovery values

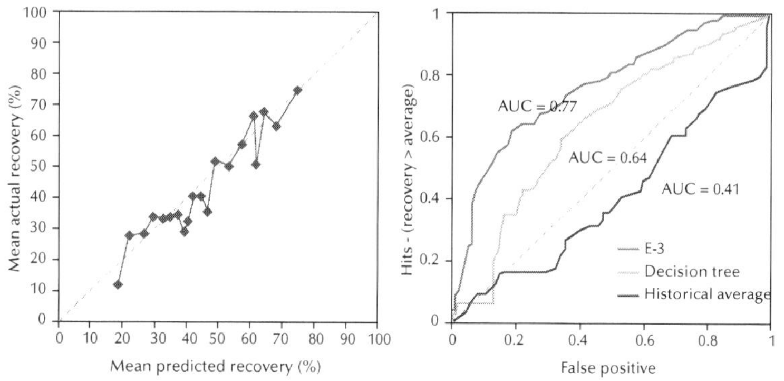

Finally, the right panel of Figure 4.23 displays an ROC of the ability of the E-3, DTM and constant recovery models to distinguish above-average from below-average recovery rates. To construct the ROC, model predicted recoveries were ranked from highest to lowest (for the 40% case, the scores were sorted at random). For example, say that the highest 10% of scores are sampled. In that set, a certain number of predictions of below-average recoveries are present. These would be "false alarms" as they are saying "high recovery", but the actual recoveries are below average. The percentage of the below-average scores in that sub-sample relative to the number of below-average scores is the x-value in the plot. The corresponding y-values, the "hits", are the fraction of the above-average scores in that highest sub-sample of 10% of predicted recoveries. Thus, for the E-3 model, if the model is willing to call 10% of the below-average recoveries "above average", a 10% false alarm rate, the hit rate is roughly 45%, a ratio of 4.5-to-1. Using the same criterion, the DTM has a hit rate of roughly chance, but it improves rapidly from there. As expected, since the constant model does not rank recoveries and is sampled at random, it performs roughly at chance (near the diagonal line in the plot).

CONCLUSION

This chapter has described the construction and testing of an ensemble model for recovery value, called E-3. As its name suggests, the E-3 model is a combination of random forest, gradient tree boosting and a linear regression model. Each of the tree constituents of the E-3 model have been demonstrated to reduce errors in estimating recovery values in default over commonly used constant recovery value assumptions. Also, the E-3 model has been shown to be superior to each of its constituent models. Furthermore, the E-3 model has been shown to outperform a decision tree model that had been demonstrated to offer similar predictive power as that of Moody's LossCalc model. Analysis of variable contributions in the model indicates that seniority in the capital structure is the largest determinant of recovery value in default, and that industry sector, debt class, industry trailing mean recovery rate and credit ratings are also important contributors. Also, the E-3 model achieves significant improvement over the single DTM in walk-forward, out-of-sample recovery predictions from 1991 to 2011. That is, the E-3 model has an out-of-sample MSE of 626, a one-third reduction from the MSE of 911 obtained using a constant 40% recovery value. Correlation between predicted recoveries and actual recoveries is 55%, compared with 31% and –14% relative to the DTM and historical averages, respectively. Although the E-3 model increases accuracy in predicting recovery values in default over the simpler DTM and average recovery values, that improvement is achieved at the cost of much greater complexity. Despite this complexity, the model can be embedded in a spreadsheet-based application into which the user need only input values for the variables, thereby concealing its underlying complexity.

APPENDIX 4.1 FITTING THE BETA DISTRIBUTION USING THE METHOD OF MOMENTS

The probability density function for beta distribution with shape parameters α and β is given by:

$$f(x) = \frac{1}{B(\alpha,\beta)} x^{\alpha-1} (1-x)^{\beta-1}, 0 \le x \le 1$$

(A.4.1.1)

where $B(\alpha,\beta)$ is a normalising constant. Given sample data $(X_1, X_2, \ldots, X_n)$, there are several ways to estimate α and β, including maximum likelihood estimation (MLE) and method of moments. Due to the ease of implementation and numerical stability, here we introduce the method of moments estimation.

For a beta-distributed random variable X, its first and second moments are:

$$M_1 = E(X) = \frac{\alpha}{\alpha+\beta}, \text{ and } M_2 = E(X^2) = \frac{\alpha(\alpha+1)}{(\alpha+\beta)(\alpha+\beta+1)}$$

(A.4.1.2)

Solving for α and β in terms of these moments, we obtain:

$$\alpha = \frac{M_1(M_1 - M_2)}{M_2 - M_1^2}, \beta = \frac{(1-M_1)(M_1 - M_2)}{M_2 - M_1^2}$$

(A.4.1.3)

Thus, to estimate α and β from the sample data, we first estimate M_1 and M_2 by the corresponding sample moments:

$$\widehat{M}_1 = \frac{1}{n}\sum_{i=1}^{n} X_i, \widehat{M}_2 = \frac{1}{n}\sum_{i=1}^{n} X_i^2$$

(A.4.1.4)

Plugging M_1 and M_2 into the previous equation yields the method of moments estimate:

$$\hat{\alpha} = \frac{\widehat{M}_1(\widehat{M}_1 - \widehat{M}_2)}{\widehat{M}_2 - \widehat{M}_1^2}, \hat{\beta} = \frac{(1-\widehat{M}_1)(\widehat{M}_1 - \widehat{M}_2)}{\widehat{M}_2 - \widehat{M}_1^2}$$

(A.4.1.5)

APPENDIX 4.2 SUMMARY OF THE RANDOM FOREST ALGORITHM

The process of implementing the random forest algorithm can be summarised as follows:

1. Draw B bootstrap samples D^1, D^2 ..., D^B with replacement from the training dataset for a given prediction year t.
2. For each bootstrap sample D^b, one generates recursively an unpruned regression tree R^b by the following steps until the pre-specified minimum node size is reached.

a. At each node, randomly chose m variables from the total p variables. As a rule of thumb, one can use $m = [p/3]$. Note that bagging (or bagged regression trees) is the special case when $m = p$.

b. Among the chosen m variables, $X_1, X_2, \ldots, X_m$, the standard tree-fitting algorithm is to select the best split variable j and the best split point s according to:

$$\min_{j,s}\left\{\min_{c_1}\sum_{x_i \in K_1}(r_i - c_1)^2 + \min_{c_2}\sum_{x_i \in K_2}(r_i - c_2)^2\right\}$$

(A.4.2.1)

where r_i is the dependent variable (normalised recovery value) for observed data i and the split regions $K_1(j, s)$ and $K_2(j, s)$ are defined respectively by:

$$K_1(j, s) = \{X \mid X_j \leq s\}, K_2(j, s) = \{X \mid X_j > s\} \quad \text{(A.4.2.2)}$$

if X_j is a continuous variable. On the other hand, if X_j is a categorical variable with q unordered levels, there will be $2^{q-1} - 1$ ways of splitting these q levels into disjoint regions, and it becomes extremely likely that the algorithm will favour some split in X_j for a large q given the large number of choices. As such, one should avoid including categorical variables with a large number of levels to avoid over-fitting.

For any split (j, s), note that the optimisation can be further simplified to:

$$\min_{j,s}\left\{\sum_{x_i \in K_1(j,s)}(r_i - \hat{c}_1)^2 + \sum_{x_i \in K_2(j,s)}(r_i - \hat{c}_2)^2\right\}$$

(A.4.2.3)

where $\hat{c}_h = \text{average}(r_i \mid x_i \in K_h(j, s))$ for $h = 1,2$.

3. After one has grown an ensemble of de-correlated trees R1, R2..., RB, the prediction on a new data point x is calculated as the average prediction from all the trees in the forest:

$$\hat{R}(x) = \frac{1}{B}\sum_{b=1}^{B} R^b(x)$$

(A.4.2.4)

Random forests have only two meta-parameters, the number of trees in the forest (B) and the number of variables chosen at random at each node (m). As noted by Breiman (2001) and subsequently Liaw and Wiener (2002), the RF algorithm is usually not sensitive to their values and does not over-fit when a large B is specified. In practice, with a growing number of predictors it is necessary to build more trees. A simple way to check if we have enough trees in the forest is to compare the prediction result based on a subset of the forest to that based on the full forest – when the performance is similar, enough trees have grown and there is no need to increase B further.

APPENDIX 4.3   SUMMARY OF GRADIENT TREE BOOSTING ALGORITHM

The processes can be summarised as follows.

1. Initialise $\hat{F}_0(x) = \hat{f}_0(x) = \arg\min_c \sum_{i=1}^{N} L(r_i, c)$, where r_i represents the normalised recovery rates.
2. Then, iteratively for $m = 1$ to M:
   a. For $i = 1, 2, \ldots, N$ compute the pseudo residuals according to the negative gradient:

$$z_{im} = -\left[\frac{\partial L\left(r_i \hat{F}_{m-1}(x_1)\right)}{\partial \hat{F}_{m-1}(x_1)}\right], 1 \leq i \leq N$$

(A.4.3.1)

   b. Fit a regression tree $\hat{f}_m(x)$ of size J to the pseudo residuals z_{im} and denote the terminal split regions as $K_m^{[1]}, K_m^{[2]}, \ldots, K_m^{[W_m]}$. See Step 2b in Appendix 4.2 or the details.
   c. Find the gradient descent step size $\lambda_m = \left(\lambda_m^{[1]}, \lambda_m^{[2]}, \ldots, \lambda_m^{[W_m]}\right)$ by computing:

$$\lambda_m^{[j]} = \arg\min_{=} \sum_{x_i \in K_m^{[j]}} L\left(r_i, \hat{F}_{m-1}(x_i) + +\right), \quad j = 1, \ldots, W_m$$

(A.4.3.2)

   d. Update $\hat{F}_{m-1}(x)$ to $\hat{F}_m(x)$ by

$$\hat{F}_m(x) = \hat{F}_{m-1}(x) + v\sum_{j=1}^{W_m} \lambda_m^{[j]} 1\left(x \in K_m^{[j]}\right)$$

(A.4.3.3)

where $0 < \nu < 1$ is a shrinkage parameter that scales the contribution from each tree and the indicator function:

$$1\left(x \in K_m^{[j]}\right) = 1 \text{ if } x \in K_m^{(j)} \text{ and } 1\left(x \in K_m^{(j)}\right) = 0 \text{ if } x \notin K_m^{(j)}$$

(A.4.3.4)

3. Finally, for a new data point x, the predicted recovery value is obtained by $\hat{R}(x) = \hat{F}_M(x)$.

Successful implementation of the above GTB algorithm requires careful tuning of three meta-parameters: the size of the trees J that determines the depth of variable other two parameters; the number of boosting iterations M that controls the prediction risk on the training dataset; and the shrinkage ν that affects the learning rate. First, J is commonly set small (less than six) to reduce unnecessary increase of variance. For the other two parameters, Friedman (2001) suggests a simple strategy that uses a very small ν, which in turn requires large values of M. However, if M is set too large, the algorithm tends to fit the training data too well, which causes overfitting and poor performance on the test dataset. As a result, we adopt an early stopping approach and select the proper size of M by examining the prediction risk with respect to M on a validation sample.

APPENDIX 4.4   CALCULATING VARIABLE IMPORTANCE
Variable importance for random forest

Due to the random sampling of observations (see step 1 in the RF algorithm in Appendix 4.2), not all observations are used for each individual tree in the forest. These data are called "out-of-bag", or OOB, for that particular tree. In an RF model, permutation-based average OOB MSE reduction was favoured as a measure for variable importance (Grömping, 2009).[13] The details of this approach are as follows.

For a particular tree b in the forest, the OOB mean squared error is the MSE calculated on the OOB observations for this tree:

$$MSE_b^{OOB} = \frac{1}{|OOB_b|} \sum_{i \in OOB_b} \left(y_i - \hat{y}_{i(b)}\right)^2$$

(A.4.4.1)

Here, OOB_b denotes the set of OOB observations for tree b, $|OOB_b|$ denotes the cardinality of this set (ie, the number of OOB observations for tree b,) and $\hat{y}_{i(b)}$ denotes the prediction made by tree b for the OOB observation y_i.

MSE_b^{OOB} measures the accuracy of RF on tree b. If the predictor x_k does not have any predictive power at all, we would expect no difference in the predictive power of the RF algorithm if we randomly permute the values of x_k within the OOB data before we make OOB predictions. The difference of OOB MSE with or without permutation is given by:

$$D(x_k, b) = \frac{1}{|OOB_b|} \sum_{i \in OOB_b} \left(y_i - \hat{y}_{i(b) \text{ with } x_k \text{ permuted}} \right)^2$$

$$- \frac{1}{|OOB_b|} \sum_{i \in OOB_b} \left(y_i - \hat{y}_{i(b)} \right)^2$$

(A.4.4.2)

Accordingly, the average OOB MSE increase due to permutation is calculated as the average increase over the entire B trees in the forest:

$$VI(x_k) = \frac{1}{B} \sum_{b=1}^{B} D(x_k, b)$$

(A.4.4.3)

If x_k is a predictor with good predictive power, we expect $VI(x_k)$ to be substantially larger than the case if x_k has no predictive power at all. As a result, $VI(x_k)$ gives a measure of variable importance for random forests.

Variable importance for gradient tree boosting

For a single regression tree, Brieman (1996) suggested using the sum of squared improvements at all splits determined by the predictor as the relative influence of that predictor. That is, for a single regression tree b and a particular predictor x_k, the relative importance is obtained by:

$$I(x_k, b) = \sum_{j=1}^{J} \psi_j^2 \left(\text{predictor } x_k \text{ is used in splitting the tree node } j \right)$$

(A.4.4.4)

where ψ_j^2 is the maximum sum of squared improvement over a constant fit over the entire region of current node j.

For GTB where M trees are constructed iteratively, Friedman (2001) generalised the formula above to calculate variable importance for predictor x_k over all the boosted trees:

$$VI(x_k) = \frac{1}{M} \sum_{b=1}^{M} I(x_k, b)$$

(A.4.4.5)

Variable importance for linear regression

Consider a linear regression model with p predictors:

$$y_i = \beta_0 + x_{i1}\beta_1 + \ldots + x_{ip}\beta_p + \varepsilon, \, i = 1, \ldots n$$

(A.4.4.6)

where the fitted response is given by $\hat{y}_i = \hat{\beta}_0 + x_{i1}\hat{\beta}_1 + \ldots + x_{ip}\hat{\beta}_p$. The coefficient of determinant R^2 indicates the proportion of the variation in y determined by the p predictors, and can be written as:

$$R^2 = \frac{\text{Regression Model Sum of Squares}}{\text{Total Sum of Squares}} = \frac{\sum_{i=1}^{n}(\hat{y}_i - \bar{y})^2}{\sum_{i=1}^{n}(y_i - \bar{y})^2}$$

(A.4.4.7)

To access the variable importance for linear regression, naturally we would like to find out each predictor's contribution to the overall R^2. If the p predictors are uncorrelated, each individual contribution is the R^2 obtained when including only that predictor in the linear model. However, when the predictors are correlated, the sum of these individual contributions is often much higher than the overall R^2. The classical approach to decompose overall R^2 in the presence of correlated predictors requires calculating the sequential R^2 contribution when we add a new predictor into the existing model.

The difficulty of the decompositional approach is that sequential R^2 contributions depend on the order of variables entering into the model. Lindeman, Merenda and Gold (1980) proposed to average the sequential R^2 contribution for a given predictor based on all possible $p!$ orderings. That is, for a given ordering of the p predictors $r = (r_1, r_2, \ldots r_p)$, if $r_j = x_k$, the sequential R^2 contribution for predictor x_k is defined as the increase in R^2 when x_k enters the model:

$$seqR^2\left(x_k;r\right)= R^2\left(\left\{r_1,r_2,\ldots r_{j-1}\right\}\cup\left\{x_k\right\}\right)- R^2\left(\left\{r_1,r_2,\ldots r_{j\ldots1}\right\}\right)$$

(A.4.4.8)

In the above definition, we have used $R^2(M)$ to represent R^2 for the linear model specified by the predictor set M. The variable importance, or the average sequential R^2 contribution, for x_k in the linear regression model is therefore obtained by:

$$VI\left(x_k\right)=\frac{1}{q!}\sum_r seqR^2\left(x_k;r\right)$$

(A.4.4.9)

Relative variable importance

Finally, for all RF, GTB and linear regression, we scale $VI(x_k)$ to get relative variable importance that sums up to 100%:

$$RVI\left(x_k\right)=\frac{VI\left(x_k\right)}{\sum_{k=1}^{p}VI\left(x_k\right)}$$

(A.4.4.10)

---

4   The only models for recovery value in default are Moody's LossCalc (Gupton and Stein, 2002), Standard & Poor's (2008) Recovery Value Rating and Citi's decision tree model (Benzschawel, Haroon and Wu, 2011), with only Moody's and Citi's being available commercially.

5   As claims in default consist of both principal and accrued interest, and because for consistency recovery values are expressed in units of percentage of face value, there are cases where recovery rates exceed 100%. For simplicity, we assume that all recovery rates are capped at 100%.

6   For a description of the Box–Cox transformation and its applications, see Sakia (1992).

7   We use the fact that Φ, Φ^{-1}, F and $\hat{F}^{-1}$ are all continuous and strictly increasing functions.

8   We also observed that in the DTM, country of jurisdiction had very little predictive power with regard to recovery value in default (see Benzschawel et al, 2013).

9   That is, it appears that information regarding whether the default event is triggered by missing interest payment, filing Chapter 11 or another type of event, has some predictive power for recovery.

10 For each split the fitted value is given by the average response in the sub-region specified by the split. The sum of squared errors in region R_k is calculated as $\sum_{x_i\in R_k}\left(y_i-c_k\right)^2$, where $c_k = E(y_i|x_i\in R_k)$.

11 Details of the RF algorithm, including how the split is calculated at each node along with the stopping criteria, can be found in Appendix 4.2.

12 The *argmin* operator in $F^* = \text{argmin}_F L(r, F)$ returns the function F^* that minimises the sum of error functions $\sum_{i=1}^{N}L[r_i,F(x_i)]$.

13 In fact, $\hat{f}_0(x)=\text{argmin}_c\sum_{i=1}^{N}L\left(r_i,c\right)$, where r_i are the recovery rates and L is the squared error loss function.

---

14 For the linear regression $y = X\beta + \varepsilon$, the OLS estimator for β is given by $\hat{\beta} = \left(X^T X \right)^{-1} X^T y$.

15 Of course, new variables in year $t + 1$ can be used for development in the model to score recoveries at $t + 2$.

16 Another well-known approach uses average impurity reduction but is subject to bias (see Grömping, 2009).

5

The Corporate Bond Credit Risk Premium

With the introduction of interest rate swaps in the early 1980s, lenders and investors were able to minimise their exposure to changes in interest rates, even for very long-dated commitments.[1] Arguably, the interest rate swap is one of the most useful innovations produced using financial engineering techniques. No longer must long-term investors worry about fluctuations in interest rates, they can mitigate that exposure by choosing to swap fixed rate for floating rate debt. Despite this success, only latterly have market participants begun to unravel the components that underlie the excess yields over those of credit benchmarks (eg, US Treasuries or swaps) required as compensation for investing in default-risky assets. Although the early work of Jones, Mason and Rosenfeld (1984) suggested that compensation for default accounted for only a small fraction of the credit spread, they attributed that result to a failure of their model of spreads rather than an inherent feature of risky bond yields.

Elton *et al* (2001) were the first to quantify the dominant role of corporate bonds' non-default spreads to Treasuries (ie, the credit risk premium) over the spread compensation for default, and interpreted that as a phenomenon to be explained. Using the logic embedded in Equation 5.1, Elton *et al* decomposed the yield spreads over Treasuries from single-A rated corporate bonds into their compensation for default, s_d, and the remaining portion which they interpreted as the credit risk premium, s_λ. That is, the yield necessary to compensate for expected losses in default for a bond of duration T, whose issuer's expected cumulative default rate to time T is p_T, and whose expected loss in default as a fraction of its face value is LGD can be approximated as:

$$s_d = -\frac{1}{T}\ln[1 - p_T \cdot LGD] \qquad (5.1)$$

As explained in Appendix 5.1, Equation 5.1 is simply a rearrangement of the price yield formula combined with the notion from risk-neutral pricing theory that the spread value is the expectation of the nominal cashflows adjusted for default probability and discounted at the risk-free rate.

Note that the spread compensation for default is designated as s_d and the credit risk premium as s_λ. The value of s_d can be viewed as the yield spread to US Treasuries necessary to account for the loss of cashflows due to the firm's default. That is, an investor who receives a yield spread over US Treasuries equal to s_d receives only an amount equal to the expected return from an equivalent-duration US Treasury security. For now, we will use the term "credit risk premium" to refer to the entire spread compensation over that necessary for the present value of expected cashflows to equal that of an equal-duration US Treasury bond above the compensation for default. However, it may also contain compensation for liquidity/illiquidity.[2]

To demonstrate evidence of the risk premium, Elton *et al* used historical default rates from the rating agencies for double-A rated corporate bonds, and assumed a recovery value (ie, 1-LGD) in default of 40%. Benzschawel (2012) reported a more systematic study of the credit risk premium for corporate bonds by rating, results which are summarised in Figure 5.1. This figure shows average cumulative 4.5-year default probabilities (PDs) by rating category from Sobehart and Keenan's (2002, 2003) hybrid probability of default (HPD) model for the corporate bonds in Citi's BIG and High Yield Indexes over the period 1994–2010.[3] 4.5-year cumulative default rates were used as that term corresponds roughly to the average duration of the bonds in those indexes. The figure also shows average monthly spreads by rating category over the 17-year period along with the spread compensation for default using Equation 5.1, average PDs by rating from the HPD model assuming a 40% recovery value in default. The last column of the table presents differences by rating category between average spreads and spread due to default.

Figure 5.1 Average credit spreads due to default and non-default spreads by agency rating category (1994–2010)

S&P Credit Rating	4.5 Year Implied PD	Average Spread (bp)	Spread Due to Default (bp)	Non-Default Spread (bp)
AAA	0.3%	70	1	69
AA+	0.3%	87	4	82
AA	0.4%	88	5	83
AA–	0.5%	104	6	98
A+	0.6%	113	8	105
A	0.7%	122	9	112
A–	0.9%	137	11	126
BBB+	1.0%	160	14	146
BBB	1.3%	178	17	161
BBB–	1.6%	223	21	201
BB+	1.9%	126	25	301
BB	2.3%	166	10	336
BB–	2.7%	383	36	347
B+	3.8%	438	51	386
B	5.7%	511	77	433
B–	8.2%	588	113	476
CCC+	11 .8%	891	164	727

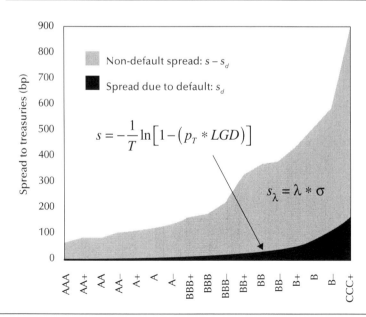

Non-default spread: $s - s_d$

Spread due to default: s_d

$$s = -\frac{1}{T} \ln\left[1 - \left(p_T * LGD\right)\right]$$

$$s_\lambda = \lambda * \sigma$$

The lower portion of Figure 5.1 presents graphically by rating category the average values of the default spread (dark area) and the non-default spread (lighter area). The dark area corresponds to average values of s_d over the period, with the light area representing the excess spread values of the credit risk premium, s_λ. The average value of the credit risk premium ranges from 69bp for triple-A rated bonds to 727bp for triple-C rated ones, but is five to 10 times larger than the average spread compensation for default regardless of rating category.

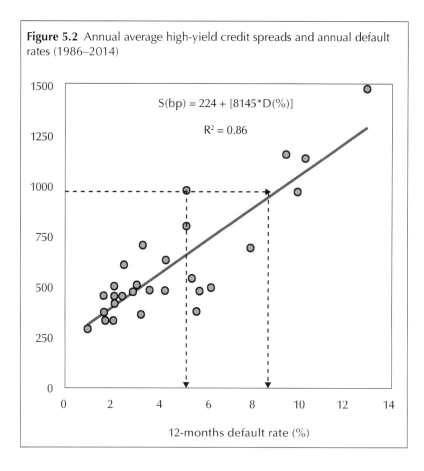

Figure 5.2 Annual average high-yield credit spreads and annual default rates (1986–2014)

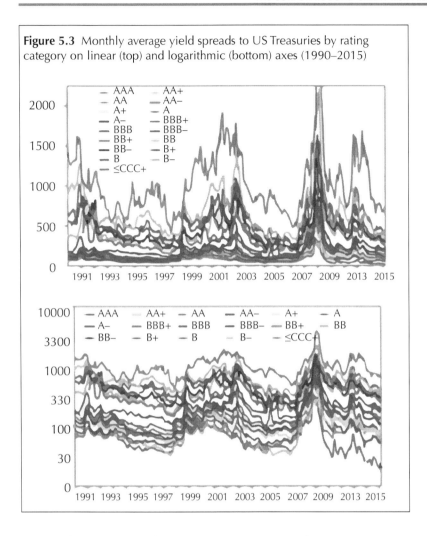

Figure 5.3 Monthly average yield spreads to US Treasuries by rating category on linear (top) and logarithmic (bottom) axes (1990–2015)

Although Figure 5.1 shows average values of the risk premium, default rates vary over the credit cycle, as do credit spreads. Perhaps by determining the relationship between credit spreads and default rates one could make inferences as to PDs from current values of credit spreads, or vice versa. Then, applying this knowledge to individual credits, one could determine what a given difference in credit spread implies regarding probability of default, or how a change in default probability would impact a bond's credit spread. Unfortunately, this has not proven possible. For example, consider Figure 5.2, which displays annual average high-yield credit spreads against their corresponding default rates for the period 1986–2014. Although overall spread levels and defaults are highly correlated ($R^2 = 0.86$), that relationship is not sufficiently strong to be useful for accurate prediction of overall spread levels, much less credit spreads for individual bonds. The dashed lines in Figure 5.2 show that errors can be large. For example, in 2008 the average high-yield credit spread was 912bp but the default rate was only 5.2%, as opposed to the regression-implied value of 8.3%.

A key to understanding the credit risk premium comes from observations of historical monthly average yield spreads to Treasuries by rating categories as shown in Figure 5.3. The top panel of the figure depicts average spreads plotted on a linear (ie, arithmetic) credit spread axis, whereas the bottom panel shows the same data on a logarithmic axis (note also, because of the convex relationship between yield and price, that spreads plotted on a logarithmic scale more linearly represent price differences). Clearly, spread values on both scales vary widely over the credit cycle. However, when plotted on logarithmic axes, it is clear that credit spreads by rating (ie, bond prices) move in tandem over time across rating categories. This suggests that although default rates and the credit risk premium may not be perfectly correlated, spread moves for default-risky credits, regardless of rating, are all affected similarly by changes in a single common factor.

Insight into the factor controlling the non-default spread, s_d, comes from examination of the volatility of credit spreads over time. For example, the connected grey dots in the top panel of Figure 5.4 show that logarithms of average monthly spread volatilities are a linear function of rating category. Furthermore, average rolling five-year monthly volatility-to-average spread ratios (grey points referenced to right axis)are all similar at about 0.3 for all rating categories. Importantly, that result implies that the market charges the same average spread per unit of spread volatility regardless of credit quality. Finally, the volatilities of the rolling spread-to-volatility ratios (black triangles)are also constant across rating categories.

Figure 5.4 Top: spread volatility by rating (left axis) and ratio of volatility to spread (right axis) and the volatility of the five-year rolling volatility-to-spread ratio; bottom: Merton-type structural model used to estimate default probabilities to compute default spreads, s_d.

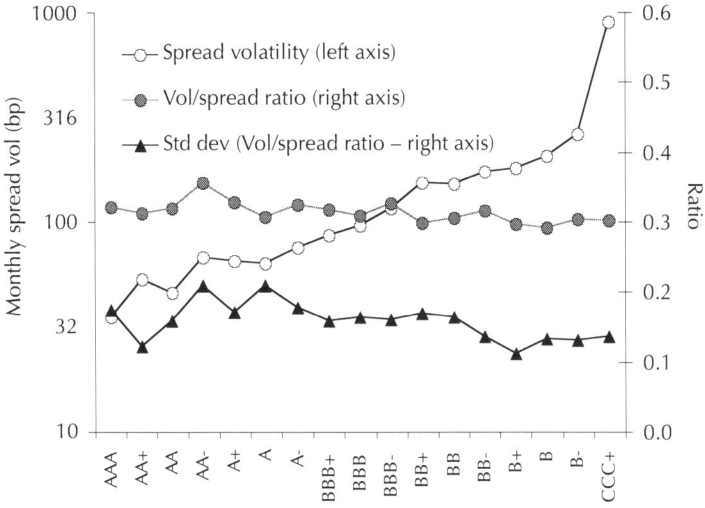

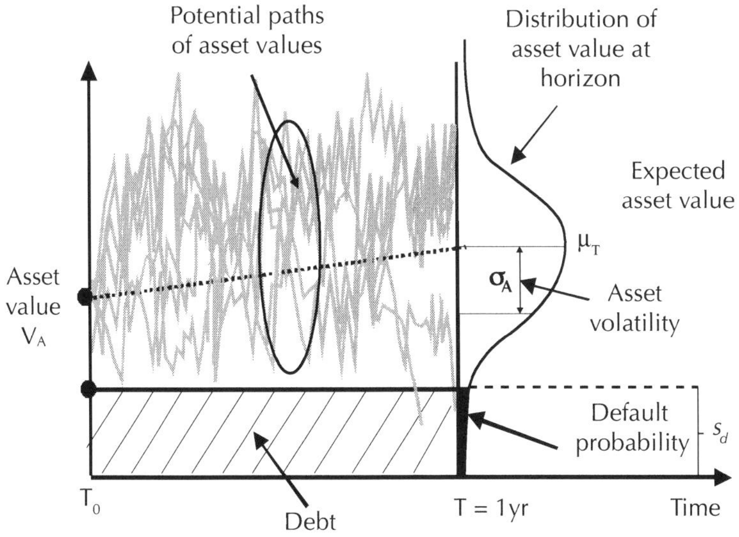

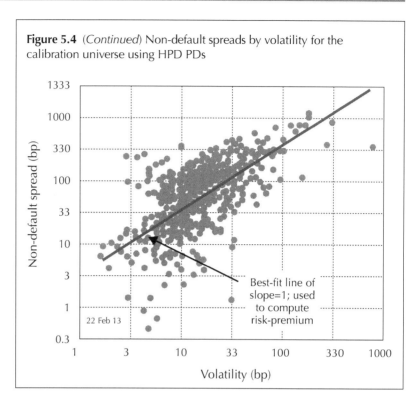

Figure 5.4 (*Continued*) Non-default spreads by volatility for the calibration universe using HPD PDs

The results in the upper panel of Figure 5.4 suggest that the credit risk premium might be related to spread volatility. This was tested by first computing values of default spreads s_d for bonds in Citi's investment-grade and high-yield indexes using the PDs from the HPD model. As illustrated in the middle panel of Figure 5.4, one can think of firms' cumulative default probabilities to time T, denoted p_T, within the structural model framework of Merton (1974) as the likelihood that a given firm is insolvent at time T. Then, given p_T and an assumed value for LGD (in this case, an average value of 60%), one can use Equation 5.1 to determine the spread value necessary to compensate for expected losses from default for each bond. By subtracting the value of s_d from the bond's overall spread, s, one can determine value of the non-default spread s_λ. The resulting values of s_λ for the corporate bonds in Citi's BIG and High Yield indexes (Citigroup, 2013) appear on a logarithmic scale as of log spread volatility in the bottom panel of Figure 5.4. If, as required by the hypothesis that the market charges the same amount on average per a function unit of volatility regardless of its source, then the relationship between non-default spread and spread volatility should have a slope of 1.0 in log–log coordinates. In fact, the grey line in the bottom panel of Figure 5.4 with slope equal to 1.0 fits the points well. Note that all points on the grey line have the same ratio of spread to volatility, and this ratio is designated as λ_t and $\lambda_t \sigma = s_\lambda$ as the spread value of a given bond's daily credit risk premium.[4]

Historical analyses of non-default spreads versus volatility such as those in Figure 5.4 indicate that, at least to a very good first approximation, lines having a slope of 1.0 fit the data well. Accordingly, one can compute historical values of the daily average ratio of spread-to-volatility (ie, λ_t) from lines of slope 1.0 fit to historical data. The resulting values of λ_t appear in Figure 5.5. The left panel of Figure 5.5 shows values of shows values of λ_t since 1999, whereas the right panel shows λ_t over the past year. The dashed line in each plot is the average value of λ_t, which is 4.9bp per unit of spread volatility. The plots also show that, as of 2013, the spread per unit of volatility has been consistently below average. That is, investors have been willing to accept less spread per unit of volatility than average, even amid the relatively low levels of spread volatility (the light grey area). Presumably, this willingness to accept near record low levels of spread per volatility reflects investors' quest for yield amid the US Federal Reserve's qualitative easing programme.

To summarise, for the original calculations of the credit risk premium, bonds' credit spreads were decomposed into the compensation for default s_d and into compensation for spread volatility s_λ as:

$$s_d = -\frac{1}{T}\ln[1 - p_T \cdot LGD] \text{ and } s_\lambda = \lambda\sigma \tag{5.2}$$

where T is the duration of the bond, p_T is the cumulative default probability to time T, LGD is the expected loss from default, σ is the spread volatility and λ is the current price of spread volatility (ie, the Sharpe ratio), which is the same for all credits. As mentioned, in the initial model one-year spreads from fitted spread curves are used to calculate the risk premium, so that quantity is denoted as λ_1. That is, the subscript 1 is used to denote that λ is determined

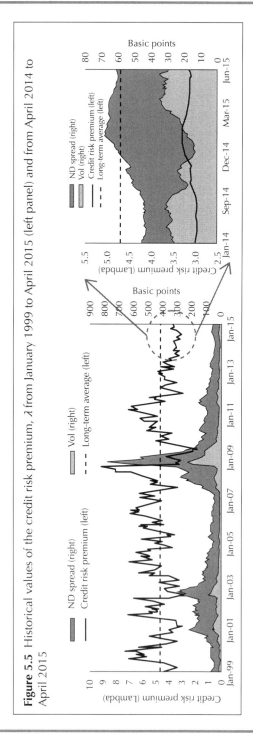

Figure 5.5 Historical values of the credit risk premium, λ from January 1999 to April 2015 (left panel) and from April 2014 to April 2015

from firms' one-year implied credit spreads as described in detail in Appendix 5.2.[5] Accordingly, when estimating λ_1 the one-year cumulative default rate p_1 is used along with the assumption that $T = 1$. Noting this, and combining the two expressions in Equation 5.2, one can write the overall spread to US Treasuries on day t for bonds having a maturity of one year as:

$$s = \lambda_1 \sigma - \ln[1 - p_1 \cdot LGD] \qquad (5.3)$$

In fact, the approach to modelling one-year credit spreads as represented in Equation 5.3 can be viewed as an amalgamation of Merton's structural default model, risk-neutral pricing theory (Hull and White, 1995) and the CAPM (Traynor, 1962; Sharpe, 1964). That is, the model requires physical probabilities of default from the structural model, risk-neutral theory to convert PDs to spread compensations for default and the Sharpe ratio from the CAPM to provide the rationale for estimating risk premium as the average daily spread value per unit of volatility.

Limitations and objectives
Since the introduction of the model of the credit risk premium in 2011, numerous successful applications to problems in credit portfolio management have been developed. These include:

❏ estimating default probabilities for sovereign bonds (Benzschawel *et al*, 2011);
❏ hedging cash bond exposure to changes in the credit risk premium (Benzschawel and Su, 2014);
❏ measuring the risk premium and embedded leverage in corporate bond spreads (Benzschawel, Lee and Li, 2013) and credit default swaps (Benzschawel, Su and Xin, 2015);
❏ replicating pension liabilities (Benzschawel, Su and Bernstein, 2015); and
❏ estimating the risk premium in the municipal bond market (Benzschawel and Su, 2015).

Despite these successes, several aspects of the original framework are less than satisfactory. First, as described in Appendix 5.3, the early method has proven problematic for determining a consistent risk premium for bonds of all maturities from 100-day trailing volatilities. That is, the method does not include a reliable way to infer the risk premiums from longer-maturity bonds from a short series of trailing bond spreads. That is why, as a temporary solution, it was decided to fit credit spread versus maturity curves to each firm's bonds, and impute one-year spreads from firms' term structure of credit spreads. Finally, as discussed below, it is possible to infer values of embedded leverage in short-maturity corporate bond spreads (see Frazzini, Kabiller and Pedersen, 2012; Asness, Frazzini and Pedersen, 2012; Frazzini and Pedersen, 2012, 2014) from our measurements of the short-dated credit risk premium (Benzschawel, Lee and Li, 2013).[6] However, due to the inability to measure the risk premium for longer-dated bonds, it is not possible to infer reliable values of embedded leverage for bonds having durations longer than one year.

All those aforementioned problems are addressed in this chapter, resulting in a more comprehensive, computationally efficient and theoretically appealing framework. Specifically, the following describes in detail how to approximate price volatilities using spread duration volatilities from individual bonds before calculating the credit risk premium. That method makes it unnecessary to infer one-year spreads for each firm, and also enables us to estimate the risk premium from the entire universe of bonds for which we have HPD model PDs and a minimum of 33 days of trailing credit spread data.[7]

MEASURING THE RISK PREMIUM: REVISED METHOD
Recall that a key assumption underlying the model is that the credit risk premium on a given day (ie, the average value of the spread to Treasuries per unit of spread volatility), λ_t, is constant for all bonds. That is, bonds' non-default duration-weighted spreads are assumed to be related linearly to the values of their trailing spread volatilities. The CAPM provides the theoretical basis for that assumption, and the results presented in Figure 5.4 provide the empirical support for that view. Given the limitations of that

approach, it appears preferable to use spread values of bonds of all maturities to estimate the daily risk premium rather than one-year imputed spreads by firm. To do this, it is first necessary to calculate values of bonds' non-default spreads from reasonably reliable estimates of their firms' cumulative default probabilities along with the bonds' short-term volatilities (as proxies for their instantaneous volatilities). Then, one must fit the ensemble of bonds' non-default spreads, a function of their spread volatilities, with a line of slope equal to 1.0 as required by the CAPM and the assumption of a fixed daily risk premium.[8]

Estimating firms' term structures of default

The first step in the new process is to estimate term structures' cumulative default probabilities (ie, cumulative default probabilities versus time) for each firm in the calibration universe. That is, each bond issuer's daily term structures of cumulative PDs from one to 10 years are determined from the HPD model. The HPD model can generate PDs at yearly intervals from one to 10 years, but it is necessary to accommodate durations of bonds of maturities out to 30 years. To do this, each firm's one-year forward default probability for each year beyond 10 is calculated using their marginal default probability from the HPD model between nine and 10 years. For each firm, curves are fit through estimated PDs on their bonds from one to 10 years according to the following algorithm. Let T be the time in years to maturity of a bond (YTM), d equals the truncated value of T (ie, the largest integer smaller than T) and p_T the firm's cumulative default probability to time T. Then, for a given bond of maturity T, the cumulative default probability is calculated according to the following rules:

❑ If $d = 0, 1, 2 \cdots, 9$, then $p_T = \{p_d + [(T - d) * (p_{d+1} - p_d)]\}$; else
❑ If $d \geq 10$, then calculate the marginal probability m from year nine to year 10 as $m = (p_{10} - p_9)/(1 - p_9)$ so that the cumulative probabilities of default for years d and $d + 1$ are given by $p_d = 1 - (1 - p_{10}) \cdot (1 - m)^{d-10}$, and $p_{d+1} = 1 - (1 - p_{10}) \cdot (1 - m)^{d-9}$. Then, the cumulative default rate for any annual maturity t greater than 10 years can be calculated as $p_T = p_d + [(T - d) \cdot (p_{d+1} - p_d)]$.

Figure 5.6 displays PDs for individual bonds (the dots) and curves fitted to term structures of default fit to firms' bonds PDs in accordance with the procedure described above. That is, the bonds' PDs (ie, the dots) for maturities of 10 years or less come directly from the HPD model, whereas PDs for longer-dated maturities are inferred from the marginal default rates between years nine and 10 as described above.

Figure 5.6 Default probabilities for individual bonds (dots) and cumulative default curves (lines) fit to firms PDs from the HPD model (March 18, 2015)

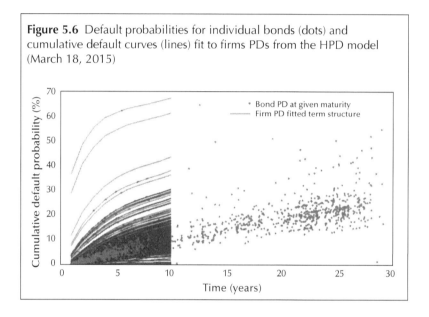

Spread volatilities, spread duration, volatilities and beta

Recall the working assumption that the "fair" risk premium on any given day is independent of credit rating, duration and volatility.[9] However, the results in Appendix 5.3 demonstrate clearly that this is not the case, at least when applying the original method. To examine this, ratios of non-default spreads to volatilities were computed for the bonds in the calibration universe. The resulting spread-to-volatility ratios are presented versus duration and versus volatility in the left and right portions of Figure 5.7, respectively. The grey line in the left figure is the result of a locally weighted scatterplot smoothing (LOWESS)[10] and illustrates the dependence of the measured average ratio of spread-to-short-term volatility on duration. The fitted curve is flat at short maturities, but there is a positive trend of spread-to-volatility ratios around the area of median duration that flattens again for longer-dated maturities.

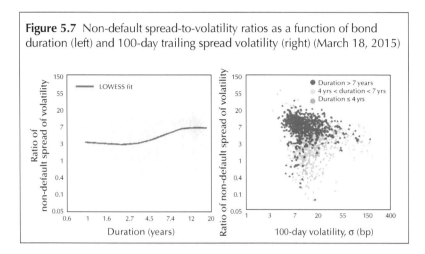

Figure 5.7 Non-default spread-to-volatility ratios as a function of bond duration (left) and 100-day trailing spread volatility (right) (March 18, 2015)

Another assumption of the market-implied (MKI) PD model that follows from the CAPM is that the risk premium should be independent of the volatility. The right panel of Figure 5.7 is a plot of ratio of non-default spreads to 100-day spread volatilities, with points from each duration class shown by a different shade of grey. Results by volatility are consistent with those in the left panel for duration. That is, credit risk premiums determined from spread volatilities are generally higher for longer-duration bonds. Interestingly, in the longest duration bucket, credit risk premiums appear to decrease as volatility increases.

The two observations above illustrate the need to adjust the risk premium calculated using trailing 100-day spread volatility for both duration and spread volatility. One way to combine these factors is by using volatilities of their spread durations (ie, spread times duration).[11] Thus, for each bond i, its 100-day spread duration volatility is defined as $\sigma_{v,i}$ to distinguish it from the 100-day spread volatility σ in Equations 5.2 and 5.3. Note that bonds' spread durations are closely related to their individual price volatilities. Also, the beta of bond i (ie, β_i) is defined as the ratio of that bond's spread duration volatility to the average spread duration volatility corresponding to $\beta = 1$ (as determined below). That is:

$$\beta_i = \frac{\sigma_{v,i}}{\sigma_{v,\beta=1}}$$

(5.4)

where $\sigma_{v,\beta=1}$ is the spread duration volatility of the bond whose $\beta = 1$.

The value of $\sigma_{v,\beta=1}$ is determined by examining spread duration volatilities of bonds near the medians of distributions of credit ratings and volatilities (recall from the top panel of Figure 5.4 that logarithms of average spread volatilities increase linearly with decreasing agency credit rating). The first step is to assign bonds to a three-by-three matrix of durations and ratings, with each dimension containing roughly one-third of the bonds in the calibration universe. The resulting nine buckets are shown in Table 5.1, with each cell having roughly an equal numbers of bonds. The three volatility categories consist of bonds rated triple-A to single-A inclusive; single-A minus to triple-B plus; and triple-B and below. Buckets are also created of bonds having durations from zero to three-and-a-half years; greater than three-and-a-half years to seven-and-a-half years; and greater than seven-and-a-half years. Figure 5.8 shows that roughly one-ninth (ie, 11%) of the bonds in the calibration universe fall into each bucket.

Table 5.1 Percentages of bonds in Citi's investment-grade and high-yield indexes in each duration rating bucket

		Agency Rating		
		AAA to A	A– to BBB+	BBB to CCC
Duration (years)	0 – 3.5	7.3%	10.7%	14.4%
	3.5 – 7.5	7.8%	11.0%	13.1%
	> 7.5	13.6%	13.1%	9.0%

Figure 5.8 provides a visual representation of the distribution of bonds' spread duration volatilities stratified by rating category. The grey dots represent the distribution of bond's volatility of spread duration by each rating category, and we highlight in grey those

bonds with median duration of three-and-a-half to seven-and-a-half years. Clearly, the median bucket inscribed by the thicker rectangles captures well the mid-range of bonds' rating and duration distribution.

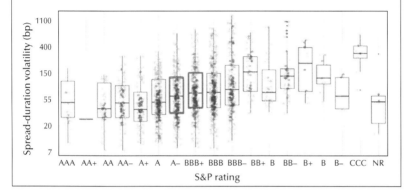

Figure 5.8 Distributions of bonds' spread duration volatilities by agency rating category percentages of bonds in Citi's investment-grade and high-yield indexes in each duration rating bucket

The market beta (ie, $\beta = 1$) is defined as the average spread duration volatility of the bonds in the median bucket of Table 5.1, the one highlighted in a rectangle (ie, bonds rated single-A minus to triple-B plus, and having durations from three-and-a-half years to seven-and-a-half years). Then, one can compute betas for individual bonds, β_i, as defined in Equation 5.4. Also, the median value of s_λ in the central bucket is identified as the one whose spread duration of the bond in our calibration universe whose value of β_i is closest to 1.0 (ie, having the minimum value of $\sigma_{v,i} - \sigma_{v,\beta=1}$). Then, the ratio of the median non-default spread-to-spread duration volatility at $\beta = 1$ (ie, its risk premium relative to spread duration volatility) is defined as Ψ_β and designated as the risk premium λ on day t. That is:

$$\psi_\beta = \frac{s_{\lambda,i}}{\sigma_{v,\beta\cong1}} = \lambda_t \qquad (5.5)$$

One can also calculate values of Ψ_i for individual bonds as ratios of their non-default spreads to 100-day trailing spread duration volatilities, and their use is described below. Importantly, once one has the median spread duration volatility for the β = 1 bucket, it is possible to calculate median values of β for all the other buckets based on the ratios of their spread duration volatilities to that for the β = 1 bucket. Median values of β determined in this way are displayed by rating duration bucket in Figure 5.10. As expected, beta increases for longer-duration bonds and as volatility increases (ie, as bonds' credit qualities move downward from investment-grade to high-yield).

Table 5.2 Values of β by rating duration bucket

		Agency Rating		
		AAA to A	A– to BBB+	BBB to CCC
Duration (years)	0 – 3.5	0.4	0.5	0.8
	3.5 – 7.5	0.8	1.0	1.3
	> 7.5	2.3	2.7	3.1

Figure 5.9 Left: bond duration versus beta; right: density distribution of values of β from our sample of investment-grade and high-yield bonds (May 15, 2015)

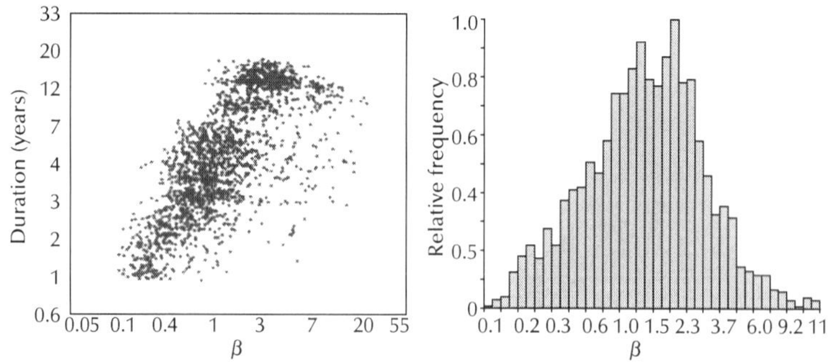

The left panel of Figure 5.9 shows bonds' durations as a function of β_i. The plot shows a near linear relationship between bonds' βs and their durations. The right panel of Figure 5.9 displays the relative frequency of values of β for the bonds in the calibration sample of investment-grade and high-yield corporate bonds. When values of β are scaled in logarithmic units as in the right panel of Figure 5.9, their distribution is roughly Gaussian (mean = 1.2; median = 1.0; skew = −0.08; kurtosis = −0.14).

Deriving the credit risk premium

Recall that one objective is to find a general relationship between λ and bonds' values of $\sigma_{v,i}$ so that the non-default spread for any bond whose beta is known can be written as:

$$s_{\lambda,i} = \lambda_t * f(\beta_i) * \sigma_{v,i} \qquad (5.6)$$

Equation 5.6 implies that one can adjust bonds' spread duration volatilities $\sigma_{v,i}$ by a factor related to their values of β_i. To do this, consider first the top panel of Figure 5.10, which displays ratios of values of bonds' spread to spread duration volatilities, designated as Ψ_i, to that at $\beta = 1$, Ψ_β, as a function of their individual betas, β_i. If there is a single risk premium, ratios of Ψ_i / Ψ_β would be described well by the horizontal line through the point Ψ_β at $\beta = 1$. In fact, the grey line in the figure is the result of LOWESS process and illustrates the dependence of Ψ_i on β_i. That is, ratios of Ψ_i / Ψ_β are greater than 1.0 for bonds with betas less than 1.0 and less than 1.0 for bonds with betas greater than 1.0.

Our approach is to adjust values of bonds' $\sigma_{v,i}$ based on the LOWESS fit and their values of β_i to compute adjusted values of Ψ_i such that the resulting LOWESS line is horizontal and passes through Ψ_β at $\beta = 1$. The middle panel in Figure 5.10 shows the adjustment function, $f(\beta_i)$, determined from the LOWESS fit in the top panel. Finally, the bottom panel of Figure 5.10 plots ratios of Ψ_i to Ψ_β with values of Ψ_i computed using adjusted values of $\sigma_{v,i}$. First, the latter plot indicates that a horizontal line passing through the point Ψ_β is a reasonable fit to the data, while acknowledging the considerable variability of individual ratios about that line. The plot also shows in different shades of grey, ratios of Ψ_i to Ψ_β by duration bucket. There appears to be no systematic deviation from the horizontal line for bonds in any duration bucket.

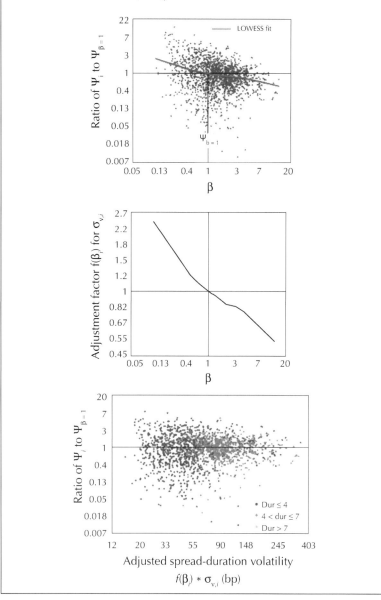

Figure 5.10 Left: ratios of Ψ_i to $\Psi_{\beta=1)}$ as a function of bonds' betas, β_i; middle: correction factors $f(\beta_i)$ for day t to be applied to bonds' 100-day trailing spread duration volatilities to obtain average constant values of Ψ_i; right: ratios of Ψ_i to $\Psi_{\beta=1}$ as a function of bonds' adjusted spread duration volatilities (ie, $(\beta_i) * \sigma_{v,i}$)

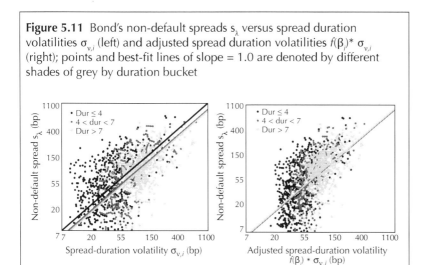

Figure 5.11 Bond's non-default spreads s_λ versus spread duration volatilities $\sigma_{v,i}$ (left) and adjusted spread duration volatilities $f(\beta_i)^* \sigma_{v,i}$ (right); points and best-fit lines of slope = 1.0 are denoted by different shades of grey by duration bucket

Figure 5.11 shows how the adjustment function $f(\beta_i)$ serves to align spread-to-volatility ratios obtained for bonds of different durations. The figure displays bonds' non-default spreads s_λ as a function of their spread-durations $\sigma_{v,i}$ (left panel) and their adjusted spread durations $f(\beta_i)^*\sigma_{v,i}$ (right panel). Bonds in different duration buckets (0-4 years, 4-7 years, and >7 years) are plotted in different shades of grey as are their best-fit lines of slope equal to 1.0. When spread duration volatility is unadjusted, average non-default spreads for bonds in the 0–4-year duration bucket (black symbols) are largest for a given level of spread duration volatility as indicated by the black line in the left panel of Figure 5.11. Average non-default spreads for bonds in the 4–7-year duration bucket (dark grey symbols and line) have intermediate values per unit of duration-adjusted volatility, with non-default spreads for the longer-duration bonds having the smallest average spread values. The right panel shows those same non-default spread values, but with spread duration volatilities adjusted by the $f(\beta_i)$ function in Equation 5.6. That plot shows that, after adjustment, best-fit lines of slope equal 1.0 are now nearly identical.

Properties of the credit risk premium

Recall from Equation 5.5 that the value of the daily risk premium λ_t is calculated as the ratio of the median non-default spread to the spread duration volatility for the bond in the middle spread duration bucket whose value is closest to $\beta = 1$. We call the value of that ratio $\Psi_{\beta=1}$. Daily values of λ_t calculated from 1999 to May 2015 are given by the black function in Figure 5.12. That plot also presents in light grey the values of the risk premium calculated from the original model using firms' one-year imputed non-default spreads and spread volatilities. The average value of the risk premium calculated from Equation 5.5 (ie, the new one) is 4.4bp per unit of adjusted spread duration volatility, and is given by the dark grey dashes in Figure 5.12. The two series, while far from identical, track each other well. The divergence between the two series reflects differences in market preference for short-dated credit (old method) versus a more balanced portfolio (new method). For example, consider in Figure 5.12 the period beginning in 2013, near the start of the Fed's quantitative easing (QE) programme. Although sometimes close, the new credit risk premium is above that for the original one determined from firms' one-year imputed spreads. This likely reflects investors' preferences for short-dated corporates as a substitute for US Treasuries, and as protection from the effects of an anticipated tapering of QE. This is consistent with the historically steep term structure of corporate bond spreads by maturity (see Su and Benzschawel, 2015).

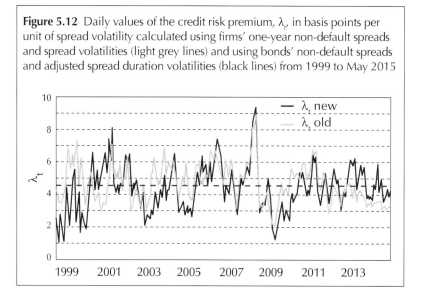

Figure 5.12 Daily values of the credit risk premium, λ_t, in basis points per unit of spread volatility calculated using firms' one-year non-default spreads and spread volatilities (light grey lines) and using bonds' non-default spreads and adjusted spread duration volatilities (black lines) from 1999 to May 2015

The top portion of Table 5.3 presents statistics on distributions of daily values of λ_t from the original and revised model over the period 1999–2015. In general, distributions of risk premiums are similar; mean values of λ_t differ by only 0.3bp per unit of volatility over the 16-year period, and the standard deviations differ by only 0.2bp. Both distributions are nearly Gaussian, with little skew or kurtosis (although kurtosis for the new lambda is lightly greater, see below). The lower portion of Table 5.3 shows the results of analysis of mean reversion in the time series of the risk premium as an Ornstein–Uhlenbeck (1930) autoregressive process where:[12]

$$d\lambda_t = \eta(\mu_\lambda - \lambda_t)dt + \sigma_\lambda dW_t \qquad (5.7)$$

and where μ_λ and σ_λ are the mean and standard deviation of the time series of λ_t, W_t is a Weiner process (random Brownian motion with mean of 0 and standard deviation of 1.0) and η is the half-life of mean reversion.[13] The fact that the slope of the best-fit regression line is essentially zero (ie, –0.01) indicates little drift in the risk premium over time. The half-lives of risk premium mean reversion are 88 and 83 business days (just over one-third of a year) for the new and old risk premiums, respectively.

Table 5.3 Top: comparison of distributions of historical values of new and old credit risk premium calculations (1999–2015); bottom: analysis of mean reversion in new and old historical risk premiums

Statistics	New	Old
Mean	4.4	4.7
Median	4.4	4.6
Range	8.7	7.3
Maximum	9.6	9.2
Minimum	1.0	1.9
Standard deviation	1.4	1.2
Skewness	0.3	0.4
Kurtosis	0.7	0.1
Mean reversion	**New**	**Old**
Slope	–0.01	–0.01
Half life (days)	88	83

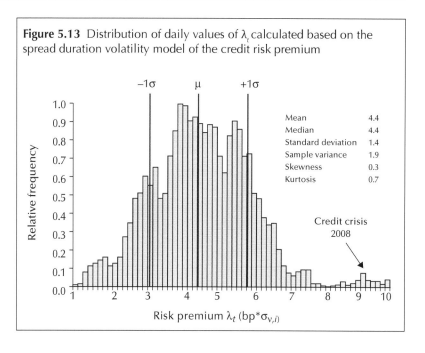

Figure 5.13 Distribution of daily values of λ_t calculated based on the spread duration volatility model of the credit risk premium

Figure 5.13 presents a relative frequency diagram of the new risk premium based on the adjusted spread duration volatility. Aside from the large values of the risk premium during the liquidity crisis of 2008, the distribution of daily values of λ_t is roughly Gaussian.

CREDIT SPREADS AND DEFAULT PROBABILITIES

We have used the HPD model for generating default probabilities for commercial and industrial firms for over a decade, and have developed numerous strategies for beating credit indexes based on that model (Benzschawel *et al*, 2014). However, the HPD model cannot generate estimates of PDs for sovereign nations and private firms owing to the lack of available financial ratios and tradable equity prices required as inputs to the model. In addition, structural models provide relatively poor estimates of PDs for financial firms (Benzschawel, 2012). In fact, although these measures of the credit risk premium have proven useful for numerous applications since their original publication, the initial model was intended primarily to allow us to estimate PDs for sovereign bond issuers (Benzschawel *et al*, 2011). One application of the market-implied PD model described herein is to estimate PDs for private and financial firms, and sovereign obligors. Accordingly, this section presents tests of the internal consistency of the risk premium model in reproducing credit spreads of bonds and default probabilities of issuers in the calibration sample used to generate values of λ_t and $f(\beta_i)$.

To begin, consider the model for credit spreads developed in the previous sections as embodied in Equations 5.5 and 5.6:

$$s_m = \left[\lambda_t * f(\beta_i) * \sigma_{v,i}\right] - \frac{1}{T}\ln[1 - p_T \cdot LGD] \qquad (5.8)$$

where s_m is the model spread and all other terms are as defined earlier. Assume that one knows only a bond's duration, T, current spread, s_m, spread duration volatility, $\sigma_{v,i}$ and has an estimate for its recovery value in default, 1-LGD. Then, using the values of λ_t and $f(\beta_i)$ calculated from the calibration universe of bonds using HPD PDs, one can calculate that bond's market-implied cumulative PD, designated as p_T. In fact, as shown in the left panel of Figure 5.14, using λ_t and 100-day spread volatilities but no adjustment factor causes the model to overestimate actual spreads for short-duration bonds (black symbols) and underestimate spreads for longer-duration bonds (light grey symbols), the same bonds from which the risk premium was estimated. It was the failure of the original model to calculate consistent values of s_m using 100-day spread volatilities for bonds of all durations that resulted in the choice to settle for the one-year inferred spread method of Equation 5.3 (ie, the old method).

The predicted spreads in the other panels of Figure 5.14 were generated from values of λ_t calculated using spread duration volatilities, but without (middle) and with (right) the spread adjustment for beta, $f(\beta_i)$. Both fits to actual spreads are better than using only spread volatilities, but the beta-adjusted method provides a more consistent fit to spread estimates regardless of durations using adjusted spread duration volatilities bonds of all durations. The consistency of Equation 5.8 to determine λ_t is more easily seen from the three plots in Figure 5.15, which display predicted and actual spreads by duration bucket. These are the same data that appear in the right panel of Figure 5.14 but plotted on separate axes, which more clearly reveal the lack of bias when using Equation 5.8 to predict market spreads on the calibration universe.

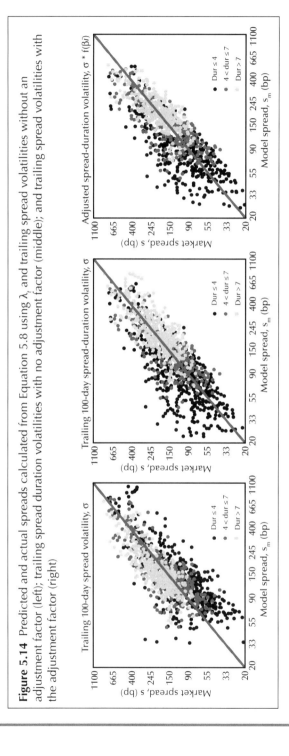

Figure 5.14 Predicted and actual spreads calculated from Equation 5.8 using λ_t and trailing spread volatilities without an adjustment factor (left); trailing spread duration volatilities with no adjustment factor (middle); and trailing spread volatilities with the adjustment factor (right)

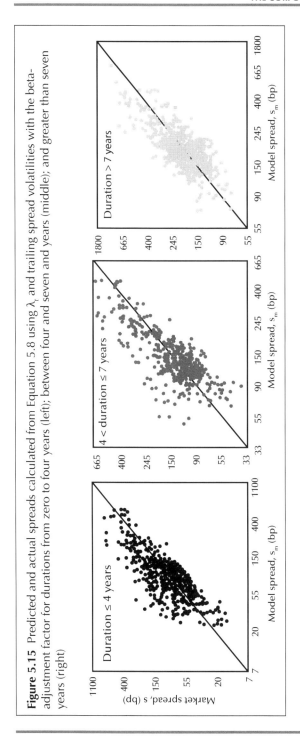

Figure 5.15 Predicted and actual spreads calculated from Equation 5.8 using λ_t and trailing spread volatilities with the beta-adjustment factor for durations from zero to four years (left); between four and seven and years (middle); and greater than seven years (right)

We also tested the consistency of the model in Equation 5.8 to re-generate cumulative default probabilities for firms in the calibration universe using only values of λ_t and $f(\beta_t)$, along with knowledge of their 100-day trailing credit spreads and an assumed recovery value of 40% in default.[14] The left panel of Figure 5.16 shows the relationship between cumulative default probabilities, p_T, from the HPD model (used to estimate non-default spreads for the derivation of λ_t and $f(\beta_t)$) and their corresponding values of p_T calculated from the MKI model using bond spreads and Equation 5.8. The figure reveals no systematic deviations between the two measures. Note that the variability of the PDs about the best-fit line is not a problem with the model, but there is considerable variability of values of firms' credit risk premium ratios, Ψ_t, about their average values. The lower plot shows average values of market-implied P_T (the dots) by decile of cumulative PDs from the HPD model along with their 95% confidence intervals (the lines). Perfect agreement between the models is shown by the dashed line of slope 1.0 inset in the figure.

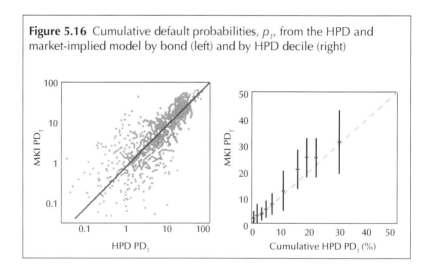

Figure 5.16 Cumulative default probabilities, p_T, from the HPD and market-implied model by bond (left) and by HPD decile (right)

Term structures of cumulative PDs for individual firms were generated to examine the consistency of the MKI model to mimic PDs generated by the HPD model. To do this, for each of the 2,000+ bonds in the calibration universe, credit spreads and volatilities were used to generate term structures of default probabilities. First, from Equation 5.8, bonds' default credit spreads at time T, $s_{d,T,i}$ were generated as:

$$s_{d,T,i} = max\left[s_i - \lambda_t * f(\beta_i) * \sigma_{v,i}, 1\right] \tag{5.9}$$

where all symbols are as described above. Note that Equation 5.9 puts a lower bound of 1bp on the default spread. Using the value of T, $s_{d,T,i}$ in Equation 5.9, one can solve for the value of the market-implied cumulative PD to time T, $p(MKI)_{T,i}$ as:

$$p(MKI)_{T,i} = \frac{1}{LGD} * (1 - e^{-T*s_{d,T,i}}) \tag{5.10}$$

which is just a rearrangement of the PD spread relationship in Equation 5.1.

To estimate term structures of cumulative PDs for bonds in the calibration sample, cases for which issuers have at least five bonds outstanding were treated differently from bonds of issuers with less than five. An illustration of the fitting procedure for issuers with more than four bonds in the sample is illustrated in the left panel of Figure 5.17. That is, firm's market-implied cumulative default probabilities were calculated for their bonds, $p(MKI)_{T,i}$ from their bond spreads using Equation 5.10. Then, logarithms of bonds' $p(MKI)_{T,i}$ values were plotted versus the logarithms of their durations, T and the points were fit using an ordinary least-squares regression. This procedure is equivalent to an exponential curve fitting of the original term structure, whose corresponding plot on linear axes appears in the middle panel of Figure 5.17.

Figure 5.17 Example of one firm's market-implied cumulative PDs versus tenor on log–log (left) and linear (right) axes; right: generic term structure of cumulative PDs versus rating category used for firms with less than five bonds available for scoring

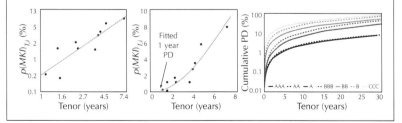

Accordingly, to generate estimates of one-year PDs from MKI that are consistent with those of the HPD model, a correction was applied to firms' one-year PDs imputed from the MKI model. That is, an adjustment factor for each rating category, $a_{1,Rating}$, is applied where $Rating = (AAA, AA-, \ldots, C)$ such that:

$$a_{1,\,Rating} = \frac{Median[p(HPD)_{1,\,Rating}]}{Median[p(MKI)_{1,\,Rating}]} \tag{5.11}$$

and

$$p(MKI)'_{1,i,\,Rating} = a_{1,\,Rating} * p(MKI)_{1,i,\,Rating} \tag{5.12}$$

for bonds in each rating category at $T = 1$. For example, applying the correction to the bonds whose values of $p(MKI)_{1,i}$ appear in the left panel of Figure 5.18 gives rise to the values of $p(MKI)'_{1,i,\,Rating}$ in Figure 5.19. Although not necessary on all days, the corrections in Equations 5.11 and 5.12 serve to ensure consistency between PDs at one-year generated by MKI and HPD models. Note also that adjustment factors, $a_{1,\,Rating}$, are only applied for values less than one. This is necessary to ensure the monotonicity of term structures of default by rating category, and has proven to be the only necessary direction of adjustment.

Figure 5.18 Inferred values of cumulative default probabilities derived from term-structure fits using the MKI model, $p(MKI)_{T,i}$, as functions of corresponding HPD default probabilities; comparisons are shown at one, three and 10-year tenors in left, middle and right panels, respectively

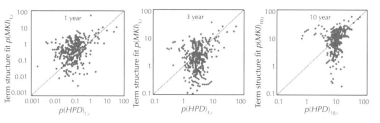

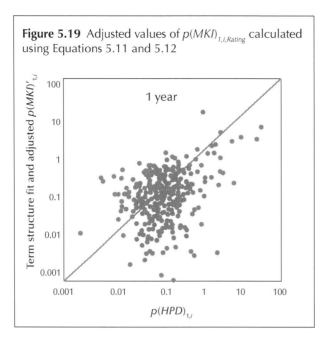

Figure 5.19 Adjusted values of $p(MKI)_{1,i,Rating}$ calculated using Equations 5.11 and 5.12

The consistency of predicted spreads and market spreads, and HPD and MKI PDs, from bonds used to derive the risk premium are important for two reasons. First, it enables generation of MKI PDs whose values are, at least on average, consistent with those of the HPD model since those are the bonds from which daily estimates of λ_t and $f(\beta_i)$ are derived. In addition, the values of λ_t and $f(\beta_i)$ and Equation 5.8 can be used to derive PDs from private firms whose spreads, durations and expected losses in default are available. Finally, for sovereign and municipal bonds, the general form of Equation 5.8 can be used to derive market-implied PDs, although each asset class will require its own set of default probabilities and calibration universe to generate asset class-specific values of λ_t and $f(\beta_i)$.

EMBEDDED LEVERAGE IN CORPORATE BONDS
Recall that to have a consistent risk premium, it was necessary to apply a beta-related adjustment, $f(\beta_i)$, to bonds' spread duration volatilities. Although the adjustment function changes slightly from day to day, the general shape is similar across days. In gen-

eral, relative to $\beta = 1$, lower beta spread duration volatilities must be adjusted upward and higher volatilities downward to derive a constant risk premium for bonds of all durations and ratings. This enables us to back out market spreads and default probabilities for private firms and financial companies consistent with those used to determine the risk premium. Since spread duration is a reasonable proxy for price volatility and logarithms of credit spreads are linearly related to bond prices, the need for an adjustment would appear to contradict the single risk premium hypothesis. Furthermore, such a correction would be at odds both with the CAPM and commonsense. Since our measure of bonds' Ψ_i values are analogous with Sharpe ratios, in the absence of technical or other factors investors should be drawn to the assets that provide the largest return for their volatilities. Although one might expect to observe temporary deviations in the risk premiums across asset classes and smaller deviations within an asset class, the systematic deviations reported above for corporate bonds would appear problematic.

Fortunately, some analyses (Asness, Frazzini and Pedersen, 2012; Frazzini, Kabiller and Pedersen, 2012; Frazzini and Pedersen, 2012; 2014) provide insight into the cause of the consistently higher values of Ψ_i for low-beta bonds and lower values for high-beta assets. As shown in the graphs in Figure 5.20, those authors have documented consistently higher Sharpe ratios for low-beta credits relative to Sharpe ratios for high-beta ones across a wide variety of asset classes, including corporate bonds. For example, the upper left panel of Figure 5.20 displays Sharpe ratios of US equity market returns by beta decile from lowest (1) at about 0.65 to highest (10) at about 0.3, with the middle range Sharpe ratio of 0.5 typical of reported equity risk-adjusted returns. Other panels show similar results for global equity, US Treasury bonds, corporate credit by duration (similar to the top panel of Table 5.1) and agency rating, commodities and foreign exchange. The only deviation from the trend of higher risk-adjusted returns for lower-beta credits is reported for the sovereign bond market.

Frazzini and Pedersen interpret the dependence of Sharpe ratios on beta as the result of "embedded leverage" in high-beta assets. They claim that an important feature of a financial instrument is its embedded leverage – the amount of market exposure per unit of

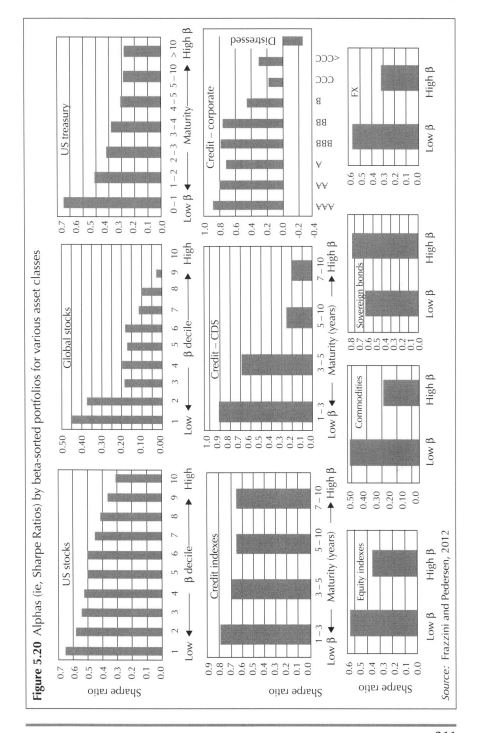

Figure 5.20 Alphas (ie, Sharpe Ratios) by beta-sorted portfolios for various asset classes

Source: Frazzini and Pedersen, 2012

committed capital. That is, since an investor can match the returns of an index with a fractional investment in higher-beta assets, the market requires a premium for that leverage in terms of a lower risk-adjusted return. The reverse is true for lower-beta credits, for which investors must lever up to match index returns, thereby warranting a higher excess return. The importance of embedded leverage arises from investors' inability (or unwillingness) to use outright leverage to achieve their desired market exposures. For example, investors may not be able to use outright leverage, since banks face regulatory capital constraints and hedge funds must satisfy their margin requirements.

Figure 5.21 Adjustment factors $f(\beta_i)$ applied to $\sigma_{v,i}$ versus bonds' betas, β_i, (left axis) and embedded leverage (right axis) implied by $f(\beta_i)$ (March 2, 2015)

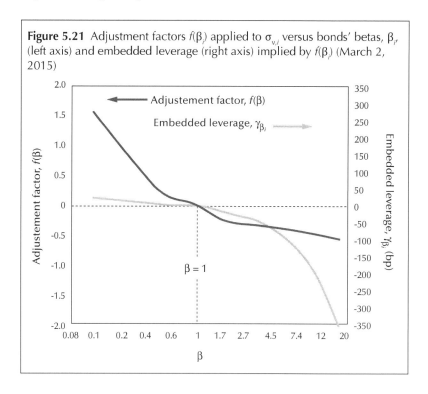

The analyses of Frazzini and colleagues above support our claim that the reason ratios of bonds' non-default spreads to their spread duration volatilities, Ψ_i, vary with beta (higher for lower-beta bonds and lower for high-beta ones) is due to the embedded leverage in those bonds. If so, it is possible to derive the spread value of embedded leverage from the adjustment factor, $f(\beta_i)$, that we apply to bonds spread duration volatilities, $\sigma_{v,i}$, to derive a constant risk premium for all bonds. For example, consider Figure 5.21, which displays the adjustment factors $f(\beta_i)$ versus bonds' values of β_i (left axis) and the spread values of embedded leverage, γ_i, derived from that correction (right axis). The values of embedded leverage are calculated as the negative of the amount of spread adjustment necessary to make average non-default spread to spread duration volatility ratios a constant. That is, spreads for low-beta bonds must be adjusted downward and those for high-beta bonds upward. For example, bonds whose β_i is 0.4 require a –10bp adjustment in non-default spread for their average values of Ψ_i to equal $\Psi_{\beta=1}$. The embedded leverage in Figure 5.21 is the negative of that adjustment as it is the excess or spread, so in the case of γ_i at a β of 0.4, the embedded leverage is a positive 10bp. Conversely, if β is 2.7, the embedded leverage is negative at –30bp. Finally, the figure indicates that the embedded leverage can be quite large for very high-beta bonds, reaching levels as high as 300–400bp for the typically few extremely volatile bonds.

Given the ability to measure the embedded leverage in corporate bond prices, we examined how spread values of embedded leverage change with changes in market conditions. Of particular interest was determination of how embedded leverage is affected by stresses to market liquidity, such as those which occurred during the credit crisis of late 2007–09. To that end, Figure 5.22 presents values of γ_{β_i} versus β_i for selected dates spanning the period from October 2006 until March 2015. The figure shows that during non-crisis liquidity conditions (ie, excluding 2008), embedded leverage functions of β follow the typical pattern shown in Figure 5.21. That is, embedded leverage for all bonds having $\beta < 1$ is roughly 10–25bp on any given day, whereas embedded leverage for bonds with $\beta > 1$ becomes increasingly negative as β increases.

The more extreme embedded leverage curves given by the thicker light grey and dark grey lines in Figure 5.22 were obtained in August and October 2008, just before and after the default of Lehman Brothers, respectively. Although the leverage for low-beta bonds had already increased from roughly 20bp to 100bp a month before the Lehman default, the estimated leverage premium for bonds with $\beta < 1$ spiked up to nearly 300bp. Equally dramatic is the rise in the discount for embedded leverage estimated for bonds having $\beta > 1$. Those values of γ_β peak around minus 200–300bp for bonds with the largest betas in times of normal liquidity, but during the credit crises had widened to roughly 800bp.

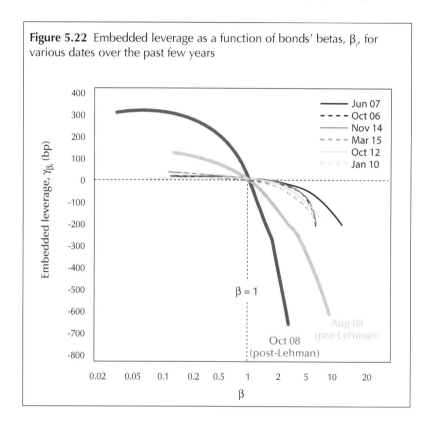

Figure 5.22 Embedded leverage as a function of bonds' betas, β_i, for various dates over the past few years

PREDICTING THE CREDIT RISK PREMIUM

In Chapter 3, it was shown that the ratio of the current average high-yield corporate bond spreads to one-year predicted default rates from the HT 2.0 model can predict one-year directional changes in yield spreads with 80% accuracy (those results appear in Figure 3.12). To the extent that fluctuations in high-yield spreads are due to changes in the credit risk premium, one ought to be able to predict the credit risk premium as well given its current level relative to the predicted one-year default rate, D_p. We tested that using the new time series of values of λ_t shown in Figure 5.12. That is, for each month from January 1999 to March 2014, we computed ratios of the current value of λ_t to the predicted default rate.[15] We then computed future one-year changes in the values of the risk premium (ie, $\lambda_{t+12} - \lambda_t$). The results of that analysis are presented in Figure 5.23. The top panel of the figure shows monthly ratios of the credit risk premium to the D_p rate from 2000 to 2013. The grey dashes in the figure show the trailing expanding average ratio of λ_t to the predicted default rate. The bottom panel of Figure 5.23 displays probabilities of correct and incorrect predictions of directional changes in $\lambda_{t+12} - \lambda_t$ for each month from January 2003 to March 2014. As for high-yield corporate bond spreads, one-year changes in λ_t are related to ratios of λ_t to D_p. That is, high λ_t-to-D_p ratios (ie, greater than 1.5) signal lower values of λ_t at the end of next year with an accuracy of 70%, whereas lower ratios signal increases in the credit risk premium over the next year with 57% accuracy. Also, note that when correct the average absolute one-year change in λ_t is greater by 30–50% than the change in λ_t when incorrect.

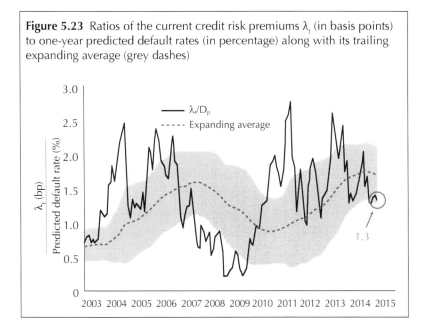

Figure 5.23 Ratios of the current credit risk premiums λ_t (in basis points) to one-year predicted default rates (in percentage) along with its trailing expanding average (grey dashes)

Figure 5.23 (*Continued*) One-year changes in the credit risk premium versus monthly ratios of current values of λ_t to the predicted high-yield default rate

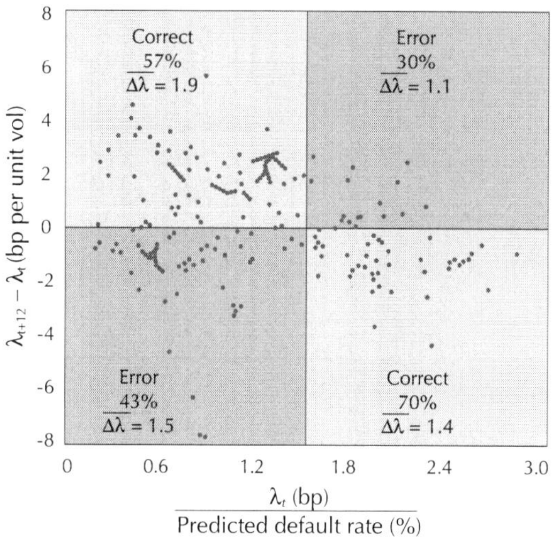

CONCLUSION

The chapter began with a description of the relationship between the cost of default and the overall compensation for investing in default-risky corporate bonds. It was shown that the compensation for loss of cashflows due to default is only a small fraction of corporate bonds' yield spreads over Treasuries. The relationship among logarithms of monthly credit spreads by rating category indicated that a single factor, called the risk premium, λ_t, is the major contributor to bond spreads and that, on any given day, its average value is a roughly constant fraction of bonds' price volatilities regardless of credit quality. Based on those findings, an initial provisional method of measuring daily values of the risk premium was presented that used firms' imputed one-year credit spreads and simple trailing spread volatilities. Although useful as an interim measure, that original approach has several limitations. Those limitations include the inability to measure the risk premium using individual bonds at durations longer than one year and the inability to estimate values of embedded leverage for those bonds.

The remainder of the commentary focused on extending the model of the risk premium to longer-duration bonds by substituting spread duration volatilities, $\sigma_{v,i}$, for spread volatilities. In addition, it was shown that a beta-related adjustment factor, $f(\beta_i)$ as applied to $\sigma_{v,i}$ was required to ensure a constant risk premium across bonds of different credit ratings and durations. We argued and presented evidence from other markets that the necessity of the adjustment factor is the result of bonds' embedded leverage, γ_β, whereby low- and high-beta corporate bonds have greater and lesser risk-adjusted returns relative to the average return, respectively. In addition, that hypothesis enables us to assess daily values of embedded leverage versus β_i from $f(\beta_i)$. Estimates of γ_β obtained before, during and after the credit crisis confirm that the yield spread value of embedded leverage spikes dramatically during liquidity crises, thereby supporting the notion that our adjustment reflects the influence of embedded leverage on bond returns. Finally, it was demonstrated that ratios of the current risk premium λ_t to model-based forecasts of one-year default rates predict one-year directional moves in λ_t at well-above chance levels.

APPENDIX 5.1   THE YIELD VALUE OF DEFAULT

As described briefly above, the yield spread over US Treasuries due to default can be derived from the price yield formula with the assumption from risk-neutral pricing theory that the present value of a set of cashflows is their expected likelihood of receipt discounted at the risk-free rate. To illustrate this as applied to the yield value of a risky security, consider a single cashflow of US$1 to be received at time T in the future as shown in Figure A.5.1.1. From bond mathematics, we know that we can find a discount factor y_T applied to the US$1 such that, when discounted back from T to the present, will equal the market value PV. That is:

$$PV = 1e^{-y_T T}$$

(A.5.1.1)

If the cashflow at T will be received with certainty, then according to risk-neutral pricing theory, the fair value of PV is the value of US$1 discounted at the risk-free rate, r_T, between time 0 and T. That is, for a certain cashflow we can substitute r_T for y_T in Equation A.5.1.1.

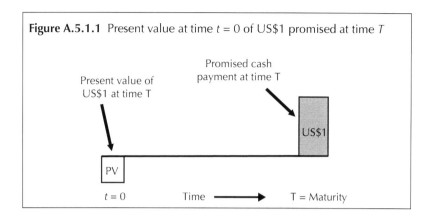

Figure A.5.1.1 Present value at time $t = 0$ of US$1 promised at time T

For discounting uncertain cashflows, we add a factor to r_T, call it s_T such that $y_T = r_T + s_T$ when discounting. In addition, we represent the uncertain cashflow as an expected value, $E[1]_T$ in this case. If the obligor does not default, we receive US$1 at time with the probability $1 - p_T$; otherwise, we receive the recovery value R with probability p_T. Thus, one can express the expected value of the US$1 to be received at time as the weighted sum of receiving the US$1 or the recovery value. That is:

$$E[1]_T = [(1 - p_T) * 1 + p_T R]$$
(A.5.1.2)

Based on the foregoing and risk-neutral pricing theory, we can rewrite Equation A.5.1.1 for a default-risky cashflow as:

$$e^{-T(r_T + s_T)} = e^{-Tr_T}[(1 - p_T) * 1 + p_T R]$$
(A.5.1.3)

where s_T reflects the additional yield required to compensate for the likelihood of not receiving the full US$1 at T. By taking the natural logarithms of both sides of Equation A.5.1.3 and rearranging, we can express the spread compensation owing to default as:

$$s_T = -\frac{1}{T} ln[1 - (p_T * LGD]$$
(A.5.1.4)

which is the expression in Equation 5.1 of the main chapter. Note that in the text, for simplicity, we represent a stream of cashflows from a bond as a single cashflow to be received at the duration of the bond.

APPENDIX 5.2 MARKET-IMPLIED PDS: INITIAL MODEL

As mentioned in the chapter, an undesirable but initially useful part of our procedure for estimating the risk premium was to first use the term structure of firms' bond spreads to impute one-year spreads for each issuer by fitting the term structures using a modified Nelson–Siegel (1987) procedure. For example, Figure A.5.2.1 illustrates how firms' one-year spreads are inferred from curves fit to its bonds of various maturities. The figure shows spreads to US Treasuries at half-year intervals from 0.5 to 30 years. The points are fit using the Nelson–Siegel method, and used to infer spreads for firms having less than four bonds outstanding.[16] Otherwise, firms' one-year spreads are determined from curves fit to its individual bonds.

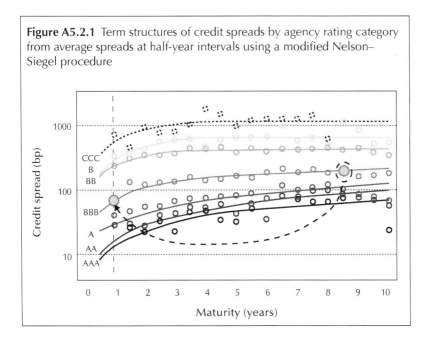

Figure A5.2.1 Term structures of credit spreads by agency rating category from average spreads at half-year intervals using a modified Nelson–Siegel procedure

Using this method, we derive inferred one-year spreads for all the firms in our calibration sample (the firms in Citi's BIG and High Yield indexes having HPD scores). Then, for each firm we calculate the one-year default spread according to the risk-neutral pricing formula given by:

$$s_{D,1} = -\frac{1}{T} ln[1 - (p_1 * LGD]$$

(A.5.2.1)

where T is the duration of the bond (assumed to be 1.0) and LGD is the loss given default (ie, 1 – recovery value). Recall that the default spread in Equation A.5.2.1 is the increment in yield over an equivalent duration US Treasury necessary to break even with the expected return on the Treasury given expected losses due to default.

We then calculate the one-year non-default spread $s_{ND,1}$ by subtracting the default spread from the full one-year spread, s_1, assuming $LGD = 60\%$. That is:

$$s_{ND,1} = s_1 - s_{D,1} \qquad \text{(A.5.2.2)}$$

We also calculate the 100-day trailing volatility of one-year bond spread, σ_1, using an exponential weighting scheme with half-life of 33 days. Then, the risk premium λ inferred from the calibration universe is given by:

$$\lambda = \frac{\text{mean}(s_{ND,1})}{\text{mean}(\sigma_1)} \qquad \text{(A.5.2.3)}$$

Then, given the value λ and a bond's one-year spread, spread volatility and an $LGD = 60\%$, one can impute a one-year default spread as:

$$s_{D,1} = s_1 - \lambda\sigma_1 \qquad \text{(A.5.2.4)}$$

At this point, we now have the one-year non-default spread and spread volatility $(\sigma_1, s_{D,1})$, and we can plot these in a diagram as shown in Figure A5.2.2. The diagonal line in the figure is the zero-p_1 line (ie, $\lambda\sigma_1$) and the curved line is the best fit to the thousands of dollar-denominated corporate bonds in Citi's indexes. The line is constructed by fitting a line of the form:

$$\ln(s) = \ln(\sigma) + \ln(\lambda) + Ae^{Bn(\sigma)} \qquad \text{(A.5.2.5)}$$

Then, to derive the implied p_1 for the given firm, we project the point (σ_1, s_1) onto the fitted fair value line defined by Equation A.5.2.5 along a line from the point to the line as illustrated for the circled point in Figure A.5.2.2. That projection yields the point (σ_1^*, s_1^*). Recalling that the credit spread is modelled as:

$$s = \lambda_t\, \sigma + \frac{1}{T}\ln[1 - p_T \cdot LGD] \qquad \text{(A.5.2.6)}$$

using (σ_1^*, s_1^*), noting that $T = 1$ for the one-year implied spreads, and assuming $LGD = 60\%$, we can rearrange Equation A.5.2.6 to solve for p_1 as:

$$p_1 1 = \frac{1 - e_{tt}^{(\lambda\sigma_1^* - s_1^*)}}{LGD} \qquad (A.5.2.7)$$

Figure A5.2.2 One-year imputed credit spreads versus volatilities (straight line) and best-fit relationship between log spread and log volatility (curved line); the vector adjustment procedure is also illustrated

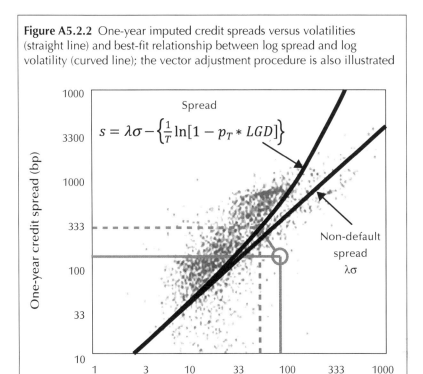

APPENDIX 5.3   PROBLEM WITH GENERALISING λ FROM ONE-YEAR IMPLIED SPREADS

In this section, we illustrate our difficulty in generalising our initial measurement of the credit risk premium to bonds of maturities longer than about four years. For example, we can solve for λ_1 using our previous method as described in detail in Appendix 5.2. Then, one can test the generality of estimates of λ_1 by comparing the spreads implied for individual bonds of given maturities, s_m, from firms in the calibration sample s_T with those measured in the market, s. These are the firms whose cumulative default probabilities p_T up to their durations, T, are able to be derived from the HPD model as described above. That is one can test the consistency of estimates of λ_1 by using bonds cumulative default rates for their durations, values of their trailing 100-day spread volatilities (see endnote 3), assuming an LGD = 60% and solving for the spread, s_T using the following:

$$s_T = \lambda_1 \sigma - \frac{1}{1}\ln[1 - p_1 * LGD]$$

(A.5.3.1)

To the extent that $s_m = s$ is the extent to which the estimate of λ_1 generated from one-year implied spreads generalises to bonds of all maturities.

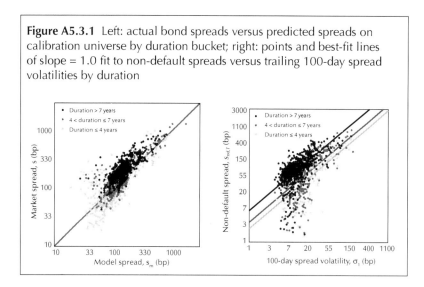

Figure A5.3.1 Left: actual bond spreads versus predicted spreads on calibration universe by duration bucket; right: points and best-fit lines of slope = 1.0 fit to non-default spreads versus trailing 100-day spread volatilities by duration

The left panel of Figure A.5.3.1 presents plots of predicted spreads from the model, s_m, and firms' actual bond spreads, s (recall that the bond spreads in Figure A.5.3.1 are those used to estimate firms' one-year spreads for estimating λ as described in Appendix 5.2). Bonds' spreads are coded by duration buckets (zero to four years, four to seven years and greater than seven years) as indicated in the figure. To the extent that the risk premium is consistent across durations, all points should be distributed roughly symmetrically about the negative diagonal for which $s_m = s$. Not surprisingly, this appears roughly true for bonds having durations of less than four years (the light grey circles) as the risk premium was determined using short duration (ie, one-year) imputed spreads. However, for the durations between four and seven years and greater than seven years, the dark grey and black symbols, respectively, the points appear to lie mostly above the negative diagonal. That is, spreads predicted by the model tend to be smaller than those actually obtained for longer-duration bonds. This implies that the risk premium measured using one-year spreads is too low for the longer-dated bonds.

The right panel of Figure A.5.3.1 displays by duration bucket bonds' non-default spreads versus trailing 100-day volatility, and confirms the underestimation of the risk premium at longer durations. That is, lines of slope equal to 1 fit to log non-default spread versus log spread volatility, while axes shift vertically as duration increases, indicative of a greater return per unit of short-term volatility for longer-dated bonds. Thus, if one uses the λ obtained from the one-year spreads, it would underestimate the price of risk for bonds with durations longer than four years.

1   Salomon Brothers brokered the first currency swap in 1981 between IBM and the World Bank, and interest rate swaps followed shortly thereafter.
2   As the results reported herein are based on average spread values, bonds' relative liquidity/illiquidity is assumed not to introduce bias into the present results.
3   The credit spreads and bond indicative data come from the corporate bonds in Citigroup's BIG index and High Yield Cash Pay index (see Citigroup Index, 2013).
4   For simplicity, this chapter presents only a brief description of how the points in Figure 5.4 were determined. In fact, as described in Benzschawel and Lee (2011) and briefly in Appendix 5.2, a Nelson–Siegel (1987) procedure was used to determine one-year equivalent spreads (ie, $T = 1$) for all firms in the sample, and these are the values that appear in Figure 5.4. Also, spread volatility was computed on the trailing 100 daily spread values, but an exponential decay with a half-life of 1.5 months (ie, 33 days) was imposed on trailing spread values.
5   Motivation for the decision to use one-year imputed spreads is described in detail in Appendix 5.3. One objective of this chapter is to describe a more general method for determining the risk premium directly from bond's credit spreads.
6   The "embedded leverage effect", also called "Buffet's alpha", refers to the fact that lower volatility credits tend to offer investors slightly greater returns per unit of volatility than higher volatility assets. The inference is that investing in higher-yielding (higher beta) credits with respect to an index provides investors with implicit leverage relative to an index investment. The market charges a premium for that leverage. The reverse is true for lower beta credits, for which investors must lever up to match index returns, but in return those investors receive a premium relative to the index issue.

7   Although ideally one would use a series of 100 days of trailing spreads to estimate spread volatilities, given the use of a spread contribution half-life of 33 days, 33 days would seem to be a sufficient period from which to estimate spread volatilities for newly issued bonds or bonds whose spread histories are limited.

8   Note the use of bonds' 100-day trailing volatilities as estimates of instantaneous spread volatilities (or maybe even markets' views of future near-term volatilities). At the time of writing, this method appears as the most practical option.

9   The notion of a constant risk premium (CRP) for all credits in deeply embedded within financial theory, beginning with the work of Markowitz (1959) and Sharpe (1964, 1994). Also, the role of CRP as a guiding principle is akin to the efficient markets hypothesis (EMH). Although the strict assumptions of both CRP and EMH are routinely violated (see Fama and French, 2003, for a discussion of this point), they both serve as benchmarks against which explanations for deviations (market segmentation, liquidity, implicit leverage, supply and demand, etc) are based.

10   LOWESS was originally proposed by Cleveland (1979) and further developed by Cleveland and Devlin (1988). At each point in the dataset, a low-degree polynomial is fitted to a subset of the data, with explanatory variable values near the point giving more weight to points near the point whose response is being estimated and less weight to points further away.

11   Note that in the original model of Equations 5.2 and 5.3 using one-year non-default spreads and 100-day spread volatilities, the spread durations were roughly 1.0 for all firms.

12   A detailed explanation of how to analyse mean reversion in financial time series can be found in Dixit and Pindyck (1994).

13   The half-life of mean reversion is the time it would take for the process to move halfway back to its mean after a move away if $\sigma_\lambda = 0$. For example, if $\eta = 0$, it would be Brownian motion.

14   Although in practice recovery values from the E-3 Model (Benzschawel and Su, 2013) are used to estimate LGD, we used a constant recovery value of 40% of face for both estimating the risk premium and for testing the consistency of the model.

15   Note that we update one-year predicted default rates from our HT 2.0 model monthly.

16   For firms having less than four bonds outstanding, the shape of the curve nearest to the bonds' spreads is used to provide the best fit to the bonds. The method is described in detail in Benzschawel and Lee (2011).

6

The Credit Default Swap Risk Premium

Chapter 5 presented methods for calculating the risk premiums and embedded leverage in corporate bonds. In this chapter, we will apply a similar analysis to the US corporate CDS market, and compare properties of CDS risk premiums and embedded leverage to those in the cash bond market. The plan of this chapter is to first present briefly the rationale for the approach, followed by the derivation of the CDS risk premium and a comparison of its properties with corporate bond risk premiums. This will be followed by a description of embedded leverage in the CDS market, along with a demonstration of the ability of ratios of current CDS risk premiums to one-year predicted default rates to predict one-year changes in the CDS risk premium.

THE CDS RISK PREMIUM

Since the rationale and procedure for computing market risk premiums in the corporate bond market is shown in Chapter 5, only a brief discussion of the general approach will be described herein. The main assumption of this approach to measuring risk premiums in the CDS market is that one can decompose the CDS premiums into compensation for expected losses (LGD) given a credit event, called the "default premium", s_d, and the remainder of the premium, called the non-default premium, s_λ. That is, the CDS premium for contract i is:

$$s_i = s_{\lambda,i} + s_{d,i} \qquad (6.1)$$

Given this assumption and approximating the entire set of quarterly CDS premiums as a single cashflow at its effective duration T_i, one can solve for $s_{d,i}$ if one has values of $p_{T,i}$ and LGD_i, the cumulative default probability of firm i to time T_i and the LGD, respectively We estimate firms' values of $p_{T,i}$ using Citi's HPD model (Sobehart and Keenan, 2002, 2003; Benzschawel, 2013) and bonds' LGD_i from Citi's E-3 model for recovery value in default (see Chapter 4). Then, using Equation 6.2, we can solve for $s_{d,i}$ as:[1]

$$s_{d,i} = -1/T_i \ln[1-(p_{T,i} \cdot LGD_i)] \qquad (6.2)$$

The graph and table in Figure 6.1 show averages of monthly values of s_i, $s_{\lambda}i$ and $s_{d,i}$ by agency rating category from roughly 700 CDS from 2003 to 2015. The dark area in the graph corresponds to average values of s_d over the period, with the light area representing average values of the credit risk premium, s_{λ}.[2]

As for their corporate bond counterparts, CDS premiums across rating categories are dominated by non-default premiums. For example, the table in Figure 6.1 indicates that the average monthly CDS premium for single-A rated firms is 138bp, with only 49bp due to expected payouts from credit events; the other 89bp is the non-default-related premium. In fact, average values of non-default CDS risk premiums range from 160bp for triple-A rated CDS to 891bp for CDS rated triple-C and below, but non-default premiums are roughly two to three times larger than the average spread compensation for default regardless of rating category.

To help understand the role of the credit risk premium in CDS spreads, consider Figure 6.2 in which the top panels display historical monthly average CDS premiums by rating category with analogous plots of corporate bond spreads in the lower panels. The left panels of Figure 6.2 show average spreads plotted on linear (ie, arithmetic) CDS premium and bond spread axes, whereas the right panels display the same data on logarithmic axes.[3] Several things are worth noting. First, spread values for CDS and bonds on both linear and logarithmic scales vary widely over the credit cycle. Also, when plotted on logarithmic axes, it is clear that, at

Figure 6.1 Cumulative average 4.5-year default probabilities of CDS reference entities by rating category and average of monthly CDS premiums due to default and non-default spreads (2003–15)

Agency rating	Probability of default	Total premium	Premium Due to Default	Non-Default premium
AAA	3.5%	219	58	160
AA+	2.6%	190	52	139
AA–	2.9%	147	39	108
A+	2.7%	132	40	92
A	3.0%	138	49	89
A–	4.2%	158	56	103
AA	4.4%	183	66	117
BBB+	5.2%	209	73	136
BBB	5.6%	232	82	151
BBB–	6.4%	267	90	178
BB+	7.4%	333	106	227
BB	8.3%	433	127	306
B+	8.7%	490	146	344
BB–	10.3%	541	166	375
B	11.2%	620	197	424
B–	12.9%	749	234	515
<CCC+	22.5%	1599	708	891

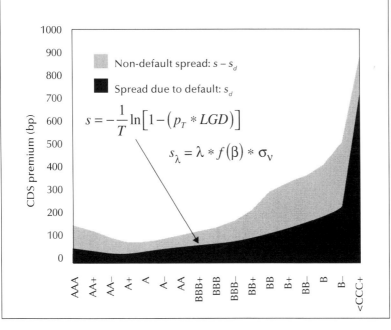

Non-default spread: $s - s_d$

Spread due to default: s_d

$$s = -\frac{1}{T} \ln\left[1 - \left(p_T * LGD\right)\right]$$

$$s_\lambda = \lambda * f(\beta) * \sigma_v$$

CDS premium (bp)

least in general, CDS premiums and credit spreads by rating each move in tandem over time across rating categories. Although the historical CDS premium series are more volatile than the corporate series, their patterns are similar.[4] That is, although default rates vary widely from triple-A to triple-C rated firms, moves in both CDS premiums and bond spreads to Treasuries, regardless of rating, are affected similarly by changes in a single common factor. That factor is the credit risk premium.

Figure 6.2 Monthly average CDS premiums (top panels) and bond spreads (lower panels) by rating category on linear (left) and logarithmic (right) axes (2003–15)

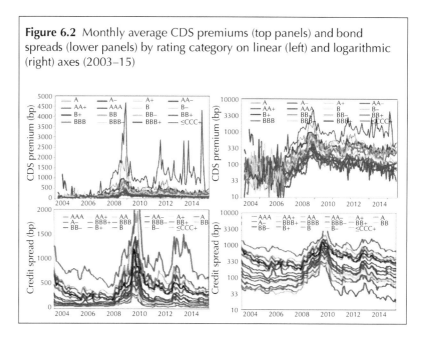

Further insight into the factor controlling the non-default CDS premiums and cash bond spreads, s_d, comes from examination of the volatility of credit spreads over time. For example, the left panel of Figure 6.3 displays average CDS premium volatilities by rating category (black symbols; left axis) and ratios of average CDS premiums to their volatilities (grey symbols, right axis). A similar plot for cash bonds in Citi's investment-grade and high-yield indexes (Citigroup Index Group, 2013) appears in the right panel. Note that axes scales in both groups are identical, with volatilities plotted in logarithmic units. The pattern of results from CDS and cash bonds is similar. Note that, for both CDS premiums and corporate bond spreads, logarithms of volatilities increase linearly with rating categories and are roughly of the same magnitude. Furthermore, ratios of CDS volatilities-to-premiums are roughly constant across rating categories, as are cash bond volatilities-to-spreads. However, the average spread-to-volatility ratio for CDS is about 0.5, whereas the corresponding ratio for corporate bonds is 0.3. Importantly, that result implies the market charges the same average spread per unit of spread volatility regardless of credit quality.

Figure 6.3 Average volatilities (left axes) and volatility-to-spread ratios (right axes) by rating category for historical CDS premium (2003–15) (left) and cash bond spreads (1994–2015) (right)

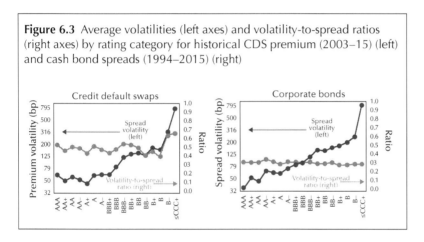

CALCULATING THE DAILY CDS RISK PREMIUM

This section will describe methods for calculating the daily risk premium in the CDS market. The procedure is analogous to that described for corporate cash bonds in Chapter 5. To begin, one requires a set of closing values of CDS premiums and durations for a large sample of CDS.[5] In addition, one must determine each reference obligor's cumulative default probability to the duration T_i of their CDS, denoted $p_{T,i}$. As for cash bonds, we use default probabilities obtained from either the Sobehart–Keenan HPD model or, if the $p_{T,i}$ from the HPD model is not available, we use the $p_{T,i}$ from Citi's market-implied PD model (Benzschawel and Lee, 2011; Benzschawel and Assing, 2012).[6] Then, given $p_{T,i}$ and an assumed value for LGD_i (in this case, a value 1.0 minus the reference recovery value for the CDS), one can use Equation 6.2 to determine the spread value of default for each CDS, $s_{d,i}$. By subtracting the value of $s_{d,i}$ from the CDS overall spread premium, s_i, one can determine value of the non-default premium $s_{\lambda,i}$. It is also necessary to compute the volatility of each obligor's CDS spread premium duration (ie, premium times duration) and define its 100-day trailing spread-duration volatility as $\sigma_{v,i}$.[7]

Given values of s_i, $s_{d,i}$, $s_{\lambda,i}$ and $\sigma_{v,i}$ for each CDS$_i$ sample on a given day, one can calculate the market beta (ie, $\beta = 1$) as the average CDS spread duration volatility in the 40–60th percentile bucket of spread duration volatilities. We designate $\sigma_{v,\beta=1}$ as the CDS premium duration volatility that corresponds to $\beta = 1$. Given the value of $\sigma_{v,\beta=1}$, we can determine the beta of CDS$_i$ (ie, β_i) to be the ratio of that CDS's premium duration volatility to $\sigma_{v,\beta=1}$. That is:

$$\beta_i = \frac{\sigma_{v,i}}{\sigma_{v,\beta=1}}$$

(6.3)

We also designate the median value of $s_{\lambda,i}$ in the 40–60th percentile bucket as $s_{\lambda,\beta=1}$ and designate the ratio of the median non-default spread to spread duration volatility at $\beta = 1$ (ie, its risk premium relative to CDS premium duration volatility) as Ψ_β and designate that value as the risk premium λ_t on day t. That is:

$$\Psi_\beta = \frac{s_{\lambda,i}}{\sigma_{v,\beta\cong1}} = \lambda_t$$

(6.4)

One can also calculate values of Ψ_i for individual CDS as ratios of their non-default premiums to 100-day trailing CDS premium duration volatilities as:

$$\Psi_i = \frac{s_{\lambda,i}}{\sigma_{v,i}}$$

(6.5)

A critical assumption underlying this method is that the "fair" risk premium on any given day is independent of credit rating, duration and volatility.[8] If so, one might expect that values of Ψ_i should be roughly equal to Ψ_β. In fact, as was demonstrated for the corporate bond market in Chapter 5, values of Ψ_i are highly dependent on their values of β_i. For example, the left panel of Figure 6.4 shows the dependence of Ψ_i for corporate bonds, with the analogous plot of values of Ψ_i from CDS at the right.

The black line in each figure results from a LOWESS, and illustrates the dependence of Ψ_i on β_i. The pattern of results is similar across markets; the average ratios are above 1.0 for $\beta_i < 1$ and less than 1.0 for $\beta_i > 1$. As described in greater detail below, we attribute the β_i-related deviations of Ψ_i from Ψ_β to reflect the embedded leverage in financial assets whose $\beta_i \neq 1$, as demonstrated for a variety of asset classes by Asness and colleagues (Asness, Frazzini and Pedersen, 2012; Frazzini, Kabiller and Pedersen, 2012; Frazzini and Pedersen, 2012; 2014).

Figure 6.4 Ratios of Ψ_i to $\Psi_{\beta=1}$ as a function of betas, β_i for corporate bonds (left) and corporate CDS (right)

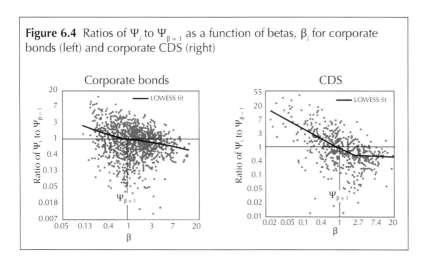

Assume for the moment that, as asserted above, the cause of the dependence of Ψ_i on β_i in Figure 6.4 is attributable to embedded leverage in financial assets (we will return to this point later). Then, we wish to find a relationship between λ_t and CDS β_i so that the non-default spread for any CDS whose beta is known can be written as:

$$s_{\lambda,i} = \lambda_t * f(\beta_i) * \sigma_{v,i} \tag{6.6}$$

and the resulting model of the spread premium for CDS_i can be written as:

$$s_i = [\lambda_t * f(\beta_i) * \sigma_{v,i}] + \frac{1}{T_i} \ln[1 - p_{T,i} \cdot LGD_i] \tag{6.7}$$

where all terms are as defined above.

Equation 6.6 adjusts assets' spread duration volatilities $\sigma_{v,i}$ by a factor related to their values of β_i. For example, consider the ratios of Ψ_i/Ψ_β in the right panel of Figure 6.4. The approach adjusts values of bonds' $\sigma_{v,i}$ based on the LOWESS fit and their values of β_i to compute adjusted values of Ψ_i such that the resulting LOWESS line is horizontal and passes through Ψ_β at $\beta = 1$. The left panel of Figure 6.5 shows the adjustment function, $f(\beta_i)$ determined from the LOWESS fit in the right panel of Figure 6.4. The right panel of Figure 6.5 plots ratios of Ψ_i to Ψ_β with values of Ψ_i computed using adjusted values of $\sigma_{v,i}$. The resulting plot of adjusted ratios indicates that a horizontal line passing through the point Ψ_β is a reasonable fit to the data while acknowledging the considerable variability of individual ratios about that line, particularly for low values of β_i.

TIME SERIES OF THE CDS RISK PREMIUM

Recall from Equation 6.4 that the value of the daily risk premium λ_t is calculated as the ratio of the non-default CDS premium to spread premium duration volatility for the CDS in the 40–60th percentile premium duration bucket. The value of that ratio is designated as $\Psi_{\beta=1}$. Daily values of λ_t calculated from January 2003 to May 2015 are given by the black function in Figure 6.6. Figure 6.6 also presents in light grey the values of the corporate bond risk premium from Benzschawel, Su and Xin (2015). The average value of the CDS risk premium is 1.3, twice that of the average corporate risk premium of 0.67. Despite the difference in absolute levels of the CDS and cash bond risk premiums, the two series track each other well except during the credit crisis of late 2007–09. Recall that the CDS minus cash bond basis for high-yield bonds moved from its more typical level of about +50bp to over –600bp during the crisis (Bai and Collin-Dufresne, 2011).

Figure 6.7 displays distributions and summary statistics of monthly values of λ_t from corporate CDS (left panel) and bonds (right panel) over the period 2003–15. As indicated earlier, average values of CDS risk premiums are about twice those of corporate bonds, but values of means and median premiums within each market are similar to each other. That is, average values of λ_t are good measures of central tendency of risk premiums for both CDS and corporate bonds. Also, both distributions are skewed toward higher values. One difference is the distribution CDS λ_t has a negative kurtosis indicative of narrower tails than a normal distribution, whereas corporate bond λ_t has fatter than normally distributed tails.

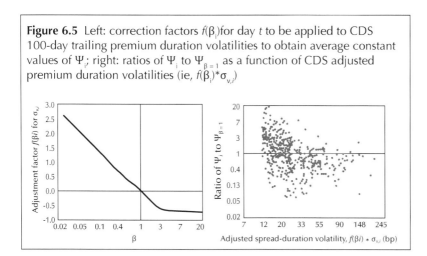

Figure 6.5 Left: correction factors $f(\beta_i)$ for day t to be applied to CDS 100-day trailing premium duration volatilities to obtain average constant values of Ψ_i; right: ratios of Ψ_i to $\Psi_{\beta=1}$ as a function of CDS adjusted premium duration volatilities (ie, $f(\beta_i)^*\sigma_{v,i}$)

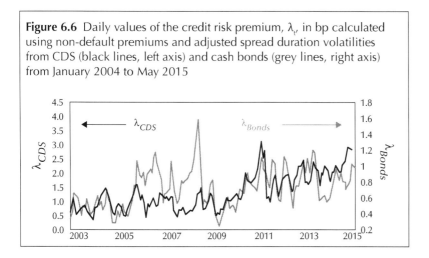

Figure 6.6 Daily values of the credit risk premium, λ_t, in bp calculated using non-default premiums and adjusted spread duration volatilities from CDS (black lines, left axis) and cash bonds (grey lines, right axis) from January 2004 to May 2015

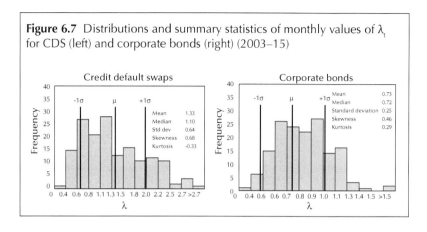

Figure 6.7 Distributions and summary statistics of monthly values of λ_t for CDS (left) and corporate bonds (right) (2003–15)

EMBEDDED LEVERAGE IN CDS PREMIUMS

Recall that to have a consistent risk premium, it was necessary to apply a beta-related adjustment, $f(\beta_i)$, to CDS spread duration volatilities. This was also necessary for corporate bonds. Since spread duration volatility is a reasonable proxy for price volatility, and logarithms of credit spreads are linearly related to bond prices, the need for an adjustment would appear to contradict the single risk premium hypothesis. Furthermore, such a correction would be at odds with both the CAPM and commonsense. Since our measure of bonds' Ψ_i values are analogous to Sharpe ratios, in the absence of technical or other factors, investors should be drawn to the assets that provide the largest return for their volatilities. Although one might expect the observed deviations in levels of the risk premiums across asset classes and smaller deviations within an asset class, the systematic deviations we observe for bond and CDS markets would appear problematic.

As described in Chapter 5, several analyses (Asness, Frazzini and Pedersen, 2012; Frazzini, Kabiller and Pedersen, 2012; Frazzini and Pedersen, 2012; 2014) provide insight into the cause of the consistently higher values of Ψ_i for low-beta bonds and lower values for high-beta assets. Those authors have documented consistently higher Sharpe ratios for low-beta credits relative to Sharpe ratios for high-beta ones across a wide variety of asset classes, including corporate bonds. Frazzini and Pedersen interpret the dependence of Sharpe ratios on beta as the result of embedded leverage in low- and high-beta assets. They define embedded leverage as the amount of market exposure per unit of committed capital. For example, since an investor can match the returns of an index with a fractional investment in higher-beta assets, the market requires a premium for that leverage in terms of a lower risk-adjusted return. The reverse is true for lower-beta credits, for which investors must lever up to match index returns, thereby providing implicit leverage to high-beta investors and warranting a higher excess return.

Importantly, the analyses of Frazzini and colleagues above support the claim that the variation with beta of ratios of CDS nondefault spreads to their spread premium duration volatilities, Ψ_i (higher for lower-beta bonds and lower for high-beta ones) is due to the embedded leverage in those assets. If so, it is possible to derive the CDS premium values of embedded leverage from the adjustment factor, $f(\beta_i)$, that are applied to bonds spread duration volatilities, $\sigma_{v,i}$, to derive a credit risk premium for all CDS. For example, consider the left panel of Figure 6.8, which displays the adjustment factors $f(\beta_i)$ versus CDS values of β_i (left axis) and the spread values of embedded leverage, γ_i, derived from that correction (right axis). The values of embedded leverage are calculated as the negative of the amount of CDS premium adjustment necessary to make average non-default CDS premiums to premium duration volatility ratios a constant. That is, spreads for low-beta CDS must be adjusted downward and those for high-beta bonds upward. For example, CDS whose β_i is 0.4, require a –17bp adjustment in non-default premium for their average values of Ψ_i to equal $\Psi_{\beta=1}$. The embedded leverage in Figure 6.8 is the negative of the spread adjustment as it is the excess premium. Therefore, in the case of γ_i at $\beta = 0.4$, the embedded leverage is a positive 17bp.[9] However, if β_i is 2.7, the embedded leverage is negative at –72bp. Finally, the figure indicates that the embedded leverage can be quite large for very high beta CDS, reaching levels as high as –500bp to –600bp for extremely volatile CDS.

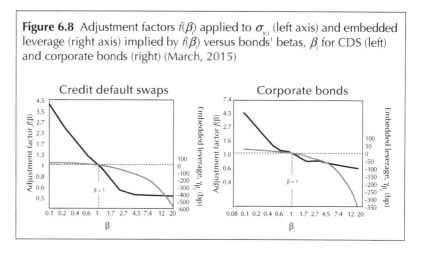

Figure 6.8 Adjustment factors $f(\beta_i)$ applied to $\sigma_{v,i}$ (left axis) and embedded leverage (right axis) implied by $f(\beta_i)$ versus bonds' betas, β_i for CDS (left) and corporate bonds (right) (March, 2015)

For comparison with embedded leverage in CDS premiums, the right panel of Figure 6.8 presents similar analysis from measures of embedded leverage in corporate bond spreads. The general pattern of embedded leverage for CDS and corporate bonds is similar. However, closer inspection reveals that for both high- and low-beta assets, CDS embedded leverage is greater than that for corporate bonds. In fact, we infer that the differences in embedded leverage between cash bonds and CDS premiums in Figure 6.8, along with the higher risk premium on CDS, reflects embedded leverage in CDS for financing cash bonds. That is, average CDS premiums are roughly twice those of cash bonds, and the corresponding spread differences provide a measure of the implicit financing of a long position in the underlying deliverable bond provided by selling protection via CDS.

One feature of the ability to measure the embedded leverage in credit spread premiums, is that it is possible to examine how values of embedded leverage change along with fluctuations in market conditions. For example, the left panel of Figure 6.9 from Benzschawel, Su and Xin (2015) shows how patterns of embedded leverage (ie, values of γ_{β_i} versus β_i) for corporate bonds changed in response to the credit stresses to market liquidity during the credit crisis of late 2007 to 2009. In periods of non-crisis liquidity conditions, embedded leverage functions of β follow the typical pattern shown in Figure 6.8. That is, embedded leverage for all bonds having β < 1 is roughly 10–25bp on any given day, whereas embedded leverage for bonds with β > 1 becomes increasingly negative as β increases. The more extreme embedded leverage curves given by the light grey and dark grey lines in Figure 6.9 were obtained in August and October 2008, just before and after the default of Lehman Brothers, respectively. Although the leverage for low-beta bonds had already increased from roughly 20bp to 100bp a month before the Lehman Brothers default, the estimated leverage premium for bonds with β < 1 spiked upward to nearly 300bp. Equally dramatic is the rise in the discount for embedded leverage estimated for bonds having β > 1. Values of $γ_β$ peak around minus 200–300bp for bonds with the largest betas in times of normal liquidity, but during the credit crises had widened to roughly 800bp.

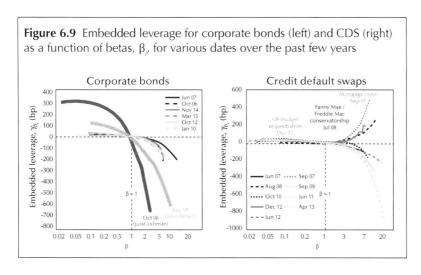

Figure 6.9 Embedded leverage for corporate bonds (left) and CDS (right) as a function of betas, $β_i$, for various dates over the past few years

The right panel of Figure 6.9 presents the analogous series of embedded leverage functions for CDS relative to the credit crisis and other events. Under "normal" conditions (ie, pre- and post-credit crisis), embedded leverage functions for corporate bonds and CDS are similar and consistent with those in Figure 6.8. However, during periods of financial stress, embedded leverage in cash bonds and CDS diverge. That is, whereas both positive and negative embedded leverage in corporate bonds increases in times of stress, CDS embedded leverage reverses, with low-beta CDS having negative embedded leverage and high-beta credits offering above-average risk-adjusted returns. Of course, this is reflected in the increase in the CDS versus cash bond basis and the divergence between corporate bond and CDS risk premiums in Figure 6.6.

PREDICTING THE CDS RISK PREMIUM

In Chapter 4, it was shown that the ratio of the average high-yield corporate bond spreads to one-year predicted default rates from Citi's HT 2.0 model can predict one-year directional changes in yield spreads with 65–80% accuracy. That is, when the current high-yield spread to predicted default (D_p) ratio is above average, high-yield spreads are lower one year later 80% of the time. Conversely, when the spread to predicted default ratio is below average, high-yield spreads widen 65% of the time. In addition, when predictions of tightening or widening are correct, the spread moves are 50–100% larger than when incorrect.

Recall from Chapter 5 that one-year changes in λ_t for corporate bonds are related to ratios of λ_t to the predicted default rate, D_p. That is, high λ_t-to-D_p ratios signal lower values of λ_t one year later with an accuracy of 70%, whereas lower ratios signal increases in the credit risk premium over the next year with an accuracy of 57%. To the extent that risk premiums in corporate bond and CDS markets are related, one ought to be able to predict one-year changes in CDS risk premiums based on ratios of CDS λ_t versus D_p. To test this, monthly ratios of the current value of the CDS λ_t to predicted default rates were computed and evaluated relative to one-year changes in the CDS risk premiums (ie, $\lambda_{t+12} - \lambda_t$). The results of that analysis appear in Figure 6.10. The left panel of the figure shows monthly ratios of the CDS risk premium to the one-year default rate, D_p, from 2003 to 2015. The dashes in the figure depict the trailing expanding average ratio of λ_t to the predicted default rate. The right panel of Figure 6.10 displays probabilities of correct and incorrect predictions of directional changes in $\lambda_{t+12} - \lambda_t$. Results for the CDS risk premium are similar to those for the cash bonds premiums. That is, directional predictions of one-year changes in the risk premiums are about the same (ie, in the 60–70% range), and when correct are larger than directional changes when incorrect. In general, these results support the idea that changes in CDS indexes might be useful to hedge changes in cash bond risk premiums.

Figure 6.10 Left: ratios of the CDS premiums, λ_t (in bp) to one-year predicted default rates (in percentages); the trailing expanding average (grey dashes) is also shown; right: one-year changes in CDS risk premiums versus monthly ratios of current values of CDS λ_t to the predicted high-yield default rate

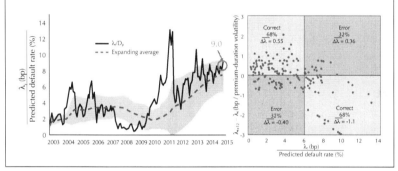

CONCLUSION

This chapter has presented the underlying rationale for estimation of the credit risk premium in the CDS market, along with results of calculations of historical CDS risk premiums and embedded leverage in those CDS spread premiums. To do this, the methodology used was analogous to that described in Chapter 5 for calculations of risk premiums and embedded leverage in corporate bond markets. In addition, this analysis enabled comparisons of the CDS market with those of cash corporate bonds. The chapter began with a description of the relationship of the CDS premium due to default relative to the overall compensation for buying CDS. As for corporate bonds, the compensation for expected loss of cashflows due to default is only a fraction of CDS premiums. It was also demonstrated that a single factor, the risk premium, λ_t, is the major contributor to CDS premiums and that, on any given day, its average value is roughly a constant fraction of CDS price volatilities regardless of credit quality.

The remainder of the chapter focused on determining the time series of CDS risk premiums and its properties along with a comparison with corporate ones. Also, as for corporate bonds, it was found necessary to derive a beta-related adjustment factor $f(\beta_i)$ applied to CDS premium duration volatilities to ensure a constant risk premium across CDS. We argue that, as for corporate bonds, the necessity of the beta-related adjustment factor is the result of embedded leverage, γ_β, in CDS premiums. In addition, the embedded leverage hypothesis enables derivation of daily spread values of embedded leverage versus β_i based on the adjustment function $f(\beta_i)$. Estimates of γ_β obtained before, during and after the credit crisis confirm that the yield spread values of embedded leverage are altered dramatically during liquidity crises. In addition, differences between changes in CDS and corporate bond embedded leverage under conditions of financial stress reflect the observed changes in the CDS versus cash bond spread basis. Finally, it was shown that, as for high-yield corporate credit spreads and corporate bond risk premiums, ratios of current CDS risk premiums to predicted one-year default rates predict one-year directional moves in λ_t at well-above chance levels.

1 Detailed descriptions of the derivation of Equation 6.1 from risk-neutral pricing theory and the price yield formula, along methods for determining firms' cumulative default probabilities and LGDs can be found in Benzschawel, Su and Xin (2015) and Appendix 5.1.

2 The non-monotonicity in the non-default premium is the result of wide CDS spreads for some highly rated obligors during the credit crisis of 2008–09.

3 Note that because of the convex relation between yield and price, spreads plotted on a logarithmic scale are more representative of linear differences in prices.

4 The greater volatility of the CDS premium series over that of corporate bonds reflects the facts that CDS quotes are only available on about 700 obligors, as opposed to several thousand for corporate bonds. The volatility is particularly large before the CDS "Big Bang" in April 2009 that served to standardised CDS contracts (MarkIt Partners, 2009).

5 For example, we use premiums by maturity from roughly 700 CDS marked daily by Citi's credit derivative traders.

6 A detailed description of the method for determining cumulative default probabilities p_T from the models appears in Benzschawel, Su and Xin (2015).

7 Note that CDS spread duration volatilities are closely related to their individual price volatilities.

8 The notion of a constant risk premium for all credits in deeply embedded within financial theory, beginning with the work of Markowitz (1959) and Sharpe (1964, 1994). Also, the role of CRP as a guiding principle is akin to the efficient markets hypothesis (EMH). Although the strict assumptions of both CRP and EMH are routinely violated, they both

serve as benchmarks against which explanations for deviations (eg, market segmentation, liquidity, implicit leverage, supply and demand) are based.

9   The scaling of the axes and the small (roughly 20bp) amount of embedded leverage for low-beta CDS are difficult to see from this plot.

7

The Municipal Build America Bond Risk Premium

Chapters 5 and 6 described methods for calculating the risk premiums and embedded leverage in corporate bond and CDS markets. In this chapter, similar methods will be used to provide insight into the compensation for credit risk and embedded leverage in the municipal Build America Bond (BAB) market. Motivation for this analysis is both to measure the credit risk premium in the municipal bonds as well as to determine if that information can be used to derive relative value trading strategies in BABs. BABs were chosen for this analysis because, unlike most other municipal bonds, they are taxable, thereby enabling one to analyse their yields using the same techniques that are typically applied to corporate bonds. Nevertheless, the approach is less straightforward than for cash and CDS markets in that there are no well-established methods for assigning probabilities of default to municipal bonds, reliably estimating their relative values, or any known attempts to measure municipal bond risk premiums.

The chapter will begin with a description of municipal bonds, BABs and the BAB market. This is followed by a description of the relationship between municipal and corporate bond agency ratings and default rates. A necessary precursor to measuring the municipal bond risk premium requires inferring default probabilities for municipal bonds and a method for estimating their recovery values in default. Since there is no known model for estimating credit cycle-dependent default probabilities (PDs) for municipal bonds, the approach uses facts regarding municipal bond defaults and a comparison of their relationship to corporate bond defaults. Using those relations, methods will be described for estimating term structures of municipalities' PDs, and how those PDs can be used along with the municipal BAB recovery values to determine the spread compensation for default (and, by inference, BAB non-default spreads). Then, as for corporate bonds, the spread compensation for default is subtracted from BAB spreads to Treasuries to generate non-default spreads. BABs' non-default spreads are then used with their spread duration volatilities to compute ratios of non-default spread to spread duration volatilities. By examining deviations of bonds' non-default spread duration volatilities from a constant ratio, we derive a beta-related adjustment factor to ensure a constant risk premium based on BABs whose betas are equal to 1. Finally, from the beta-based adjustment factor, we infer the embedded leverage in the municipal BAB market as we have done for US corporate bonds and CDS as described in previous chapters.

OVERVIEW OF MUNICIPAL BONDS

Municipal bonds are the debt obligations of states, their political subdivisions, and certain agencies and authorities. There are more than 50,000 state and local government issuers of municipal bonds, and proceeds from those bond issues are typically used to finance public projects such as water and sewer systems, schools, roads and public buildings. Under existing federal income tax law, the interest income from municipal bonds is exempt from federal income taxes. In addition to offering tax advantages, municipal bonds have historically low default rates (less than 1% of bonds issued have defaulted). Individual ownership of municipal bonds grew from approximately US$130 billion in 1980 to US$3.7 trillion in 2011. A majority of municipal bonds issued and outstanding are exempt from federal income taxes. Of the more than US$3.4 trillion of municipal issues outstanding as of March 31, 2012, more than US$2.7 trillion were tax-exempt issues, while taxable municipals outstanding accounted for US$630 billion (Bond Buyer, 2013).

There are two basic types of municipal bonds.

❑ General obligation bonds: Principal and interest are secured by the full faith and credit of the issuer, and usually supported by either the issuer's unlimited or limited taxing power. In many cases, general obligation bonds are voter-approved.

❑ Revenue bonds: Principal and interest are secured by revenues derived from tolls, charges or rents from the facility built with the proceeds of the bond issue. Public projects financed by revenue bonds include toll roads, bridges, airports, water and sewage treatment facilities, hospitals and subsidised housing. Many of these bonds are issued by special authorities created for that particular purpose.

One of the primary reasons that municipal bonds are considered separately from other types of bonds is their special ability to provide investors with tax-exempt income. Interest paid by the municipal issuer to bond holders is often exempt from all federal taxes, as well as state or local taxes depending on the state in which the issuer is located. Since traditional municipal bonds are often tax-exempt, one needs to consider tax rates when comparing yields of municipal bonds to corporate bonds or other taxable bonds. This relationship can be represented as follows:

$$r_m = r_c(1 - t)$$
(7.1)

where r_m is interest rate of the municipal bond, r_c is the interest rate of a comparable taxable bond, and t is the tax rate. For example, if $r_c = 10\%$ and $t = 38\%$, then $r_m = 10\% * (100\% - 38\%) = 6.2\%$. Thus, a municipal bond that pays 6.2% generates equal interest income after taxes as a corporate bond that pays 10% (assuming all else equal). The marginal tax rate t at which an investor is indifferent between holding a corporate bond yielding r_c and a municipal bond yielding r_m is:

$$t = 1 - (r_m / r_c)$$
(7.2)

Alternatively, one can calculate the taxable equivalent yield of a municipal bond and compare it to the yield of a corporate bond as $r_c = r_m(1 - t)$.

BUILD AMERICA BONDS

In 2009, BABs were created as a new class of municipal bonds under Section 1531 of Title I of Division B of the American Recovery and Reinvestment Act. BABs are taxable municipal bonds that carry special tax credits and federal subsidies for either the bond issuer or the bondholder. As BABs are taxable, one can analyse their yields using the same techniques that are typically applied to corporate bonds (eg, on a yield spread to US Treasuries). BABs enable state and municipal governments to tap additional sources of capital from investors who could not otherwise benefit from the tax advantage of regular municipal bonds.[1] For statutory reasons, BABs were only issued during 2009 and 2010. However, during this period more than US$180 billion worth of BABs were issued, constituting roughly 30% of all municipal bond issuance. The tax subsidy is for the life of the BABs, and some BABs still have over 20 years remaining before maturity.[2]

Under the BAB programme, municipalities issue bonds with taxable coupon payments, but they receive a subsidy from the federal government to offset their borrowing costs. The existing BAB tax subsidy is set at 35% of the BAB. This is the same as the highest marginal federal income tax rate and the highest marginal corporate income tax. For example, assume a state government issues a BAB with 5% taxable interest rate. The US Treasury pays the state $0.35 \times 5\% = 1.75\%$, making the state's effective borrowing cost 3.25%. An investor in a BAB receiving the 5% coupon is subject to taxes. If this investor is in the highest federal marginal income tax bracket, they would then receive $(1 - 0.35) \times 5\% = 3.25\%$ net of federal taxes. Therefore, suppose the state government issued a regular municipal bond at 3.25%. An individual investor buying the regular municipal bond receives the full 3.25% and pays no tax. Thus, for a taxable investor, the regular municipal bond with 3.25% coupon has the same out-of-pocket cost as the BAB with the 5%.

The success of the BAB programme has been well-documented. First, the fact that taxable interest rates tend to be higher than tax-exempt yields makes regular municipal bond yields relatively unattractive investments for pension funds, foreign investors and investors in low tax brackets. The introduction of taxable municipal bonds increases the investor base, thereby enabling a broader group of investors to finance state and local government projects. This goal has apparently been realised, as the US Treasury (2011) estimates that state and local governments have reaped over US$20 billion in present value savings from issuing BABs, and analysis by Ang, Bhansali and Xing (2010) indicates that BAB issuers were able to obtain financing at an average of 54bp cheaper than issuing in the regular municipal bond market. In fact, the success of the BAB programme fuelled clamour from issuers and the municipal finance industry for it to be reinstated (Puentes, Sabol and Kane, 2014).

MUNICIPAL BONDS: RATINGS, CREDIT TRANSITIONS, DEFAULTS AND RECOVERIES

Although municipal bonds are similar to their corporate counterparts in coupon style, quoting convention and valuation, they differ in several respects that complicate their analysis. For example, the panels in Figure 7.1 present a comparison between corporate and municipal bond agency ratings distributions (top panel of page 249), default rates (bottom panel of page 249), recovery values in default (bottom panel of page 250) and credit ratings transitions (top panel of page 250). Note the huge disparity among the credit qualities of issuers on the municipal and corporate bond markets in the upper panel of page 249. That is, although corporate issuer ratings span both investment-grade and high-yield rating categories, municipal bond issuers nearly all have investment-grade ratings.

Implicit in the comparison between municipal and corporate bond distributions on the same agency rating scale is the assumption that ratings for both asset classes represent equal amounts of riskiness. In fact, in 2002 Moody's published the first study of municipal defaults by agency rating category (Washburn, 2002) in which they demonstrated substantial differences in default rates for similarly rated corporate and municipal issuers. Moody's also published an updated version of those results (Tudela, Medioli and Van Praach, 2012), and those appear in the bottom panel of Figure 7.1 on page 249. That figure shows average cumulative default rates by rating category and time horizon for municipal bonds ((second panel of page 249) and corporate bonds ((third panel of page 249) issued between 1970 and 2011. Figure 7.1 indicates that, aside from default probabilities of higher-quality issuers in years one and two, cumulative default rates for all similar ratings and time horizons are higher for corporations than for municipalities. In particular, those differences tend to increase with tenor. For example, the 10-year cumulative default rate for double-B rated corporate bonds (43%) is nearly twice that for single-B municipal bonds (22%). Differences are evident for all maturities and all tenors. In fact, Moody's has published an adjusted rating scale for municipalities that relates expected default rates between municipal and corporate issuers. As we shall see below, correcting for these differences is a critical step in estimating the risk premium in the BAB municipal bond market.

Another important consideration for estimating expected gains and losses when investing in municipal bonds is their likelihoods of transitioning among rating categories; presumably changes in ratings are accompanied by relative changes in their credit spreads. The two lower panels of Figure 7.1 on page 249 display one-year rating transitions for municipal bonds and corporate bonds, respectively. Comparison of the one-year transitions to default from bonds in each rating category confirms these results in that, for all rating categories, corporate default rates are higher than those for municipal bonds. The cells on the diagonal of the matrix represent the probabilities of bonds of a given rating remaining in their same category after one year. Comparison of the corresponding transitions for municipal and corporate issuers indicates that, for all rating categories, 4–10% more of corporate obligors transition out of their current rating than municipalities. For example, the probability of a municipal issuer transitioning out of the single-A rating category is 6.66% (100–93.34%), and that same probability for a single-A rated corporation is 13.64% (100–86.36%). Furthermore, inspection of the direction of the ratings changes in each rating category reveals that the ratio of downgrades to upgrades is greater for corporate issuers than for municipal ones. For example, for Baa-rated issuers, the one-year downgrade-to-upgrade ratio for municipals is (0.49/1.51) = 0.32, whereas that same ratio for corporate issuers is (4.04/4.37) = 0.92. Presumably, the greater rating stability of municipal issuers is reflected in lower price

Figure 7.1 Top: municipal and corporate bond rating distributions (December 2011); bottom: cumulative default rates by rating category and time horizon for municipal (top) and corporate (bottom) issuers

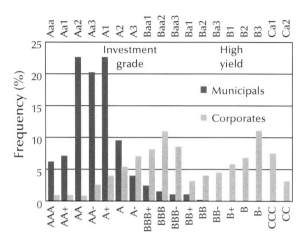

Municipals

| Time horizon (in years) | | | | | |
Rating	Year 1	Year 2	Year 3	Year 4	Year 5
Aaa	0.0000%	0.0000%	0.0000%	0.0000%	0.0000%
Aa	0.0327%	0.0348%	0.0370%	0.0396%	0.0424%
A	0.0097%	0.0119%	0.0154%	0.0193%	0.0217%
Baa	0.0635%	0.0725%	0.0807%	0.0897%	0.0974%
Ba	1.4152%	1.5590%	1.6243%	1.6986%	1.7836%
B	5.8550%	7.7081%	9.3205%	10.6397%	11.5998%
Caa–C	15.8449%	16.5785%	16.5785%	16.5785%	16.5785%

Corporates

| Time horizon (in years) | | | | | |
Rating	Year 1	Year 2	Year 3	Year 4	Year 5
Aaa	0.0000%	0.0000%	0.0000%	0.0262%	0.0995%
Aa	0.0078%	0.0187%	0.0423%	0.1060%	0.1774%
A	0.0207%	0.0950%	0.2205%	0.3443%	0.4720%
Baa	0.1815%	0.5063%	0.9295%	1.4342%	1.9384%
Ba	1.2049%	3.2192%	5.5685%	7.9575%	10.2153%
B	5.2361%	11.2958%	17.0435%	22.0544%	26.7936%
Caa–C	19.4758%	30.4940%	39.7172%	46.9039%	52.6218%

Figure 7.1 (*Continued*) Top panels: average one-year rating transition rates for municipal issuers and corporate issuers (1970-2011). Bottom panel: defaulted bond recovery rate distributions, municipal versus corporate

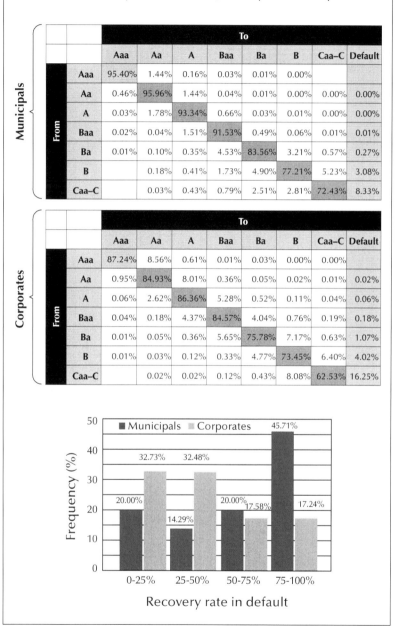

volatility of municipal bonds, suggesting that municipal bonds might have greater volatility-adjusted returns than equally rated corporate bonds.

Much effort has been put into collecting data on defaults and developing models to estimate firms' default probabilities. However, much less effort has been devoted to modelling recovery value in default, and much less data regarding recovery values exist. This is surprising since the expected losses from default on a bond depend not only on the probability of default, but also on the recovery value in default. That is, the expected loss on a bond, EL, can be calculated as:

$$EL = p_T * (1 - RV) \qquad (7.3)$$

where p_T is the cumulative default rate to time T, RV is the recovery value in default and $(1 - RV)$ is also called the LGD. As described below, a critical component of determining the risk premium for BABs requires estimating their expected losses from default. Hence, it is important to use reasonable estimates of recovery values in default in those calculations.

Presumably owing to a scarcity of models for recovery value in default, portfolio managers and broker–dealers commonly assume a constant value for RV, typically around 40% of face value for corporate issuers.[3] The value of 40% is based on early reports of Hickman (1958), Altman and Nammacher, (1984) and Altman and Kishore (1996), and our analysis of Moody's default and recovery database confirms this value. Benzschawel and Su (2013) have confirmed an average recovery value of 40% for corporate bonds on a sample of over 5,000 corporate bond recoveries. However, as shown in Figure 7.2, the distribution of corporate bond recovery values around 40% is extremely broad, covering nearly the entire range between 0% and 100% of face value, the distribution is bimodal and the most common recovery value is around 20%.

Moody's (Washburn, 2002) has analysed distributions of recovery values in default for corporate bonds and municipalities, and those results appear in the final chart of Figure 7.1. Clearly, recovery values in default for municipal bonds (the lighter bars) are consistently greater than those for corporate bonds. Moody's

(2007) provided a more detailed study of LGD for various classes of municipal bonds. Those values appear for each sector in Table 7.1 (note that, unlike Figure 7.1 which plots recovery value, Table 7.1 plots loss given default where $LGD = (1 - RV)$. Note that, consistent with the recovery values in Figure 7.1, most losses given default are 30% or less (recover rates greater than 70%). In fact, losses in default for general obligation bonds of states and localities and water and sewer bonds are only in the 5–10% range. Conversely, project financing such as toll roads and bridges, stadium and airports tend to have lower recovery rates, which are roughly similar to those of corporate bonds. The values of LGD shown for the sectors in Table 7.1 are important as they will be used along with estimates of default probabilities to calculate the spread compensation for default for BABs as described in the next section.

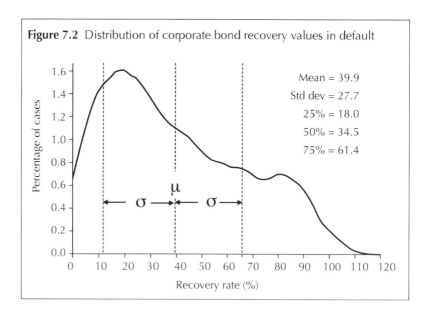

Figure 7.2 Distribution of corporate bond recovery values in default

Table 7.1 Average loss given default ($LGD = 1 - RV$) rates for municipal sectors

Sector	Type of obligation	Loss given default
State and local government and public enterprise:		**5–10% range**
General obligation and water/sewer enterprise	State government general obligation	5%
	Local government (including instrumentalities, territories and commonwealths) general obligation	10%
	Water/sewer enterprise	10%
	State revolving fund	10%
State and local government and public enterprise: other		**10–30% range**
	State lease obligation and special tax	10%
	Local government lease obligation and special tax	15%
	Mass transit	15%
	Higher education – public	15%
	Airport/port general revenue	15%
	Toll roads and bridges – established	15%
	Housing – affiliated/actively managed	15%
	Electric and gas – transmission only	15%
	Electric and gas – generation and joint power authority	30%
	Solid waste/resource recovery	30%
	Parking enterprise	30%

Table 7.1 (*Continued*)

State and local government and public enterprise: other (*continued*)	Lottery revenue	30%
	Special assessment/tax increment – established	30%
	Government-affiliated projects	30%
Not-for-profit corporation		**45–55% range**
	Higher education – private	45%
	Hospitals (not-for-profit) including multi-state hospital systems	45%
	Other not-for-profit	45%
	Long-term care/senior living	55%
Limited recourse project financing		**45-55% range**
	Military housing	45%
	Toll roads and bridges - start-up	55%
	Special assessment/tax increment – start-up ("dirt bonds")	55%
	Charter schools	55%
	Housing – conduit/not actively managed	55%
	Airport/port special facility	55%
	Hotel/convention centre	55%
	Stadiums and other projects	55%

Source: Moody's Investors Service

SPREAD COMPENSATION FOR LOSSES FROM DEFAULT AND THE CREDIT RISK PREMIUM

The reason that the differences between corporate and municipal default rates and recovery values are important is that our method for determining the risk premium requires estimating bonds' expected losses from default. To do this requires reliable estimates physical default probabilities and recovery values in default. Although several useful models have been developed to estimate corporate bonds' physical default[4] and recovery values in default,[5] no such models exist for municipal bonds. Although average default probabilities by agency rating categories exist for municipal bonds (see Figure 7.1), actual default probabilities fluctuate greatly in dependence on the credit cycle and are rarely near average values. Before discussing our approach to assigning default and recovery values for municipal BABs, we will describe briefly the rationale behind our estimation of the risk premium and, in particular, its dependence on reliable estimates of bonds' default risk and recovery values.

As described in previous chapters, we can view bonds' yield spreads, s, over their corresponding benchmark yields (eg, US Treasuries) as composed of two main factors: the spread compensation for not receiving the cashflows owing to default, s_d, and the compensation for fluctuations in the non-default-related portion of the spread that we call the credit risk premium, s_λ. That is $s = s_\lambda + s_d$.

For example, Figure 7.3 shows monthly average values of s_d and s_λ by agency rating for corporate bonds in Citi's BIG and High Yield indexes (Citi Index Group, 2013) over the period 1998–2014. The spread compensation for default, s_d, represented by the dark area in the figure, was calculated using average monthly PDs by rating from the Citi's HPD model (Sobehart and Keenan, 2002; 2003; Benzschawel, 2013) and assuming a 40% recovery value in default. The lighter area is the non-default spread, s_λ and is determined as the difference between the entire spread, s, and the default spread s_d. The figure indicates that the spread compensation for default is negligible for most investment-grade bonds. Even for high-yield bonds, the non-default spread is much larger for all credit ratings than the default spread.

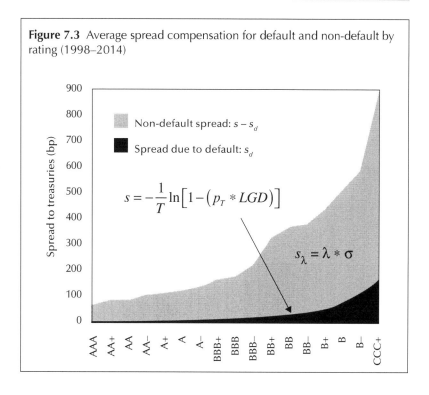

Figure 7.3 Average spread compensation for default and non-default by rating (1998–2014)

For computational convenience, we can treat a bond's cashflows as a single payment occurring at its duration T. Then, we can estimate the bonds' spread compensation from default as:

$$s_d = -\frac{1}{T}\ln[1-(p_T \cdot \mathrm{LGD})]$$

(7.4)

where p_T is the cumulative default probability of the issuer up to time T and LGD is determined from Table 7.1. Recall from previous chapters that Equation 7.4 is based on the idea that the spread value of default can be derived from the price yield formula, with the assumption from risk-neutral pricing theory that the present value of a set of cashflows is their expected likelihood of receipt discounted at the risk-free rate.

Our motivation for determining bonds' values of s_d is to reveal their credit risk premiums as the remainder after subtracting their default-related yield spreads to Treasuries from their overall spreads. Thus, to solve for s_d one needs estimates of cumulative default probabilities p_T and values of LGD for each bond. In addition, one requires a method for estimating an obligor's cumulative default probabilities p_T over the entire range of durations of its bonds.

We know of no model available to reliably estimate term structures of default probabilities for municipal bond issuers. Accordingly, we devised a method for estimating BAB issuers' PDs based on their credit ratings and historical default rates, along with some suggestions provided by the credit rating agencies. Our method for determining the term structure of an obligor's p_T consists of first determining the agency rating of the issuer and indicative data on the given BAB. As an example, consider a local general obligation (GO) BAB from an issuer rate A/A2 by S&P/Moody's with 7.2 years left until maturity, a duration of 5.0 years and trading at 120bp over the US Treasury yield curve. Thus, we already know that $T = 5$ for input to Equation 7.4, but we also need to determine p_5 and LGD to solve for s_d.

In general, to solve for a BAB issuer's p_T is to use estimates of current default rates for corporate bonds by rating and the historical relationship between corporate and municipal default rates. Although we have no reference bonds in the municipal market for which we have estimates of physical PDs, one typically has several useful pieces of information for making reasonable inferences regarding municipal bond default probabilities. First we have agency ratings for both corporate bonds and many municipal bonds. Also, each day one can generate term structures of default probabilities from Citi's HPD model for a large number of corporate bonds (over 30,000). For example, Figure 7.4 shows term structures of cumulative default probabilities by agency rating category from one to 10 years from Citi's HPD model for June 10, 2015.[6] Importantly, these term structures of corporate cumulative default rates rise and fall with changes in the economic cycle. We use the credit cycle-dependent corporate term structures by rating from Figure 7.4 in combination with the corporate and municipal default rates in Figure 7.1 to derive credit cycle-dependent municipal default rates. That is, based on ratios of historical default rates for corporate and municipal bonds, we have developed scaling factors by rating and tenor to go from corporate to municipal firm PDs. For example, the corporate-to-municipal default ratios at one year are shown in the top and middle panels of Figure 7.5, with adjustment factors by tenor for A/A2 rated bonds shown in the bottom panel. The top and middle panels of Figure 7.5 indicate that, for investment-grade rated municipal bonds (BBB/Baa3 or better), one-year municipal bond default rates are to be adjusted downward from corporate rates by factors of 0.5 for AAA/Aaa and AA/Aa rated municipal bonds, 0.15 for A/A bonds and 0.20 for BBB/Baa issues.

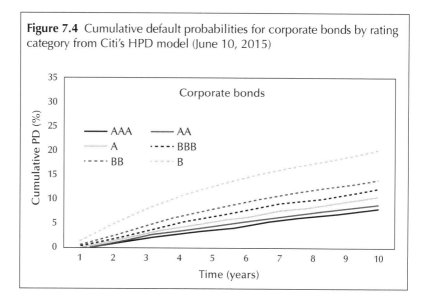

Figure 7.4 Cumulative default probabilities for corporate bonds by rating category from Citi's HPD model (June 10, 2015)

An example of the resulting term structure of PDs for municipal bonds by agency rating and tenor are presented in Figure 7.6. The figure reveals that, consistent with the ratios of municipal to corporate bond defaults by rating, PDs for investment-grade municipal bonds have lower average cumulative PDs than their corporate counterparts, whereas high-yield municipal default rates are higher.[7] To determine cumulative annual municipal issuer default rates from 11 to 30 years, we extrapolate from the 10-year cumulative PD using the one-year marginal default rate between nine and 10 years. We also do this for corporate cumulative default rates.

Figure 7.5 Ratios of corporate-to-municipal bond default ratios by agency ratings, and adjustment factors for rating-based default rates from corporate default curves

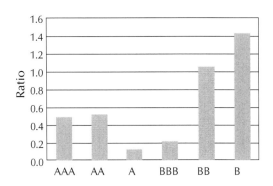

Rating	Corporate 1-yr PD	Muni 1-yr PD	Physical ratio	Factor
AAA	0.0000	0.0000	100%	50%
AA	0.0610	0.0327	53.61%	50%
A	0.0730	0.0097	13.29%	15%
BBB	0.2880	0.0635	22.05%	20%
BB	1.3360	1.4152	105.93%	100%
B	4.0470	5.8550	144.68%	150%

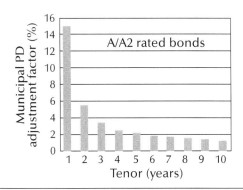

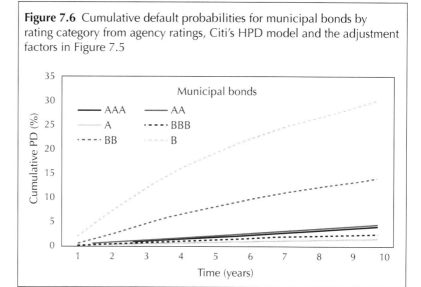

Figure 7.6 Cumulative default probabilities for municipal bonds by rating category from agency ratings, Citi's HPD model and the adjustment factors in Figure 7.5

Returning to the example of the seven-year bond from the A/A2 issuer, we are now able to estimate the cumulative PD at its five-year duration point, p_5. This is the value of 1.3% given by the single-A rating curve in Figure 7.7.[8] Using this method, one can estimate a value of p_T for any municipal bond having an agency rating. We recognise that agency ratings often lag market perceptions of credit quality as embedded in credit spreads (Benzschawel, 2012). However, we are comfortable using a ratings-based estimation method as we assume that: (i) on average, agency ratings for a large number of issuers are roughly correct; (ii) average values of default probabilities will not bias estimates of the daily market-wide risk premium; and (iii) the overwhelming majority of municipal bond issuers have investment-grade ratings (ie, low default rates) and high recovery values in default (see Table 7.1).

Finally, to estimate bonds' losses in default, we use the table of LGDs in Table 7.1. For our example of a local general obligation bond, we use the average value of LGD = 10%. Inputting the values of T, p_T, and LGD into Equation 7.4, we get:

$$s = -\frac{1}{T} \ln[1 - p_T \cdot LGD]$$

$$= -\left(\frac{1}{5}\right) \ln[1 - (0.013 * 0.1)]$$

$$= 0.0003$$

Thus, the spread compensation for default is negligible (ie, 0.3bp), even for a seven-year single-A rated municipal bond. Then, given the spread of the non-default spread, $s_{d'}$ is calculated as:

$$s_\lambda = s - s_d$$
$$= 120.0bp - 0.3$$
$$= 119.7bp$$

(7.5)

Thus, given low default rates and high recovery values relative to corporate bonds, default spreads for most municipal bonds are relatively small. Therefore, the potential for errors in PDs due to our assumption regarding the use of average default rates by rating should be small.

CALCULATING BAB BETAS AND THE DAILY RISK PREMIUM

Having demonstrated how non-default spreads can be obtained for BABs using Equation 7.4, consider how to estimate the overall credit risk premium using as a model calculation of the daily risk premium in the corporate market. Recall that the key to understanding the credit risk premium comes from an analysis of the relationship between non-default credit spreads and spread volatility. That is, our model of the risk premium is:

$$s = [\lambda_t * f(\beta_i) * \sigma_{v,i}] + \frac{1}{T} \ln[1 - p_T \cdot LGD]$$

(7.6)

where λ_t is the daily value of the risk premium, $f(\beta_i)$ an adjustment factor related to the beta of bond i with respect to the universe of bonds to account for embedded leverage (see below) and $\sigma_{v,i}$ is the bond's spread duration volatility. The right portion of Equation 7.6 is spread compensation for default in Equation 7.4.

Calculating spread duration volatilities

The method as applied to the municipal BABs is to first estimate values $\sigma_{v,i}$ for all the BABs in our sample. From values of $\sigma_{v,i}$ one can derive their values of β_i. Then, from values of β_i one can calculate λ_t. Finally, using λ_t we derive the beta-adjustment function and its associated values of embedded leverage. Each of these computations is demonstrated below.

Recall from Chapter 5 that the spread duration volatility for bond i is calculated as:

$$\sigma_{v,i} = \frac{1}{\sum_{t=0}^{-99} w_t} * \sqrt{\sum_{t=0}^{-99} \left(s_{v,i,t} - \overline{s_{v,t}}\right)^2 * w_t}$$

(7.7)

where $s_{v,i,t}$ is the yield spread to US Treasuries on day t multiplied by the bond's duration on that day, t is days from the valuation date (ie, $t = 0$) and w_t is a negative exponential weighting function with a 33-day half-life defined as:

$$w_t = e^{-0.021*t}$$

(7.8)

Importantly, note that bonds' spread durations are closely related to their individual price volatilities via the logarithmic relationship between bond prices and yields.[9]

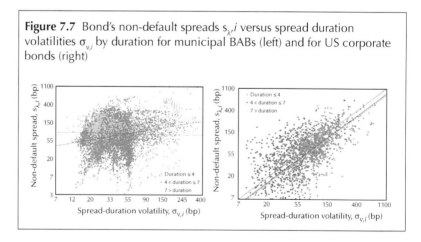

Figure 7.7 Bond's non-default spreads s_λ, i versus spread duration volatilities $\sigma_{v,i}$ by duration for municipal BABs (left) and for US corporate bonds (right)

Values of BAB's non-default spreads, s_λ, on November 10, 2015, appear as a function of their spread duration volatilities, $\sigma_{v,t}$, in the left panel of Figure 7.7. Values for bonds in different duration buckets appear in different shades of grey, and a similar plot for US corporate bonds is presented in the right panel of Figure 7.7. BABs' non-default spreads show much less correlation with their spread duration volatilities than corporate bonds, although bonds in both markets display a dependence on duration. Finally, note that on any given day, there are roughly 15,000 BABs for which we have credit spreads and ratings compared to the roughly 3,000 corporate issues.

Calculating bond betas

Given values of bonds' spread duration volatilities, we define the beta of bond i (ie, β_i) to be the ratio of that bond's spread duration volatility to the average spread duration volatility corresponding to $\beta = 1$ (as determined below). That is:

$$\beta_i = \frac{\sigma_{v,i}}{\sigma_{v,\beta=1}}$$

(7.9)

where $\sigma_{v,\beta=1}$ is the spread duration volatility of the bond whose $\beta = 1$. To determine $\sigma_{v,\beta=1}$ on day t, we first rank values of $\sigma_{v,\beta=1}$ and calculate their percentiles. Then, as shown in Figure 7.8, we designate the value of $\sigma_{v,i}$ at the 50th percentile of the ranked values as $\sigma_{v,\beta=1}$.

The left panels of Figure 7.9 display the relationship between duration and bond βs for BABs (top) and the frequency distribution of BAB βs (bottom). For comparison, similar plots for US corporate bonds appear in the right panels. The figure illustrates that spread volatilities of BABs tend to be much less correlated with duration and much more narrowly distributed about $\beta = 1$ than their corporate counterparts. Frequency distributions of β for BABs and corporate bonds (bottom panels) also exhibit important differences. Those plots reveal that the distributions of BAB βs are bimodal with a median β less than one, whereas corporate bonds are much more normally (ie, Gaussian) distributed with a mode slightly greater than one. In addition, the distribution of BAB βs has a very long upper tail, with little density in any one region, but extending up to values of 20 or more for extreme cases. This is illustrated in the upper left panel of Figure 7.9, for which the vertical dashed line divides the region of BAB βs above and below 3.0.

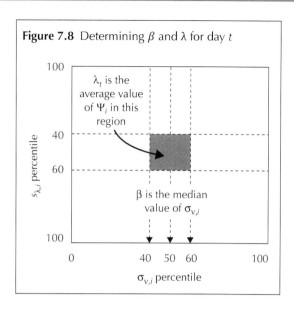

Figure 7.8 Determining β and λ for day t

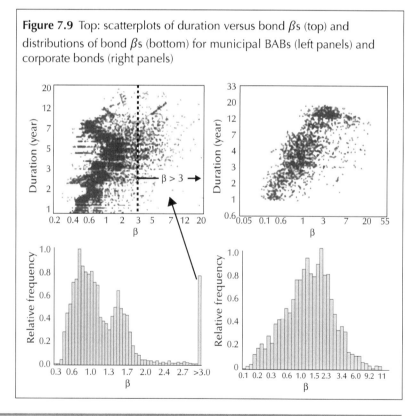

Figure 7.9 Top: scatterplots of duration versus bond βs (top) and distributions of bond βs (bottom) for municipal BABs (left panels) and corporate bonds (right panels)

Calculating the risk premium, λ_t

To calculate the BAB risk premium on day t (ie, λ_t) we first define Ψ_i for bond i as the ratio of its non-default spread to its spread duration volatility. That is:

$$\Psi_i = \frac{s_{\lambda,i}}{\sigma_{v,i}}$$

$$(7.10)$$

Given values of Ψ_i for the bonds in our sample, the risk premium on day t, λ_t is calculated as the average value of Ψ_i for all N bonds having values of $s_{\lambda,i}$ and $\sigma_{v,i}$ between the 40th and 60th percentiles as shown by the grey area in the centre of Figure 7.8. That is, we designate the ratio of the average non-default spread to spread duration volatility near $\beta = 1$ (ie, its risk premium relative to spread duration volatility) as Ψ_β, and designate that value as the risk premium λ on day t. That is:

$$\lambda_t = \frac{1}{N} \sum_{x=1}^{N} \Psi_x$$

$$(7.11)$$

for values of Ψ_x whose value of Ψ_i are from bonds with values of s_λ and $\sigma_{v,i}$ that are both within their population of percentile ranges from 41 to 60.

The resulting time series of λ_t for municipal BABs from September 2009 to June 2015 appears in Figure 7.10. The top panel of the figure shows the BAB risk premium on linear axes, with the values on λ_t in logarithmic units in the lower plot. For comparison, values of λ_t for US corporate bonds are also shown. Clearly, values of λ_t for BABs are consistently higher than those of corporate bonds. That is, risk-adjusted returns in the municipal bond market are consistently larger than those for US corporate bonds. The average value of the BAB risk premium is 4.15bp per unit of spread duration volatility, whereas the average corporate λ_t is 0.78.

The lower panel of Figure 7.10 shows the same data as the top panel but for λ_t plotted in logarithmic units. Note also that the two series have been adjusted vertically to reveal similarities in their patterns over time. Although clear deviations exist between the adjusted series of λ_t for BABs and corporates, the general temporal pattern of the risk premiums is similar.

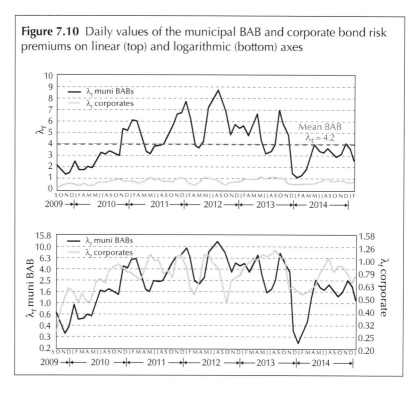

Figure 7.10 Daily values of the municipal BAB and corporate bond risk premiums on linear (top) and logarithmic (bottom) axes

To determine the factors that underlie differences in values of λ_t between BABs and corporates, we compared bond spreads to Treasuries and spread duration volatilities by rating for BABs and US corporate bonds. In particular, it seemed possible that higher municipal BAB risk premiums may result from underestimation of their spread volatilities. The left panel of Figure 7.11 displays average values of credit spreads by agency rating for BABs (light grey bars) and corporates (dark grey bars). Examples of time series of single-A credit spreads for BABs and corporates over the sample period appear in the middle and right panels of Figure 7.11. Despite the fact that, for these rating categories, historical default rates for corporates are higher than for municipal bonds, BABs yield spreads over Treasuries are consistently higher than those of similarly rated corporate bonds. Average values of spread duration volatilities by rating category are also shown for corporate bonds and BABs in the left panel of Figure 7.11. Unlike credit spreads, BAB spread duration volatilities for a given rating category are consistently below those of corporate bonds. Thus, the high values of λ_t observed for municipal BABs in Figure 7.10 are due to both higher credit spreads and lower spread volatilities. Thus, we conclude that BABs continue to offer greater risk-adjusted returns per unit of price volatility than their corporate bond counterparts.

Figure 7.11 Comparison of municipal BAB and corporate bond spreads and spread duration volatilities; top: average spreads and spread duration volatilities by rating; bottom: comparison of time series of single-A rated credit spreads

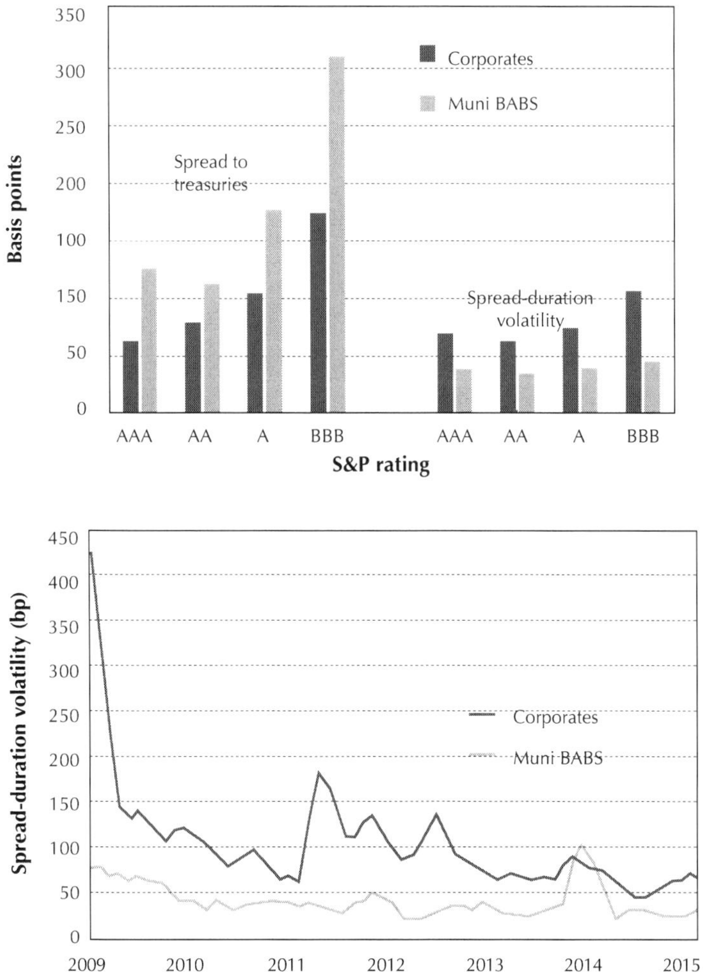

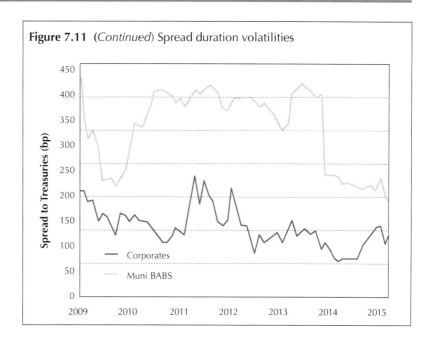

Figure 7.11 (*Continued*) Spread duration volatilities

The approach to modelling credit spreads as represented in Equation 7.6 can be viewed as an amalgamation of agency ratings, the Merton (1974) structural default model, risk-neutral pricing theory (Hull and White, 1995) and the CAPM (Traynor, 1962; Sharpe, 1964). That is, our model requires agency credit ratings for BABs, PDs for corporate bonds from the structural model, risk-neutral theory to convert PDs to spread compensations for default and the Sharpe ratio from the CAPM, which provides the rationale for estimating risk premium as the average daily spread value per unit of spread duration volatility.

SOME PROPERTIES OF THE BAB CREDIT RISK PREMIUM

This section presents statistics on the values of the daily BAB risk premium, λ_t, along with an analysis of its mean-reverting properties. To that end, consider Figure 7.12, which displays distributions of daily values of the risk premium for BABs (left panel) and US corporate bonds (right panel) over the period from September 2009 to March 2015. Although the sample period is relatively short, both means and medians of each distribution are similar, indicating that average values of λ_t are good measures of central tendency for both

BABs and corporate bonds. In addition, although the λ_t distribution for BABs exhibits some positive skew, whereas corporate λ_t values are symmetric about their mean, both BAB and corporate distributions have fat tails (ie, kurtosis well below 3.0).

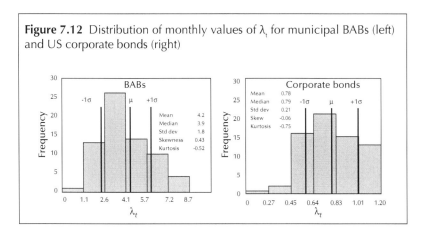

Figure 7.12 Distribution of monthly values of λ_t for municipal BABs (left) and US corporate bonds (right)

We calculated the time it would take for a positive or negative deviation in the risk premium from its average to revert back to its mean. This requires solving for the half-life of mean reversion in time series of monthly BAB and corporate bond values of λ_t. To do this, we assume that the risk premium can be modelled as an autoregressive process (Uhlenbeck and Ornstein, 1930) in which:[10]

$$d\lambda_t = \eta(\mu_\lambda - \lambda_t)\, dt + \sigma_\lambda\, dW_t \qquad (7.12)$$

where μ_λ and σ_λ are the mean and standard deviation of the time series of λ_t, W_t is a Weiner process (random Brownian motion with mean of 0.0 and standard deviation of 1.0) and η is the half-life of mean reversion.[11] The fact that the slope of the best-fit regression lines to each time series is essentially zero (ie, 0.11 and 0.0 in Table 7.2) indicates little drift in either risk premium over time. The half-lives of risk premium mean reversion are 2.2 months and 3.5 months for the BAB and corporate bond risk premiums, respectively. Thus, for an upward or downward spike in the BAB risk premium, in the absence of another shock to the risk premium, it would take slightly more than two months to retrace one-half of that move.

Table 7.2 Analysis of mean reversion in risk premiums for BABs and corporate bonds

Mean reversion	BABs	Corporates
Slope	0.11	0.0
Half-life (months)	2.2	3.5

EMBEDDED LEVERAGE ADJUSTMENT

Recall from Chapters 5 and 6 that one implication of the CAPM is that bonds' and CDS risk premiums on a given day (ie, values of Ψ_i) are a constant value, at least on average.[12] This implies that BABs' non-default spreads should be a constant fraction of their trailing spread duration volatilities. For the same reason, BABs' ratios of $\Psi_i / \Psi_{\beta = 1}$ as a function of their betas should be roughly 1.0 and should be well fit by a horizontal line. The top panel of Figure 7.13 shows BABs' ratios of $\Psi_i / \Psi_{\beta = 1}$ versus their betas. The LOWESS regression fit to the data (black lines)indicates large deviations from a ratio of one, with low-beta bonds having greater returns per unit of spread duration volatility and lower risk-adjusted returns for high-beta bonds. In fact, we find a similar, if less dramatic, pattern of deviations from uniform values of $\Psi_i / \Psi_{\beta = 1}$ for corporate bonds (see Chapter 5). Our approach is to adjust values of bonds' $\sigma_{v,i}$ based on the LOWESS fit and their values of β_i to compute adjusted values of Ψ_i such that the resulting LOWESS line is horizontal and passes through Ψ_β at $\beta = 1$. That adjustment factor, $f(\beta_i)$, is included in the definition of the credit spread in Equation 7.6 in which bonds' non-default spreads are represented as $s_{\lambda,i}$ where:

$$s_{\lambda,i} = \lambda_t^* f(\beta_i) * \sigma_{v,i} \tag{7.13}$$

The middle panel in Figure 7.13 shows the adjustment function $f(\beta_i)$ determined from the LOWESS fit in the top panel for municipal BABs on April 10, 2015. Finally, the last panel of Figure 7.13 displays ratios of Ψ_i to Ψ_β with values of Ψ_i computed using adjusted values of $\sigma_{v,i}$. The latter plot indicates that a horizontal line passing through the point Ψ_β is a reasonable fit to the data, meanwhile acknowledging the considerable variability of individual ratios about that line. The plot also shows the ratios of Ψ_i to Ψ_β by duration bucket plotted in different shades of grey. There appears to be no systematic deviation from the horizontal line for bonds in any duration bucket.

Recall that a key assumption underlying our approach is that the credit risk premium on a given day λ_t is a constant ratio of spreads to Treasuries per unit of spread duration volatility for all bonds. Since our measure of bonds' Ψ_i values are analogous to Sharpe ratios, in the absence of technical or other factors, deviations in uniformity of the risk premiums as a function of β_i (ie, the need for the $f(\beta_i)$ adjustment factor) would appear problematic. Furthermore, such a correction would be at odds both with the CAPM and commonsense. However, as we argued in Chapters 5 and 6 on the corporate and CDS risk premium, β-related deviations of Ψ_i from $\Psi_{\beta=1}$ result from embedded leverage in corporate bond spreads (Asness, Frazzini and Pedersen, 2012; Frazzini, Kabiller and Pedersen, 2012; Frazzini and Pedersen, 2012, 2014). That is, low-beta assets have larger risk adjusted returns than average, whereas high-beta assets have lower Sharpe ratios.[13]

In accordance with the rationale for the $f(\beta_i)$ adjustment, one can measure the embedded leverage on a given day as the amount of spread adjustment required to offset deviations from horizontal in the LOWESS curve in Figure 7.13. Figure 7.14 displays average spread values for BABs and US corporate bonds by agency rating category. For all rating categories, yield spreads to US Treasuries are greater for BABs than for corporate bonds. The latter result is surprising because default probabilities for municipal bonds are half or less than those for equivalently rated corporate bonds (see Figure 7.1), and BABs' recovery values in default are generally higher than those of corporate bonds (see Figure 7.1 and Table 7.1). This result also implies that borrowing rates for taxpayers, who fund municipal debt payments, are greater than their similarly risky, or even less risky, corporate counterparts. This spread difference is unlikely due to a relative lack of liquidity in the municipal bond market as the number of municipal bonds far exceeds those of corporate borrowers.

Figure 7.13 Top: ratios of Ψ_i to $\Psi_{\beta=1}$ as a function of BAB betas, β_i; bottom: correction factors $f(\beta_i)$ for day t to be applied to bonds' 100-day trailing spread duration volatilities to obtain average constant values of Ψ_i

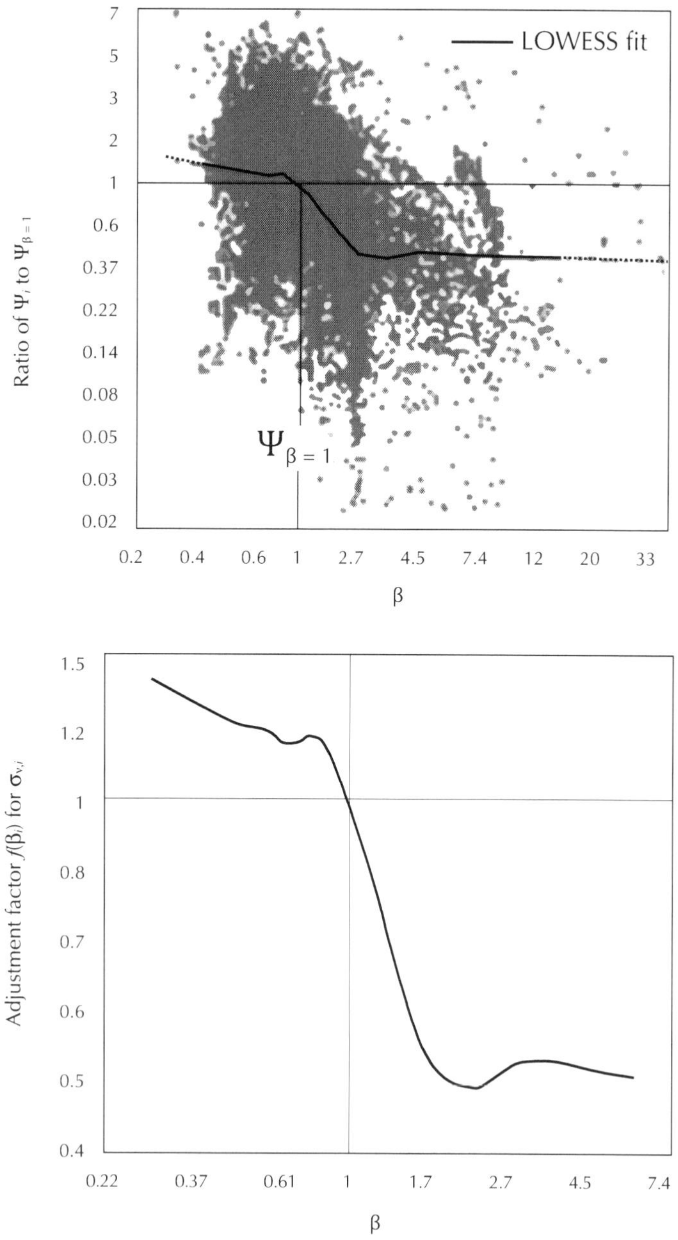

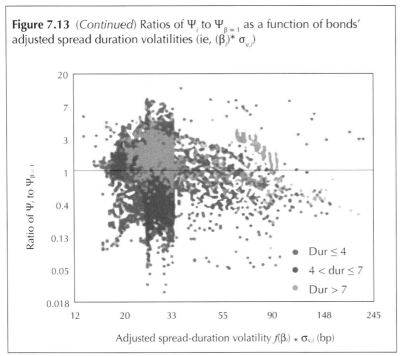

Figure 7.13 (*Continued*) Ratios of Ψ_i to $\Psi_{\beta=1}$ as a function of bonds' adjusted spread duration volatilities (ie, $(\beta_i)^* \sigma_{v,i}$)

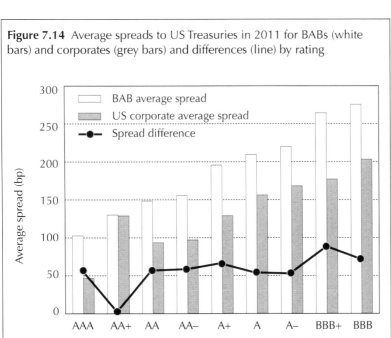

Figure 7.14 Average spreads to US Treasuries in 2011 for BABs (white bars) and corporates (grey bars) and differences (line) by rating

Municipal bond strategists suggest several reasons for the 50–100bp spread advantage of BABs over similarly rated corporate bonds (Rai, Friedlander and Muller, 2015). First, although the number of BAB issues far exceeds those of corporate bonds, BAB issue sizes tend to be smaller, so investors are concerned with potential lack of liquidity. Also, since the BAB programme has been discontinued, the stigma of an orphaned product adds to fears of illiquidity in the asset class. Rai and Friedlander (2015) argue that, despite these factors, the large size of the BAB market, BABs' large spread advantage over corporate bonds, investors' overblown fears of early BAB refunding and the long durations of many BABs all contribute to making BABs an attractive investment relative compared to equally rated corporate bonds.

RELATIVE VALUE OPPORTUNITIES IN THE BAB MARKET

If the foregoing analysis is correct, one ought to be able to design BAB trading strategies that consistently outperform the average BAB return. To that end, we examined returns on BAB portfolios of equal weight that were rebalanced monthly with strategies based on one-year spreads and spread volatilities. Thus, for these analyses, we assume that simulating trades using one-year imputed credit spreads for each issuer will not bias results obtained with actual BABs.[14] To begin, we turned our series of daily one-year spreads into a series of 26 monthly spreads from our sample of 1,023 municipal issuers as illustrated in the left side of Figure 7.15. Then, for each month in the sample period, each issuer was assigned to one of nine cells with equal numbers of bonds per cell (ie, 1023 / 9 – 114 bonds per cell). The cells were constructed based on BAB one-year spreads and volatilities as shown on the right side of Figure 7.15. That is, the bins are:

❑ high spread – low volatility;
❑ high spread – medium volatility;
❑ high spread – high volatility;
❑ medium spread – low volatility;
❑ medium spread – medium volatility;
❑ medium spread – high volatility;
❑ low spread – low volatility;
❑ low spread – medium volatility; and
❑ low spread – high volatility.

The cells in the figure are coded by the risk-adjusted return expected based on our previous findings on their ratio of spread to volatility.

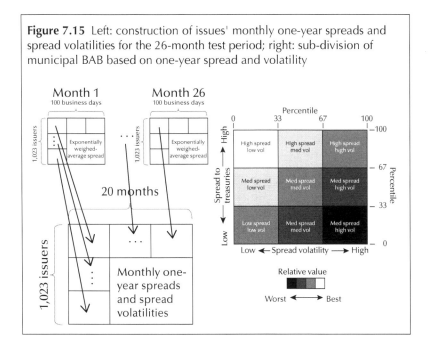

Figure 7.15 Left: construction of issues' monthly one-year spreads and spread volatilities for the 26-month test period; right: sub-division of municipal BAB based on one-year spread and volatility

The trading strategy is to overweight the one-year imputed BABs in the highest spread bucket in each volatility bucket (ie, buckets 1, 2 and 3 above) while underweighting BABs in the lowest spread bucket (ie, buckets 7, 8 and 9). Monthly cumulative non-compounded returns for each of the nine spread and volatility buckets appear in Figure 7.16. Those returns include coupon interest plus spread moves. Returns from the high (1, 2, 3), medium (4, 5, 6) and low (7, 8, 9) spread buckets are coded in dark grey, black and light grey in the figure. Several features of these results are worth noting. First, consistent with our previous analysis, returns from BABs in the high spread bucket of each volatility bucket (high, medium and low) and coded in dark grey had the largest returns. Furthermore, spreads in the lowest volatility bucket had higher returns than any of the medium or low spread buckets (buckets 4–9), even those with high volatility. Also, for high spread BABs, returns vary monotonically with volatility: high volatility BABs have the largest returns and low volatility BABs have smallest returns. However, for medium and low spread BABs, BABs in the median 33–67% volatility bucket have lower returns than BABs in the low 0–33% volatility bucket.

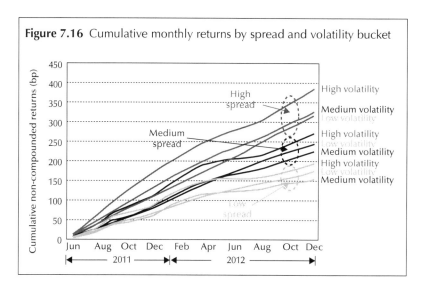

Figure 7.16 Cumulative monthly returns by spread and volatility bucket

We also examined cumulative returns by spread and volatility bucket according to issuer type and issuer size, and these results appear in Figure 7.17. Returns by issuer type and issuer size are consistent with the pattern of overall returns in Figure 7.16. The dark ellipses show that for all high spread buckets, high BABs with high spread volatilities have the largest returns, almost always followed by returns from medium spread buckets, with the smallest returns coming from low volatility BABs. In particular, the figures show that BABs with high spreads in the lowest volatility bucket consistently outperform high volatility bonds in medium and low spread buckets. Also, the grey circles show that, for medium and low spread buckets, low spread volatility BABs almost always have higher returns than medium volatility BABs. Both of these results are inconsistent with CAPM and offer promise of outsized returns relative to equal volatility portfolios.

Figure 7.17 Cumulative non-compounded returns from the nine spread and volatility cells for different issuer types (left) and issuer sizes (right)

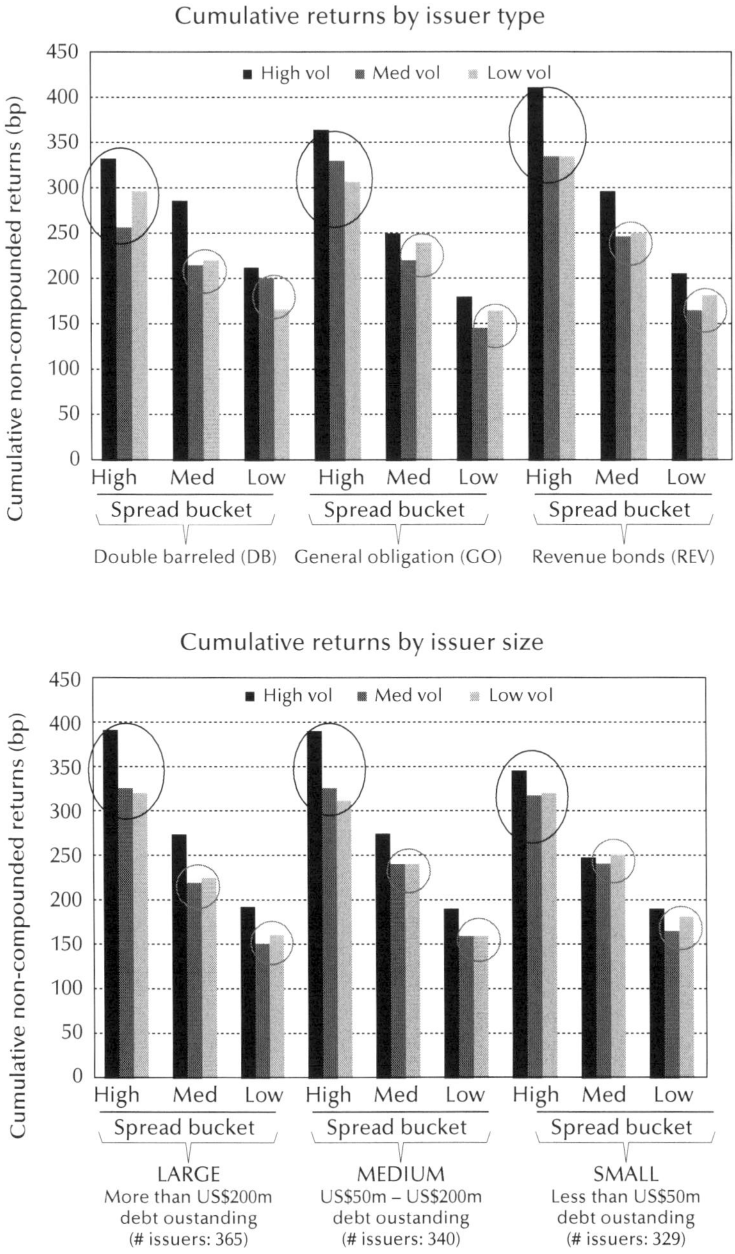

Cumulative returns by issuer type

Cumulative returns by issuer size

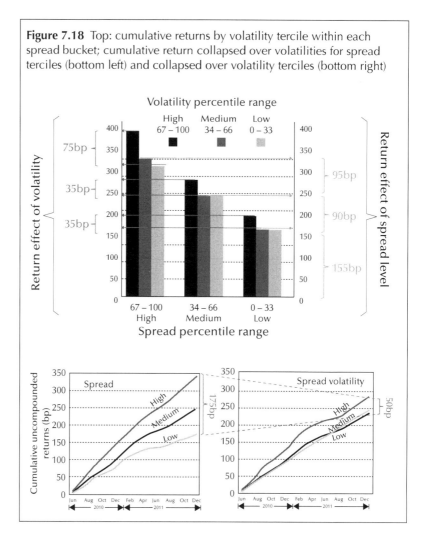

Figure 7.18 Top: cumulative returns by volatility tercile within each spread bucket; cumulative return collapsed over volatilities for spread terciles (bottom left) and collapsed over volatility terciles (bottom right)

We also investigated the relative effects of spread and volatility on one-year imputed BAB returns. According to the strict CAPM, spreads and volatilities should have equal effects on returns as their ratio should be a constant. Although the results in Figure 7.17 reject this for the BAB universe, we wished to measure it directly. Accordingly, the plot in the left panel of Figure 7.18 shows returns for high, medium and low spread terciles and by volatility tercile within each spread bucket. Inspection of the figure reveals that, within each spread bucket (0–33, 33–67, 67–100), spread matters more than volatility. That is, for the 0–33% spread bucket, spreads vary by 155bp, while the volatility range is 35bp and for the 33–67% spread bucket, spreads increase by an average of 90bp, although variations in volatility are only of 35bp. Finally, the average spread increment is 95bp as one moves from the middle spread bucket to the 67–100% bucket, while its volatility increment is only 75bp. The middle and right panels isolate the effects of spread bucket and volatility bucket, respectively, and confirm results in the top panel. That is, the effect of varying spread is three times greater than variations in volatility (175bp versus 50bp).

Finally, we examined combined returns from the high, medium and low volatility buckets within each of the three spread buckets (ie, such as those in the lower left panel of Figure 7.18) relative to that average of one-year BAB returns in the sample (ie, the index). The results appear in Figure 7.19, where the top panel shows cumulative returns from each spread bucket (the lines) versus the BAB one-year index (the bars). Note that because each spread bucket contains an equal number of bonds from each of the three volatility buckets, the CAPM would not predict differential returns. The graph shows that returns from the medium spread bucket (the dark grey line) are very close to the return for the index equivalent to the returns from the medium spread bucket. The figure also shows that cumulative returns from the high spread buckets, the black are above the index and the low spread bucket returns (grey lines) are below. The graph in the middle panel of Figure 7.19 displays monthly differences in returns from the high spread bucket versus the BAB index. Investing in a volatility matched high spread group of BABs underperformed the index (and then only slightly) in one of the 19 months tested. The table of average returns and volatilities from the high spread BABs and the index in Figure 7.19 indicates that the high spread BABs outperform the index by 5bp per month (it outperforms the low spread BABs by even more) and by 55bp on an annual basis, a 33% margin.

Figure 7.19 Top: cumulative returns by spread group; middle: monthly return differences; bottom: summary statistics

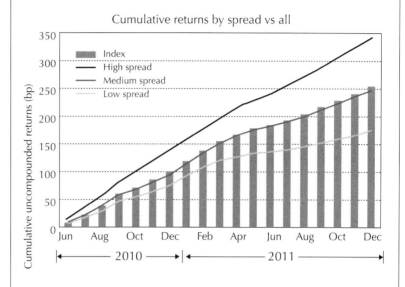

Cumulative returns by spread vs all

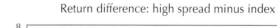

Return difference: high spread minus index

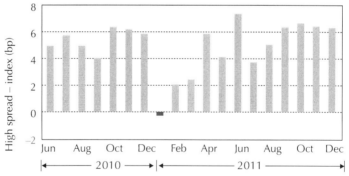

	Monthly			Annualised		
	Indx	Hi	Diff	Indx	Hi	Diff
Mean:	13	18	5	160	216	55
Std dev:	3.5	2.8	1.8	12.1	10.2	6.1
Inf ratio:	3.6	6.1	2.6	12.4	21.0	9.1

CONCLUSION

In this chapter, we applied techniques used to measure risk and relative value in the corporate bond and CDS markets to a subset of municipal bonds called BABs. The first section of the chapter described properties of BABs, their credit ratings, ratings transitions and recovery value – particularly in comparison with those of US corporate bonds. Using those relations, methods were devised for estimating default probabilities and recovery values in default for municipal bonds. We showed how, by taking differences between corporate and municipal default rates into account, one can estimate credit cycle-dependent default probabilities from municipal bonds and use those values, along with tabled values of recovery values, as inputs to our risk premium calculations.

We then described how methods for estimating the corporate credit risk premium can be applied to the BABs. Using measures of non-default spread and spread to volatility ratio, we calculated daily values of the BAB risk premium and compared those values with those of US corporate bonds. We found that, despite the lower default risk for similarly rated BABs and corporate bonds, BABs return roughly 50bp more on average than corporate bonds. Furthermore, the median spread volatility for BABs is also larger than that for corporates, and daily BAB risk premiums are always greater than those for corporates. In fact, BABs' average returns per unit of volatility are roughly twice that of corporate bonds; therefore, it can be concluded that BABs are attractive investments relative to corporate bonds in terms of both absolute and risk-adjusted returns.

Somewhat surprisingly, however, BAB non-default spreads are relatively independent of spread volatilities. That is, unlike corporate bonds, BABs lack a constant risk premium (spread to volatility ratio). Also, in conflict with the CAPM theory, we find that portfolios of high-, medium- and low-volatility BABs having the highest spreads outperform equivalent-volatility BABs having medium and low spreads. In fact, low volatility BABs with the highest spreads consistently outperform BABs with similar volatilities with medium and low spreads. Finally, it was shown that an equal volatility portfolio of high spread BABs can outperform an average volatility portfolio (ie, the index), by 55bp annually on a risk-adjusted basis.

As for corporate bonds, BABs display beta-dependent deviations from a constant risk premium, which can be attributed to embedded leverage in low- and high-beta assets. Accordingly, this reasoning allowed calculation of the first measures of embedded leverage in municipal bonds. The chapter also described the implications of these results for BAB issuers and investors. In particular, the huge advantage of BAB returns over similarly rated corporate bonds was ascribed to the fact that the BAB programme has been discontinued, to exaggerated investor fears of BAB refundings and small BAB issue sizes relative to corporate bonds. Nevertheless, these results and the views of municipal bond strategists support the view that BABs continue to offer investors attractive risk-adjusted returns relative to their corporate bond counterparts.

1   That is, the low yields on regular municipal bonds relative to similarly risky taxable bonds make them unattractive to investors who are not able to benefit from the tax credit.

2   A more detailed treatment of BABs can be found in Ang, Bhansali and Xing (2010) and Daniels *et al* (2014).

3   The only commercially available model of recovery value in default for corporate bonds is the Moody's LossCalc model (Dwyer and Korablev, 2008).

4   Examples of corporate default models include Altman (1968), Kealhofer and Kurbat (2001), Sobehart and Keenan (2002; 2003), Finger *et al* (2001).

5   Dwyer and Korablev (2008) and Benzschawel and Su (2013) have developed models for recovery value in default.

6   The HPD model generates PDs at annual intervals from one to 10 years for each firm that has tradable equity. To generate a firm's PDs from 11 to 30 years, we use its one-year marginal default rate from years nine to 10. See Chapter 5 for a detailed description of the construction of term structures of cumulative PDs for individual issuers.

7   The higher default rates for high-yield municipal bonds presumably reflects the fact the most high-yield municipal issuers began as investment grade (ie, they are "fallen angels"), and have negative credit momentum. Similar trends have been reported for corporate fallen angel firms (Fridson and Wahl, 1986).

8   For non-integer values of bonds' durations T, we define d as the truncated value of T (ie, the largest integer smaller than T) and estimate p_T for $d = 0, 1, 2 \cdots, 29$ using $p_T = \{p_d + [(T - d) * (p_{d+1} - p_d)]\}$.

9   We use bonds' 100-day trailing volatilities as estimates of instantaneous spread volatilities (or maybe even markets' views of future near-term spread volatilities).

10 A detailed explanation of how to analyse mean reversion in financial time series can be found in Dixit and Pindyck (1994).

11 The half-life of mean reversion is the time it would take for the process to move halfway back to its mean after a move away if $\sigma_\lambda = 0$. For example, if $\eta = 0$, it would be Brownian motion.

12 The notion of a constant risk premium for all credits in deeply embedded within financial theory, beginning with the work of Markowitz (1959) and Sharpe (1964, 1994). Also, the role of CRP as a guiding principle is akin to the role of the EMH (see Fama, 1965). Although

the strict assumptions of both CRP and EMH are violated routinely, they both serve as benchmarks against which explanations for deviations (market segmentation, liquidity, implicit leverage, supply and demand, etc) are based.

13   A detailed discussion of the embedded leverage effect is presented in Chapter 5.

14   To impute one-year BAB spreads, we construct spread curves by maturity for each firm in the sample using a Nelson–Siegel (1987) procedure and then impute one-year spreads for each issuer. This method is described in detail for corporate bonds in Benzschawel and Assing (2012).

Part II

NEW CREDIT MODELS AND TRADING STRATEGIES

8

Predicting Bank Defaults

As described in Chapter 1, there has been considerable success at predicting default and credit relative value for commercial and industrial firms using Merton-type structural models, such as Moody's/KMV (Vasicek, 1988; Kealhofer, 1999) model and Citi's HPD model (Sobehart and Keenan, 2002; 2003). However, generating accurate model-based estimates of PDs for financial firms has proven difficult. Some reasons for this include financials' high levels of leverage, the relative opacity of their assets and liabilities, potential support from governments, extreme risk of "tail events" and regulatory changes. Since the financial crisis of 2008–09 and the subsequent downgrade of many financial firms, investors have been increasingly interested in better assessing and managing their credit exposure to financial institutions. Also, the US Office of the Comptroller of the Currency (OCC), in accordance with the Dodd–Frank Act, has published final rules (Department of the Treasury, 2012) that remove references to credit ratings from its regulations pertaining to investment securities, securities offerings and foreign bank capital equivalency deposits.[1] Amid this backdrop, the development of accurate models for assessing bank credit risk appear critical both for managing exposure to financial firms and for compliance with federal regulations.

This chapter will describe the development and testing of time-adaptive statistical models that predict default probabilities of banks using information from their financial data as reported by the US Federal Deposit Insurance Corporation (FDIC). The model inputs are sets of financial ratios suggested in the literature to be effective in forecasting future bank failures. The model provides estimates of banks' cumulative PD profiles from one to five years out, albeit with decreasing accuracy. The model was validated through out-of-sample testing regarding its ability to predict accurately the defaults of US depository institutions between 1992 and 2012. As we find little benefit of one-year PDs models over agency ratings for already low-rated banks, we examined the performance of the bank models relative to agency ratings for banks rated above single-B minus and for those rated above single-C minus. We find that the predictive power of agency ratings drops off dramatically as the credit quality of the scoring sample increases, with much less deterioration in default prediction using the bank PD models described herein.

We will also present a detailed analysis of the contributions of financial variables to annual models developed each year (2000–12) and for each tenor (one to five years ahead). For predicting default in years one and two from the present, banks' fraction of non-performing loans, the ratios of banks' assets to their liabilities, and banks' return on equity are most important. For longer terms of three to four years, those variables give way to the ratio of net loans to bank equity and yields on earning assets. Finally, at the five-year horizon, yield on earning assets, asset size and net interest margin become the most important predictors of default.

The results described below not only provide evidence of the benefits of the adaptive statistical modelling approach over agency ratings, but also insight into short- and long-term predictors of bank failure.

MODELLING BANK DEFAULTS

The numerous bank failures amid the financial crisis of 2008–09 and the subsequent ratings downgrades of many financial firms have highlighted limitations of agency credit ratings and existing credit models to anticipate defaults for financial firms. During the crisis, many banks went from apparent solvency to default in a very short period of time, presumably reflecting the particular sensitivity of financial institutions and insurance companies to sudden declines in investor confidence. Although the credit ratings of financial firms are concentrated in the investment-grade range, results from Vazza and Kraemer (2012) as shown in Figure 8.1 demonstrate that, despite their higher credit ratings, financial firms have a faster and steeper path to default than their non-financial counterparts.[2]

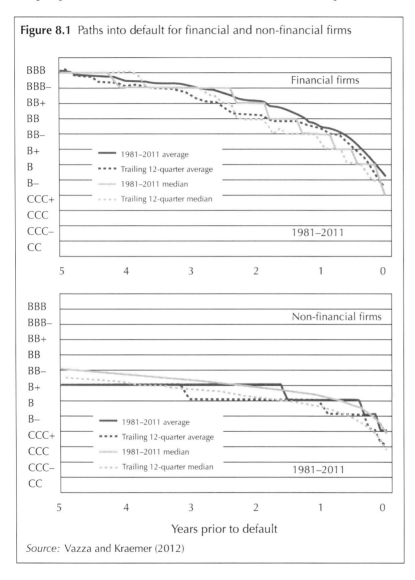

Figure 8.1 Paths into default for financial and non-financial firms

Source: Vazza and Kraemer (2012)

As highlighted in Benzschawel (2012), there are several challenges to measuring the credit quality of financial institutions. First, financial firms operate differently from most non-financial corporates, running highly levered balance sheets financed by short-term borrowing, thereby having greater exposure to market risk and funding risk.[3] As mentioned above, differences also include the relative opacity of banks' assets and liabilities, potential support from governments, extreme risk of "tail events" and exposure to regulatory changes. Although we have had success using Citi's HPD model for predicting risk of default and relative value of commercial and industrial firms, that model has proven less reliable for financial firms. There are several reasons for this.

Financial firms typically use short-term borrowing to finance long-term obligations, thereby carrying much higher leverage than similarly risky non-financial firms. As leverage is an important source of risk in structural models, Merton-type structural models typically overestimate PDs for financial firms relative to similarly risky non-financials. To correct this, structural models often embed adjustments to leverage and/or volatility for financial firms, but these modifications can cause other problems.

Although several available structural models differentiate between financial firms and industrial ones (emphasising short-term liabilities more), there are relatively few defaults by publicly traded financial firms, posing difficulties for model calibration. Thus, the financial models are calibrated to ratings upgrades and downgrades, which tend to trail perceptions of risk as indicated by credit spreads (see Benzschawel and Adler, 2002). This introduces uncertainty in mapping model outputs (a ranked risk measure) to historical default rates. Also, the asset quality of financial firms is often opaque, making it more difficult to assess the credit quality of financial firms from an examination of their financial statements.

Modelling considerations aside, it important to note that there are many banks and most are privately held firms, often unrated by major agencies. Since private firms have no publicly traded equity, Merton-type default models such as KMV and HPD cannot score those firms. As of March 2013, there were 7,019 depository institutions in the US reporting to the FDIC, with total liabilities of US$12.8 trillion.[4] For investors with broad exposure to the banking sector, it is difficult to analyse a large number of banks using fundamental analysis. Thus, rather than adapt structural models to generate PDs for financial firms, a statistical approach was chosen to estimating risk of bank failure. That is, bank defaults were modelled using an adaptive logistic regression function on information contained in banks' financial statements as published by the FDIC. The inputs to the model are financial ratios found to be effective in forecasting future bank failures, and the outputs are predictions of annual cumulative PDs for each bank from one to 30 years.

We backtested the model's ability to predict defaults of US depository institutions between 1992 and 2012. The testing dataset includes 16,520 distinct banks and 604 default events. We conducted the backtest using a walk-forward procedure. That is, to make PD predictions in any year, we only use information before that year to select model variables and calibrate the model coefficients. A walk-forward method was chosen as it best mimics how the model is to be used in practice. Estimates of PDs from the model display a high degree of accuracy in out-of-sample backtesting at predicting both relative default risk and absolute default probabilities. These aspects of performance are important for different applications, as will be discussed further below. For now, note that estimates of PDs for banks in the highest 10th percentile include 94% of the defaulting banks within the next year.[5] As described, the predictive power of the model decreases as prediction horizon is extended although the model still performs well above chance multiple years out.

CONSTRUCTING THE BANK PD MODEL
Financial variables as predictors of default

Since the pioneering work of Beaver (1966) and Altman (1968), financial modellers have realised that certain financial ratios are highly predictive of a firm's future default. The same is true for banks. For instance, we find that banks with low, especially negative, ROE are much more likely to default. Intuitively, banks with low or negative profitability will likely struggle to pay their liabilities on time and will have difficulty finding additional funding. To illustrate this effect, each panel in Figure 8.2 displays normalised distributions of ROEs for defaulting and non-defaulting banks. Distributions are shown for one-, two-, three- and four-year horizons in successive panels. Inspection of Figure 8.2 reveals that banks with low ROE are much more likely to default than those with high ROEs. Also, the predictive power of the ROE as regards default decreases with increases in the time horizon. That is, the distributions of ROEs from defaulting and non-defaulting banks are clearly apart from each other at one- and two-year horizons, but those differences narrow, becoming very small at four years out (this likely reflects the fact that financial firms with poor current ROE are no longer solvent after year two). T-tests on the differences between the distributions of ROEs for defaulting and non-defaulting banks cease to be significant over four years out.

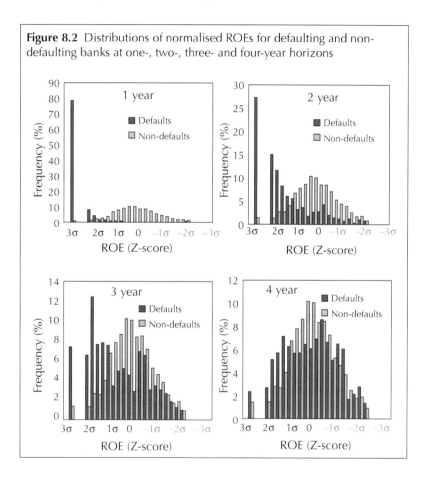

Figure 8.2 Distributions of normalised ROEs for defaulting and non-defaulting banks at one-, two-, three- and four-year horizons

A similar testing procedure as illustrated in Figure 8.2 for ROE revealed other financial ratios that are useful for default prediction. These include firms' leverage ratios, ratios of non-performing to performing loans and net loans to bank capital. A challenge in predicting default is to select an appropriate set of variables and combine them appropriately in a multivariate model. To do this, we applied a walk-forward logistic regression technique. The logistic regression function (described in the following section) is commonly used for predicting variables with binary outcomes, particularly when the inputs are non-linearly related to the desired output. The walk-forward method constructs a new model each year from the candidate variable set while adding the data from the previous year to the development sample. For variable selection in each new model, we used an automated procedure called forward stepwise selection, which is explained below.

Logistic regression

Logistic regression has similarities to the more familiar multiple linear regression method, but involves an extra step: the logistic transform. This is illustrated for a set of hypothetical input variables in Figure 8.3. The application begins with selection of a set of candidate financial variables, denoted x_i, $i = 1, \dots, n$. The inputs, x_i, could be financial ratios or other quantities. The lower portion of Figure 8.3 depicts how values of hypothetical input variables (the circles in each plot) are fit by functions, of the form:

$$f(x_i) = \alpha_i + \beta_i x_i \qquad (8.1)$$

to derive constants, α_i, and coefficients, β_i, for each input variable.

Then, for a given set of inputs, each x_i is put through its linear transform in Equation 8.1. For variable x_1 for the example in Figure 8.3, the constant $\alpha_1 = 0$ and the coefficient $\beta_1 = -3$. Thus, if $x_1 = 0.5$ as shown in the figure, $f(x_1) = -1.5$. Hypothetical functions and outputs for x_2 and x_n are also shown in Figure 8.3.

The resulting outputs of the first stage of the logistic regression, the values $f(x_i)$, are summed at an intermediate stage whose output z can be represented as:

$$z = \beta_0 + \sum_{i=1}^{n} \beta_i x_i \qquad (8.2)$$

where:

$$\beta_0 = \sum_{i=1}^{n} \alpha_i$$

(8.3)

For the example in Figure 8.3, the resulting value of z is assumed to be -1.2. The value of z from Equation 8.2 is then put through the logistic transform, which serves to constrain the output of the regression to a value between 0 and 1. For example, for the default model, the resulting value is given as:

$$\varphi(z) = \frac{1}{1 + e^z}$$

(8.4)

Figure 8.3 Logistic regression function; linear transformations of financial variables (lower plots) are summed at an intermediate stage and put through the logistic transform (top graph), which converts the output to a value between 0 and 1 (0% and 100%)

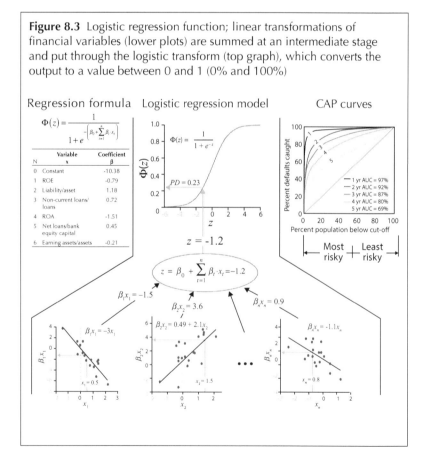

Automated selection of input variables

Note that the method involves deriving a new model each year, incorporating into the learning sample the data from each successive year's defaulting and non-defaulting firms. As the factors that influence defaults and their relative contributions may change over time, we chose an adaptive procedure for selecting variables for each annual model. A set of 20 candidate financial ratios was selected that have been shown to be predictive of subsequent default. Since the distributions of different financial ratios can also vary widely, those ratios were converted into standard normal distributions before testing their usefulness as inputs to each annual model.

The process of model construction begins with only the logistic function and no variables chosen for inclusion. Then, for each candidate input variable, we build a logistic default model by selecting values of α_i and β_i for each variable that enables the best prediction of default on the development sample. That is, for each input variable x_i, we solve for α_i and β_i in the following equation:

$$\varphi(z) = \frac{1}{1 + e^{-(\alpha_i + \beta_i x_i)}} \tag{8.5}$$

The variable with the greatest predictive power with respect to default is chosen as the first input variable. As described in further detail below, we chose the Bayesian information criterion (BIC), developed by Schwartz (1978), as the measure of predictive power. The Bayesian information criterion (BIC), measures how well the model fits the data, but also imposes a penalty for having too many variables, thereby guarding against overfitting the data. After selection of the first variable, the process is repeated to select a second variable, and so on until model performance ceases to improve. Once all the variables for the model are selected, the value of the constant β_0 and coefficients β_i $(i = 1, \dots, n)$ for each of the variables are refit to minimise the error in the logistic regression equation:

$$\varphi(z) = \frac{1}{1 + e^{-(\beta_0 + \sum_{i=1}^{n} \beta_i x_i)}} \tag{8.6}$$

An illustration of the results of variable selection is presented in Figure 8.4. The top portion of the left panel displays the logistic regression equation, with the table below lists the input variables to the model in the order in which they are selected. That is, variables are listed in descending order of their predictive power. The BIC values resulting from inclusion of each variable are also displayed. The right portion of Figure 8.4 is a plot of the BIC values that result from the inclusion of each variable. For instance, the model starts with only a constant term whose BIC value is 8,174. The variable selection procedure determined that banks' ROE provides the largest predictive power of all candidate variables, and its inclusion in the model achieves a BIC of 4,274. After selection of the ROE, the procedure is run again, picking the liability/asset ratio as the best of the remaining candidate variables, bringing the BIC down to 3,738. This procedure continued until the BIC could no longer be decreased. At that point, six variables had been selected and their corresponding coefficients appear in the left table of Figure 8.4.

Figure 8.4 Left: one-year bank PD model equation, variables and corresponding coefficients (light grey: less risky; dark grey: more risky), with variables listed in the order selected; right: BIC for each successive variable selected

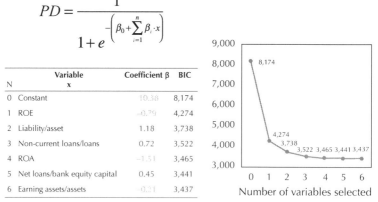

$$PD = \frac{1}{1 + e^{-\left(\beta_0 + \sum_{i=1}^{n} \beta_i \cdot x\right)}}$$

N	Variable x	Coefficient β	BIC
0	Constant	10.38	8,174
1	ROE	−0.79	4,274
2	Liability/asset	1.18	3,738
3	Non-current loans/loans	0.72	3,522
4	ROA	−1.51	3,465
5	Net loans/bank equity capital	0.45	3,441
6	Earning assets/assets	−0.21	3,437

Converting model scores to default probabilities

Values of $\Phi(z)$ from the model can be shown to be highly correlated with default probability (see right panel of Figure 8.3). That is, the model appears to perform well at ranking the relative default risk of US banks. However, when outputs of the model (ie, values of $\Phi(z)$) were linked to actual physical default probabilities, the resulting values proved less than satisfactory. Accordingly, in this section we link values of $\Phi(z)$ from the bank model to default probabilities from the HPD model.

The approach to transforming values of $\Phi(z)_i$, for $i = 1,...,5$, where i indicates the model for a given default year contingent upon survival to year $i - 1$, is straightforward. For those banks that have PDs from the HPD model, we plot HPD PDs versus values of $ln\Phi(z)_i$ from the bank model as shown in the left panel of Figure 8.5 for the one-year model (ie, $i = 1$). Then, we fit the points with a second-order polynomial of the form:

$$PD_i = a_i + [b_i * ln\Phi(z)_i] + [c_i * ln\Phi(z)_i^2] \tag{8.7}$$

as shown by the grey line in left panel of Figure 8.5 for which $i = 1$, and $a_1 = 5.5$, $b_1 = 0.68$ and $c_1 = 0.02$. It is important to note that we impose monotonicity on the function in Equation 8.7 to ensure that the conversion from $ln\Phi(z)$ to PD does not change the ordering of banks as regards their default risk. Thus, the transformation in Equation 8.7 merely serves to convert model outputs to physical PDs and does not alter the CAP curves shown in the right panel of Figure 8.3.

Figure 8.5 Mappings between bank model outputs, $\ln\Phi_i(z)$ and HPD PDs; left: best-fit order 2 polynomial of HPD PDs to $\ln\Phi_i(z)$; right: best-fit order polynomial 2 to $\ln\Phi_1(z)$ for $\ln\Phi_i(z)$ for $i = 1, ... , 5$ models

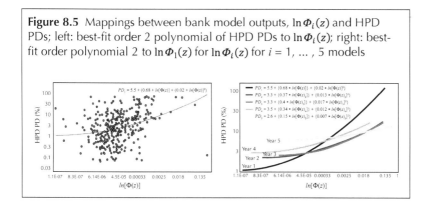

The right panel of Figure 8.5 shows the mapping from $ln\Phi(z)$ to PD function for the one-year model (ie, $i = 1$) using the black line, along with the functions for models for years two to five. The coefficients of a_i, b_i and c_i for each of the curves are inset in the graph. Finally, note that these mapping functions are only used for the current set of models. Although the mapping in Figure 8.5 is for December 5, 2013, this mapping can be updated daily to reflect changes in banks' PDs from the HPD model.

WALK-FORWARD BACKTESTING

The bank models were backtested by constructing annual series of one- to five-year models using all available US bank data from 1992 to 2012. The number of non-defaulting banks and defaulting banks in the sample by year are given by the dark grey bars (left axis) and the light grey bars (right axis), respectively, in Figure 8.6. Note that there were roughly 14,000 banks in the sample in 1993, but that number had declined to around 7,000 by 2012. Also, there are three apparent waves of defaults: one in the early 1990s, a small one around the year 2000 and a surge of bank failures during the global financial crisis.

Figure 8.6 Number of non-defaulting banks (dark grey bars, left axis) and defaulting banks (light grey bars, right axis) banks by year in the development dataset

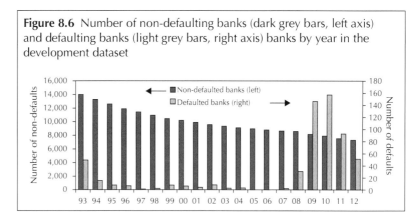

To determine out-of-sample performance of the model, we used a walk-forward procedure as illustrated in Figure 8.7 for the one-year model. The test set is sufficiently large, with a total of 499 defaulters out of 11,114 distinct banks, to provide a strong test of model performance. As the model needs a minimum number of years of data for development, data from the years 1992–99 were used to construct the first annual model (select variables and calibrate the weights) for each horizon for one to five years. The one-year model for 1999 was then used to score all non-defaulting banks at the beginning of 2000, and its ability to predict defaults in 2000 was determined. Predictions from models for years two to five tested only banks that had survived to the model year. Thus, for the two-year model, firms surviving until 2001 were scored with its 1999 model, and so forth for the longer horizons. To generate the set of models for year 2000 (ie, used to predict defaults in 2001–05 for one- to five-year models), we added the data from year 2000 to the set from 1992 to 1999. Variables were selected and coefficients determined, and the model was tested on the corresponding test sample for the given horizon. That procedure was repeated annually until 2012. Of course, from models at horizons longer than one year, testing was achievable only to year 2012 minus the horizon year. We adopted the walk-forward procedure because it most realistically estimates the performance of the model as it will be deployed in practice.

Figure 8.7 Illustration of the walk-forward development and testing procedure for the one-year models; a new model is developed each year from 1999 to 2011 using data from all previous years and tested on defaulted and non-defaulted banks in each subsequent year from 2000 to 2012; for models with two- to five-year horizons, test samples consisted of firms surviving until year X+2 to X+5, respectively

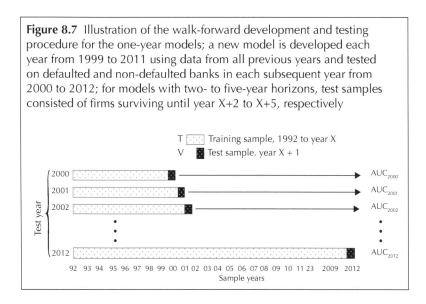

To evaluate model performance at separating banks that will default from non-defaulters, we generated CAP curves for the one- to five-year model horizons. The cumulative resulting CAP curves

for test years 1999–2012 are displayed in Figure 8.8. For example, to generate the one-year curve (black line), we first rank all banks over the entire 13-year test period from highest to lowest by their one-year PDs from the models. Then, for successive intervals in the ranked population, we calculate the cumulative fraction of default-ing banks contained within that interval. The interpretation of CAP curves is straightforward; for any criterion, the fraction of default-ers caught above the population percentile measures the discrimi-natory power of the model. For example, the CAP curve for the one-year model at the 10% population criterion caught 94% of the banks that defaulted within the following year over the period 1999–2012.

Figure 8.8 Left: CAP curves for predictions of bank defaults for one- to five-year models using walk-forward testing from 1999 to 2012; right: values of the one- to five-year CAP curves at critical thresholds, with corresponding values from the chance line also shown

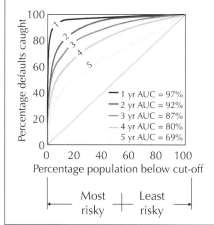

	Percent defaults caught			
	Population inside cut-off			
	10%	20%	30%	50%
One year	94	96	97	98
Two year	90	87	91	97
Three year	68	78	85	92
Four year	55	67	74	86
Five year	40	52	60	71
Chance	10	20	30	50

The higher and steeper the CAP curve over the diagonal chance line, the better the model is at discriminating defaulters from non-defaulters. The table on the right in Figure 8.8 displays values of the CAP curves for each of the model horizons for various values of the population cut-off. The left-most values in the table show that the 10% of banks ranked riskiest by the one- to five-year models capture 94%, 80%, 68%, 55% and 40% of the defaulting banks, respectively. Not surprisingly, those data reveal that the power of the models decline as the prediction horizon extends beyond one year, but even the five-year model is performing well above chance, capturing 40% of the banks that default in the fifth year after model development and scoring. Finally, it is important to note that even though the models are only regenerated on an annual basis, the financial data from the banks is available to update bank default scores on a quarterly basis, and that is how the model is to be used in practice.

PERFORMANCE OF THE BANK MODEL RELATIVE TO AGENCY CREDIT RATINGS

We next evaluate the extent to which the bank default models offer advantages over using agency ratings for assessing bank risk. In addition, we examine the models' abilities to predict defaults for banks not already recognised by the agencies as risky. That is, "How well do the models predict defaults for banks with credit ratings above triple-C, single-B and so on?" To address those questions, we performed the series of studies reported in this section.

Of particular interest to investors is the riskiness of smaller and/or lower-rated financial firms, particularly savings and loans (SNL) and bank holding companies (BHCs). This is because debt from those financial firms is often placed in trust-preferred securities (TRUPs). As returns and payouts from TRUPs are highly dependent on defaults and ratings downgrades, those investors are particularly interested in accurate assessments of default probabilities and signals of deteriorating credit quality. To test this, we examined the relative predictive power of ratings by Kroll, which are best known in this space, and the bank default models for SNL and BHCs.

To test the predictive power of the regression model versus agency ratings, we first determined those financial firms that have both model scores and Kroll agency ratings. Kroll has three categories of financial firms: BHCs, SNL and banks (not identified). We obtained Kroll ratings for as many financial institutions as possible over the period 2000–12. The number of banks having Kroll ratings and bank model scores appear in Figure 8.9, broken down by BHCs and SNL. Clearly, it appears that Kroll rates significantly fewer financial firms than are scored by the bank model. This is partly due to Kroll not rating new banks within the first three years of their existence. It is also possible that we received only partial data on

Kroll bank ratings. Nevertheless, as shown in Figure 8.9 there are roughly 1,000 firms each year having both Kroll ratings and bank model scores, and these are typically the lower rated portion of the financial services firms. Importantly, as shown in Table 8.1, there are at least a reasonable number of defaults for testing model, at least when results are aggregated over the 13-year test period.[6]

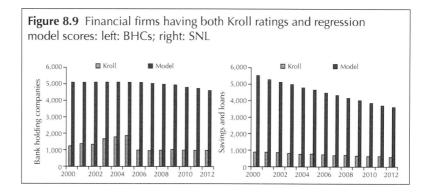

Figure 8.9 Financial firms having both Kroll ratings and regression model scores: left: BHCs; right: SNL

Table 8.1 Number of defaults for testing one- to five-year models

	Number of defaults				
	Horizon (years)				
	1	2	3	4	5
BHC	61	121	172	215	317
SNL	109	214	312	403	459

To test the predictive power of the bank models versus agency ratings, we first determined those financial firms that have both model scores and agency ratings. The left panel of Figure 8.10 shows the Kroll rating scale, where ratings range from single-A plus to default (D). The middle and right panels of Figure 8.10 display the distributions of BHCs and SNL by Kroll credit ratings, respectively, for financial firms having both Kroll credit ratings and bank model scores. Note that Kroll does not rate many banks or SNL at A+ or A–. Of course, there are relatively few very low rated (single-C plus to single-C minus) financial institutions as it is very difficult for low-rated financial institutions to survive for long. Note also that there are fewer SNL than BHCs in the sample.

Figure 8.10 Kroll rating scale for financial firms (left) and distributions of bank holding companies (middle) and savings and loans (right) with both bank model scores and Kroll credit ratings

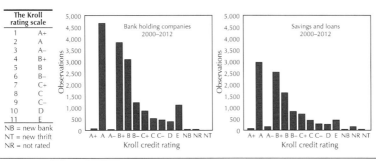

We computed CAP curves for predicting bank defaults using Kroll agency ratings and the bank model. Figure 8.11 displays CAP curves for BHCs (top) and SNL (bottom) for predicting default in years one to four. The curves for Kroll ratings and the Citi bank model are presented in each graph for comparison. A useful measure of predictive power from CAP analysis is the AUC, which is the percentage of the area under each CAP curve. The AUCs for Kroll ratings and the bank model are inset in each plot.

Table 8.2 Areas under the CAP curves for Kroll agency ratings and bank models for BHCs and SNL

	Horizon (Years)							
	1		2		3		4	
	BHC	SNL	BHC	SNL	BHC	SNL	BHC	SNL
Kroll	96	97	92	91	84	83	73	77
Citi	98	99	96	99	91	89	85	83
C-K	2	2	4	8	7	6	8	6

Several features of the data in Figure 8.11 are of interest. First, it is clear that both the bank default model and the Kroll agency ratings order banks' risk at better than chance levels, even out to four years. It is also evident that the predictive accuracy for both models decreases as the year of prediction gets farther out in time.[7] Visual inspection of AUCs in the top and bottom panels is sufficient to conclude that each model's performance for BHCs and SNL are similar. This is confirmed by values of AUCs listed in tabular form in Table 8.2 for each model and year (these same values are inset in each plot in Figure 8.11). That is, AUCs for BHCs and SNLs within each model vary at most by 4% and often only by 1%.

Figure 8.11 and Table 8.2 also allow quantitative comparisons of performance between Kroll ratings and the bank default models. Again, visual inspection of the CAP curves in Figure 8.11 is sufficient to conclude that the adaptive regression model performs better than Kroll ratings, particularly as the time horizon increases. Notably, for one-year predictions the models are both quite good: AUCs for the bank model are 98% and 99% for BHCs and SNLs, respectively, with AUCs for Kroll ratings being 96% and 97%. Still, as shown in the last row of Table 8.2, the bank default model edges out Kroll ratings even at one year, with that advantage tending to increase with the prediction horizon. In fact, for all eight CAP curves in Figure 8.11 AUCs for the adaptive regression model are greater than those for Kroll ratings.

Despite the success of the bank default model in predicting defaults, market participants have remarked that predicting bank defaults at short horizons is not difficult. That is, they claim that bank failures tend to be rapid and fairly obvious. Some suggest that deterioration of banks' credit is reflected in high levels of non-performing loans and loss of investor confidence as evidenced by rapid withdrawal of banks' necessary short-term funding. Furthermore, agency ratings are sufficient to capture those aspects of bank performance. That the Kroll ratings and bank default model have extremely high predictive power at the one-year horizon is consistent with that view. However, the predictive power of the bank model at longer horizons relative to agency ratings suggests that the bank model is adding value. We evaluate these issues in the next section.

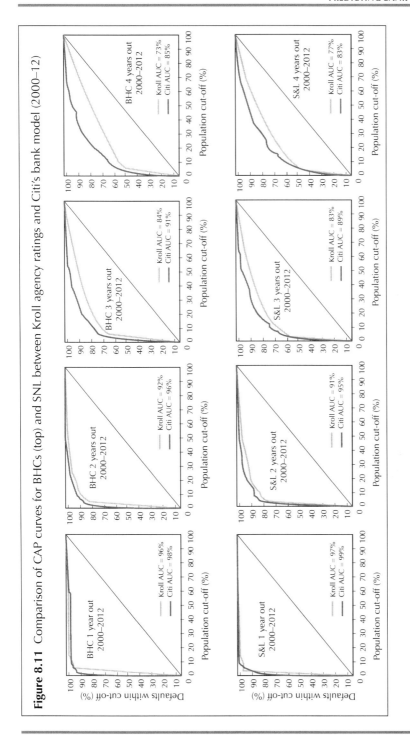

Figure 8.11 Comparison of CAP curves for BHCs (top) and SNL between Kroll agency ratings and Citi's bank model (2000–12)

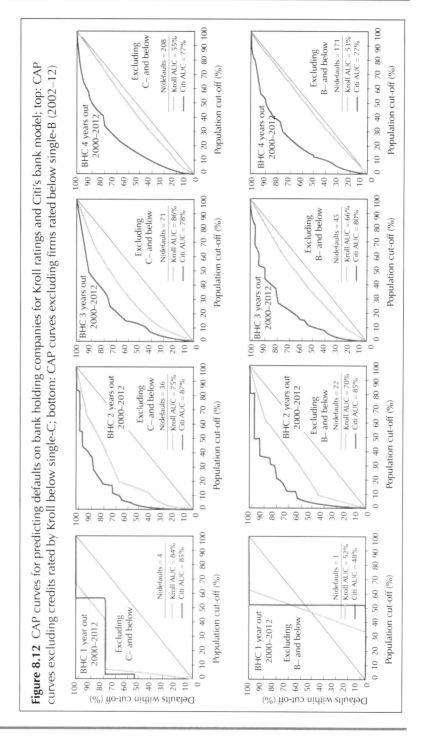

Figure 8.12 CAP curves for predicting defaults on bank holding companies for Kroll ratings and Citi's bank model; top: CAP curves excluding credits rated by Kroll below single-C; bottom: CAP curves excluding firms rated below single-B (2002–12)

PREDICTING DEFAULT FOR LESS RISKY BANKS

One way to assess the added value of bank default models, given that low-rated financials have already been recognised by agencies and investors as risky, is to exclude the riskiest obligors from the analysis of performance. To that end, in separate analyses we eliminated all those obligors rated by Kroll's below single-C (ie, single-C minus and below) and all those banks Kroll rates below single-B (single-B minus and below).[8] We then computed CAP curves and AUCs on those sub-samples as in Figure 8.11 and Table 8.2, respectively. The resulting CAP curves and table of AUCs for BHCs appear in 8.12 and the left table in Table 8.3, respectively.[9] Consider first the CAP curves in Figure 8.12. CAP curves excluding BHCs rated below single-C appear by horizon in the top panels and those excluding BHCs rated below single-B appear in the lower panels. First, note that only one firm rated below single-C and four BHCs rated below single-B default within one year. This confirms our intuition stated above, that predicting bank defaults at short horizons is not difficult given their low agency ratings. That is, the defaults that occur within one year of risk scoring occur almost exclusively for banks rated below single-C by the Kroll agency.

The pattern of CAP curves in Figure 8.12 is similar for banks rated by Kroll at or below single-C minus and single-B minus. First, for all horizons greater than one year, the bank PD model outperforms Kroll agency ratings. Also, performance appears to decrease as the time horizon increases from two to four years, but decreases in performance are greater for Kroll ratings than for the bank model. We note that for predicting defaults at the four-year horizon, the CAP curves indicated that Kroll ratings are nearly at chance, whereas the bank model is performing well above chance. Interestingly, performance of both the bank model and Kroll ratings do not appear to change significantly between BHC samples that exclude firms below single-C or single-B.

The features of the CAP curves mentioned above for BHCs are presented quantitatively as AUCs in the top portion of Table 8.3. That is, except for one year (as discussed above), AUCs from the bank model are greater than those for Kroll ratings at all tenors, by 8% to 14%. The pattern is similar when excluding either BHCs rated below C or B. That is, performance appears to drop off for both models as the prediction horizon increases, but performance drops off more dramatically for Kroll ratings, being close to chance at the four-year horizon. Also, AUCs for cases where BHCs below B and C are excluded are remarkably similar; model performances do not drop off appreciably when the criterion for inclusion in the sample is raised to B and above from C and above.

Table 8.3 Areas under the CAP curves (AUCs) excluding firms rated by Kroll as single-C-minus and below and single-B minus and below for BHCs (top) and SNL (bottom)

	Bank holding companies (BHCs)							
	Horizon (years)							
	1		2		3		4	
Exclude Below	C	B	C	B	C	B	C	B
N(defaults)	4	1	36	22	71	45	208	171
Kroll	84	52	75	70	66	66	55	53
Regression	85	48	87	85	79	80	77	77
Regression–Kroll	1	−2	12	15	13	14	12	14

	Savings and loans (SNL)							
	Horizon (years)							
	1		2		3		4	
Exclude Below	C	B	C	B	C	B	C	B
N(defaults)	3	1	27	14	71	45	116	85
Kroll	77	55	77	61	66	59	62	60
Regression	82	89	86	80	79	78	77	76
Regression–Kroll	5	34	9	21	13	19	15	16

The lower portion of Table 8.3 lists similar measures for SNL. The pattern of results mimics those for the BHCs in the upper portion. That is, the bank model outperforms Kroll ratings at all tenors when SNLs rated below C and B are excluded. Also, AUCs tend to decrease with increases in year of default prediction, but those decreases, while slight for adaptive regression model, are greater for Kroll agency ratings. Finally, the performance of both adaptive regression model and Kroll's ratings are similar when either SNLs below C and B are excluded from the analysis.

ANALYSIS OF VARIABLE CONTRIBUTIONS

From the analysis of the CAP curves and AUCs above, it is clear that the bank model continues to perform well even as the year of default prediction moves out. One of the reasons for this is that the bank model uses different sets of variables to predict default at each successive annual horizon. Accordingly, in this section we report on the contributions of the various candidate variables to the models, both over our timeframe of testing from 2000 to 2012 and for tenors of one to five years.

Consider first variables selected for the one-year model. The first portion of Table 8.4 lists the variables selected each year from 2000 to 2012 for the one-year model using the walk-forward development and testing procedure. The number associated with each variable is the order in which the variable was chosen based on its BIC. Those variables having no value associated with them in a given year were not selected for that year's model. The table shows that the most important variable for predicting one-year default is firms' ROE. The ROE was the first variable chosen for one-year models in every year. The ratio of liabilities to assets is also important for short-term default predictions, being chosen second for all years except 2010. Contributions from other variables are less consistent over time. For example, prior to 2009, earning assets to total assets is the third variable selected for all models, but was not even selected in 2010 or 2011, being selected last in 2012. Conversely, the ratio of non-current loans to loans was not selected at all in 2000, gradually increasing in its importance, such that from 2009 onward it was either the second or third most important predictor of default. Other variables having contributions to one-year default prediction are the yield on earning assets over the period from 2004 to 2009, and latterly, the return on assets (ROA), the total assets and the ratio of non-current loans to al-lowance for loan losses. Finally, note that there is a tendency for the number of important variables to increase over the testing period, with early models having only four or five variables, expanding to seven variables by 2011 (see last row of Table 8.4).

Table 8.4 Potential model variables and their order of selection for the one-year model for 2000–12

Variables	2000	2001	2002	2003	2004	2005	2006	2007	2008	2009	2010	2011	2012
					Order in which selected (1,2, ...)								
ROE	1	1	1	1	1	1	1	1	1	1	1	1	1
Liabilities / assets	2	2	2	2	2	2	2	2	2	2	3	2	2
Non-current loans / loans		5	5	5	5	4	4	4	4	3	2	3	3
Net operation income / assets	4	4	4	4	4	5	5	5	5	6	6	7	
Earning assets / assets	3	3	3	3	3	3	3	3	3	4			7
Yield on earning asset					6	6	6	6	6	5			
ROA											4	4	4
Assets											5	6	6
Non-current loans / loan loss allowance												5	5
Net loans / bank equity capital													
Annual default rate													
Assets 90 days past due / 30–89 days past due													
Net interest income / earning assets													
Net interest margin													
Num of Vars selected	4	5	5	5	6	6	6	6	6	6	6	7	7

Table 8.4 (*Continued*) Summary of variable selection, displaying probability of selection and average order if selected for the one-year model

Variables	One-year model	
	Probabitlity of selection	Average order if selected
ROE	100%	1.0
Liabilities / assets	100%	2.1
Non-current loans / loans	92%	3.9
Net operation income /assets	92%	4.9
Earning assets / assets	85%	3.5
Yield on earning asset	46%	5.8
ROA	23%	4.0
Assets	23%	5.7
Non-current loans / loan loss allowance	15%	5.0
Net loans / bank equity capital	0%	-
Annual default rate	0%	-
Assets 90 days past due / 30–89 days past due	0%	-
Net interest income / earning assets	0%	-
Net interest margin	0%	-

The second portion of Table 8.4 summarises the consistency of variable contributions to the one-year models over time, both in terms of what percentage of the 13 yearly models each variable was included, but also its average place in the hierarchy of contributions if selected. As mentioned, ROE was selected as the first variable using the BIC 100% of the time, with the ratio of Liabilities to Assets also chosen in all models, but having an average in the order of 2.1 owing to its third position in the 2010 model. The percentage of non-current loans and net operating income to assets is in 92% of the annual models at roughly fourth and fifth rank, whereas the fraction of earning assets is in 85% of the models, but when included has an average rank of 3.5. After those variables, contributions drop off rapidly, with the yield on earning assets in 46% of the models, but only at a rank of 5.8, followed by ROA and total assets at 28%. Finally, non-current loans to loan loss allowance is in 15% of the annual one-year models at a rank of fifth. Variables never included in any of the annual one-year models are: net loans to bank equity capital; annual default rate; ratio of assets 90 days past due to those 30–60 days past due; net interest income to earning assets; and net interest margin.

Table 8.5 presents summaries of the consistency of variable contributions to the two-, three-, four- and five-year models over time, analogous to that shown for the one-year model as seen in the second portion of Table 8.4. The figures reveal shifts in the importance of various predictive variables over time. For example, the ROE, most important for the one-year model, becomes successively unimportant for predicting default in later years, not even being included on any of the annual four- or five-year models. Liabilities to assets, also important at one year, declines immediately to around 30% at two years and remains at about that frequency, but never of greater importance than a rank of third. Conversely, net loans to bank equity capital, not included in any one-year models, is in every model at two and three years, maintaining its contribution, albeit in lesser amounts, out to five years. Meanwhile, the yield on earning assets, only marginally important at one year, becomes more important at longer horizons, being one of the most important at three to four years.

Table 8.5 Summary of variable selection, displaying probability of selection and average order if selected for annual two-, three-, four- and five-year bank default models

Two-year model		
Variables	Probabitlity of selection	Average order if selected
Non-current loans / loans	100%	1.1
Net loans / bank equity capital	100%	3.6
ROE	92%	2.7
Yield on earning asset	85%	4.2
Earning assets / assets	85%	4.3
Assets 90 days past due / 30–90 days past due	31%	5.8
Annual default rate	23%	5.3
Liabilities / assets	23%	5.7
Assets	23%	5.7
Net interest income / earning assets	15%	8.0
Net operation income /assets	0%	-
Net interest margin	0%	-
ROA	0%	-
Non-current loans / loan loss allowance	0%	-

Three-year model		
Variables	Probabitlity of selection	Average order if selected
Net loans / bank equity capital	100%	1.8
Non-current loans / loans	100%	2.1
Yield on earning asset	92%	4.3
Net operation income /assets	69%	3.9
Liabilities / assets	31%	3.0
Annual default rate	23%	2.0
Assets	23%	5.7
Assets 90 days past due / 30–90 days past due	23%	6.0
ROE	15%	4.5
Net interest income / earning assets	15%	9.0
Net interest margin	8%	10.0
Non-current loans / loan loss allowance	8%	11.0
Earning assets / assets	0%	-
ROA	0%	-

Table 8.5 (*Continued*)

Four-year model		
Variables	**Probabitlity of selection**	**Average order if selected**
Yield on earning asset	77%	2.3
Non-current loans / loans	69%	2.4
Net operation income /assets	69%	2.7
Annual default rate	31%	2.0
Liabilities / assets	31%	3.0
Net loans / bank equity capital	31%	4.0
Assets 90 days past due / 30–90 days past due	23%	1.3
Assets	15%	4.0
ROA	8%	6.0
Net interest margin	8%	7.0
Net interest income / earning assets	8%	8.0
ROE	0%	-
Earning assets / assets	0%	-
Non-current loans / loan loss allowance	0%	-

Five-year model		
Variables	**Probabitlity of selection**	**Average order if selected**
Yield on earning asset	54%	2.6
Assets	46%	4.0
Net interest margin	38%	3.6
Earning assets / assets	31%	1.0
Annual default rate	31%	2.5
Net loans / bank equity capital	23%	2.7
Assets 90 days past due / 30–90 days past due	23%	3.0
Liabilities / assets	23%	4.3
Net interest income / earning assets	23%	6.
Non-current loans / loans	15%	8.0
Net operation income /assets	8%	2.0
ROA	8%	2.0
ROE	0%	-
Non-current loans / loan loss allowance	0%	-

Figure 8.13 Description and comparison of important variables for bank defaults at one- to five-year horizons

One-year model

- Most important variables:
  - Return on equity
  - Liabilities / assets
  - Percent of non-performing loans

- Number of variables tends to increase with length of training period
  - Early models have four to five variables; later models have six to seven variables

Two-year model

- Most important variables:
  - Fraction of non-current loan
  - Net loans/ bank equity capital
  - Return on equity
  - Yield on earning assets
  - Earning assets / assets

- Biggest changes from one- to two-year models:
  - Net operating income / assets have become relatively unimportant at two years
  - Liabilities / assets have lost importance

Three-year model

- Most important variables:
  - Net loans / bank equity capital assets
  - Non-current loans / loans
  - Net operating income/ assets

- Biggest changes from one- and two-year models to three-year model
  - Earning assets / assets are insignificant at 3 years
  - ROE has continued to decrease in importance between 1 and 3 years

Four-year model

- Most important variables:
  - Yield on earning assets
  - Net current loans/ loans
  - Net operating income / assets

- Biggest changes from one- through three-year models to four-year model
  - Non-current loans are insignificant at 4 years
  - Net interest margin has not been important for years one to three

Five-year model

- Most important variables:
  - Yield on earning assets
  - Assets
  - Net interest margin
  - Earning assets / assets

- The consistency of variable selection tends to decrease as prediction horizon increases

A summary of the changes in variables as the annual prediction horizon increases from one to five years appears in Figure 8.13. The most important variables for each annual prediction horizon are listed followed by a description of the changes that occurred from the previous years' model. For example, in predicting default from one to two years, ROE has become less important and the ratio of liabilities to assets is no longer in the model, whereas the fraction of non-current loans has become important along with the ratio of net loans to bank equity capital. In moving from the two- to three-year horizon, ROE is no longer in the model, whereas net loans to bank equity capital, which entered the model at two years, is now most important. When predicting default between three and four years, the value of non-current loans is no longer in the model, whereas the current yield on earning assets has become most important. Finally, at five years the current yield on earning assets remains most important along with net interest margin, with the fraction of current loans and operating income to assets no longer included. In general, quality of assets is most important in near-term default predictions, giving way to operating income and the yield on earning assets as the important determinants of default at longer horizons. It is important to remember that our models are for marginal annual defaults. Thus, variables important for modelling defaults in early years remain important for cumulative default prediction, just not for predicting marginal defaults pending survival to later years.

A quantitative analysis of the variable contributions over time is presented in Table 8.6. The left portion in the figure shows the likelihood of each variable being selected for the default models by horizon in each year over the period from 2000 to 2012. The table at the right displays the average order of selection if the variable was included in the model at the listed horizons. Consider first the probabilities of variable selection. Those probabilities have been colour-coded for convenience, with variables included in 76% to 100% of the annual models for a given horizon coded in black, those included between 11% and 75% in dark grey, and those in 10% or less in light grey. Although ROE and the ratio of liabilities to assets are included in all one-year models, their contributions drop off rapidly at two to five years. Also, performance on earning assets (earning assets to assets) is important at one- and two-year hori-

Table 8.6 Probabilities of variable selection by model horizon (left) and average order of inclusion if selected at given horizon (right) for annual models over the period 2000–12

Variables	Probability of selection					Average order if selected				
	1y	2y	3y	4y	5y	1y	2y	3y	4y	5y
ROE	100%	92%	15%	0%	0%	1.0	2.7	4.5	-	-
Liabilities / assets	100%	23%	31%	31%	23%	2.1	5.7	3.0	4.0	4.3
Non-current loans / loans	92%	100%	100%	69%	15%	3.9	1.1	2.1	2.4	8.0
Net operation income / assets	92%	0%	69%	69%	8%	4.9	-	3.9	2.7	2.0
Earning assets / assets	85%	85%	0%	0%	31%	3.5	4.3	-	-	1.0
Yield on earning asset	46%	85%	92%	11%	54%	5.8	4.2	4.3	2.3	2.6
ROA	23%	0%	0%	8%	8%	4.0	-	-	6.0	2.0
Assets	23%	23%	23%	15%	46%	5.7	5.7	5.7	4.0	4.0
Non-current loans / loan loss allowance	15%	0%	8%	0%	0%	5.0	-	11.0	-	-
Net loans / bank equity capital	0%	100%	100%	31%	23%	-	3.6	1.8	3.0	2.7
Annual default rate	0%	23%	23%	31%	31%	-	5.3	2.0	2.0	2.5
Assets 90 days past due / 30–89 days past due	0%	31%	23%	23%	23%	-	5.8	6.0	1.3	3.0
Net interest income / earning assets	0%	15%	15%	8%	23%	-	8.0	9.0	8.0	6.7
Net interest margin	0%	0%	8%	8%	38%	-	-	10.0	7.0	3.6

zons, but is not included in three- and four-year models, with only moderate contributions to five-year models. The grey-scale coding in Table 8.6 helps to reveal some features not easily distinguished in the data. For example, the most consistently important variable is the percentage of non-current loans, included in nearly all annual models from one to three years and dropping off to 69% at four years and 15% at five years. Also, asset size, while not in all annual models, is in 15% and 46% of models in all years. For two- to four-year horizons, the yield on earning assets and net loans to bank equity capital become important, while having less influence in the one- and five-year models. Notably, the five-year models appear to have the most diversity of variable contributions, with no model in more than 54% of annual models. Finally, net interest margin appears relatively unimportant, except at the five-year horizon, with the ratio of non-current loans to loan loss allowance only included in a small fraction of models at one- and three-year horizons.

The average order of selection of each variable for each model horizon appears at the right in Table 8.6. Variables selected early in the process (averaging from 1 to 2.5) are coded in black, those in the middle set, averaging between 2.5 and 5.0, are in dark grey, and those selected above fifth on average in ligh grey. The table shows the importance of ROE in early year models; ROE was selected first in all one-year models from 2000 to 2012, with non-current liabilities second in all but one year. Again, for mid-year horizons, net operating income becomes selected in most models, averaging between 1.1 and 2.4 in selection order. Although the annual default rate is never included in more than 31% of models at any horizon, when selected at four- and five-year horizons its average order is second. The table also confirms the relative unimportance of net interest income to earning assets and net interest margin.

We conclude the analysis of variable contributions with an analysis of the consistency of the signs of the variables input into each model. That is, we measure the extent to which a variable, if selected, maintains the same sign in different years and tenors. For example, variables having positive signs are indicative of higher default risk, whereas negative inputs signal lower risk of default. Table 8.7 shows for each variable the likelihood that it is positive if selected. Again, grey-scale-coding is used to highlight variables;

Table 8.7 Analysis of variable consistency by model tenor: left: probabilities of variables having positive signs (higher default risk; black) if selected right: average values of variable contributions if selected

Variables	Probability of selection					Average order if selected				
	1y	2y	3y	4y	5y	1y	2y	3y	4y	5y
ROE	0%	0%	0%			−0.6	−0.6	−0.5		
Liabilities / assets	100%	0%	0%	0%	100%	1.0	−1.0	−1.2	−1.4	1.7
Non-current loans / loans	100%	100%	100%	100%	0%	0.6	1.1	0.9	0.6	−0.9
Net operation income / assets	17%	0%	0%	0%	100%	−0.6		−0.7	−0.7	1.4
Earning assets / assets	0%	0%				−0.5	−0.7			−8.1
Yield on earning asset	100%	100%	100%	90%		0.4	0.7	0.7	0.7	−3.
ROA	0%			0%	100%	−1.5			−0.3	1.2
Assets	100%	100%	100%	100%	50%	0.3	0.5	0.5	0.5	−1.4
Non-current loans / loan loss allowance	100%		0%			0.6		−0.4		
Net loans / bank equity capital		100%	100%	100%	0%		0.7	0.8	1.6	−0.5
Annual default rate		0%	0%	0%	25%		−0.2	−0.5	−0.3	0.0
Assets 90 days past due / 30–89 days past due		0%	0%	0%	0%		−0.6	−0.6	−0.5	−4.4
Net interest income / earning assets		0%	0%	0%	67%		−0.4	−0.6	−1.1	0.9
Net interest margin		0%	100%	100%	0%			0.5	1.2	−4.0

319

variables having 67% or greater likelihood of being positive high-lighted in black (for higher risk), those between 0% and 33% positive in dark grey (for lower risk) and grey for those in between. If a variable is not included in a model (eg, for ROE in year-four and year-five models), the corresponding cell is blank. Clearly, almost all variables, when selected for a model in a given year, are of the same sign. That is, nearly all cells with values are either 0% or 100%. Exceptions to this include assets at the five-year horizon and net operating income to assets at one year. Although some variables are of the same sign when included in models at all horizons (eg, ROE, annual default rate and net interest income to earning assets), most variables change sign when included at different horizons. However, excluding their inputs to the five-year model, all variables except percentage of non-current loans are of the same sign if included in models at shorter horizons.

CONCLUSION

To overcome limitations of Merton-type structural models in predicting default probabilities for financial firms, we built and tested adaptive statistical models to estimate default probabilities for US banks. The models are logistic regressions whose input variables are selected and calibrated based on their past effectiveness at predicting bank failures. Selection of variables in the model and their weights were updated yearly using a "walk-forward" procedure. Models were built to predict defaults at annual horizons from one to five years. Performance of the models at discriminating between defaults and non-defaults was evaluated for horizons of one to five years using a sequence of annual walk-forward out-of-sample tests from 1992 to 2012. In general, the models perform favourably at predicting defaults, even relative to our best non-financial corporate default models, with a 97% AR at one year prior to default, and decreasing, but still above-chance, predictive power out to five years. The models are designed to be updated on an annual basis, although updated financials for input to the model are available from the FDIC on a quarterly basis.

As we find that one-year PD models offer little benefit over agency ratings for already low-rated credits, we examined the performance of the bank models relative to Kroll agency ratings for credits rated above single-B minus and for those rated above single-C minus. We find that the predictive power of agency ratings drops off dramatically as credit quality of the scoring sample increases, with much less deterioration in default prediction using the bank PD model.

We also presented a detailed analysis of the contributions of financial variables to model outputs by year (2000–12) and tenor (one- to five-years ahead). For a given prediction horizon, we find great consistency among variables selected for each annual model over the period from 2000 to 2012. For predictions of marginal defaults in years one and two, return on equity and percentage of non-performing loans are major determinants of default. Those variables give way in importance at intermediate tenors (ie, three to four years) to current yield on earning assets and net loans to bank equity capital. Finally, at the five-year horizon, yield on earning assets, asset size and net interest margin become the most important predictors of default.

In a final section we analysed the consistency of the order of variable selection as well as the signs of the input variables as they reflect increases and decreases in credit quality. We find a rough, but positive, relationship between the probability of a variable being selected in each annual model and its average importance in the predictive selection hierarchy. Also, we find that variables, when selected for a given predictive tenor, are nearly always of the same sign across the years of annual model development. However, we do find that many variables change sign as the year of marginal default prediction changes, but this mostly occurs for a single year: predicting defaults between years four and five. Not only do these results provide evidence of the advantage of the adaptive statistical modelling approach over agency ratings, but they provide insight to the short- and long-term determinants of bank failure.

---

1   Section 939A of the Dodd–Frank Act requires federal agencies to review regulations that
     require the use of an assessment of creditworthiness of a security or money market instrument and any references to, or requirements in, those regulations regarding credit ratings.
     Section 939A then requires the agencies to modify the regulations identified during the
     review to substitute any references to, or requirements of, reliance on credit ratings with
     such standards of creditworthiness that each agency determines to be appropriate.

2   For example, Vazza and Kraemer (2012) report that in 2011 only 20% of all financial firms had speculative-grade ratings.

3   As of March 2013, the average liability-to equity ratio of the US banking sector was 7.8.

4   Information about aggregate bank sector size was obtained from the FDIC's "Statistics on Banking" (available at http://www2.fdic.gov/SDI/SOB/).

5   If the model were performing at chance, only 10% of the defaulters would be included in the top 10% of the population ranked by PDs from the model.

6   Note in Table 8.1 that numbers of defaults increase with model horizon. This is because we use overlapping windows in counting multi-year defaults.

7   Recall that, for each model, the prediction for each year is dependent on the firm surviving up to the year of prediction. Thus, when predicting defaults for year two, all firms that defaulted in the first year after the date of prediction are excluded from the sample.

8   It is important to keep the distinction in mind between the Kroll rating scale in the left portion of Figure 8.10 and the more familiar scales of Standard and Poor's and Moody's. As a rule of thumb, a Kroll rating of single-C is roughly equivalent to a rating by Standard and Poor's of triple-C.

9   As bank model PD scores can take any value between 0 and 1 while ratings can only take one of a small number of discrete values, bank PDs also allow for finer discrimination between institutions than ratings do. This difference also explains why the CAP curves for the bank model is a step-function while the CAP curve for ratings is a piecewise linear function. This is particularly evident when the default sample is small, as for the one-year horizon model.

9

Beating Credit Benchmarks

The performances of portfolio managers and other investment professionals are often assessed relative to pre-specified benchmark portfolios. Since the early 2000s, we have been exploring ways to help investors beat return targets using model-based measures of credit risk and relative value. In this chapter, we will describe a procedure, called the cut-and-rotate (C&R) method, which is based on estimates of PDs and relative value obtained from structural models of credit risk.[1] The C&R procedure has evolved from an initial study of credit picking "robots" in 2003. That is, several different automated credit selection algorithms were used to construct portfolios using model-based PDs and yields from bonds in investment-grade and high-yield credit indexes. Subsequent applications refined the credit picking strategies using more accurate estimates of default probabilities and adding recovery value in default to determinations of relative value. In addition, the method was applied to other cash bond benchmarks and synthetic credit indexes.

This chapter begins with a brief description of the results of our credit picking robot study. It then discusses how we refined the method to apply it to the corporate bonds in Citi's North American BIG and High Yield indexes.[2] We also present the performance of those initial studies along with results on the effects of portfolio size and transaction costs, before describing the credit-cycle dependence of the contributions of the C&R components of the strategy. The section concludes with a description of the out-of-sample performance of the C&R strategy on Citi's BIG index since 2004.

In later sections, we will describe applications of the C&R strategy to several other global credit benchmarks, including the corporate bonds in Citigroup's EuroBIG index, the Asian Broad Bond index, the Chinese Dim Sum index and the double-A rated corporate bonds in Citi's BIG index. We also discuss issues related to practical deployment of the C&R strategy. In a final section, we highlight the factors that underlie C&R strategy success.

THE BEGINNING: CREDIT PICKING ROBOTS

To provide perspective, we describe our initial study in which we deployed credit picking robots with different investment strategies to determine the optimal methods for constructing credit portfolios. As this study is described in detail in several places,[3] we reiterate it only briefly here. That initial investigation was motivated by consideration of the differential returns of two CDOs but, as explained below, the results generalise to all credit benchmarks that we have tested.

The objective was to construct portfolios and analyse returns of 100 corporate bonds using four different strategies. Portfolios were constructed from sub-samples of 2,000 bonds selected from a universe of roughly 5,000 bonds.[4] The par value of each bond in the 100-bond portfolios was set at 1%. The selection procedure ensured that all portfolios had an equal number of bonds in each agency rating category from single-B plus to single-A (10 bonds per rating category), with an average rating of triple-B minus. Only bonds with maturities between four and 12 years were considered, with no more than two bonds from a single issuer and no more than 20 bonds in any given industry sector. All selection strategies were constrained by that same set of guidelines. That is, all portfolios had the same distribution of bonds by rating, the same maturity range, and the same sector and issuer limits. Importantly, the fact that the ratings distributions were the same for all portfolios should have ensured, to the extent that the rating agencies were correct, that average default rates for each strategy would be the same.

To sum up, the portfolio guidelines for credit picking robots were:

❑ 100 credits;

- ❑ uniform ratings from single-A to single-B plus;
- ❑ an average rating of triple-B minus;
- ❑ maturities of between four and 12 years; and
- ❑ sector/issuer concentration of 20%/2%.

Figure 9.1 Credit picking robot study: left: diagram of credit picking strategies; middle: average returns per portfolio by strategy; right: average defaults per portfolio

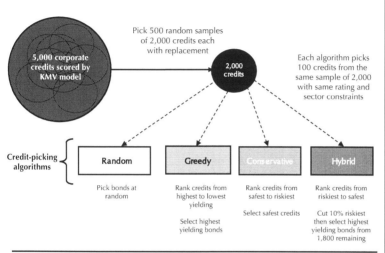

	Average annual return			
	Random	**Greedy**	**Conservative**	**Hybrid**
1994	-3.3%	-2.5%	-3.7%	-1.9%
1995	19.7%	20.3%	18.3%	20.1%
1996	6.3%	8.5%	6.1%	8.3%
1997	10.0%	11.3%	8.4%	11.7%
1998	7.1°%	4.7°%	7.6%	6.6%
1999	1.1%	3.9°4	0.4%	5.7%
2000	4.7%	2.6°4	7.7%	9.3%
2001	12.5%	17.6%	10.4%	14.0%
2002	5.9%	2.4%	9.7%	7.9%
Mean	7.1%	7.6°%	7.2%	9.1%
Std dev	6.6%	7.5%	6.2%	6.1%
Inf. ratio	1.1	1.0	1.2	1.5

Figure 9.1 (*Continued*)

	Average Defaults per Portfolio			
	Random	Greedy	Conservative	Hybrid
1994	0.00	0.00	0.00	0.00
1995	0.00	0.00	0.00	0.00
1996	0.00	0.00	0.00	0.00
1997	0.25	1.47	0.00	0.00
1998	0.11	0.40	0.00	0.00
1999	0.95	3.26	0.00	0.00
2000	0.70	0.22	0.00	0.00
2001	0.46	1.67	0.00	0.00
2002	2.68	4.82	0.00	4.73
Mean	0.57	1.32	0.00	0.53
Std Dev	0.86	1.71	0.00	1.58
Inf. ratio	1.1	1.0	1.2	1.5

The four strategies (ie, robots) for picking bonds are shown in the top panel of Figure 9.1. For each portfolio in each year, subsets of 2,000 bonds were selected from a pool of roughly 5,000 North American corporate bonds. Each algorithm was applied to the same set of 2,000 bonds to select the 100-bond portfolios, but each using different selection rules. A total of 500 portfolios were constructed by each algorithm in each year from 1994 to 2004, with subsets of 2,000 bonds selected from the 5,000 with replacement. The four credit picking strategies were the following.

❑ Random: Bonds are selected at random as long as each subsequent selection does not violate the guidelines.
❑ Greedy: Strategy ranks all bonds with respect to bond yield and fills the portfolio with the highest-yielding bonds as long as they continue to satisfy the guidelines.
❑ Conservative: Bonds are ranked with respect to expected default probability, with selection from the least risky credits that satisfy the guidelines.

❏ Hybrid: A combination of the conservative and greedy algorithms that first removes the riskiest 10% of the bonds (ie, 200) and then selects the highest-yielding credits from the remaining 90% as long as they continue to satisfy the guidelines.

Estimates of PDs for the conservative and hybrid selection methods were obtained from the Moody's/KMV model (Crosbie, 1999; Kealhofer and Kurbat, 2001).[5] PDs from the KMV model (ie, EDFs) are based on estimates of firms' asset values from their equity prices, with assets divided by the level of their debt and then scaled in units of the firm's asset volatility as determined from the volatility of its stock price.[6]

Average returns from the 500 annual portfolios are presented for each strategy in the first table of Figure 9.1. Returns from the random robot provide the benchmark for comparing returns from the other credit selection methods. Portfolios selected using the random method returned an average return of 7.1% per annum over the nine-year period, with a standard deviation of 6.6% for an information ratio of 1.1. The other three selection strategies all posted higher average returns than the random method. Consider the greedy strategy, whose average annual return is 7.6%. In 1995, 1997 and 2001, the greedy algorithm had the highest average return, but in 1998, 2000 and 2002 it performed the worst. The greedy robot achieved an information ratio of 1.0, the lowest of all strategies, including the benchmark. One might expect that the conservative algorithm, by picking the "safest" credits, would underperform the benchmark since less risky credits tend to have lower yields. However, average returns from the conservative robot were 7.2%, topping slightly those produced by random selection. Also, the volatility of returns from the conservative algorithm was less than those of the greedy and random algorithms, resulting in an information ratio of 1.2. Finally, the hybrid robot produced the largest average annual return of 9.1%, a 2% increase over the random method and 1.5% over the greedy algorithm. Importantly, it had the lowest volatility of monthly returns at 6.1%. The hybrid algorithm also has the highest information ratio at 1.5, a 50% increase over that for the random method and better than the next best ratio of 1.2 from the conservative algorithm.

It is explicit in Standard & Poor's rating criteria that the default risks are similar for all credits having similar ratings. However, average default rates by strategy, shown by year in the lower table of Figure 9.1, suggest strongly that this is not the case. In some years (ie, 1994, 1995 and 1996) none of the bonds in any of the portfolios defaulted, but both the random and greedy algorithms picked credits that defaulted in all other years. The random method, with an overall average of 0.57 defaults, had just over one default in every two portfolios. In comparison, the 1.32 average defaults per greedy algorithm portfolio are about 2.5 times that for the random method, despite identical ratings distributions. Furthermore, the conservative strategy had no defaults in any year. This is particularly impressive in that 2002 saw a record number of high-yield defaults (Altman and Bana, 2003), and also had the highest default rates for the other strategies. The lack of defaults in portfolios picked by the conservative robot suggests that: (i) the equity-based KMV credit model is useful for ranking the riskiness of credits; and (ii) agency ratings lag the market in recognising deteriorating and improving credits.

The major implications of the study of the credit picking robots are as follows:

❏ Selecting bonds with the highest yields, while outperforming in low default years, underperforms on a risk-adjusted basis owing to higher defaults. This results from agency credit ratings lagging market perceptions of credit risk.
❏ Since the conservative robot underperforms the random one in years of no defaults, but outperforms when the random method has defaults, its overall superior performance is directly related to its ability to avoid selecting bonds from firms that default.
❏ The hybrid method, by eliminating the riskiest 10% based and reaching for yield, was also relatively effective at eliminating defaults. In addition, it generated additional returns by investing in credits with high yields but relatively low risk.

BEATING CORPORATE BOND INDEXES
Initial studies: 1994–2004
The results of the credit picking robot study suggested that some version of the hybrid method might be useful for outperforming

credit benchmarks. In this section, we will describe the initial attempt to beat returns from corporate bonds in Citigroup's BIG index.[7] That study covered the period from 1994 to 2004, and is presented as background for out-of-sample results obtained since 2004. In addition to evaluating relative performance of the C&R strategy, the initial study explored separately the effects on returns of cutting the riskiest credits, the cut strategy, and then overinvesting in the highest-yielding credits, called the rotation. In addition, we evaluated the relative performance of Citi's HPD model (Sobehart and Keenan, 2002; 2003) versus Moody's/KMV model at ranking firm's default risk and relative value as input to that strategy. Although these studies were completed as long ago as the early 2000s, they are described herein to support the claim of out-of-sample testing since then, and as evidence for the out-of-sample application of this method to the credit benchmarks described below.

The C&R strategy

Analogous to the 10% cut in the robot studies the allocation was removed from the riskiest 10% of the corporate bonds in Citi's BIG index based on their KMV model EDFs, and their value was reinvested in proportion to the market weights of the remaining 90% of bonds in the index. The average credit quality of the corporate bonds in the BIG index varied greatly from 1994 to 2004, as shown by the black line in the left panel of Figure 9.2. The grey line shows the monthly average PD for the remaining bonds after the 10% cut. The figure shows that the 10% cut reduces the overall risk of the portfolio by about one-half. The middle panel of Figure 9.2 shows the boundary for the lower decile of bonds in the index. These are the values defining the 10% of bonds with the highest PDs (ie, the PD cut points), which varied from about 0.2% in 1998 to over 2% in 2002.[8]

Annual performance from 1994 to 2004 for the 10% PD-based cut strategy appears in the top row of the table in Figure 9.2. Returns are expressed as annual incremental returns in basis points relative to the index. The PD-based cut portfolios outperform the investment-grade corporate bond index by 158bp over the 11-year period, or by 14bp per annum. However, in over half of those years the difference in performance is negative or negligible. The dashed arrows between the table and the graph above it show that the cut strategy outperforms in years when credit quality is deteriorating rapidly, but underperforms, albeit usually only slightly, when credit quality is stable or improving. Thus, deploying the "cut" strategy is like buying credit protection: during benign periods, one gives up a small spread premium, but outperforms strongly when credit deteriorates.

Figure 9.2 The C&R strategy on corporate bonds in Citigroup's BIG index (1994–2004): top left: monthly average PDs (from the KMV model) of the index (black) and cut (grey) portfolios; top middle: one-year EDF cut-offs for lower 10%; top right: relative value of bonds in the consumer sector showing bonds to eliminate and underweight; bottom: annual P&L relative to the BIG index for the cut, rotate and C&R portfolios

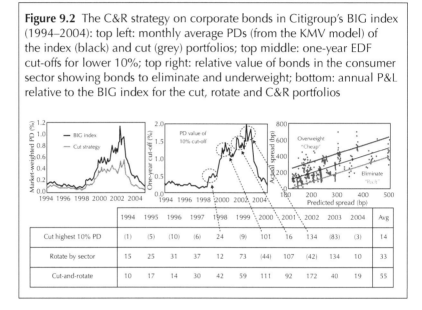

	1994	1995	1996	1997	1998	1999	2000	2001	2002	2003	2004	Avg
Cut highest 10% PD	(1)	(5)	(10)	(6)	24	(9)	101	16	134	(83)	(3)	14
Rotate by sector	15	25	31	37	12	73	(44)	107	(42)	134	10	33
Cut-and-rotate	10	17	14	30	42	59	111	92	172	40	19	55

Unlike for the robot study, instead of simply underweighting lower-yielding credits and overweighting the higher-yielding ones, the rotation algorithm was altered to keep the index's industry sectors roughly constant. To do this for a given month, the universe of bonds in the BIG index was first divided into seven industry sectors.[9] Then, bonds' yield spreads to US Treasuries for firms in each sector were regressed on a linear combination of one-year default probability and duration as:

$$s' = \gamma_0 + (\gamma_1 * Dur) + (\gamma_2 * PD) + \varepsilon, \tag{9.1}$$

Equation 9.1 was then used to generate the least squares regression line (black line) in the top right panel of Figure 9.2. The figure also shows the 10th and 90th percentile boundaries (the grey and black lines, respectively) for that sector that segregate bonds for elimination and overweighting, respectively. That is, the "rotate" strategy removes the allocation from the 10% of the bonds in each sector with the poorest relative value and doubles the allocation to the 10% of bonds having the largest spreads for their default risk and duration.

Annual excess returns from the rotate component of the strategy relative to the corporate bonds in the BIG index appear in the second row of the table in Figure 9.2. Average P&L from the rotation strategy exceeds that of the cut strategy, returning a total of 358bp over the index for the 11-year test period, or by 33bp per annum. In contrast to the 10% cut, the relative value rotation outperforms the index most years, underperforming only in 2000 and 2002. The table reveals that returns from the cut and rotate components are complementary; when the cut-based selection rule outperforms, the regression-based rotation rule underperforms, and vice versa.

The combined performance of the cut and rotate strategy over corporate bonds in the BIG index appears in the bottom row of the table in Figure 9.2. The combination performs better than either method alone; the C&R method returned an excess of 606bp over the 11-year test period, an additional 55bp per annum. Furthermore, the strategies appear additive: the PD cut method returned an additional 158bp and the regression-based rotation method returned 358bp, with the combination returning slightly less than their sum. Finally, the C&R method outperformed the index in every year in our test period, and with less risk.

The results reported above were all obtained using PDs generated by Moody's/KMV CreditEdge model. Due to licensing constraints on the KMV model, we found it preferable to test an alternative model to generate PDs for subsequent studies. Fortunately, we were able to acquire Citi's HPD model (Sobehart and Keenan, 2002, 2003), whose performance in the C&R strategy was found to exceed that of the KMV model for both investment-grade and high-yield portfolios (see Appendix I in Benzschawel, Lee and Bernstein, 2011, for a detailed comparison of the performance of HPD and KMV models as inputs to the C&R strategy). Furthermore, the HPD model has been shown to be superior at detecting corporate defaults in over a decade of out-of-sample testing (Benzschawel, 2013). Hence, we use estimates of default probabilities from the HPD model for all subsequent studies reported here.

C&R on investment-grade corporate bonds (2005–14)

We have been reporting on performance of the C&R strategy in the monthly "Corporate Markets Quantitative Review",[10] and provide an update on C&R performance through 2014 in this section. Our methods have changed little since our initial studies. The most significant change to the methodology reported by Benzschawel and Jiang (2004) concerned the addition of model-based recovery values as input to the relative value calculation used for credit rotation. That is, in 2005 we acquired Moody's LossCalc model for recovery value (Dwyer and Korablev, 2008) and incorporated those values into our relative value function.[11] Later, we built and tested our own recovery value model (Benzschawel, Haroon and Wu, 2011; Benzschawel and Lee, 2013), and have used that model since early 2012. We include a summary of our existing method in Appendix 9.1. In addition, we now calculate relative value in each sector by regressing logarithms of recovery-adjusted spread versus the sum of logarithms of PDs and durations as opposed to linear axis in the initial studies.

Aside from the addition of recovery value to the relative value function, the C&R strategy with respect to the corporate bonds in Citi's BIG index was the same as for the studies reported above. Firms' monthly PDs from the HPD model were used to determine the monthly 10% cut. Those PDs were also used along with recovery values from Moody's LossCalc and later Citi's recovery value model to determine monthly relative value functions used for rotating out of overvalued credits and to overweight undervalued ones. Returns from the C&R strategy and its components were determined separately and in combination for each month from the beginning of 2005 to December 2014. We also report on the relative contributions to C&R performance from carry (average yield spread relative to the index) and convergence (avoided bonds widening and overweight bonds tightening).

Table 9.1 presents a summary of annual returns from the corporate bonds in Citigroup's BIG index, the benchmark and the relative performance of the C&R strategy since 1994. Thus, the table shows both in- and out-of-sample results as separated by the dashed line in the figure. The left-most column shows that, over the 21-year testing period, the average yield spread to US Treasuries of the corporate bonds in the index is 148bp. However, the second column of Table 9.1 reveals that the average annual index spread has varied considerably, being as tight as 67bp in 1996 and as wide as 555bp in 2008, with a standard deviation of 101bp. Note that the mean spread change of the BIG index corporate bonds is only 1bp, indicating that average investment-grade bond spreads are mean reverting, with the index returning roughly the yield spread on its bonds over time.

Table 9.1 Annual spread performance of Citi's BIG index and relative performance of individual cut and rotate strategies and the combined C&R strategy (1994–2014)

| Year | BIG index | | Strategy | | |
	Average spread	Spread change	Cut	Rotate	Cut and rotate
1994	81	(11)	(1)	15	10
1995	78	(3)	(5)	25	17
1996	67	(11)	(10)	31	14
1997	79	12	(6)	37	30
1998	146	67	24	12	42
1999	132	(14)	(8)	73	59
2000	205	73	101	(44)	111
2001	195	(11)	16	107	92
2002	204	10	134	(42)	172
2003	108	(97)	(83)	134	40
2004	88	(20)	(3)	10	19
2005	102	14	1	12	10
2006	86	(16)	4	30	38
2007	198	112	(4)	(15)	(17)
2008	555	358	56	(10)	(8)
2009	159	(396)	(71)	614	553
2010	148	(11)	(6)	129	122
2011	137	(12)	18	30	46
2012	128	(12)	5	121	137
2013	113	(15)	(11)	27	20
2014	108	(5)	11	83	102
Sum	3117	18	162	1379	1609
Mean	148	1	8	66	77
Std. dev	101	123	46	133	118
Inf. ratio		0.0	0.2	0.5	0.7

The left and right middle columns of Table 9.1 display annual out-performance from the individual cut and rotate allocation strategies, respectively. As for the study in Figure 9.2, results are presented as basis points of out- or underperformance relative to the corporate bonds in the BIG index. The figure indicates that, although the cut strategy, by itself, underperforms the index 11 out of 21 years it out-performs the index by 8bp on average. This is slightly below the 13bp outperformance in the initial study reported in 2004. Although the 10% cut strategy alone is only marginally profitable, rotating out of the 10% of bonds with the worst relative value by sector value and doubling the allocation to the 10% having the greatest spread for their risk is much more profitable. The rotate strategy alone outperformed the index by an average of 66bp annually since 1994, with an infor-mation ratio of 0.5. Despite the overall attractiveness of the rotation strategy, it did produce annual losses in 2000, 2002, 2007 and 2008.[12]

The right-most column of Table 9.1 shows the results of the com-bined C&R strategy, which outperforms the index in 19 of the 21 years tested and eight of the 10 out-of-sample years (the C&R strat-egy also outperformed the index in 2015 by 39bp). On average, the C&R strategy outperforms the 148bp annual return of the index by 77bp, a 50% improvement, with an information ratio of 0.7. In fact, the only underperformance came during the height of the credit crisis in 2007 and 2008 when the C&R strategy underperformed by 17bp and 8bp, respectively, while the index spread rose by 112bp and 358bp, its two largest annual increases. In addition, the following year saw the largest annual outperformance of 553bp. Finally, note that when the C&R strategy outperforms, it outperforms by 85bp on average, whereas the average underperformance is only 13bp.

We also examined sources of annual excess profit and loss (P&L) of the C&R strategy over the index in terms of the portion result-ing from positive carry (the C&R portfolio having a greater aver-age spread than the index) and convergence (C&R avoiding spread widening of excluded bonds and profiting from spread tightening of overweight bonds). That analysis appears in Figure 9.3. The fig-ure shows that the majority of the P&L in the C&R strategy comes from convergence (light grey bars), with only slight contributions from positive carry (dark grey bars). Although rotation into bonds having greater spread for their risk would tend to produce positive carry, that advantage is offset by exclusion of the riskiest credits whose spreads tend to be the largest.

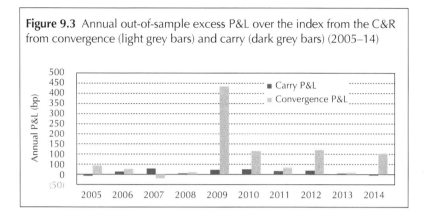

Figure 9.3 Annual out-of-sample excess P&L over the index from the C&R from convergence (light grey bars) and carry (dark grey bars) (2005–14)

Optimising the C&R criteria

For these studies, a constant criterion of 10% was used for both cutting the riskiest and rotating bonds based on relative value. The choice of the 10% criteria was arbitrary, decided upon in the early robot picking and index beating studies. At that time, optimising the C&R criteria did not seem appropriate given considerations regarding over-fitting the data. Given over a decade more of data we sought to determine if different criteria might be preferable, both the cut and rotate criteria were altered separately from 0% to 40%, and returns and information ratios were computed for each combination of criteria.

The top panel of Figure 9.4 displays average annual total returns from the C&R strategy for the 0–40% range of criteria for cuts and rotations, with the lower plot showing information ratios for each set of parameters. It appears that our 10% cut and 10% rotation criteria are roughly optimal, given considerations of risk-adjusted returns and transactions costs. For example, note that the current 10% C&R criteria, highlighted in each panel, produces roughly a 7% annual return (about 200bp due to credit spread) with an information ratio of 0.6. However, the lower panel indicates that the best information ratio is obtained with a cut of 5% and a rotation of 32% in each sector. Although the optimal parameters increase the excess return over the index by 50bp per annum, the information ratio increases only marginally from 0.6 to about 0.65. To the extent that there would be increased costs associated with the larger rotation, altering the rotation criterion would not seem worthwhile. Still, decreasing the cut to 5% might be of value. Nevertheless, the results in Figure 9.4 provide little incentive for changing the C&R criteria from 10%.

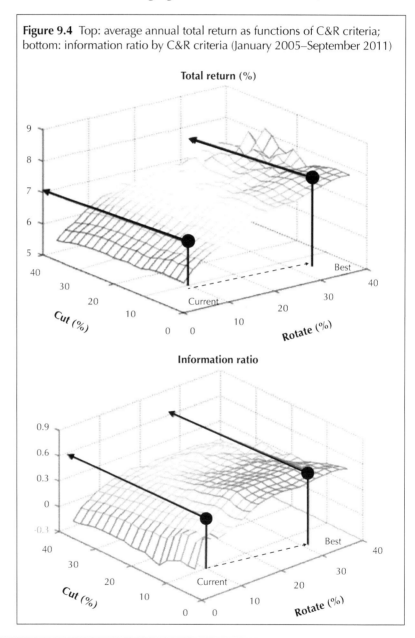

Figure 9.4 Top: average annual total return as functions of C&R criteria; bottom: information ratio by C&R criteria (January 2005–September 2011)

C&R ON CITI'S EUROBIG INDEX

Latterly, we have applied our C&R strategy to other global cred-it benchmarks. We first report on the ability of the C&R strategy to outperform the corporate bond returns from Citigroup's Euro Broad Investment Grade (EuroBIG) index.[13] We were able to ob-tain monthly price and composition data on the index beginning in 2004, and have tracked the performance of the index and our C&R strategy since then. As for the North American BIG index study, we used Citi's HPD model to estimate default probabilities of EuroBIG bonds for the cut and relative value analysis. For example, Figure 9.5 shows how recovery value adjusted spreads for corporate bonds in the EuroBIG plot as a function of default probability and dura-tion. The white circles in Figure 9.5 are bonds to be excluded owing to the 10% cut, the dark grey circles are "rich" bonds to be rotated out of, and the black circles are to receive double their allocation.

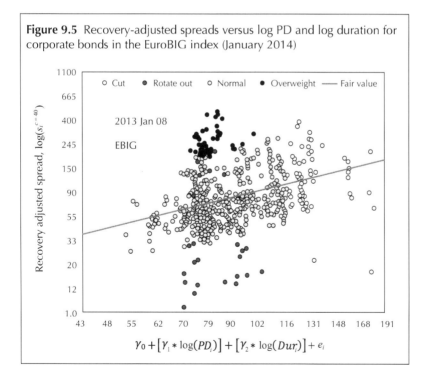

Figure 9.5 Recovery-adjusted spreads versus log PD and log duration for corporate bonds in the EuroBIG index (January 2014)

$$\gamma_0 + \left[\gamma_1 * \log(PD_i)\right] + \left[\gamma_2 * \log(Dur_i)\right] + e_i$$

Annual returns from the EuroBIG and its associated C&R strat-egy appear in the top panel of Figure 9.6. The figure shows that the C&R strategy outperforms the EuroBIG corporates in six of 10 years tested. Furthermore, the average in years of outperformance is 130bp, whereas years of underperformance average only a 40bp deficit. Hence, on average, the C&R strategy has a 69bp annual return advantage over the corporate bonds in the EuroBIG index, a value not appreciably different from the 75bp annual advantage found for the C&R on the North American BIG index.

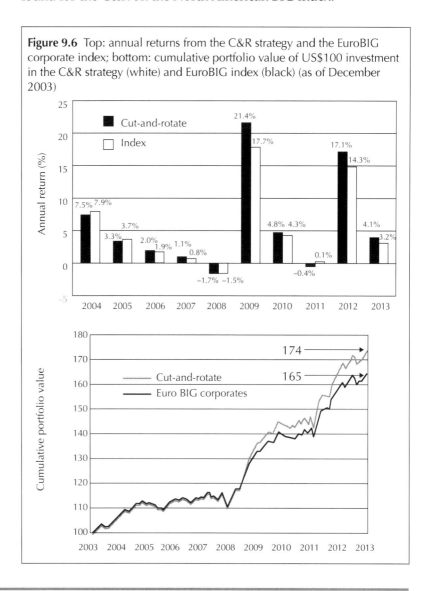

Figure 9.6 Top: annual returns from the C&R strategy and the EuroBIG corporate index; bottom: cumulative portfolio value of US$100 investment in the C&R strategy (white) and EuroBIG index (black) (as of December 2003)

The bottom panel of Figure 9.6 displays cumulative P&L from US$100 investments in either the EuroBIG index corporates (black line) or the C&R strategy on the EuroBIG (grey line) since December 2003. The figure shows that, although the corporate index returned an impressive 65% over the period, the C&R strategy returned 74%, an average outperformance of 90bp per annum since 2004. Finally, it is important to note that, unlike the North American BIG index study for which the rotation was done within industry sectors, the rotation on the EuroBIG was done without regard to obligors' sectors, currencies or country of domicile.

C&R ON CITI'S DIM SUM INDEX

In December 2010, Citi's Index Group introduced a renminbi-denominated (Yn) bond index, called the Dim Sum Offshore CNY bond index, to measure the performance of Yn-denominated (also known as "dim sum") bonds issued and settled outside mainland China. The Dim Sum bond index excludes RMB-denominated but non-RMB-settled (typically US dollar-settled) synthetic securities, convertible bonds, retail securities (mainly issued by the Chinese government and financial institutions for retail customers) and certificates of deposits (CDs). Other defining features include:

❑ fixed rate coupons only (excludes zero-coupon bonds);
❑ minimum maturity of one year;
❑ minimum issue size of RMB1 billion;
❑ no minimum S&P or Moody's rating, but defaulted bonds are excluded;
❑ denominated and settled in RMB;
❑ weighting is by market capitalisation;
❑ rebalancing one per month (end of month);
❑ reinvestment of cashflows at end-of-month Eurodeposit rate; and
❑ value calculated daily from Citi trader and Interactive Data Corporation prices.

Table 9.2 presents the major characteristics of the 30 bonds in the Dim Sum index as of January 2014, including a summary of duration and yield by credit quality, maturity and sector.

Table 9.2 Citi's Dim Sum (offshore Yn) index characteristics (January 2014)

Sector	Duration	Yield
Dim sum index	2.97	3.93
Investment grade	3.15	3.29
High yield / not rated	2.59	5.32
0-5 Years	2.41	3.87
5+ Years	7.91	4.39
Govt / govt sponsored	3.83	3.05
Corporate	2.42	4.49
❏ Industrial	2.36	4.90
Manufacturiing	2.13	4.00
Services	2.37	5.80
Consumer	2.35	3.71
Energy	4.39	3.46
Transportation	2.26	4.32
Other	1.90	3.69
❏ Utilities	1.92	4.00
Telecoms	1.61	5.06
Gas	2.29	3.40
Other	1.90	3.69
❏ Finance	2.71	3.96
Banking	2.27	3.62
Life insurance	3.71	4.32
Leasing	3.41	5.39

We applied the C&R method to the bonds in Citi's Dim Sum index over the period February 2011 to December 2013. As for our other studies, we used estimates of PDs from HPD model to estimate default probabilities for firms in the Dim Sum index. However, not all issuers in the Dim Sum index had tradable equity, a requirement for estimating PDs from HPD. To estimate PDs for firms without tradable equity, we estimated PDs using the market-implied PD model (Benzschawel and Lee, 2011; Benzschawel and Assing, 2012). That model requires only a short series of credit spreads and the daily spread value of volatility to infer firms' PDs. Also, for our relative value analysis we estimated values of recovery in default from our decision-tree model.

Each month from February 2011 to December 2013 we plotted bonds' recovery value adjusted spreads against the logarithms of their PDs and durations. An example of the resulting regression for December 2013 appears in Figure 9.7, where the grey line is the least squares fit to spreads of the Dim Sum index bonds. Then, we applied the C&R criteria to the bonds in the Dim Sum index by first removing the allocation from the 10% of the bonds with the largest PDs and redistributing that allocation among the remaining 90%. The riskiest 10% of the bonds in December 2013 are indicated by the grey circles in Figure 9.7. After the cut, we removed the allocation from the "richest" 10% of bonds, the points coded in white in the figure, and doubled the allocation to the 10% of the "cheapest" bonds, the black circles in Figure 9.7.

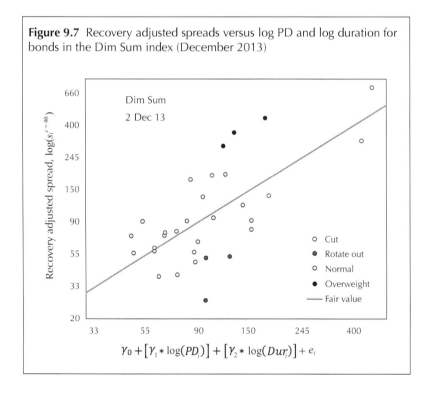

Figure 9.7 Recovery adjusted spreads versus log PD and log duration for bonds in the Dim Sum index (December 2013)

$$\gamma_0 + \left[\gamma_1 * \log(PD_i)\right] + \left[\gamma_2 * \log(Dur_i)\right] + e_i$$

Each month, we compared the returns from the C&R strategy with those of a similar investment in the Dim Sum index. Those results are summarised in Figure 9.8. The left panel shows monthly outperformance (light grey bars) and underperformance (dark grey bars) of the C&R strategy relative to the index. The figure shows that the C&R outperforms the Dim Sum index in only 17 of 32 months. However, as shown in the middle tables, the C&R strategy outperforms on an annual basis in all three years tested (top), and the 7.4bp average return in months of outperformance is two times that of the average loss of –3.6bp when the C&R underperforms. Over the 32-month test period, the C&R method had an average annual return of 3.44% as opposed to 3.17% for the Dim Sum index, a 27bp annual advantage. Finally, the right panel of Figure 9.8 shows that the cumulative compounded return from US$100 invested in the C&R strategy tops that of the Dim Sum index by just over 30bp per annum since April 2011.

Figure 9.8 C&R strategy on Citi's Dim Sum index; left: monthly excess returns of C&R minus the index; middle: table of returns by year (top) and performance statistics; right: cumulative compounded returns from C&R and the Dim Sum index

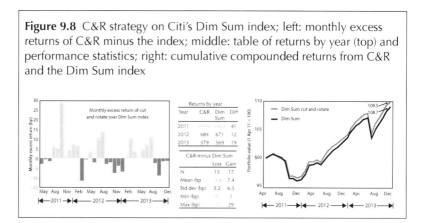

C&R ON CITI'S ASIAN BROAD BOND INDEX

We also tested the C&R strategy on Citi's Asian Broad Bond index (ABBI). The ABBI consists of investment-grade and high-yield US dollar-denominated debt issued by governments, agencies and corporations domiciled in Asia (ex-Japan). The ABBI provides a comprehensive measure of the Asian fixed income market across various asset classes and credit sectors. Figure 9.9 displays the profile of the ABBI by maturity and sector (left panel), geographical distribution (middle) and agency ratings (right panel). At the end of 2012, there were 629 bonds, 82% of which were investment grade, with 12% having maturities longer than 10 years, but with a slight overweight for bonds shorter than five years. A quarter of the bonds are government or government-sponsored entities, with nearly three-quarters being corporate issues. By country, China has the largest weighting at 27%, followed by Korea (18%), Indonesia (12%) and Hong Kong (11%), with less than 10% from India, Philippines, Malaysia and Singapore. Finally, nearly 40% of the bonds in the ABBI are rated triple-B and 34% are single-A, dropping to 12% for double-B, with double-A and single-B contributing 7% and 5%, respectively.

Figure 9.9 Characteristics of Citi's ABBI; left: maturity and sector profile; middle: geographical distribution; right: agency rating distribution

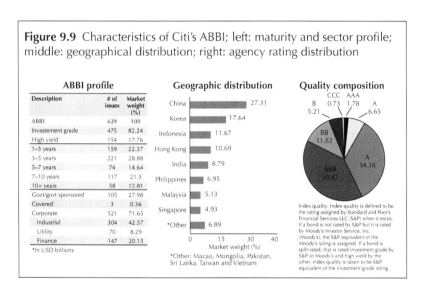

Description	# of issues	Market weight (%)
ABBI	629	100
Investement grade	475	82.24
High yield	154	17.76
1–3 years	159	22.37
3–5 years	221	28.88
5–7 years	74	14.64
7–10 years	117	21.3
10+ years	58	12.81
Govt/govt sponsored	105	27.98
Covered	3	0.36
Corporate	521	71.65
Industrial	304	42.57
Utility	70	8.29
Finance	147	20.15

*In USD billions

*Other: Macao, Mongolia, Pakistan, Sri Lanka, Taiwan and Vietnam

Index quality: Index quality is defined to be the rating assigned by Standard and Poor's Financial Services LLC (S&P) when it exists. If a bond is not rated by S&P but it is rated by Moody's Investor Service, Inc. (Moody's), the S&P equivalent of the Moody's rating is assigned. If a bond is split-rated, that is rated investment grade by S&P or Moody's and high yield by the other, index quality is taken to be S&P equivalent of the investment-grade rating.

We applied the C&R method to the corporate bonds in Citi's ABBI over the period 2009–13. Similar to the Dim Sum index, we used the HPD model to estimate PDs for ABBI issuers when available, filling in with PDs from the market-implied model for issuers without tradable equity. Again, we obtained values from our recovery value model to adjust spreads of all bonds to a constant 40% level, as shown in Figure 9.10. To construct the C&R portfolios each month from December 2008 to December 2013, we eliminated the allocations from the 10% of the bonds with the largest PDs (white circles), followed by removing the allocation from the 10% with the worst relative values (dark grey circles) and doubling the allocation to the "cheapest" bonds (black circles).

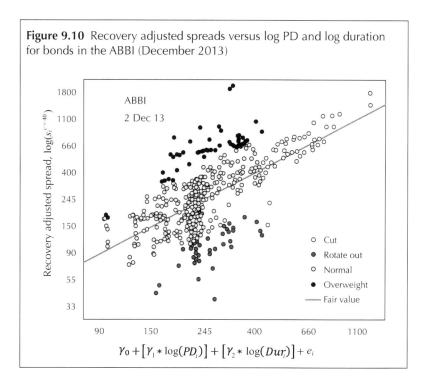

Figure 9.10 Recovery adjusted spreads versus log PD and log duration for bonds in the ABBI (December 2013)

Annual returns from the C&R strategy and the ABBI are presented in the top panel of Figure 9.11. The C&R strategy (black bars) outperforms the ABBI (white bars) in four of the five years tested. Moreover, in the four years of outperformance by the C&R strategy, its average return was 205bp over the ABBI, while in 2011 it only underperformed by only 42bp. On average, the C&R method has a 155bp annual return advantage over the bonds in the ABBI. The bottom two panels display cumulative compounded annual returns from the C&R and ABBI strategies in tabular and graphical form, respectively. Over the 5.1 years between December 2008 and December 2013, the C&R strategy generated over 9% more than the ABBI. Again, as for the C&R strategy on the Dim Sum index, the 10% cut and the rotation were performed on the entire portfolio with no attempt to balance country or sector contributions.

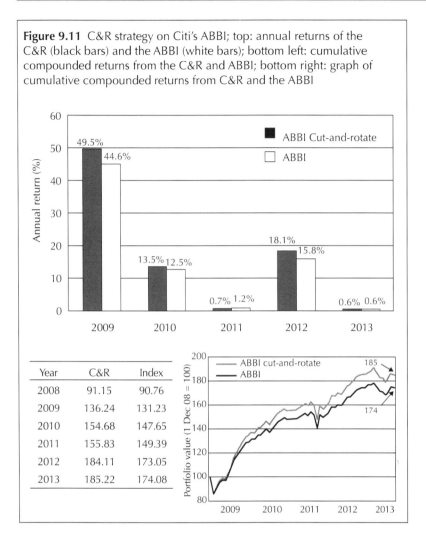

Figure 9.11 C&R strategy on Citi's ABBI; top: annual returns of the C&R (black bars) and the ABBI (white bars); bottom left: cumulative compounded returns from the C&R and ABBI; bottom right: graph of cumulative compounded returns from C&R and the ABBI

Year	C&R	Index
2008	91.15	90.76
2009	136.24	131.23
2010	154.68	147.65
2011	155.83	149.39
2012	184.11	173.05
2013	185.22	174.08

C&R ON DOUBLE-A CORPORATE BONDS

Although we demonstrated that the C&R strategy consistently outperforms corporate bonds in Citi's BIG index, we also examined if the C&R strategy can outperform the subset of the BIG index corporate bonds rated from double-A plus to double-A minus. The reason for choosing double-A rated bonds for analysis is because double-A bond returns from Citi's BIG index form the credit component of Citi's Pension Liability index (CPLI), a popular benchmark for pension fund managers (Bader and Mah, 1995; Bernstein, 2010).[14] Firms' have latterly been abandoning defined benefit plans for 401K plans, yet these firms have nearly 70 years of future liabilities to manage, and many plans remain underfunded. Hence, an important objective for fund managers is not only to continue to generate the equivalent of double-A bond returns, but to make up for existing deficits. Since the C&R strategy has outperformed every benchmark tested so far, it seemed important to test it on double-A rated credits.

Accordingly, we applied the C&R strategy to the double-A rated bonds in Citi's BIG index from January 2006 to March 2013. As before, PDs were generated by the HPD model and from the market-implied model to fill in when HPD PDs were unavailable. Again, values from our recovery value model were used to adjust spreads of all bonds to a constant 40% level. Also, to construct the C&R portfolios each month, we eliminated the allocations from the 10% of the double-A rated bonds with the largest PDs, followed by removing the allocation from the 10% with the worst relative value, and doubling the allocation to the "cheapest" bonds. Unlike the earlier study on the BIG index, no attempt was made to balance industry sector allocations for this study.

The top panel of Figure 9.12 shows the average PD over the test period for the benchmark double-A rated bonds in the BIG index (black line), the effect on average default risk of the rotate (dashed black), the cut (light grey) and the C&R strategy (dark grey). Not surprisingly, the C&R strategy greatly reduces the portfolio's default risk relative to that of the double-A universe, decreasing the risk by about half. The light grey lineshows that cutting the riskiest 10% of the bonds accounts for nearly all of the risk reduction, whereas the rotate strategy has minimal effect relative to the risk of the double-A benchmark portfolio.

The bottom panel of Figure 9.12 displays annual excess returns relative to one-month US T-bills for the double-A rated BIG index corporates (black bars), the C&R strategy (white bars), the rotate strategy alone (light grey bars) and the cut strategy alone (dark grey bars). The figure shows that both the C&R and the rotate alone strategies outperform the double-A bond benchmark in most years. The double-A corporate benchmark returned an average excess return of 4.50% per annum, whereas the C&R strategy averaged 5.27%, an annual outperformance of 78bp. For the first time in our studies we observed that the rotate strategy alone performed best. That is, the rotate strategy generated an annual average excess return of 5.43%, topping the double-A benchmark by 94bp and the C&R strategy by16bp. We also observed that, for the first time, the cut strategy alone underperformed the benchmark with an excess return of 4.33% per annum, 16bp less than the benchmark.

The third and final panel of Figure 9.12 presents cumulative annual uncompounded excess returns for the various portfolios of double-A-rated corporate bonds. Consistent with our analysis of annual returns, the figure shows that the rotate strategy (dark grey line) has the highest uncompounded excess return over the period at 38.0%, topping the 31.4% return of the double-A benchmark (black line) by 7.6% over the seven-year period. The C&R strategy (dashed black) also tops the benchmark at 36.9%, but with only a 5.5% advantage over the period. Clearly, if pension managers could realise these excess returns provided by the rotate strategy, given the effects of compounding, they could quickly make up deficits in defined benefit plans. Finally, one can observe that the 30.3% cumulative uncompounded return of the cut strategy alone (light grey line) underperforms the benchmark by 1.1% over the period.

Figure 9.12 C&R strategy on double-A rated bonds in Citi's BIG index broken down by index, C&R, cut only and rotate only; top: average one-year default rates; middle: annual excess returns over one-month T-bills; bottom: cumulative uncompounded excess returns

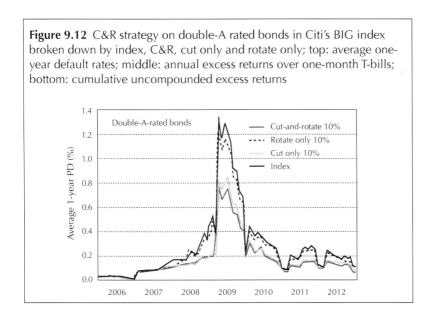

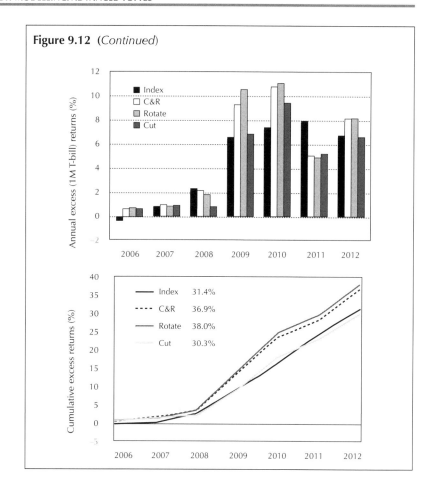

Figure 9.12 (*Continued*)

THE C&R STRATEGY IN PRACTICE

Although the C&R strategies consistently outperform credit benchmarks, there are challenges in applying these strategies for practical portfolio management. For example, it is difficult, if not impossible, to buy all the bonds in the benchmarks studied above, and monthly rotations on entire portfolios would likely be prohibitively expensive. Still, there are a number of viable options for practical deployment of the C&R method, including:

❑ deployment of the strategy on a smaller number of credits;
❑ lag into the strategy from new investments and redemptions;

❏ use of CDS on corporate credits; and

❏ construct an exchange-traded fund (ETF) based on the C&R strategy.

We consider each of these methods below.

C&R on subsets of benchmark bonds

We were interested in the extent to which the C&R method could be applied to index-tracking portfolios of various sizes while still outperforming the reference index. Accordingly, we (Benzschawel, Lee and Bernstein, 2011) studied the effects of portfolio size, transactions costs and turnover rate on C&R performance by constructing monthly US BIG index tracking portfolios of 50, 100, 200 and 500 bonds from January 2001 to January 2007. 100 portfolios of each size were generated to minimise the sampling bias, and results were analysed with and without transaction costs. We also constructed 100 portfolios of 200 bonds selected from the index bond universe at random to serve as a benchmark. Finally, we applied constraints of maximum monthly turnover of 5% or 10% of the portfolio.

Table 9.3 displays annual excess returns over the US BIG index by portfolio size for 5% and 10% monthly turnover limits. Results for the random 200-bond benchmark-tracking portfolio are also shown. Regardless of portfolio size and turnover, the C&R strategy outperforms random tracking portfolios of 200 credits. Note that the absolute levels of returns decrease with increasing portfolio size but their standard deviations decrease more, such that larger portfolios have lower absolute, but higher risk-adjusted, returns. The greater return with smaller portfolios presumably results from the fact that the rotate strategy necessarily selects bonds whose average richness and cheapness are more extreme.

The excess returns in Table 9.3 do not include the costs of monthly portfolio adjustments, either to maintain the C&R strategy or those required to merely track the index. To estimate the costs for implementing the C&R strategy, transaction costs were assumed for each bond based on the issuing firm's credit rating, the bond's time since issuance, and issue size.[15] As shown in Table 9.4, transactions costs reduce significantly excess P&L and information ratios over returns in the BIG index. That is, including transactions costs lowers average returns by about 50bp across portfolio sizes for the 5% turnover case, with decreases in information ratios of between 0.5 and 0.9. Transactions costs are larger for the 10% of turnover cases at just over 90bp per annum, and information ratios decrease by 0.6 for the 50-bond portfolios to 1.6 for the 500-bond portfolios.

Table 9.3 Effect of portfolio size and turnover limits on outperformance of the C&R strategy

| | Monthly turnover = 5% | | |
Size	μ	σ	Info. ratio
50	92	122	0.8
100	85	103	0.8
200	74	82	0.9
500	65	54	1.2
Random*	18	42	0.4

| | Monthly turnover = 10% | | |
Size	μ	σ	Info. ratio
50	133	146	0.9
100	123	123	1.0
200	103	95	1.1
500	74	57	1.3
Random*	11	41	0.3

*Random portfolio has a size of 200

Despite these seemingly large transaction costs, their practical implications are questionable. That is, the analysis does not account for transactions that would necessarily be incurred to maintain any index replication strategy with a much smaller number of bonds. In fact, because the index composition changed nearly completely over the 11-year period of the study, a replicating portfolio would require many buys and sells. For example, compare the effects of transactions costs on the 200-bond benchmark and C&R portfolios in Table 9.4. Transactions costs for the 5% case (top panel) decrease the random benchmark returns by 48bp, but reduce the C&R returns by only 52bp. Similarly, for 10% turnover (bottom panel), the 200-bond benchmark return decreases by 83bp, but decreases in returns from the C&R strategy are only slightly greater at 94bp. Thus, transactions costs should be considered in the context of alternative portfolios that might be constructed. From that perspective, the cost of the substitutions required by the C&R strategy for any size portfolio that mimics the index would likely not be much greater than maintenance of a similar-sized tracking portfolio.

Table 9.4 Effects of transactions costs on average returns and information ratios of C&R portfolios

| | | Monthly turnover = 5% | | | |
| | | Change | | Result | |
Size	Return before costs	Return	Info. ratio	Return	Info. ratio
50	92	−52	−0.5	40	0.3
100	85	−52	−0.5	33	0.3
200	74	−52	−0.6	22	0.3
500	65	−41	−0.9	14	0.3
Random*	18	−48	−1.1	−30	−0.7

| | | Monthly turnover = 10% | | | |
| | | Change | | Result | |
Size	Return before costs	Return	Info. ratio	Return	Info. ratio
50	133	−94	−0.6	39	0.3
100	123	−90	−0.7	33	0.3
200	103	−94	−1.0	7	0.1
500	74	−91	−1.6	−15	−0.3
Random*	11	−83	−2.0	−72	−1.7

*Random portfolio has a size of 200

Lagging into the C&R strategy through portfolio attrition

One approach for investment firms to take advantage of the C&R strategy is to deploy the strategy gradually over time. For example, for funds that experience regular inflows and redemptions (eg, mutual funds, insurance companies and pension funds), selling the riskiest bonds and bonds with poor value to meet redemptions and putting new money into bonds with lower risk and high relative value would result, over time, in portfolios that approach those consistent with the C&R criteria.

We have used this strategy over the years to help clients analyse and adjust the risk–reward characteristics of their credit portfolios. For example, consider the table in Figure 9.13, which depicts characteristics of a sample of high-yield corporate bonds from a portfolio that we have analysed. The first few columns contain bonds' indicative information, to which we add information on default risk, credit momentum, implied credit ratings and relative value. The column on the right indicates which action the C&R strategy implies for the bond. That is, the portfolio is analysed with respect to the relative value plot in the lower portion of Figure 9.13, where the grey line is the best fit to the entire set of corporate bonds, with the solid circles representing bonds in the portfolio. As in the previous plots, the white circles represent bonds whose PDs put them in the riskiest 10% of the corporate bond index population (ie, bonds to be cut), the grey symbols indicate bonds with poor relative value (ie, to be rotated out) and the black circles are bonds to overweight. These classifications appear in the right-most column of the table in Figure 9.13.

The risk and relative value of the portfolio in Figure 9.13 is summarised in the top left panel of Figure 9.14. The right-most columns of that table show an average par-weighted Z-score deviation of -0.02σ from fair value for an average relative value (R-Val) of -4bp. The negative sign is indicative of a portfolio having average spreads below that which the market is paying on average for that combination of risks. Given the analysis in Figure 9.13, bond transactions were made, with the resulting portfolio summary in the lower left table of Figure 9.14 and the resulting relative value plot at the lower right (the relative value plot in the upper right is reproduced from Figure 9.13). The summary shows that the rotations have left the

Figure 9.13 Sample portfolio of high-yield bonds (March 28, 2013)

Bonds							Credit analytics					Relative value		
Par amt (US$)	Ticker	Description	CUSIP	S&P rating	OAS (bps)	Duration (years)	One-year PD (%)	One-month momentum	Three-month momentum	Implied rating	PD model	Z-score	R val (bps)	Cut and rotate
1,000	AVA	9.0 04/19	05349	B–	714	3.45	9.58	0	–0.04	c3	MKI	–0.01	–5	Cut
1,000	BAC	5.7 1/24/22	06051	A–	195	7.13	0.12	–0.04	–0.01	a1–	HPD	–0.90	–159	Rotate out
250	BBD	4.25 01/16	09775	BB	261	2.63	1.68	–0.06	–0.05	b1	HPD	–0.77	–174	Rotate out
60	BBT	5.625 perp	54937	A–	148		0.10	–0.03	+0.00	a1+	HPD			Include
1,000	BC	7.375 09/23	11704	BB–	472	7.51	1.09	+0.07	–0.03	b2–	HPD	–0.36	–128	Include
994	BCF	10.0 02/19	12157	B–	570	1.74	1.82	–0.05	0	b1–	MKI	+0.63	+196	Include
1,000	BDC	5.5 09/22	07745	BB	343	6.18	0.28	–0.14	–0.00	b3	HPD	–0.26	–66	Include
1,000	BEA	5.25 04/22	05538	BB+	308	5.96	0.10	–0.20	–0.09	a1–	HPD	–0.04	–8	Include
4,500	BMC	4.5 12/22	05592	BBB+	229	7.85	0.48	–0.11	0	b3–	HPD	–1.20	–278	Rotate out
2,000	BME	6.5 08/20	09061	B+	409	4.57	0.92	0		b1+	MKI	–0.22	–63	Include
1,000	BME	6.5 '20 (sub)	09061	B+	462	3.98	0.92	0		b1+	MKI	+0.05	+16	Include
500	BOR	9.5 10/15	56808	NCE	699	2.22	4.51	0	+0.01	c3–	MKI	+0.48	+192	Include
500	BRC	4.525 01/23	11162	BB+	328	7.88	0.11	–0.09	–0.01	a1–	HPD	–0.14	–31	Include
1,000	CCI	7.125 11/19	22822	B+	297	1.48	0.22	+0.07	0	b3	HPD	+0.47	+80	Rotate out
1,000	CCI	2.381 12/17	14987	B+	157	4.45	0.22	+0.07	0	b3	HPD	–1.15	–180	Rotate out
1,000	CCI	3.849 04/23	14987	B+	198	8.34	0.22	+0.07	0	b3	HPD	–1.18	–236	Rotate out
250	CCK	4.5 01/23	22818	BB+	315	7.91	0.51	–0.06	–0.07	b3–	HPD	–0.74	–201	Rotate out

risk characteristics relatively unchanged, but have increased the relative value of the portfolio from –4bp below average to +27bp above average.

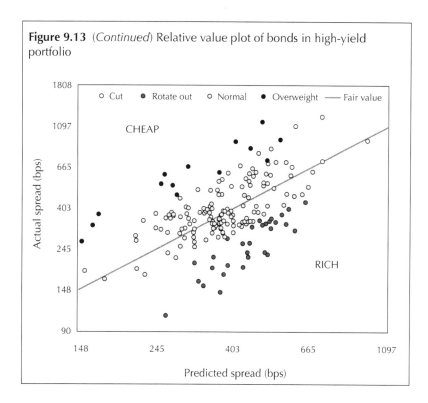

Figure 9.13 (*Continued*) Relative value plot of bonds in high-yield portfolio

The long/short CDS rule-based investment (RuBI)

One might also to apply the C&R strategy in the corporate CDS market. In 2004, we proposed a method for generating long/short trades using CDS in the North American corporate credit default swap index series (CDX.NA.IG) based on the C&R strategy.[16] The CDX.NA.IG consists of 125 of the most liquid CDS referencing North American investment-grade firms whose industry sectors generally span the range of those in the credit market. The terms of the index CDS are five years at issue, and the index is reconstituted every six months. Implementation of the C&R strategy as deployed in the CDS market are summarised below.

Figure 9.14 Portfolio summaries and relative value plots before (top) and after (bottom) bond transactions to improve relative value

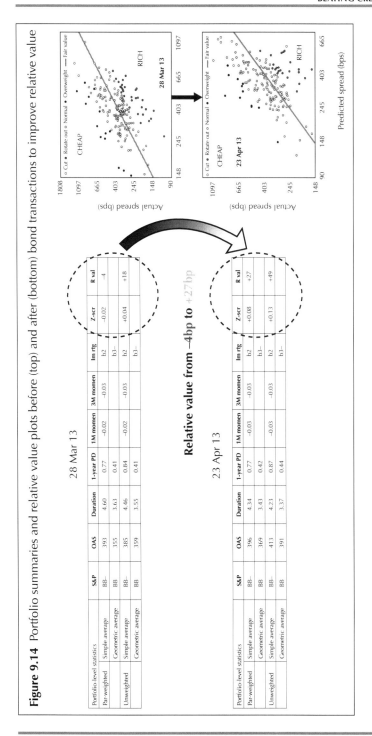

Relative value from −4bp to +27bp

The main features of the long/short CDS RuBI strategy are:

❏ eliminate from consideration the three CDS with the largest PDs (risk), and with the best and worst relative value (model error);
❏ buy protection on 20 CDS with the "worst" relative value (ie, the smallest spreads given their PDs and recovery values);
❏ sell protection on 20 CDS with the "best" relative value (ie, the largest spreads given their PDs and recovery values); and
❏ optimisation constraints on long/short CDS mismatch:
❏ 0.5% for dV01-weighted beta;
❏ 10% for estimated recovery rate;
❏ two maximum sector difference; and
❏ 0.5% mismatch between cumulative long and short PDs.

Unfortunately, since the CDX index was introduced in late 2003, until latterly we have had very little history on which to validate that strategy. However, Benzschawel and Lee (2012) published a detailed analysis of performance of the long/short CDS strategy since 2003, as described herein. In addition, we update its performance since that report.

The determination of CDS relative value and the CDS elimination criteria for the RuBI trade are illustrated in the left and middle panels of Figure 9.15. The left panel shows spread premiums on July 1, 2010, for over 400 five-year CDS plotted versus the PDs of their reference obligors from the HPD model. The best-fit line to those CDS is shown, with CDS having better than average relative value above the line and CDS with poorer relative value below. The same line is used to determine the "rich" and "cheap" CDS in the CDX.NA.IG as shown in the middle panel of Figure 9.15. That plot also shows the three CDS with best and worst relative value that are eliminated, along with the CDS whose reference obligors have the largest PDs. Finally, the diagram also shades in grey, the 20 credits of good and poor relative value, respectively, on which credit protection is sold and bought.[17] Note that there are two expected sources of P&L from the CDS RuBI strategy. First, each trade is designed to have positive carry: the difference in premiums between long and short CDS positions. The other potential source of P&L comes from convergence of rich and cheap credits to fair value.

We report the performance of three-month long/short CDS RuBI trades initiated monthly from 2004 to 2012. Each monthly trade consisted of a US$10 million investment in 20 long CDS and 20 short CDS positions (US$250,000 per CDS) in the current on-the-run five-year CDS. Thus, at any one time our simulations contained three overlapping trades, with partial overlap of constituent CDS.[18] Recall that there are two potential sources of P&L for the RuBI trades: (i) positive carry from selling protection on CDS with wide spreads and buying protection on CDS whose spreads are relatively tight; and (ii) CDS having spreads above average tightening toward the average and the widening of rich CDS spreads toward the average. This convergence is evident in the RuBI trades as illustrated in the right panel of Figure 9.15. The darkest region in the plot shows the near-steady P&L from the positive carry on the long/short CDS positions. The carry accounts for about a quarter of the P&L from the RuBI trades (12% of the 50% cumulative return). The other 75% of the RuBI return results from the convergence of the CDS to fair value (ie, the grey line shown in the middle panel of Figure 9.15).

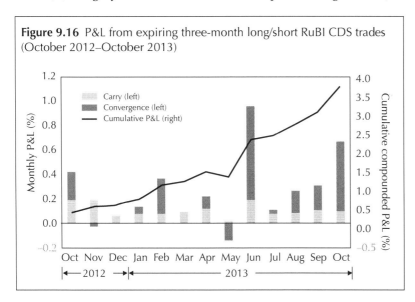

Figure 9.16 P&L from expiring three-month long/short RuBI CDS trades (October 2012–October 2013)

Figure 9.16 displays monthly returns from the simulated RuBI strategy from October 2012 to October 2013. The market-neutral RuBI strategy posted positive P&L in 11 out of 13 months in the period. The figure

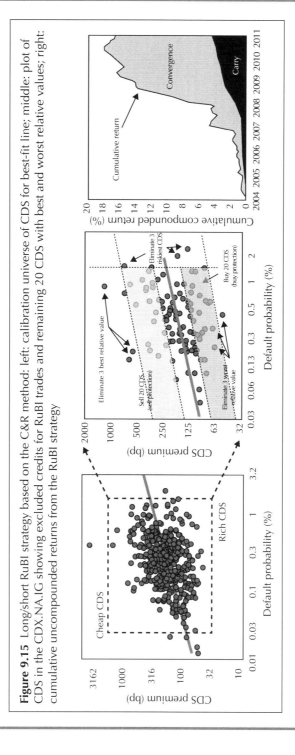

Figure 9.15 Long/short RuBI strategy based on the C&R method: left: calibration universe of CDS for best-fit line; middle: plot of CDS in the CDX.NA.IG showing excluded credits for RuBI trades and remaining 20 CDS with best and worst relative values; right: cumulative uncompounded returns from the RuBI strategy

also breaks out P&L from carry (light grey bars) and convergence (dark grey bars). As is consistent with the historical tests shown in the right panel of Figure 9.15, P&L from convergence makes up the bulk of the returns from the RuBI strategy. That is, the RuBI trade had monthly convergence P&L of 33bp with a 20bp monthly return from carry.

Cut-and-rotate ETF/ETN

Another approach to deploying the C&R strategy would be to construct an ETF or exchange-traded note (ETN) consistent with the C&R strategy. For example, bonds in the fund would only be those not in the 10% of the riskiest credits and, for any sector, only the 10% with best relative value. Also, authorised participants might only be allowed to contribute securities or make redemptions in the fund if they improve its relative value as assessed by the C&R criteria.

This could also be done in CDS, as we (Benzschawel and Lee, 2012) presented the outlines of a funded and unfunded ETN on the RuBI strategy. The RuBI note could be traded either over-the-counter (OTC) or as an ETN or ETF.[19] The structure of such a note is relatively straightforward. Consider an investor that wishes to invest US$10,000 in the long/short RuBI trade at its current value. The current value of the trade on any given day is the net asset value (NAV) of the sum of one-third of the value of each of the three underlying open monthly RuBI trades that serve as the current basis of the index.[20] Thus, a US$10,000 initial investment would be apportioned with a US$3,333.33 investment in each of the three open CDS contracts. In addition, it is assumed that the funded note would pay three-month Libor on the amount of the principal invested in each contract (for further details on the RuBI note, please see our report).

WHY DOES THE C&R STRATEGY WORK?

A strategy that consistently outperforms benchmarks would appear to run counter to the efficient markets hypothesis (Fama, 1965). That is, given the information available in the marketplace, one should not be able to consistently achieve returns in excess of average market returns on a risk-adjusted basis. Nevertheless, we have described herein all the benchmarks upon which we have tested the C&R strategy and have yet to underperform in any of the cases. Accordingly, it is natural to ask: "How and why does the C&R strategy work?" In fact, we claim to have come to some understanding of the basis for the consistent outperformance of the C&R strategy. We here present a brief summary of our understanding derived from several decades of research on the relation between default risk, credit ratings and corporate bond spreads. In short, our method takes advantages of the following facts and their interactions.

❑ Most credit benchmarks are defined, at least in part, by agency credit ratings.

❑ Agency ratings lag the markets' perception of credit risk (Benzschawel and Adler, 2002). In fact, by the time agency ratings change, bond spreads are already at the average of the category to which they have changed, but begin to move a year or more prior to that action.

❑ Idiosyncratic changes in firms' equity prices, on average, lead changes in the bonds' spreads to US Treasuries (Benzschawel, 2012), and equity-based credit models (HPD and KMV) capture this effect. Reasons for this include that the equity market has advantages over the bond market with respect to analyst coverage, trading volume and market frictions (less cost, smaller sized execution and more alternatives for going long and short).

❑ Firms whose credits ratings have been recently downgraded/upgraded have downward/upward ratings momentum relative to firms having identical, but stable, ratings (Altman and Kao, 1992; Bangia *et al* (2002); Christensen, Hansen and Lando (2004); Lando and Skødeberg, 2002).

❑ The ratings upgrade-to-downgrade ratio is roughly 0.7 per year on average (Vazza and Kraemer, 2011).

❑ A downward change in rating results in larger average spread widening than spread tightening from a rating upgrade (Benzschawel and Assing, 2012). This is due to the asymmetry between spread changes between higher (smaller spread change) and lower (greater spread change) and ratings changes.

❑ Bonds with higher volatilities have higher default risk (Merton, 1974) and lower spread compensation per unit of volatility (Asness, Frazzini and Pedersen (2012); Frazzini, Kabiller and Pedersen (2012); Frazzini and Pedersen (2013). This has been termed "the embedded leverage effect" or "Buffet's alpha".

CONCLUSION

To better understand how to select assets for credit portfolios, we constructed portfolios using several automated credit picking methods (ie, credit picking "robots") and examined the relative risks and performances of the selected portfolios. In an initial study, the robots selected multiple 100-bond portfolios from the same large set of North American corporate bonds each year from 1994 to 2002 using identical issuer, sector and credit rating constraints. Each robot used a different credit picking algorithm: random selection (benchmark); selecting the highest-yielding credits (greedy); choosing the least-risky bonds based on default probabilities (conservative); or choosing the highest-yielding credits after removing the riskiest ones (hybrid). All three non-random credit picking algorithms outperformed the random benchmark on an absolute return basis. However, the greedy robot, which picked only the highest-yielding credits, had the lowest risk-adjusted return, even below the benchmark, and the highest annual default rate. Meanwhile, the conservative robot, by choosing the least risky credits, had both a higher absolute and risk-adjusted return with a lower average default rate than the benchmark. Finally, the hybrid robot, which cut out the riskiest credits and then selected by yield, outperformed all strategies in both absolute and risk-adjusted returns.

Results from the credit picking studies inspired development of an algorithm to outperform corporate credit benchmarks by cutting allocations from the riskiest assets in the target benchmark along with those having the worst relative value, and overweighting high-value credits. Our initial studies focused on outperforming returns from corporate bonds in investment-grade and high-yield indexes. We also analysed separately the benefits of cutting the riskiest bonds and of rotating out of the "richest" credits into the "cheapest" ones. Over an initial test period from 1994 to 2004, we found that although both the individual "cut" and "rotate" strategies underperformed the index in some years, in combination, the C&R strategy outperformed corporate bonds in the index in every year initially tested. More specifically, we find that cutting the allocation from 10% of the bonds with the greatest default risk underperforms credit indexes when credit spreads are stable or improving, but outperforms during periods of credit spread widening.

Conversely, the rotation strategy performs best in stable and improving credit environments, only underperforming when credit quality deteriorates. We also found similar patterns of results in the high-yield and credit default swap markets.

In a separate set of studies for the period 1997 to 2007, we explored the effects of portfolio size and monthly credit substitution limits on performance of the C&R strategy over similar portfolios that tracked a broad investment-grade bond index. We found that C&R portfolios with as few as 50 bonds with similar average statistics as the index consistently outperformed 50-bond index-tracking benchmark portfolios.

After a seven-year hiatus, in 2011 we examined and reported on how the C&R strategy would have performed on investment-grade portfolios since 2004, and described some enhancements to our methodology. The only major alteration in our methods from earlier studies was to use a relative value function that incorporated bonds' estimated recovery values in default in addition to their default probabilities and durations. The absolute and risk-adjusted "out-of-sample" returns from 2005 to 2013 are similar to our earlier findings, as are contributions from the cut and rotate components. In fact, in the 19-year test period, the method only underperformed the investment-grade benchmark in 2007 (by 17bp) and 2008 (by 9bp) amid outsized index spread widening during the credit crisis. Finally, we tested various combinations of cut and rotation percentages away from our original 10% assumptions, but found no convincing evidence to alter our current adjustment criteria.

Given the success of the C&R method on North American credits, we examined the effectiveness of the strategy of outperforming: (i) the corporate bonds in a European investment-grade bond index; (ii) a portfolio of double-A rated bonds from a North American bond index; (iii) the Chinese Dim Sum index; and (iv) an Asian broad bond index. With the exception of the double-A rated bond study, those later analyses were limited by the shorter time series of available returns than in the earlier studies. Still, we find that the strategy, with no adjustment, outperforms the index benchmark on all those indexes tested. Finally, we report an update of our study of the C&R strategy as embodied in long/short CDS trades.

The chapter concluded with a discussion of issues regarding the implementation of the C&R strategy by various types of institutional clients, and provided suggestions for practical deployment of the method.

1   We used Moody's KMV model, a commercially available product, for our original studies (Crosby, 1999; Kealhofer and Kurbat, 2001) and later acquired Sobehart and Keenan's (2002, 2003) HPD model. Both models use information from the equity market, along with balance sheet and income statement information, to assess the default risk of public firms.

2   See Benzschawel et al (2004). See also Citigroup (2011, 2013) for a description of constituents in the benchmark indexes.

3   See McDermott, Skarabot and Kroujiline (2002, 2003); Benzschawel et al (2003); Benzschawel, Lee and Bernstein (2011); and Benzschawel (2012).

4   The universe of bonds available for selection were corporate bonds in Citigroup's BIG and High Yield indexes (Citigroup Index, 2011). For the high-yield index, only bonds that were not in bankruptcy or default and had no variable coupons were included in the sample. 10–20% of the firms with bonds in our sample did not have EDFs from the KMV model, and these were excluded from the sample. For an additional description of the bond database, see Benzschawel and Adler (2002).

5   The PD calculation in the KMV model is based on a Merton-type structural model of default risk (Merton, 1974) where the credit risk is driven by the firm's value process. The estimated PD of a firm is driven by two main inputs: the asset volatility of the firm and its leverage defined as the default point divided by the market value of the firm's assets. The EDF methodology is based on the following steps: (i) use the firm's equity price and equity volatility to estimate its asset value and volatility; (ii) identify the default point (based on financial information) and estimate the distance-to-default; (iii) the measure of default risk; and (iii) scale the distance-to-default to match historical default probabilities over a given time horizon.

6   Citi's BIG and High Yield indexes are also described in Citigroup Index Group (2013).

7   The corporate bonds in the Citigroup BIG index are all investment grade and have been marked-to-market at every month-end since January 1985. The size criterion for the index has grown from a minimum of US$25 million in 1985, US$50 million in 1992, US$100 million in 1995, US$200 million in 2001 and US$250 million in 2005. The index is rebalanced every month. For a description of the Citi indexes, see Citigroup (2013).

8   These results were first presented in Benzschawel and Jiang (2004).

9   The sectors are consumer, energy, finance, manufacturing, service, transportation and utilities.

10 For an example, see Lee and Benzschawel (2014).

11 The decision to include recovery values in the relative value calculation is based on our finding that differential effects of recovery values from Moody's LossCalc model were evident in credit spreads for investment-grade and high-yield credit default swaps.

12 One may be curious about the 8bp underperformance of the C&R strategy in 2008, given that the cut strategy alone generated 56bp of outperformance while the rotate method by itself lost only 10bp. The underperformance resulted from the cut causing the high-yielding bonds within the higher 10% of default risk to be excluded prior to their potential inclusion in the rotate strategy. It is important to remember that this anomaly occurred amid the credit crisis of 2007–08.

13 The EuroBIG bond covers all sectors of the investment-grade fixed income market that are accessible to institutional investors, and measures their performance and risk characteristics (for further information, see Citigroup Index Group, 2013). Much like its North

American counterpart, the EuroBIG is comprised of fixed rate bonds rated BBB–/Baa3 and above, having maturities greater than one year, but denominated in euros and having a size greater than €500 million. Note that, similar to the North American BIG index, the EuroBIG also contains sovereign, agency and other sovereign-sponsored bonds, but we are only performing C&R and comparing returns on the corporate bonds in those indexes.

14   The credit component of the CPLI, while referenced to double-A rated bonds in Citi's BIG index, actually deviates slightly from their returns. This is because returns from bonds that have been downgraded by the rating agencies over the month in question are deleted from the CPLI calculations, along with those bonds whose spreads are two standard deviations below the average double-B bond spreads.

15   Those adjustments ranged from 2bp for large, recently issued triple-As to 12bp for smaller, older triple-B bonds.

16   See Benzschawel and Jiang (2004).

17   Note that, in the parlance of CDS trading, one who is long CDS receives the premium and experiences a mark-to-market loss when the premium widens, thereby being short the credit. Conversely, one with a short CDS position pays the premium and is long the credit, benefitting if the CDS premium decreases.

18   See Benzschawel and Lee (2012) for a more detailed description of the long/short CDS RuBI strategy.

19   Given that the underlying assets are derivatives (ie, CDS), the existing regulatory environment would make it more difficult to implement the strategy as an ETN or ETF, as opposed to a note issued by a broker–dealer.

20   Recall that each month we construct a new three-month long/short CDS RuBI trade, so at any time there are three trades running concurrently, with a large degree of overlap of CDS in each. The index assumes an equal investment in each of the three open RuBI trades.

APPENDIX 9.1: ADJUSTING SPREADS FOR RECOVERY VALUE

The most significant change to our methodology concerned adding an explicit model-based recovery value to the relative value calculation used for credit rotation. In our original studies, relative value functions were computed separately for each industry sector. The decision to include recovery values in the relative-value calculation is based on our finding that recovery values from Moody's Loss-Calc model were evident in credit spreads for investment-grade and high-yield credit default swaps (CDS). To demonstrate this, we adjusted credit spreads from the same set of roughly 700 CDS using a constant recovery value of 40% or the firms' recovery values from Moody's LossCalc model. For example, the spread value of recovery can be approximated as:

$$s_0 = -\frac{1}{d} * \log\left[1 - \frac{1 - e^{-(s*d)}}{1 - R}\right]$$

(A.9.1.1)

where s and s_0 are the market spread and zero-recovery spread, respectively, d is the duration and R is the recovery value used to make the adjustment.

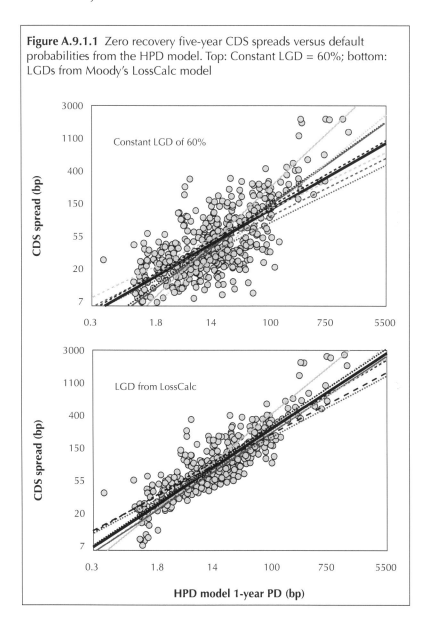

Figure A.9.1.1 Zero recovery five-year CDS spreads versus default probabilities from the HPD model. Top: Constant LGD = 60%; bottom: LGDs from Moody's LossCalc model

Figure A.9.1.1 displays zero recovery spreads as a function of default probabilities inferred from the HPD model using the constant RV=40% (top) and recovery values from LossCalc (bottom). Note that the axes are the same in both plots. Although the best-fit solid lines to the data are similar, the volatilities of zero-recovery spreads around those lines are smaller when using LossCalc. The results demonstrate that, even for investment-grade credits, the market recognises differences in recovery value and these differences are captured, at least in part, by Moody's LossCalc model. Finally, the lighter lines in the figure are fit to zero-recovery values by industry sector. The reduction of variability of those lines around the average suggests that much of the predictive power of Moody's LossCalc comes from accounting for the influence of industry sector on recovery value.

Based on the results in Figure A.9.1.1 we now evaluate bond relative value using constant recovery value spreads. But instead of a constant $R=0\%$, we assume a constant value of 40% for all firms. The calculation assumes that if R is the assumed recovery rate for the asset and c is the constant reference rate of recovery, one can estimate the spread value of recovery s_r using as:

$$s_r = s_R - s_c \qquad (A.9.1.2)$$

Having the spread value of recovery (see below) and estimates of R for all assets, one can then adjust assets' (eg, bonds, CDS, or loans) spreads to a reference rate of recovery, c, as:

$$s_R^c = s + s_r \qquad (A.9.1.3)$$

where it seems reasonable to assume that $c=40\%$, the average of senior unsecured corporate debt (Altman and Kishore, 1996).

The spread correction for default depends on the duration of the asset, d, and the reference rate of recovery, c. Then, given the bond's spread in basis points, s, its duration in years, d, and assumed recovery rate in percent, R, the spread adjusted to the reference recovery rate $c=40\%$ can be calculated as

$$s_R^c = \frac{-10000}{d} * \ln\left\{1 - \left[\frac{\left(1 - \frac{c}{100}\right)}{\left(1 - \frac{R}{100}\right)}\right] * \left[1 - \exp\left(\frac{-s}{10000} * d\right)\right]\right\}$$

$$\qquad (A.9.1.4)$$

Also, given an adjusted spread s_R^c, determined using the parameters above, the market spread can be calculated as:

$$s = \frac{-10000}{d} * \ln\left\{1 - \left[\frac{\left(1 - \frac{R}{100}\right)}{\left(1 - \frac{c}{100}\right)}\right] * \left[1 - \exp\left(\frac{-s_R^c}{10000} * d\right)\right]\right\}$$

(A.9.1.5)

The relative value function in Equation 9.1 of the text can be rewritten to accommodate the adjustment for differences in recovery value as:

$$\ln(s_R^c) = \gamma_0 + \left[\gamma_1 * \ln(p_1)\right] + \left[\gamma_2 * \ln(d)\right] - \varepsilon$$

(A.9.1.6)

where p_1 is the estimate of the one-year default probability from the HPD model and all other quantities are as defined above. Values of γ_0, γ_1 and γ_2 are determined by minimising the error term ε across the universe of credits.[1]

After converting observed market spreads to "constant recovery spreads" we regress bond's values of s_R^c for $c=40\%$ versus their durations and values one-year default probability according to Equation A.9.1.6. The coefficients for γ_0, γ_1 and γ_2 of Equation A.9.1.6 on September 25, 2011 were found to be 6.06, 0.19 and 0.26, respectively, and the resulting constant recovery spreads appear in the top panel of Figure A.9.1.2. That plot also shows the best-fit regression line to the recovery-adjusted spread values. The relative value of any bond, i, denoted z_i, is calculated with respect to the regression line as:

$$z_i = \frac{\ln(\varepsilon_i)}{\sigma_{\ln(\varepsilon)}}$$

(A.9.1.7)

where ε is as defined in Equation A.9.1.6 and $\sigma_{\ln(\varepsilon)}$, the standard deviation of the logarithms of the errors, was found to be 0.62. The lower panel of Figure A.9.1.2 displays the differences between predicted and recovery-adjusted market spreads as a function of predicted spread for September 25, 2011. The random pattern of deviations from the "fair value" line is indicative of a lack of spread-related bias in the relative value function.

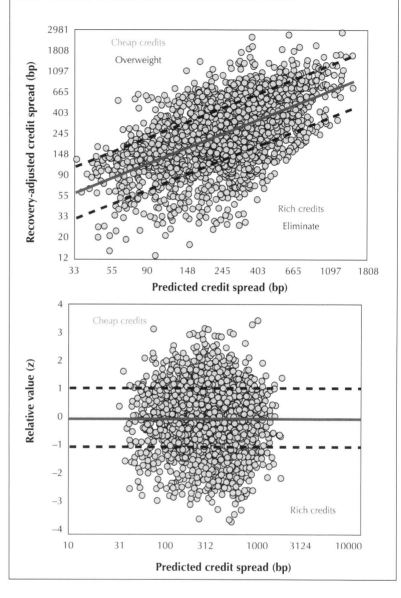

Figure A.9.1.2 Top: Actual versus predicted spreads for corporate bonds in Citi's investment-grade and high-yield indexes; bottom: residuals (ie, relative values) of bonds to best-fit line in z-score units

21 Note that we tried several variations of correction for recovery value. The method embodied in Equation A.9.1.5 produced the least differences between predicted and market spreads of those tested.

10

Hedging the Credit Risk Premium

OVERVIEW

In this chapter, we will use our understanding of the credit risk premium (see Chapter 5) to devise and test methods for hedging systematic spread moves in cash bonds due to changes in investors risk appetites and/or market volatility. Based on the ability to decompose credit spreads into default and non-default components, short positions in the North American investment-grade CDS index, *CDX. IG.NA*, provide very good hedges for changes in the credit spread premiums of cash bonds. In particular, we find that changes in *CDX. IG.NA* best track changes in bonds' risk premiums over three-month periods. Thus, we use trailing three-month changes as the basis for computing hedge ratios, β_t, between the cash bond risk premium and the CDS index. We report a comparison of performance of a naïve hedging strategy (ie, $\beta_t = 1$) with a dynamic strategy whereby the hedge ratio is determined based on the slopes of regression analyses on a rolling window of changes in the CDS index and the credit risk premium. The naïve $\beta_t = 1$ hedge performs well except during the liquidity crisis of late 2007 to 2009, whereas the dynamic hedge works well over the entire test period since 2004. These results suggest that investors can mitigate spread volatility owing to changes in the credit risk premium using the *CDX* index. In addition, it appears possible to use the *CDX* index to replicate the non-default spread (*NDS*) premium of cash bond portfolios.

INTRODUCTION

With the introduction of interest rate swaps in the early 1980s, lenders and investors were able to minimise their exposure to changes in interest rates, even for very long-dated commitments.[1] Arguably, the interest rate swap may be the most useful innovation produced using financial engineering. No longer must long-term investors worry about fluctuations in interest rates; they can hedge that exposure by choosing to swap fixed rate for floating rate debt.

Unfortunately, investors in credit spread products have no such option for hedging their exposure to systematic changes in credit spreads, and these changes can be large. Consider, for example, the top panel of Figure 10.1, which displays the average 4.5-year US Treasury yield (dark grey) and the corresponding average investment-grade bond yields (black line) since 1998. The light grey line is the estimated yield compensation for default obtained using average PDs for the bonds from the Sobehart and Keenan (2002, 2003) HPD credit model. That is:

$$s_d = -\frac{1}{T}\ln[1 - p_T \cdot LGD]$$

(10.1)

where T is 4.5 years, the average duration of the bonds, p_T, is the average cumulative default probability to time T and LGD is the expected loss in default.[2]

The lower plot compares the compensation for the risk premium and its average level over the period – that is, it displays the average monthly credit spread premium for investment-grade corporate bonds. As is evident from Figure 10.1 and elaborated in detail in Chapter 5 on the credit risk premium, the majority of the yield spread to US Treasuries for corporate bonds is due to something other than not receiving the cashflows from default. In particular, the lower portion of Figure 10.1 shows that this compensation can be as much as 800bp during times of market stress, as in 2008. Although default risk was large in 2008 (difference between light and dark grey curves), default risk was also relatively large in 2002, but the NDS was near its long-term average. Of course, during the credit crisis, bond investors incurred large mark-to-market losses on their portfolios while, at least in general, still receiving their promised cashflows.

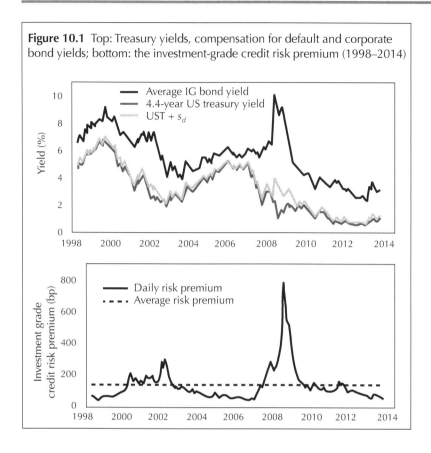

Figure 10.1 Top: Treasury yields, compensation for default and corporate bond yields; bottom: the investment-grade credit risk premium (1998–2014)

UNDERSTANDING THE CREDIT RISK PREMIUM

Since Chapter 5 contains a detailed discussion of the credit risk premium, it is reiterated only briefly here. Recall that only latterly have market participants begun to unravel the components that underlie the spread compensation for investing in default-risky assets. Although the early work of Jones, Mason and Rosenfeld (1984) suggested that compensation for default accounted for only a small fraction of the credit spread, it was Elton *et al* (2001) who first documented the role of the credit risk premium in corporate bond spreads.[3] Using the logic embedded in Equation 10.1, Elton *et al* decomposed the credit spreads of single-A rated corporate bonds into their compensation for default and the remaining portion, which they interpreted as the credit risk premium. We designate the spread compensation for default as s_d and the credit risk premium as s_λ. The value of s_d can be viewed as the spread compensation necessary to compensate for the expected loss of cashflows due to default. That is, an investor who receives a yield spread to US Treasuries equal to s_d receives only an amount equal to the expected return from an equivalent-duration US Treasury security.

Recall from Chapter 5 that we decompose bonds' credit spreads into the compensation for default s_d and into compensation for spread volatility s_λ, where:

$$s_d = -\frac{1}{T} \ln[1 - p_T \cdot LGD] \text{ and } s_{\lambda,i} = \lambda_t * f(\beta_i) * \sigma_{v,i} \tag{10.2}$$

where T is the duration of the bond, p_T is the cumulative default probability to time T, LGD is the expected loss from default, σ is the spread volatility, λ_t is the current price of spread volatility (ie, the Sharpe ratio) and λ_t is the same for all credits. Recall also that $f(\beta_i)$ is a function that corrects for the effects of β-dependent "embedded leverage" in credit spreads.

Putting those two expressions together, we can express the overall yield spread to US Treasuries on day t as:

$$s = [\lambda_t * f(\beta_i) * \sigma_{v,i}] - \frac{1}{T} \ln[1 - p_T \cdot LGD] \tag{10.3}$$

Thus, the model of spreads represented in Equation 10.3 requires physical PDs from the structural model, risk-neutral theory to convert PDs to spreads and the Sharpe ratio from the CAPM to estimate the daily spread value of volatility, λ_t. Assume that we know a bond's duration, T, market spread, s, an estimates of its default probability, p_T, and recovery value in default, 1-LGD. Then, using the values of λ_t and $f(\beta_i)$ calculated from the calibration universe of bonds using HPD PDs, one can calculate that bond's credit risk premium, $s_{\lambda,t}$, which is the quantity that we wish to hedge with the CDX index.

HEDGING BONDS' CREDIT RISK PREMIUMS

The default component of risky bonds, s_d in Equation 10.2, is issuer-specific, depending on obligors' credit qualities. For example, an investor may be comfortable bearing an obligor's default risk, but may be concerned about mark-to-market risk owing to changes in the credit risk premium. This concern is reasonable since, as demonstrated by the average spread decomposition in Figure 10.1 (see also Figure 5.1), the spread value of volatility, λ_t, dominates all obligors' bond spreads. Changes in the risk premium and its strong correlation among corporate bonds (see Figure 5.3) pose additional challenges over considerations of default risk for managers of credit portfolios. That is, values of their securities may rise or fall dramatically due to changes in s_λ, and those changes may be largely unrelated to the default risk of their holdings.

Accordingly, given the understanding of the credit risk premium, we sought the possibility of hedging the changes in investors risk appetites and market volatility as reflected in changes in the credit risk premium, s_λ. A successful and timely implementation of the hedge can help investors preserve compensation from a suitable level of default risk and also protect their portfolios against tail risk. In the following sections, we will first develop a hedging strategy for mark-to-market changes in corporate bonds' NDS using the CDS.IG.NA, followed by an extension of that hedging strategy to a portfolio of bonds.

Market NDS and the CDX index

We calculate the market volatility on day t, designated as σ_t^M, as the mean of all bonds' spread volatilities.[4] The superscript M is used to denote that it represents the market. With the value of λ_t calibrated daily, the market non-default spread is defined as:

$$NDS_t^M = s_\lambda^M = \lambda_t \cdot \sigma_t^M \qquad (10.4)$$

Figure 10.2 Left: daily values of the market NDS, NDS_t^M and the CDX. IG.NA; right: cumulative percentage changes of the market NDS, NDS_t^M and the CDX.IG.NA

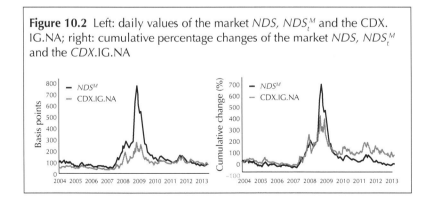

The left panel of Figure 10.2 displays the daily spread levels of NDS_t^M and *CDX.IG.NA* since 2004, while the right panel displays the cumulative changes of each of the two series. The figure shows that both series remain relatively stable prior to 2008, and they tend to co-move when the credit environment deteriorates, suggesting that it might be possible to hedge ΔNDS_t^M with $\Delta CDX.IG.NA$.

Since the goal is to hedge changes in market *NDS* (ΔNDS_t^M by simultaneous changes in short positions in *CDX.IG.NA* (ΔCDX), we expect a large value of ΔNDS_t^M to be accompanied by a large value of ΔCDX of the same sign. This is consistent with the trailing one-month and three-month correlations between the two series in Figure 10.3, which spike upward during the credit crisis of 2007–08. Given the positive correlation under times of stress, it appears that the *CDX.IG.NA* provides at least an approximate hedge against tail risk in corporate bond spreads. In the next section, we will determine the optimal interval over which to determine the hedging parameters.

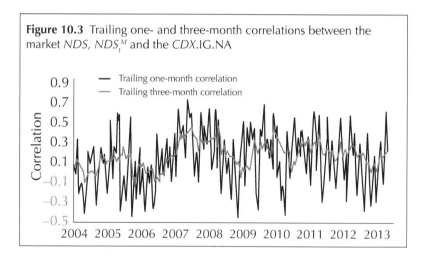

Figure 10.3 Trailing one- and three-month correlations between the market *NDS, NDS$_t^M$* and the *CDX*.IG.NA

Determining the hedging frequency

The usefulness of *CDX.IG.NA* as a hedge for NDS_t^M depends on how well ΔCDX tracks ΔNDS_t^M. The left set of panels in Figure 10.4 display scatterplots of daily (top left), weekly (top right), monthly (bottom left) and three-month (bottom right) changes in spread levels for market NDS_t^M and *CDX.IG.NA* from 2004 to 2013. Each set of changes are evaluated daily. In these plots, call receiver operating characteristics (ROCs), the upper right and lower left panels contain points whose values of ΔCDX and ΔNDS_t^M are of the same sign, positive and negative, respectively. These cases we call "hits", as P&L from a short CDX position would at least partially hedge P&L from changes in the NDS_t^M. Conversely, the upper left and lower right panels contain points whose values of ΔCDX and ΔNDS_t^M have opposite signs. In the statistical literature these cases are called "false alarms" or "false positives": cases for which a short/long CDX positions would add to gains/losses from long/short exposures to NDS_t^M, respectively.[5] Visual inspection is sufficient to reveal that on a single-day basis there is little relationship between ΔCDX and ΔNDS_t^M, and the correlation between those two series is 20%. Thus, hedging $\Delta NDS_{t=1}^M$ with $\Delta CDX_{t=1}$ would be relatively ineffective, even counterproductive. However, as the tenor of the hedging frequency increases from one day to three months, there is a concomitant increase in the relationship between ΔCDX_t and ΔNDS_t^M such that there are very few false positives for three-month changes. In fact, the correlations increase to 38%, 54% and 74% as the hedging interval increases to one week, one month and three months, respectively.

The ROCs for values of Δt equal to one day, one week, one month and three months appear in the right panels of Figure 10.4. The ROCs confirm that daily and weekly changes in ΔCDX and ΔNDS are only weakly correlated, and are therefore not suitable for the hedge. On the other hand, monthly and three-month ΔCDX and ΔNDS move much more closely in tandem, with the three-month Δt being best. As a result, we suggest using three-month changes as the appropriate hedging frequency.

Having decided upon a three-month hedging frequency, we evaluated the likelihood that the largest values of $\Delta NDS_{\Delta t=3M}^M$ would correspond to the largest values of $\Delta CDS_{\Delta t=3M}$. That is, the ROC analysis in Figure 10.4 examined only the correspondence in signs of changes in CDX and NDS and not their magnitudes. To that end, we selected the 30% largest positive and 30% largest negative three-month changes in NDS (ie, $\Delta NDS_{\Delta t=3M}^M$ and plotted those changes against the corresponding values of $\Delta CDX_{\Delta t=3M}$. Thus, for this study the sample excluded 40% of the cases having the smallest absolute values of three-month changes in $NDS_{\Delta t=3M}^M$.

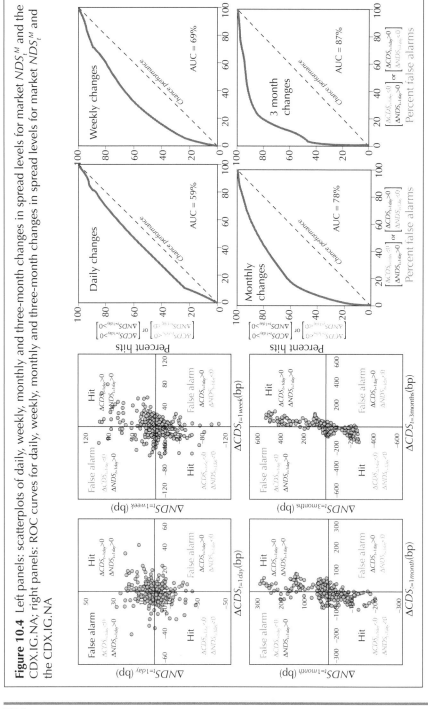

Figure 10.4 Left panels: scatterplots of daily, weekly, monthly and three-month changes in spread levels for market NDS_t^M and the CDX.IG.NA; right panels: ROC curves for daily, weekly, monthly and three-month changes in spread levels for market NDS_t^M and the CDX.IG.NA

The upper left panel of Figure 10.5 presents a scatterplot of $NDS^M_{\Delta t=3M}$ versus $\Delta CDX_{\Delta t = 3M}$ after removal of the smallest 40% of absolute changes in $NDS^M_{\Delta t=3M}$ and their associated values of $\Delta CDX_{\Delta t = 3M}$. The corresponding ROC curve appears at the upper right. The ROC curve was constructed in a similar manner to that for the three-month changes in Figure 10.4, except that the ROC in Figure 10.5 excludes the values of $\Delta CDX_{\Delta t = 3M}$ associated with the 40% of the smallest absolute changes in $NDS^M_{\Delta t=3M}$. Eliminating the 40% of the smallest changes in $NDS^M_{\Delta t=3M}$ improves the performance of the hedge, as evidenced by increasing the AUC3 to 93% from its value of 87% with the full sample of $NDS^M_{\Delta t=3M}$ and $\Delta CDX_{\Delta t = 3M}$.

Figure 10.5 Left panels: scatterplots of the 30% (top) and 10% (bottom) largest changes in three-month market NDS^M_t against the largest values of three-month ΔCDX; right panels: ROC curves for the 30% (top) and 10% (bottom) largest changes in three-month market NDS^M_t against the largest values of three-month market ΔCDX

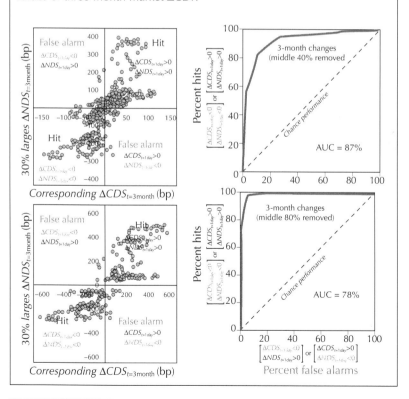

The lower panels of Figure 10.5 illustrate the performance of $\Delta CDX_{\Delta t = 3M}$ as a hedge for $\Delta NDS^M_{\Delta t=3M}$ when the smallest 80% of the changes in $NDS^M_{\Delta t=3M}$ are excluded. The scatterplot of only the largest and smallest 10% of the changes in $NDS^M_{\Delta t=3M}$ and corresponding $\Delta CDX_{\Delta t = 3M}$ values reveals only a few false alarms and, in those cases, the magnitudes of the changes in $CDX_{\Delta t = 3M}$ are relatively small. The usefulness of $\Delta CDX_{\Delta t = 3M}$ for hedging large absolute values of $\Delta NDS^M_{\Delta t=3M}$ is further quantified by the corresponding ROC whose AUC is near perfect at 99%.

Hedging strategy and optimal hedge ratio

Given the foregoing, we wish to determine the optimal hedge ratio β such that the hedged portfolio, which earns a spread difference of $[\Delta NDS - (\beta \cdot \Delta CDX)]$, minimises risk as measured by the variance of the hedging portfolio. We call the case where $\beta = 1$, the "naïve" hedging strategy. Also, for the simple case in which β is a constant, the minimum variance linear predictor of ΔNDS based on ΔCDX is given by:

$$E(\Delta NDS) + \frac{Cov(\Delta NDS, \Delta CDX)}{Var(\Delta CDX)} \cdot [\Delta CDX - E(\Delta CDX)] \qquad (10.5)$$

We can show that $Var(\Delta NDS - \beta \cdot \Delta CDX)$ is minimised by the optimal hedge ratio:

$$\beta^* = \frac{Cov(\Delta NDS, \Delta CDX)}{Var(\Delta CDX)} \qquad (10.6)$$

This is called the minimum variance (MV) hedge ratio (Johnson, 1960), and it is equivalent to the slope of the best-fit line from a least squares regression of ΔNDS on ΔCDX.

Dynamic hedging strategies, on the other hand, use $\beta = \beta_t$ and make frequent adjustments to the hedging portfolio. A simple method is to perform a linear regression based on a rolling window of time series data, where the optimal hedge ratio is found by estimating the time-varying slope. We carry out the hedging strategy according to the following steps.

❏ Trigger the dynamic hedge at date t only when the level of $NDS^M_{(t-1)}$ is greater than 200bp. This threshold will not be breached under most market conditions, but is necessary in times of market stress. If the dynamic hedge is not triggered, we default to using the naïve hedge ratio $\beta = 1$.

❏ Find the previous 20 trading days' trailing three-month changes in levels of NDS and $CDX.IG.NA$ (ie, $\Delta NDS_{\Delta t = 3M}$ and $\Delta CDX_{\Delta t = 3M}$). For notational convenience, we express the daily series of three-month changes as:

$$N = (N_{t-20}, N_{t-19},...,N_{t-1}) \text{ and } C = (C_{t-20}, C_{t-19},...,C_{t-1}) \quad (10.7)$$

accordingly, where:

$$N_i = NDS_i - NDS_{i-3M}, \; C_i = CDX_i - CDX_{i-3M} \quad (10.8)$$

❏ The optimal hedge ratio is given by $\beta^{*M} = \hat{\beta}^M_{t|t-1}$ from the fit of the regression:

$$N = \beta_{t|t-1} C + \epsilon, \quad (10.9)$$

where $\beta_{t|t-1}$ means the hedge ratio is based on all information up to date $t-1$.

Analysis of hedging performance

Based on the hedging strategy discussed in the previous section, Figure 10.6 plots the estimated dynamic hedge ratio over time where our portfolio is examined every three months. Again, when the dynamic hedge is not triggered, β_t is assumed to be the naïve hedge ratio of 1.

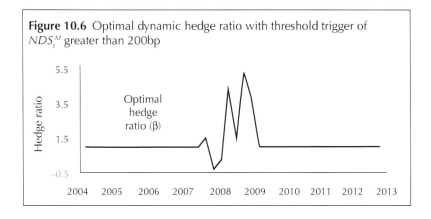

Figure 10.6 Optimal dynamic hedge ratio with threshold trigger of NDS^M_t greater than 200bp

One way to judge the hedging performance is by the amount of variance reduction (VR) in P&L produced by the hedge when compared with an unhedged portfolio. That is:

$$VR = \frac{Var(\text{Unhedged Portfolio}) - Var(\text{Hedged Portfolio})}{Var(\text{Unhedged Portfolio})}$$

(10.10)

For the naïve hedge with a constant $\beta = 1$, we find that $VR = 35\%$. For the dynamic hedge, $VR = 85\%$ is a significant improvement over the naïve hedge. This is confirmed in Figure 10.7, which displays much flatter differences for the dynamically hedged portfolio.

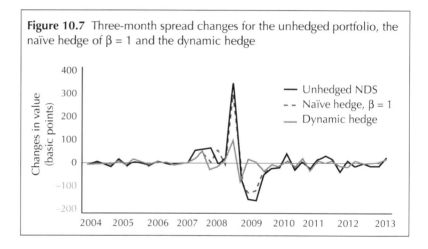

Figure 10.7 Three-month spread changes for the unhedged portfolio, the naïve hedge of $\beta = 1$ and the dynamic hedge

Finally, we evaluate the hedging performance of the *CDX.IG.NA* in terms of cumulative P&L of hedged and unhedged credit portfolios. A perfectly hedged portfolio will be P&L neutral and will have a constant value of zero for the cumulative change in portfolio value. Assume the spread level of the portfolio at the previous balancing period is S_{t-1} (in basis points) and the current spread level is S_t, the change in portfolio value from V_{t-1} to V_t, is:

$$V_t = V_{t-1} \cdot \frac{1 + S_{t-1}/10000}{1 + S_t/10000}$$

(10.11)

Figure 10.8 displays cumulative portfolio changes for the hedged and unhedged portfolios. The plot shows the effectiveness of the dynamic hedge at reducing the tail risk from large moves in the credit risk premium. The fact that even the unhedged NDS position (black line in Figure 10.8) has a cumulative P&L of roughly zero over the 10-year test period illustrates the mean reverting characteristic of the credit risk premium, s_λ. However, the unhedged portfolio has larger deviations from zero P&L during the period than either the naïve hedge or the dynamic hedge. Although the static hedge matches well the performance of the dynamic hedge for much of the time between 2004 and 2007, and 2010 and 2013, it fails nearly as badly as the unhedged portfolio during the liquidity crisis of 2008 and 2009. Meanwhile, the dynamic CDX hedge, while performing its worst during the crisis, still provided a good hedge for the changes in NDS during that period.

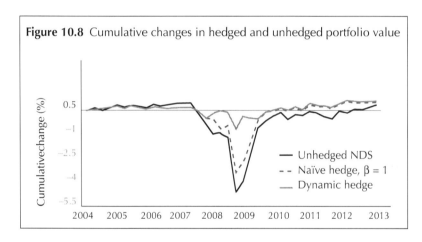

Figure 10.8 Cumulative changes in hedged and unhedged portfolio value

Another advantage of the dynamic hedge is illustrated in Figure 10.9, which displays distributions of daily series of three-month changes in basis points for the unhedged portfolio and three-month hedged P&L. Both the unhedged and hedged portfolios have mean P&L values near zero. However, the standard deviation of the three-month unhedged P&L is 75bp, whereas the naïve hedge reduces that volatility to 61bp. Nevertheless, the 28bp volatility of three-month spread changes for the dynamic portfolio is about one-third that of the unhedged portfolio and under half that of the static portfolio.

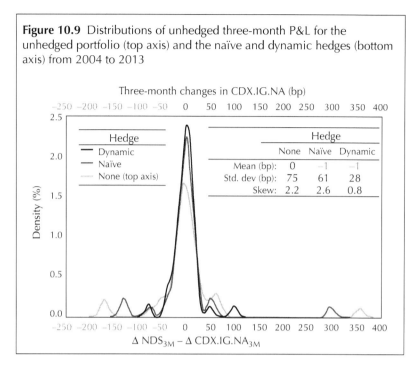

Figure 10.9 Distributions of unhedged three-month P&L for the unhedged portfolio (top axis) and the naïve and dynamic hedges (bottom axis) from 2004 to 2013

Hedging the risk premium for a portfolio of bonds

Recall that a key finding in our model of the credit risk premium is that, at least on average, the market charges roughly the same amount of spread per unit of volatility regardless of the underlying credit quality. In other words, λ_t, calculated from market each day, does not depend on credit ratings or spread volatility *per se*. In light of this, assume we have a bond portfolio consisting of N bonds: B_1, B_2, ... B_N with weights in the portfolio indicated by w_1, w_2, ... w_N such that $\sum_{i=1}^{N} w_i = 1$. Then, the non-default exposure of this portfolio can be characterised by:

$$NDS_t^P = \sum_{i=1}^{N} w_i \cdot (\lambda_t \cdot \sigma_{i,t}) = \lambda_t \sum_{i=1}^{N} w_i \cdot \sigma_{i,t}$$

(10.12)

where $\sigma_{i,t}$ is the spread volatility for bond i calculated on date t. Consequently, the optimal hedge ratio for this portfolio, P, is given by:

$$\beta^{*P} = \frac{Cov\ (\Delta NDS^P, \Delta CDX)}{Var(\Delta CDX)} = \frac{Cov\ (\sum_{i=1}^{N} w_i \cdot \Delta NDS_i, \Delta CDX)}{Var(\Delta CDX)}$$

$$= \frac{\sum_{i=1}^{N} w_i \cdot Cov\ (\Delta NDS_i, \Delta CDX)}{Var(\Delta CDX)} \tag{10.13}$$

For each individual bond in the portfolio, the optimal hedge ratio for that bond is:

$$\beta_i^* = \frac{Cov\ (\Delta NDS_i, \Delta CDX)}{Var(\Delta CDX)} \tag{10.14}$$

which we estimate by following the same steps as described above. We now have:

$$\beta^{*P} = \sum_{i=1}^{N} w_i \beta_i^* \tag{10.15}$$

That is, the optimal hedge ratio for the whole portfolio is the weighted average of the optimal hedge ratio for each member bond in the portfolio. In the extreme case where the portfolio contains all bonds in the market in equal weights, the optimal hedge ratio becomes exactly the optimal hedge ratio β^{*M} for the market NDS as demonstrated in the previous sections.

CONCLUSION

In this chapter, we used our understanding of the credit risk to evaluate the investment-grade CDS index as a hedge for the credit risk premium of bonds in an investment-grade corporate bond index. The chapter began with only a brief description of the credit risk premium as the topic was described in detail in Chapter 5. Short positions in the North American investment-grade CDS index were shown to provide very good hedges for changes in the credit spread premiums of cash bonds when hedging changes in bonds' risk premiums over three-month periods. We reported a comparison of performance of a naïve hedging strategy where $\beta_t = 1$ with a dynamic strategy whereby the hedge ratio is determined based on the slopes of regression analyses on a rolling window of changes in the CDS index and the credit risk premium. A static $\beta_t = 1$ hedge performed well historically except during the liquidity crisis of late

2007 to 2009, whereas the dynamic hedge works well over the entire test period since 2004. These results suggest that investors can mitigate spread volatility owing to changes in the credit risk premium using the *CDX* index.

Finally, since one can hedge changes in the cash bond risk premium with changes in *CDX.IG.NA*, it would appear possible to use the *CDX* index to replicate the non-default spread premium of cash bond portfolios. That is, one could replicate the risk premium of a long position in the cash bonds with a long position in the *CDX* index. This could prove useful for synthetically replicating with the *CDX* a portion of a less liquid cash bond portfolio that may be necessary to liquidate when market conditions become strained. This may also be useful for replicating returns from longer-dated liabilities for which bonds may be scarce or unavailable. An example of this as applied to pension liabilities is considered in the following chapter.

1   Salomon Brothers brokered the first currency swap in 1981 between IBM and the World Bank, and interest rate swaps followed shortly thereafter.

2   As explained in Appendix 5.1, Equation 10.1 is simply a rearrangement for the price yield formula combined with the notion from risk-neutral pricing theory that the spread value is the expectation of the nominal cashflows adjusted for default probability and discounted at the risk-free rate.

3   It may also contain a premium for liquidity/illiquidity. For now, we use the term "credit risk premium" to refer to the entire spread compensation over and above that necessary for the present value of expected cashflows to equal that of an equal-duration US Treasury security.

4   For each single bond, its volatility is calculated as the standard deviation of exponentially weighted bond spreads over the previous 100 days.

5   The term "false alarm" originated from the literature on statistical decision theory, whereby the original development of ROC analysis was applied to detection of signals in noise, and an incorrect response would be to indicate a signal when none was present. We use it here for consistency, but it is synonymous in this case with inconsistent P&L from changes in *CDX* and *NDS*. A detailed description of constructing these curves appears in Chapter 1 and an example appears in Figure 1.16.

11

Managing Pension Fund Liabilities

De-risking pension liabilities and making up for liability shortfalls are important problems for many pension fund managers. In this chapter, these issues will be addressed using techniques developed in Chapters 5, 9 and 10 for estimating the credit risk premium and beating and hedging global credit benchmarks. That is, we present methods to match and outperform the spread return of the double-A rated corporate bonds that underlie the spread liabilities of the Citigroup Pension Liability index (CPLI). We begin by demonstrating, as we have for matching the investment-grade corporate risk premium in Chapter 10, how the five-year North American CDS index (CDX.IG.NA) can serve as a proxy for the spread portion of the double-A rated corporate bonds underlying the CPLI. That is, the credit spread return of the bonds underlying the CPLI can be reasonably replicated by selling protection on the CDX.IG.NA. The rationale for our approach, verified herein, is that the main drivers of monthly returns on the double-A bonds underlying the CPLI are fluctuations in the credit risk premium, and furthermore that the CDX.IG.NA serves as a reasonable proxy for changes in that premium.

To address pension liability shortfalls, we applied a variation of our cut-and-rotate (C&R) strategy to the double-A rated corporate bonds underlying the CPLI. We report that, as for other credit benchmarks, removing allocations from the 10% with the largest default risk, while underweighting/overweighting the richest/cheapest 10% of bonds, one can outperform the double-A CPLI benchmark spread returns. Finally, we show that the ratio of the existing CPLI spread premium to the predicted default rate from the HT 2.0 model (see Chapter 3) can predict the directions of one-year spread moves in the double-A bond spread component of the CPLI with an accuracy of over 70%.

CITIGROUP PENSION LIABILITY INDEX

The CPLI is a popular pension liability benchmark consisting of the return from a customised liability payout schedule out to 70 years. The CPLI standard liability curve is shown in Figure 11.1, but other payout structures have been added (Bernstein and Li, 2013). Importantly, the CPLI liabilities (or any pension's particular liabilities) are discounted using the Citigroup Pension Discount Curve (CPDC). The CPDC is calculated using a set of double-A rated corporate bonds from Citi's Broad Investment Grade (BIG) index (Citigroup, 2013) with some modifications,[1] and is intended to correspond roughly to the term structure of zero-coupon double-A rated corporate bond yields. The constituent bonds used to determine the CPDC are specified monthly.

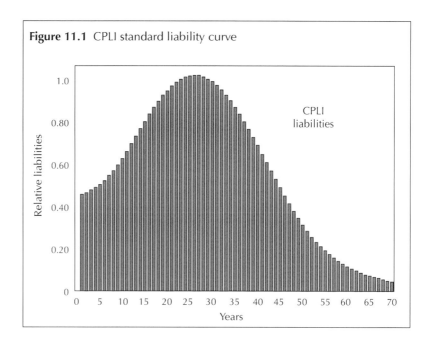

Figure 11.1 CPLI standard liability curve

To maintain a funded status, pension managers with funds bench-marked to the CPLI must match (or beat) the monthly returns on the term structure of yields determined from the double-A rated corporate bonds. Note that, for any given pension, the concern is about the returns of its specific liabilities based on the discount curve, but we can use the return of the CPLI as a proxy for those returns. The CPLI and CPDC were developed at Salomon Brothers in 1994 (Salomon Brothers, 1994; Bader and Ma, 1995) to provide pension plan sponsors with a method for determining their discount rates. Since then, the CPLI has proven popular as a benchmark for determining US corporate pension liabilities and has undergone various enhancements and extensions since its introduction (Bernstein, 2010; Bernstein and Li, 2013).

One can decompose the monthly return on the CPLI liabilities into two parts: a rate component and a spread component. Figure 11.2 shows the rate and spread portions of the discount curve as of June 30, 2014.[2] Hedging these two parts can be approached separately. The top panel of Figure 11.2 depicts the interest rate and credit spread returns as represented out to 30 of the 70 years of the CPLI. The largest component of the CPLI liabilities is the contribution from interest rates whose value can be discounted using the Libor curve. Importantly, one can replicate the interest rate return using Treasury bonds/strips matched in duration and convexity to the CPLI or via interest rate swaps. Thus, benefit plans can hedge their interest rate exposure to monthly changes in the CPLI using highly liquid instruments. The credit spread contribution is the total liabilities minus the Treasury liabilities at those maturities.

Despite the success of the CPLI as a pension liability benchmark, it has not proven possible to replicate exactly the returns on the CPLI using available assets. For example, the bottom panel of Figure 11.2 presents the distribution of differences in percentage of returns from the double-A rated bonds in Citi's BIG index and the returns on the double-A bonds in the CPLI from 1995 to 2014. Although just over one-third of the monthly returns are within +/−1bp, for some months the differences can be substantial.

This inability to replicate returns results from the way pension liabilities (as proxied by the CPLI) are calculated, relative to returns calculated on an actual portfolio of assets (see Bernstein, 2013, for

Figure 11.2 Top: sample term structure of CPLI interest rate and credit spread components; middle: monthly maturity roll-down effect on CPLI liabilities; bottom: distribution of difference between CPLI returns and a "perfect" hedge portfolio

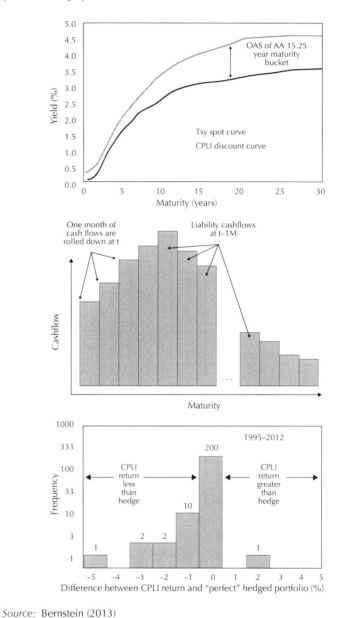

Source: Bernstein (2013)

an extensive discussion of this). Briefly, for a set of assets, or even a typical bond benchmark, one calculates monthly returns as the percentage changes in the values of the assets. For the bond benchmark, the constituents remain constant over a month. However, for a portfolio of assets the constituents can change over a month, as return calculations incorporate the values of items as they are bought or sold. Although for the CPLI (or pension liabilities more generally) monthly returns are also calculated as the percentage change in value of the liabilities, there are important differences, as outlined below.

❑ Although it is possible to calculate returns from a portfolio of bonds to explicitly hedge the spread exposure of the liabilities as of the beginning of the month, the set of bonds used to create the CPDC changes from the beginning of the month to the end of the month, and these changes can be difficult to predict.

❑ It is possible to predict those bonds entering or leaving the set due to rolling out of the index or due to new issuance since the candidate bonds for the index are lagged by one month.

❑ However, ratings changes cause unpredictability in the discount curve calculation. For example, if an issuer is downgraded out of the double-A rating category its bonds leave the set used to calculate the discount curve, often to dramatic effect (see bottom panel of Figure 11.2).

❑ Additional unpredictability results from an exclusion rule, based on an outlier test that eliminates bonds from a particular month's discount curve bond set.

❑ Even if the bonds in the CPLI were specified beforehand and one could construct a "perfect" hedging portfolio, the lack of liquidity and scarcity of the underlying bonds, particularly at longer-dated maturities, impose a practical limitation on sourcing the underlying securities.

❑ Finally, whereas specific bonds roll down their own yield or spread curves, the liabilities roll down the CPDC – which cannot be replicated using the bonds that underlie the CPLI (see middle panel of Figure 11.2).

The effects of the features of the CPLI described above are such that CPLI returns can be characterised as the portion of the credit spread premium term structure determined from a basket of double-A rated credits that excludes the risk of their downgrade and default risk (ie, for taking only "spread risk"). Accordingly, it has been difficult to replicate the spread return of the CPLI liabilities or to de-risk the liabilities of fully funded pension plans.

MATCHING THE CPLI SPREAD PREMIUM
The credit risk premium
In Chapter 10, we demonstrated that the CDX.IG.NA provides a reasonable hedge (or replication) for the non-default portion of the returns from corporate bonds. That work was based on the earlier observations of Benzschawel and Lee (2011) and Benzschawel and Assing (2012), and described in Chapter 5, indicating that:

❑ one can calculate the portion of a bond's yield spread to US Treasuries due to default s_d, thereby revealing its non-default spread, s_λ;
❑ on a given day, t, bonds' non-default spreads are related linearly to their spread volatilities, σ, such that $s_\lambda = \lambda_t * \sigma$, where we call s_λ the credit risk premium and λ is the basis points of yield per unit of non-default spread volatility; and
❑ although the value of λ_t fluctuates over time with the price of spread risk (ie, the yield compensation per unit of spread volatility) on any given day, the same value of λ_t describes well the relationship between non-default spread and spread volatility, ignoring the effect of embedded leverage.

To illustrate, the top panel of Figure 11.3 shows averages of monthly spreads by agency rating category from 1999 to 2014 for corporate bonds in Citi's BIG and High Yield indexes.[3] The dark region in the top panel shows average spread compensation for 4.5-year cumulative default probabilities (PDs) by rating category. The PDs were generated from Sobehart and Keenan's (2002, 2003) HPD model. The dark area corresponds to average values of s_d over the period, with the more lightly shaded area showing average values of the credit risk premium s_λ. The average value of the credit risk premium ranges from 69bp for triple-A rated bonds to 727bp for triple-C rated ones, but is five-to-10 times larger than the average compensation for default regardless of rating category. The lower panel of Figure 11.3 presents daily values of the credit risk premium (ie, λ_t) since 1999.

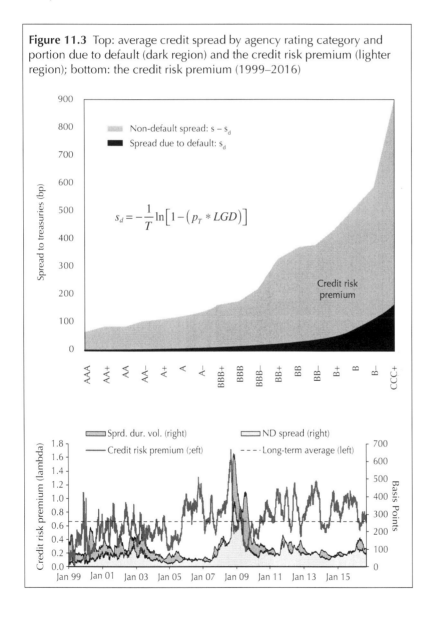

Figure 11.3 Top: average credit spread by agency rating category and portion due to default (dark region) and the credit risk premium (lighter region); bottom: the credit risk premium (1999–2016)

$$s_d = -\frac{1}{T}\ln\left[1-\left(p_T * LGD\right)\right]$$

MATCHING THE DOUBLE-A BOND RETURNS WITH CDX.IG.NA

Note that, as shown in the top panel of Figure 11.3, nearly the entire spread of double-A rated corporate bonds is due to the risk premium, rather than compensation for not receiving cashflows due to default. Given our understanding of the credit risk premium and the ability to hedge changes in market NDS (ΔNDS_t^M) by simultaneous changes in CDX.IG.NA (ΔCDX) as described in Chapter 10, it seemed possible that one could replicate, at least approximately, spread returns from the double-A rated constituents of the CPLI using the CDX.NA.IG. Accordingly, we evaluated the effectiveness of the CDX.IG.NA as a proxy for three-month returns of double-A bonds that underlie the CPLI liabilities.

As Chapter 10 contains a detailed description of hedging changes in cash bond risk premiums with the CDX.IG.NA, calculations of hedge ratios are presented only briefly in this section.

Naïve (static) hedge

For the static (ie, naïve) hedge, we can show that Var($\Delta CPLI - \beta \cdot \Delta CDX$) is minimised by the optimal hedge ratio:

$$\beta^* = \frac{Cov(\Delta CPLI, \Delta CDX)}{Var(\Delta CDX)}$$

(11.1)

This is equivalent to the slope of the best-fit line from a least squares regression of $\Delta CPLI$ on ΔCDX.

Dynamic hedge

For the dynamic hedge, we let $\beta = \beta_t$ and make adjustments to the hedge using a regression on a rolling window of time series data, where the optimal hedge ratio is estimated as the time-varying slope of changes in the CPLI versus the CDX.IG.NA. In general, we use the naïve hedge ratio $\beta = 1$ and only apply the dynamic hedge at date t when the level of $CPLI_{t-1}$ is greater than 200bp. This threshold is only breached in times of market stress. We calculate trailing three-month changes in the CPLI and CDX.IG.NA for the previous 20 trading days (ie, $\Delta CPLI\Delta_{t=3M}$ and $\Delta CDX\Delta_{t=3M}$). We express the daily series of three-month changes as:

$$N = (N_{t-20}, N_{t-19}, \ldots, N_{t-1}) \text{ and } C = (C_{t-20}, C_{t-19}, \ldots, C_{t-1}) \quad (11.2)$$

where $N_i = CPLI_i - CPLI_{i-3M}$ and $C_i = CDX_i - CDX_{t-3M}$. The optimal hedge ratio is given by $\beta^{*M} = \hat{\beta}^{*M}_{t|t-1}$ from the regression: $N = \beta_{t|t-1} C + \epsilon$, where $\beta_{t|t-1}$ means the hedge ratio is based on all information up to date $t-1$.

To apply the hedging strategy described above to the N bonds, $B_1, B_2, \ldots B_N$, in the CPLI, we assign each bond their corresponding weight, $w_1, w_1, \ldots w_N$, such that $\sum_{i=1}^{N} w_i = 1$. Then, the exposure of the CPLI portfolio designated using the superscript P to the risk premium whose proxy is the CDX.IG.NA can be characterised as:

$$\beta^{*P} = \frac{Cov\,(\Delta\,CPLI^P, \Delta\,CDX)}{Var(\Delta\,CDX)} \quad (11.3a)$$

$$= \frac{Cov\,(\sum_{i=1}^{N} w_i \cdot \Delta\,CPLI_i, \Delta\,CDX)}{Var(\Delta\,CDX)} \quad (11.3b)$$

$$= \frac{\sum_{i=1}^{N} w_i \cdot Cov\,(\Delta\,CPLI_i, \Delta\,CDX)}{Var(\Delta\,CDX)} \quad (11.3c)$$

where the asterisk (*) is used to indicate the dynamic hedging strategy. As different bonds will have different amounts of exposure to changes in the credit risk premium, the optimal hedge ratio for each bond is calculated as:

$$\beta_i^* = \frac{Cov\,(\Delta CPLI_i, \Delta CDX)}{Var(\Delta CDX)} \quad (11.4)$$

which we estimate by following the same steps as described above. Given each bond's β_i^*, we can estimate the total amount of risk premium exposure in the portfolio β^{*P} as:

$$\beta^{*P} = \sum_{i=1}^{N} w_i \beta_i^* \quad (11.5)$$

That is, the optimal hedge ratio for the whole portfolio is the weighted average of the optimal hedge ratio for each bond in the portfolio.

THE CDX.IG.NA AS A PROXY FOR THE DOUBLE-A BONDS IN THE CPLI

Figure 11.4 displays the analogous results for the CPLI as those of Figures 10.7 to 10.9 for replicating the credit risk premium of Citi's corporate bond indexes. Accordingly, the top-left panel of Figure 11.4 displays the dynamic hedge ratio between returns of the double-A bonds in the CPLI and CDX.IG.NA from 2005 to 2013. As for matching changes in the risk premium in Figure 10.8 when the dynamic hedge is not triggered, β_t is equivalent to the naïve hedge ratio of $\beta_t = 1$. The lower left panel of Figure 11.4 shows that the naïve hedge works well in matching the double-A bond returns in all years except during the liquidity crisis of late 2007 to 2009, whereas the dynamic hedge works well over the entire test period since 2005.

Recall that we can evaluate the effectiveness of the CDX.IG.NA in replicating the double-A rated bond returns by analysing its effect in reducing the variance of the unhedged double-A bond returns. The right portion of Figure 11.4 displays distributions of daily series of three-month changes in basis points for the unhedged double-A portfolio and three-month hedged P&L. Both the unhedged and hedged portfolios have mean P&L values near zero. However, the standard deviation of the three-month unhedged P&L is 55bp, whereas the naïve hedge reduces that volatility to 41bp, a 25% reduction. The 23bp volatility of three-month spread changes for the dynamically hedged portfolio is just under half of the unhedged portfolio and just above half that of the static portfolio. In particular, the figure illustrates that the largest changes in monthly P&L are offset by the CDX.IG.NA hedge.

Finally, Figure 11.5 displays cumulative monthly spread changes in percentage from the unhedged double-A rated bond portfolio and the naïve and dynamically hedged portfolios. The figure reveals that, unhedged, the double-A portfolio had a maximum cumulative spread widening of over 4% during the credit crises of 2007–09, which it recouped by 2010. The naïve $\beta_t = 1$ hedge also results in spread widening, but only about 2.5% during the credit crisis, also recovering to ultimately match the cumulative spread changes in the unhedged double-A portfolio. Not only does the dynamic hedge not experience the spread widening during the crisis, but it is slightly overaggressive: the net credit spreads actually tightened during the crisis, and the dynamic portfolio maintained that advantage until the end of 2013.

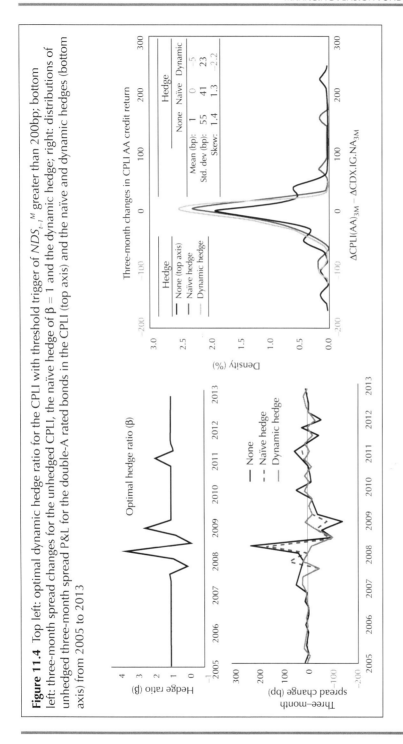

Figure 11.4 Top left: optimal dynamic hedge ratio for the CPLI with threshold trigger of $NDS_{t-1}{}^M$ greater than 200bp; bottom left: three-month spread changes for the unhedged CPLI, the naïve hedge of $\beta = 1$ and the dynamic hedge; right: distributions of unhedged three-month spread P&L for the double-A rated bonds in the CPLI (top axis) and the naïve and dynamic hedges (bottom axis) from 2005 to 2013

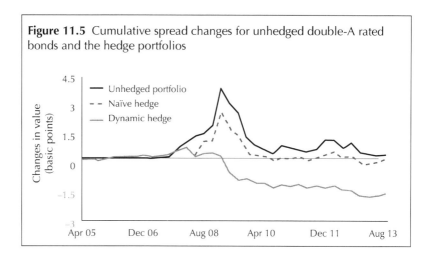

Figure 11.5 Cumulative spread changes for unhedged double-A rated bonds and the hedge portfolios

OUTPERFORMING DOUBLE-A CORPORATE BONDS
The cut-and-rotate method

In 2003, we (Benzschawel *et al*, 2003) described a method for systematically selecting corporate bonds based on their risk and relative value that has since been shown to consistently outperform credit benchmarks (Benzschawel, Lee and Bernstein, 2011; Benzschawel *et al*, 2014). As that strategy, the cut-and-rotate (C&R), is described in detail in Chapter 9, it is described only briefly herein.

Below we summarise the main steps in the C&R strategy, with graphical representations of both the "cut" and the "rotate" sub-strategies on corporate bonds in Citi's BIG index presented in Figure 11.6. The first step after specifying the benchmark portfolio is to generate one-year default probabilities for all the constituent bonds from the Sobehart–Keenan model. Then, the allocation is removed from the 10% of the bonds with the highest PDs (note, as shown in the left panel of Figure 11.6, the "cut" strategy reduces the overall default risk of the portfolio). The right panel of Figure 11.6 illustrates the application of the rotate strategy on the corporate bonds in one particular industry sector of Citi's BIG index. We divide the corporate bond universe into seven sectors: consumer, energy, finance, manufacturing, service, transportation and utilities. Each industry sector's credit spreads were fit with a line of form:

$$\log(s_i^{c=40}) = \gamma_0 + [\gamma_1 * \log(PD_i)] + [\gamma_2 * \log(Dur_i)] + \varepsilon \qquad (11.6)$$

where PD_i is the one-year default probability for the firm issuing bond, i, Dur_i is the duration of bond i and $s_i^{c=40}$ is the equal-recovery adjusted spread as described in Benzschawel, Lee and Bernstein (2011).

The C&R strategy can be summarised by the following steps.

❏ Select a benchmark bond index.
❏ Eliminate the allocation from the 10% of the riskiest bonds (using a PD model) and distribute that allocation proportionally among the remaining 90% of credits.
❏ Remove the allocation from the 10% of the richest bonds by industry sector and double the allocation to the cheapest 10% (the rich bonds are those with the least spread for their default risk, recovery value and duration, while cheap bonds have the largest spreads).
❏ Re-compute the risk and relative value of all benchmark bonds each month.

Figure 11.6 Left: monthly average market-weighted default probabilities of corporate bonds in Citi's BIG index, and after the cut-only, rotate-only and cut-and-rotate operations; right: example of the rotate strategy on the consumer sector in 2004, showing rich and cheap bonds

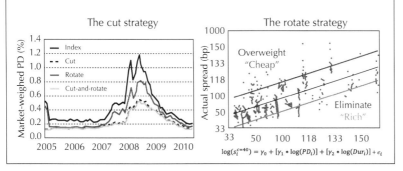

Equation 11.6 was then used to generate the least squares regression line (black line) in the right panel of Figure 11.6. The figure also depicts the 10th and 90th percentile boundaries (the black

and dashed black lines, respectively) for that sector that segregates bonds for elimination and overweighting, respectively. That is, the "rotate" strategy removes the allocation from the 10% of the bonds in each industry sector with the poorest relative value, and doubles the allocation to the 10% of bonds in that sector having the largest spread for their default risk and duration.

Figure 11.7 displays the results of the C&R strategy on the corporate bonds in Citi's BIG index. The top portion of the figure shows the 10% PD level cut-off for eliminating corporate bonds. The dashed grey circles show the level of PD cut-off related to positive returns from the cut strategy alone. The dashed arrows illustrate the relation of returns from the cut strategy relative to those of the index (row three of the table). The relative returns indicate that returns from the cut strategy are similar to buying credit protection: one gives up some minimal spread during the majority of years when credit is improving or stable, but massively outperforms in the roughly one-third of the time when credit is deteriorating. That outperformance is sufficient that the cut strategy alone outperforms the index by an average of 8bp over the 20-year test period.

Annual excess returns from the rotate component of the strategy relative to the corporate bonds in the BIG index appear in the fourth row of the table in Figure 11.7. Average P&L from the rotation strategy exceeds that of the cut strategy, returning a total of 1298p for the index over the 20-year test period, or 65bp per annum. In contrast to the 10% cut, the relative value rotation outperforms the index most years, underperforming only in 2000, 2002, 2007 and 2008. The table reveals that returns from the cut and rotate components are complementary: when the cut-based selection rule outperforms, the regression-based rotation rule underperforms, and vice versa.

The combined performance of the C&R strategy relative to corporate bonds in the BIG index appears in the bottom row of the table in Figure 11.7. Overall, the combination performs better than either method alone; the C&R method returned an excess of 1509bp over the 20-year test period, an additional 75bp per annum. Furthermore, the strategies appear additive; the PD-cut method returned an additional 8bp and the regression-based rotation method returned 65bp, with the combination returning slightly less than

Figure 11.7 Top: 10% cut-off default probabilities for investment-grade corporate bonds in Citi's BIG index; bottom: table of annual returns of corporate bonds in Citi's BIG index (top rows) and relative to the BIG index corporates for cut, rotate and combined strategy (lower rows)

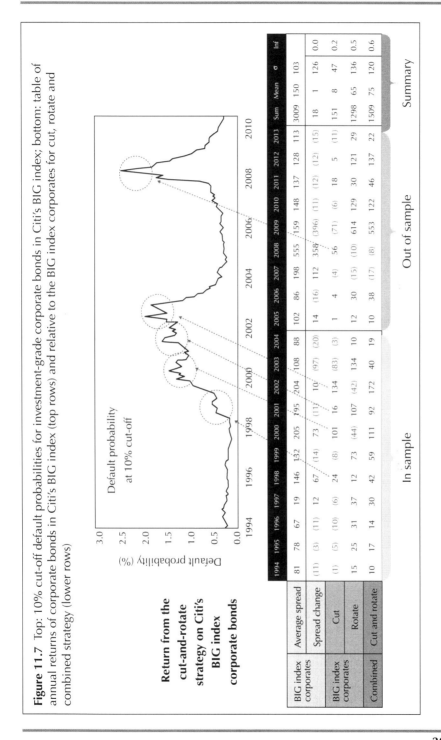

their sum. Finally, the C&R method outperformed the index in every year but two in our test period, during the credit crisis years of 2007 and 2008, and with less default risk.

Cut-and-rotate on the double-A bond portfolio

As the C&R strategy consistently outperforms corporate bonds in Citi's BIG index, we tested that strategy on the subset of the double-A rated corporate bonds in Citi's BIG index used to determine the CPLI liabilities. Although, in recent years, firms' have been abandoning defined benefit plans for 401K plans, these firms have nearly 70 years of future liabilities to manage, and many plans remain underfunded. Hence, an important objective for fund managers is not only to continue to generate the equivalent of double-A bond returns, but to make up existing deficits. Since the C&R strategy has outperformed every benchmark tested so far, it seemed important to test the C&R strategy on double-A rated bonds.[4]

Accordingly, we applied the C&R strategy to the double-A rated bonds in Citi's BIG index from January 2006 to March 2013. As before, PDs were generated by the Sobehart-Keenan HPD model and from the MKI probability model (Benzschawel and Li, 2012; Benzschawel and Assing, 2012) to fill in when PDs from HPD were unavailable.[5] Again, values from the decision-tree recovery value model (see Chapter 4) were used to adjust spreads of all bonds to a constant 40% level. To construct the C&R portfolios each month, we eliminated the allocations from the 10% of the double-A rated bonds with the largest PDs, followed by removing the allocation from the 10% with the worst relative value and doubling the allocation to the "cheapest" bonds. Unlike the earlier study on the BIG index, no attempt was made to balance industry sector allocations for this preliminary study.

The left panel of Figure 11.8 shows annual returns over US Treasuries from the double-A rated corporate bonds before (white bars) and after (dark bars) the C&R procedure. The C&R method outperformed the benchmark in six of eight years, with a tie in 2011, and 20bp of underperformance in 2007.[6] On a risk-adjusted basis (ie, above US Treasuries), the double-A corporate benchmark had an average excess return of 4.50% per annum, whereas the C&R strategy averaged 5.27%, an annual outperformance of 77bp.

Figure 11.8 Annual returns (left), cumulative compounded returns (middle) and cumulative uncompounded returns (right) from the double-A rated benchmark and the cut-and-rotate strategy

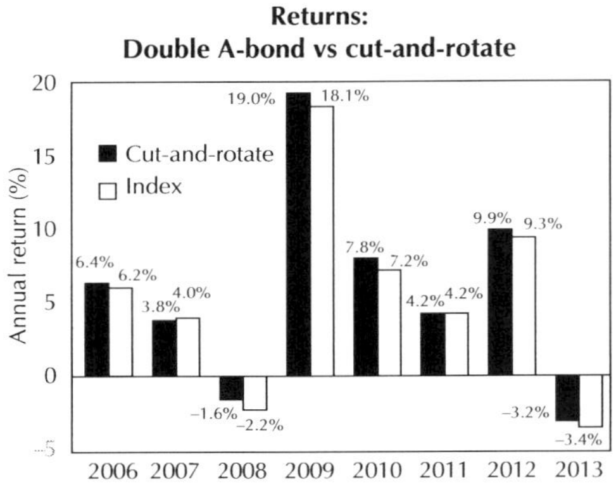

Returns:
Double A-bond vs cut-and-rotate

Cumulative compounded return			
Year	C&R	Double-A	Diff (%)
2005	100.84	100.83	0.01
2006	107.33	107.05	0.29
2007	111.47	111.30	0.17
2008	109.72	108.87	0.85
2009	130.61	128.62	1.99
2010	140.99	137.94	3.05
2011	146.95	143.73	3.22
2012	161.43	157.08	4.35
2013	156.34	151.79	4.56

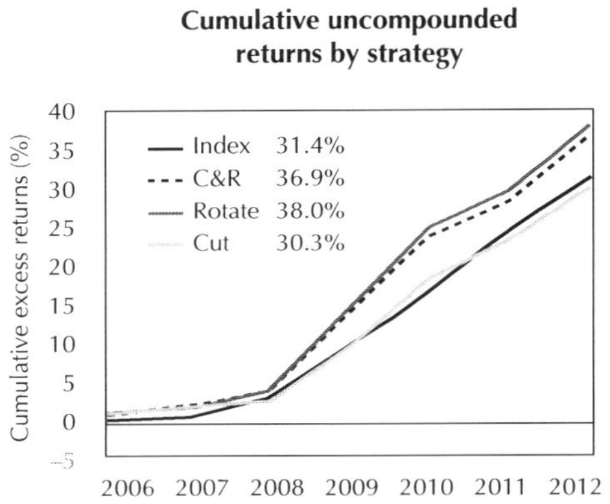

Cumulative uncompounded returns by strategy

Index 31.4%
C&R 36.9%
Rotate 38.0%
Cut 30.3%

401

The middle panel of Figure 11.8 presents annual cumulative compounded excess returns since 2005. Despite double-A rated spread losses in two of the nine years tested, both sets of cumulative returns are over 50%, with the C&R strategy returning an additional 4.56%. The right panel of Figure 11.8 presents uncompounded cumulative returns by strategy. The C&R strategy (dashed black line) tops the benchmark at 36.9%, with only a 5.5% advantage over the period. However, the figure shows that the rotate strategy alone (dark grey line) has the highest uncompounded excess return over the period since 2006 at 38.0%, topping the 31.4% return of the double-A benchmark (black line) by 7.6% over the eight-year period. For the first time in our application of the C&R strategy, we observed that the rotate strategy alone performed best. That is, the rotate strategy alone topped the double-A benchmark by 94bp and the C&R strategy by16bp. Also, for the first time we observed that the cut strategy alone underperformed the benchmark, with a deficit of 16bp, accounting for the outperformance of the rotate strategy alone. Clearly, if pension managers could realise these excess returns provided by the rotate strategy, particularly given the effects of compounding, they could quickly make up deficits in defined benefit plans.

PREDICTING CHANGES IN DOUBLE-A RATED BOND SPREADS

In Chapter 3, it was shown that the ratio of the current average high-yield bond spread to the estimated one-year default rate from our HT 2.0 model predicts one-year directional changes in average high-yield spreads with 80% accuracy (see Figure 3.13). Furthermore, in Chapter 5 we also demonstrated the ability to predict one-year changes in the credit risk premium, λ, based on the ratio of the current risk premium to the one-year predicted default rate (see Figure 5.23). Thus, we might also be able to predict one-year directional changes in the spread return of the CPLI. Accordingly, we examined if the ratio of the current CPLI spread premium to predicted default (ie, $CPLI_T$-to-Dp) could predict one-year changes in the spread return of the CPLI, $CPLI_{T+12} - CPLI_T$. Accordingly, Figure 11.9 presents 12-month changes in the CPLI spread return versus the ratio of the current CPLI double-A spread return to the predicted default rate from the HT 2.0 default rate model of Chapter 3. Results are shown for each month from 2000 to 2013. The figure indicates that, when the ratio of $CPLI_T$-to-Dp is above average, the CPLI credit spread return one-year later tends to decrease by an average of –84bp with a 73% probability. Conversely, when the ratio of $CPLI_T$-to-Dp is below its average, the CPLI credit spread one-year increases an average of 97bp with 70% probability. Note also that not only does the ratio of $CPLI_T$-to-Dp predict directional changes in the spread return of the CPLI above chance, but average losses on incorrect predictions are less than average gains when correct (–81bp versus 97bp and +37bp versus –84bp). This result, along with that supporting the CDX. IG.NA as a proxy for the double-A rated corporate bond spread return, suggests that one could anticipate directional changes in the credit spread component of the CPLI.

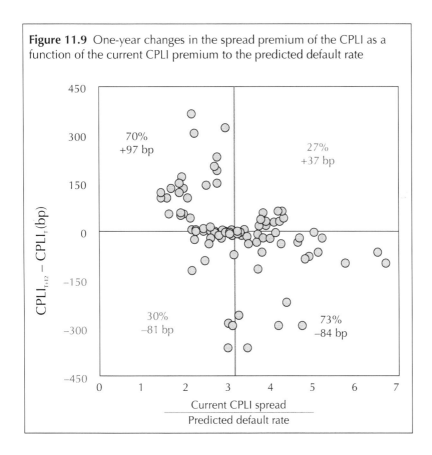

Figure 11.9 One-year changes in the spread premium of the CPLI as a function of the current CPLI premium to the predicted default rate

CONCLUSION

In this chapter, tools are presented for de-risking, outperforming and predicting changes in the double-A rated corporate bond component of the CPLI. The approach was to apply results explained in previous chapters on the corporate bonds in Citi's BIG index to the double-A rated corporate bonds underlying the credit spread portion of the returns on the CPLI. Specifically, we addressed problems of making up deficits in pension plans and the de-risking of pension liabilities. In that regard, it was demonstrated that the CDX. NA.IG could serve as an effective hedge or substitute for the credit portion of the CPLI, thereby either de-risking funded pension plans or serving as a substitute for more expensive investments in the often difficult to access cash bonds underlying the CPLI.

We also addressed problems with underfunded pension plans using methods developed to outperform the spread returns from global credit benchmarks. These included the application of the C&R strategy of Chapter 10 to the double-A rated bonds in Citi's BIG index and our ability to anticipate one-year changes in the credit spread return of the CPLI at levels much greater than chance. That is, we show that the ratio of the current CPLI credit risk premium to the predicted default rate from Citi's HT 2.0 model can predict one-year directional spread moves in the spread component of the CPLI with an accuracy of over 70%. The ability to predict changes in the credit spread component of the CPLI suggests that, with appropriate buying or selling credit protection via the CDX. NA.IG, it provides an additional method for outperforming pension liability benchmarks.

1   The SEC requires that discount rates reflect the yield of a cash-matched portfolio of securities "that receive one of the two highest ratings given by a recognised ratings agency... (for example,... Aa or higher from Moody's)".

2   Note that there are few, if any, credit instruments with durations longer than 30 years from which to estimate returns from longer-dated CPLI liabilities. Accordingly, for both interest rates and double-A credit spreads the rates for the 30-year point on the curve are assumed to extend at a constant rate from 30 to 70 years.

3   The 4.5-year cumulative default rates were used as they correspond roughly to the average duration of the bonds in those indexes.

4   The credit component of the CPLI, while referenced to double-A rated bonds in Citi's BIG index, actually deviates from their returns as described earlier in this book. Thus, this demonstration is not a direct test of the ability to outperform the spread-related liabilities in the CPLI.

5   The HPD model requires firms to have tradable equity and public financials to generate a PD. For those few firms in the BIG index without those data, we used the MKI model, requiring only a short series of credit spreads to estimate PDs.

6   Incidentally, the C&R strategy on the entire corporate bond index (see Figure 11.7) also underperformed in 2007.

12

Credit Cycle-dependent Stochastic Credit Spreads and Rating Category Transitions

This chapter will present a method for calculating value at risk (VaR) for corporate bonds using simulation methods. The simulations involve adjusting historical credit-state transition matrices for changes in default rates, ratings upgrades and downgrades, and credit spread changes as they occur over the credit-cycle dependant credit state. Transition matrices are constructed at monthly intervals out to one year, and annually out to five years thereafter. Average physical default probabilities were obtained by rating and tenor from the market-implied PD model of Benzschawel and Assing (2012), and ratings from one to five years were generated stochastically based on historical patterns of observed default rates. The time series of credit-state transition matrices were generated by inferring ratings upgrades and downgrade from estimates of the existing overall default rate referenced to historical upgrade/downgrade ratios. These economic cycle-adjusted transition matrices can be used to infer likelihoods of transitioning among various credit states given market conditions.

Given the stochastically generated credit cycle-adjusted transition matrices, we superimposed 10 stochastically generated sets of one-year credit spreads by rating on each matrix. The credit spreads were derived from spread curves fit to market data by rating category to the nodes in the credit state transition matrix at each annual tenor, with the stochastic properties of the spreads calibrated to historical spread moves.

From the resulting sets of annual credit-state transition matrices with superimposed spreads, one can calculate transition-probability inferred spreads (TIS) for bonds of various ratings over arbitrary periods. Comparisons of TIS for the spectrum of credit ratings and tenors with average market spreads agreed well, but differences were evident. Accordingly, optimisation methods were applied to make slight adjustments to transition probabilities from model-derived values to bring TIS to near coincidence with market values.

Finally, the set of matrices whose probabilities were adjusted to match market spreads were used to generate sets of iso-probability (constant VaR) spread curves by credit rating out to five years. These curves can be useful in evaluating likelihoods of expected spread moves and/or losses from default.

This chapter is divided into three major parts. The first describes the method for adjusting historical ratings transitions to be consistent with existing credit market default rates, and ratings upgrades and downgrades. The second looks at how credit spreads are superimposed on the multi-year transition matrices, and evaluates its usefulness for inferring "fair" probability weighted credit spreads for obligors of various credit qualities. That is, it explores methods for generating expected losses from existing expected default rates and terms structures of credit spreads. The final section examines the generation of stochastic default rates and stochastic credit spreads to estimate unexpected losses, and presents analyses of the relationship between expected and unexpected losses as well as estimates of VaR for bonds of various ratings categories.

CREDIT-STATE TRANSITION MATRICES

Credit rating agencies such as Moody's and Standard and Poor's (S&P) publish tables showing likelihoods of obligors transitioning from their current credit states to all other states over various time horizons. A table of one-year average credit-state transitions appears in Table 12.1, with each cell in the matrix showing the likelihood of transitioning from a current credit state on the left axis to the corresponding credit state specified on the top axis, including default.[1] Ratings transition tables have proven useful for estimating the likelihood that an obligor of known rating will have improved, deteriorated or remained stable. Furthermore, if credit

Table 12.1 Example of average one-year rating transitions from 1981 to 2010

From	To								
		AAA	AA	A	BBB	BB	B	CCC/C	D
	AAA	90.87%	8.35%	0.56%	0.05%	0.08%	0.03%	0.05%	0.00%
	AA	0.59%	90.15%	8.52%	0.55%	0.06%	0.08%	0.02%	0.02%
	A	0.04%	1.99%	91.64%	5.64%	0.40%	0.18%	0.02%	0.08%
	BBB	0.01%	0.14%	3.96%	90.50%	4.26%	0.71%	0.16%	0.27%
	BB	0.02%	0.04%	0.19%	5.79%	83.97%	8.09%	0.84%	1.05%
	B	0.00%	0.05%	0.16%	0.26%	6.21%	82.94%	5.06%	5.32%
	CCC/C	0.00%	0.00%	0.22%	0.33%	0.97%	15.20%	51.25%	32.03%
	D	0.00%	0.00%	0.00%	0.00%	0.00%	0.00%	0.00%	100.00%

Source: From Vazza and Khan (2011)

409

spreads by rating and tenor are known and superimposed on the ratings transition matrix, one could estimate the joint occurrence of transitioning from a given credit state to any other, along with its expected change in credit spread. This type of data and analysis underlies the popular VaR measure used for credit portfolio risk management. Furthermore, given a set of accurate ratings transitions and credit spreads, one could infer spread values for credit state-dependent options embedded in many corporate bonds and loans, as well as for options on CDS.

Although useful for many purposes, the suitability of using average ratings transition matrices for estimating expected losses or spread volatility is limited. This is because, as has been well-documented (Bangia, Diebold and Schuermann, 1999; Das, Fan and Geng, 2002; Keisel, Perraudin and Taylor, 2001, to name a few), values of credit-state transition probabilities are highly dependent on the credit cycle. For example, the average annual high-yield default rate has been 3.7% since 1983 (Vazza and Kraemer, 2011); however, as can be seen in the left panel of Figure 12.1, the annual high-yield default rate has varied between 0% and 12% over that period. In fact, in years with no or low default rates (eg, 1981, 2007), transitions from most credit states to default in the right-hand column of Table 12.1 would be 0%. Clearly, Figure 12.1 shows that the variations in default rates cluster into high and low periods and are not well-characterised by a normal (ie, Gaussian) distribution.

Another problem with using time-homogenous ratings transitions is that transitions among non-default states also vary over the credit cycle. As shown in the right panel of Figure 12.1, although the ratio of annual credit upgrades to credit downgrades, the "upgrade/downgrade ratio", averages 0.78 upgrades per downgrade, it varies widely from its average value. That is, the ratio has been as high as 1.25 in 2004 and 2005 when default rates were extremely low and as low as 0.25 during the tech bubble in 2002. Also, although in some years more credits are upgraded than downgraded (ie, upgrade/downgrade ratio is greater than 1.0), the opposite is usually the case. Both the variability of default rates and the upgrade/downgrade ratio affect the probabilities in Table 12.1. The credit cycle dependence of ratings transitions makes it difficult to generate accurate estimates of expected losses from either default or credit state changes using

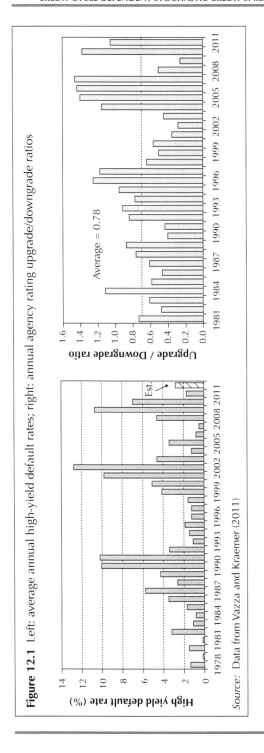

Figure 12.1 Left: average annual high-yield default rates; right: annual agency rating upgrade/downgrade ratios

Source: Data from Vazza and Kraemer (2011)

411

historical averages. To make matters worse, credit spreads also vary over the cycle and those values are only moderately correlated with default rates (Benzschawel and Lee, 2011).

Attempts have been made to generate meaningful adjustments to historical transition matrices. For example, Kavvathas (2001) derived non-time-homogenous credit rating transitions as functions of state variables. In addition, Das, Fan and Geng (2002) used a Bayesian adjustment based on estimates of changes in default probabilities from various credit models combined with a Monte Carlo simulation of the model-based PDs. Although useful, these approaches fail to adjust adequately for ratings changes among non-default states as embodied in the upgrade-to-downgrade ratio, and also remain largely untested as regards their ability to mimic the changes in credit spreads that occur over the credit cycle.

CREDIT CYCLE-DEPENDENT RATINGS TRANSITION MATRICES
As mentioned, rating transitions are reported routinely by the major rating agencies. For example, Moody's and Standard and Poor's both publish annual updated matrices of one-year historical ratings transitions for corporate firms. For practical reasons, the shortest time interval over which transitions are calculated is typically one year. This is because the number of ratings transitions over shorter intervals is insufficient for generating reliable estimates. Nevertheless, many industry practitioners are interested in short-term credit state migration. Thus, an initial objective of this chapter is to derive monthly transition matrices from the average annual rating transition matrix data. Then, those matrices are adjusted to account for the estimated annual default rate and the upgrade–downgrade ratios that correspond to existing macroeconomic conditions. Using average one-year and five-year transition matrices, one can extend the rating transition forecast to five years. The method allows investors to better quantify short-term (ie, less than one year) credit migrations as well as the expected credit risk over the multi-year life of a typical credit portfolio.[2]

Deriving monthly credit transition matrices
We derive successive time-homogenous monthly transition matrices from one to 12 months from the average annual transition

matrix reported by Standard and Poor's (Vazza and Khan, 2011) that appears in Table 12.1. To begin, let $\mathbf{P}$ be the one-year rating transition matrix. Assume that $\mathbf{P}$ is a time-homogeneous Markov transition matrix. We are interested in finding a generator $\mathbf{Q}$ for $\mathbf{P}$, (ie, $\mathbf{Q}$ is a matrix with non-negative off-diagonal entries, and each row sums to 1 such that $e^{\mathbf{Q}} = \mathbf{P}$. If a generator $\mathbf{Q}$ exists for $\mathbf{P}$, then for any $t > 0$, $\mathbf{P}_t = e^{t\mathbf{Q}}$ is a t-period rating transition matrix. However, not all transition matrices have an exact generator. Israel, Rosenthal and Wei (2001) identify the conditions for the existence (and non-existence) of an exact generator for a given matrix and the matrix $\mathbf{P}$ in Table 12.1. does not satisfy those conditions. That is, an exact generator for $\mathbf{P}$ does not exist.[3]

Although an exact generator for $\mathbf{P}$ does not exist, Israel *et al* provide a method for generating an approximation of the generator for a matrix $\mathbf{P}$ if the diagonal entries of the matrix are all greater than $1/2$ (ie, $p_{ii} > 0.5$). Clearly, the transition matrix in Table 12.1 satisfies this condition. Then, Theorems 1 and 2 in Israel *et al* (2001) state that the series:

$$\tilde{\mathbf{Q}} = (\mathbf{P} - \mathbf{I}) - (\mathbf{P} - \mathbf{I})^2 / 2 + (\mathbf{P} - \mathbf{I})^3 / 3 - (\mathbf{P} - \mathbf{I})^4 / 4 + \dots \qquad (12.1)$$

where $\mathbf{I}$ is the identity matrix, converges geometrically quickly, and has row-sums equal to zero such that $\exp(\tilde{\mathbf{Q}}) = \mathbf{P}$ exactly. In fact, matrix $\tilde{\mathbf{Q}}$ is not an exact generator for $\mathbf{P}$ because it has some non-negative off-diagonal entries. Thus, $\mathbf{P}_t = e^{t\tilde{\mathbf{Q}}}$ will also have non-negative off-diagonal entries for sufficiently small values of $t > 0$. Despite the fact that $\mathbf{P}_t$ is not a proper Markov transition matrix, any negative off-diagonal entries of $\tilde{\mathbf{Q}}$ are quite small. Thus, it is possible to replace these negative entries with zeros, and add the appropriate values back into the corresponding diagonal entries such that the row-sums equal zero. That is, once we have $\tilde{\mathbf{Q}}$ we can obtain a new matrix $\mathbf{Q}$ by:

$$q_{ij} = \max(\tilde{q}_{ij}, 0), \ j \neq i; \qquad (12.2a)$$

and

$$q_{ii} = \tilde{q}_{ii} + \sum_{j \neq i} \min(\tilde{q}_{ij}, 0) \qquad (12.2b)$$

The new matrix $\mathbf{Q}$ will have row-sums that equal zero and non-negative off-diagonal entries, but the equation $\exp(\mathbf{Q}) = \mathbf{P}$ holds only approximately. After applying the method above to obtain the generator $\mathbf{Q}$, the monthly rating transition matrix is given by $\mathbf{P}_t = \exp(t\mathbf{Q})$, where $t = 1/12$.

Optimisation

Suppose $\mathbf{R}$ is a monthly credit-state transition matrix. By the Markov property, $\mathbf{R}^{12}$ is the annual transition matrix. Since we know $\mathbf{P}$ is the actual annual transition matrix, we want to minimise the error between $\mathbf{R}^{12}$ and $\mathbf{P}$. That is, we want to solve the optimisation problem:

$$\min_{R} \left\| \mathbf{R}^{12} - \mathbf{P} \right\|^2$$

(12.3)

such that $\mathbf{R}$ is a proper Markov transition matrix. In fact, this is difficult due to high non-linearity and the large number of elements. The solution is also very sensitive to initial starting values of $\mathbf{R}$. To reduce the number of unknowns, we restrict $\mathbf{R}$ such that the one-month probability of a triple-A credit going to junk (below a triple-B-minus rating) is zero. In practice, we use the matrix expansion method to obtain an initial guess for $\mathbf{R}$ and then apply the active-set algorithm (Murty, 1988; Nocedal and Wright, 2006) to solve the optimisation. The resulting average one-month transition matrix appears in Table 12.2. We observe that all ratings are most likely to stay in the same rating for a one-month horizon. Note that the default state, D, is absorbing. Also, the investment-grade credits are highly unlikely to move into the high-yield category in one month, and vice versa.

Adjustment of monthly transitions

The one-month transition matrix in Table 12.2 is the average one-month matrix based on historical data, but market conditions are rarely coincident with historical norms. That is, we wish to embed in the transition matrix the effects of macroeconomic conditions such as the current default rate and the ratings upgrade–downgrade ratio. An assumption that underlies this approach is that the distribution of assets by rating is stable over the forecast period. Under this assumption, the annual default rate can be calculated as

Table 12.2 Average one-month rating transitions

		AAA	AA	A	BBB	BB	B	CCC/C	D
From	AAA	99.21%	0.77%	0.03%	0.00%	0.00%	0.00%	0.00%	0.00%
	AA	0.06%	99.13%	0.77%	0.04%	0.00%	0.00%	0.00%	0.00%
	A	0.00%	0.19%	99.26%	0.51%	0.03%	0.02%	0.00%	0.00%
	BBB	0.00%	0.01%	0.36%	99.15%	0.40%	0.04%	0.02%	0.01%
	BB	0.00%	0.00%	0.01%	0.55%	98.51%	0.79%	0.08%	0.06%
	B	0.00%	0.00%	0.01%	0.01%	0.61%	98.37%	0.61%	0.38%
	CCC/C	0.00%	0.00%	0.02%	0.03%	0.05%	1.86%	94.50%	3.53%
	D	0.00%	0.00%	0.00%	0.00%	0.00%	0.00%	0.00%	100.00%

the weighted sum (by rating distribution) of the transitional probabilities to the default state (ie, state "D") from all other states. Although the historical average default rate is 3.75%, in late 2012 the estimate of the one-year default rate by Hampden-Turner (2009, 2012) is 2.5%. That is, in 2012 we were in a low default environment and had been since late 2010. Accordingly, to account for that low default rate, we scale down the transitional probabilities from all other states to state D by the ratio $2.5/3.75 = 0.667$. Next, we adjust the transition matrix to account for the accompanying ratios of ratings upgrades-to-downgrades. Figure 12.2 shows that, not surprisingly, when default rates are high, the upgrade-to-downgrade ratio is low. One can approximate that relationship as:

$$U/D = 1.02 - [0.62* \; Default \; Rate \; (\%)] \tag{12.4}$$

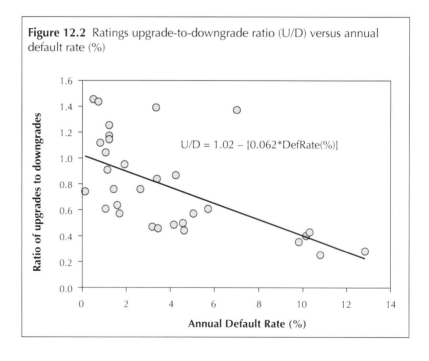

Figure 12.2 Ratings upgrade-to-downgrade ratio (U/D) versus annual default rate (%)

Although we prefer to use values of the upgrade–downgrade ratio reported by the rating agencies to make the adjustment, if not avail-

Table 12.3 Credit cycle-adjusted monthly rating transition matrix (October 2012)

From \ To	AAA	AA	A	BBB	BB	B	CCCIC	D
AAA	99.26%	0.71%	0.02%	0.00%	0.00%	0.00%	0.00%	0.00%
AA	0.06%	99.18%	0.72%	0.04%	0.00%	0.00%	0.00%	0.00%
A	0.00%	0.20%	99.28%	0.48%	0.03%	0.02%	0.00%	0.00%
BBB	0.00%	0.01%	0.38%	99.16%	0.37%	0.04%	0.02%	0.01%
BB	0.00%	0.00%	0.01%	0.59%	98.55%	0.73%	0.08%	0.04%
B	0.00%	0.00%	0.01%	0.01%	0.66%	98.49%	0.57%	0.25%
CCC/C	0.00%	0.00%	0.03%	0.04%	0.06%	2.00%	95.53%	2.35%
D	0.00%	0.00%	0.00%	0.00%	0.00%	0.00%	0.00%	100.00%

able, Equation 12.4 can provide an approximation. For example, given a default rate of 2.5%, the upgrade–downgrade ratio estimate is 0.87. The fact that the upgrade–downgrade ratio is greater than the historical average of 0.75 implies that we should adjust historical ratings transitions such that there are relatively more upgrades and relatively fewer downgrades. Using the value of 0.87 from Equation 12.4, the multiplier on the upgrade–downgrade ratio is $0.87/0.75 = 1.16$. Given that multiplier, for each rating transition to higher credit quality, we adjust the transitional probabilities to up states by the square root of 1.16, or 1.08. We adjust the transitional probabilities to down states by the inverse of 1.16, or 0.93. We leave the transitional probabilities to state D unchanged since we already incorporated those adjustments as described above. Finally, given the constraint that the sum of transitional probabilities from each state to all others is one, we obtain the transitional probability of remaining in the same credit state. The resulting one-month transition matrix is shown in Table 12.3.[4]

Multi-period transition matrices

Having generated the credit cycle-adjusted one-month transition matrix, we want to generate a multi-period transition forecast for each category out to five years (note that, after five years, average ratings transitions are used as we have little confidence in the ability to forecast the credit cycle beyond that time). The approach to generating transitions out to five years is to split the prediction period into two parts: a short period extending from one month to a year and annual periods from one to five years.

To begin, assume that monthly ratings transitions up to one year evolve according to the monthly transition matrix $\mathbf{R}$ that was derived in the previous section. For example, if one is interested in quarterly transition matrices, the Markov property implies that the three-month transition matrix should be $\mathbf{R}^3$, the six-month is $\mathbf{R}^6$, the nine-month should be $\mathbf{R}^9$ and the one-year transitions are given by $\mathbf{R}^{12}$. Examples of the three-, six-, nine- and 12-month ratings transitions appear in Table 12.4. Each matrix shows the cumulative probability of transitioning from the credit state on the vertical axis to the state given on the horizontal axis over the time period specified.

Unfortunately, the Markov property does not hold between historical one-year ratings transitions, $\mathbf{P}_1$, and five-year historical transitions, $\mathbf{P}_5$.[5] That is, it appears that additional risk factors influence ratings migrations over longer periods. Also, there is little evidence that any information present in the market would improve the accuracy of transition probabilities over historical averages for periods beyond five years. Accordingly, in the absence of more specific information, we apply a linear adjustment to one-year transitions for each year between one and five years, and apply Markov transitions to derive annual transitions thereafter. That is, starting from the one-year transition matrix $\mathbf{R}^{12}$, we interpolate linearly each year such that the two-year transition matrix is $\mathbf{R}^{12} + 1/4 \times (\mathbf{P}_5 - \mathbf{P}_1)$ and the three-year matrix is $\mathbf{R}^{12} + 2/4 \times (\mathbf{P}_5 - \mathbf{P}_1)$, and so forth. This method of adjusting rating transitions accounts for both short-term macroeconomic conditions and longer-term average transitions.

Annual ratings transitions from two to five years derived from the credit cycle-adjusted one-year matrix (in the lower right panel of Table 12.4) as described above are shown in Table 12.5. As expected, as time advances the probabilities of remaining in the initial credit states (vertical axes) decrease and the cumulative probabilities of default increase. As mentioned, to generate transition matrixes after five years, we apply the historical one-year transitions that appear in Table 12.1.

It is possible to rearrange the data in the transitions matrices in Tables 12.4 and 12.5 to construct matrices of ratings transitions for credits of a single rating category over the period from one month to five years. For example, the matrices resulting for triple-A to single-B rated credits appear in Table 12.6, with the initial rating category highlighted in each matrix. These matrices can be used to not only estimate cycle-adjusted default probabilities over long periods, but can be useful for estimating likelihoods of credit losses and, as shown below, are an important component of estimating expected gains and losses when combined with data on credit spreads.

Table 12.4 Quarterly ratings transitions matrices to one year generated from the one-month credit cycle-corrected transition matrix (initial credit states are given on the vertical axis, with the end-state on the horizontal axis)

Three-month transitions

	AAA	AA	A	BBB	BB	B	CCC/C	D
AAA	97.80%	2.11%	0.09%	0.00%	0.00%	0.00%	0.00%	0.00%
AA	0.18%	97.58%	2.12%	0.12%	0.00%	0.00%	0.00%	0.00%
A	0.00%	0.69%	97.87%	1.40%	0.08%	0.00%	0.00%	0.00%
BBB	0.00%	0.04%	1.13%	97.61%	1.09%	0.13%	0.01%	0.03%
BB	0.00%	0.00%	0.04%	1.72%	95.74%	2.13%	0.23%	0.14%
B	0.00%	0.00%	0.04%	0.06%	1.92%	95.60%	1.81%	0.78%
CCC/C	0.00%	0.00%	0.08%	0.10%	0.20%	5.65%	87.21%	6.76%
D	0.00%	0.00%	0.00%	0.00%	0.00%	0.00%	0.00%	100.00%

Six-month transitions

	AAA	AA	A	BBB	BB	B	CCC/C	D
AAA	95.66%	4.11%	0.22%	0.01%	0.00%	0.00%	0.00%	0.00%
AA	0.36%	95.23%	4.15%	0.25%	0.00%	0.00%	0.00%	0.00%
A	0.00%	1.16%	95.82%	2.75%	0.17%	0.10%	0.00%	0.00%
BBB	0.00%	0.09%	2.21%	95.12%	2.11%	0.28%	0.13%	0.01%
BB	0.00%	0.00%	0.10%	3.33%	91.72%	4.09%	0.45%	0.30%
B	0.00%	0.00%	0.09%	0.12%	3.67%	91.53%	2.95%	1.64%
CCC/C	0.00%	0.00%	0.15%	0.20%	0.48%	10.34%	76.14%	12.69%
D	0.00%	0.00%	0.00%	0.00%	0.00%	0.00%	0.00%	100.00%

Nine-month transitions

	AAA	AA	A	BBB	BB	B	CCC/C	D
AAA	93.67%	6.03%	0.39%	0.01%	0.00%	0.00%	0.00%	0.00%
AA	0.52%	92.96%	6.09%	0.42%	0.01%	0.00%	0.00%	0.00%
A	0.00%	1.70%	93.84%	4.03%	0.27%	0.14%	0.01%	0.00%
BBB	0.00%	0.14%	3.24%	92.82%	3.06%	0.45%	0.18%	0.11%
BB	0.00%	0.00%	0.17%	4.83%	87.93%	5.90%	0.67%	0.49%
B	0.00%	0.00%	0.13%	0.23%	5.27%	87.74%	4.06%	2.56%
CCC/C	0.00%	0.00%	0.21%	0.28%	0.82%	14.20%	66.57%	17.92%
D	0.00%	0.00%	0.00%	0.00%	0.00%	0.00%	0.00%	100.00%

Twelve-month transitions

	AAA	AA	A	BBB	BB	B	CCC/C	D
AAA	91.53%	7.86%	0.59%	0.03%	0.00%	0.00%	0.00%	0.00%
AA	0.68%	90.76%	7.93%	0.60%	0.02%	0.01%	0.00%	0.00%
A	0.01%	2.22%	91.92%	5.25%	0.38%	0.19%	0.01%	0.01%
BBB	0.00%	0.19%	4.23%	90.61%	3.95%	0.62%	0.23%	0.16%
BB	0.00%	0.01%	0.26%	6.23%	84.35%	7.56%	0.89%	0.71%
B	0.00%	0.00%	0.18%	0.36%	6.74%	84.22%	4.97%	3.53%
CCC/C	0.00%	0.00%	0.27%	0.37%	1.20%	17.35%	58.29%	22.53%
D	0.00%	0.00%	0.00%	0.00%	0.00%	0.00%	0.00%	100.00%

Table 12.5 Annual ratings transitions matrices from two years to five years extrapolated from the one-year credit cycle-corrected transition matrix (initial credit states are given on the vertical axis, with the end-state on the horizontal axis)

Two-year transitions

	AAA	AA	A	BBB	BB	B	CCC/C	D
AAA	84.55%	12.88%	1.93%	0.28%	0.42%	0.03%	0.01%	0.10%
AA	1.03%	83.84%	13.06%	1.67%	0.19%	0.11%	0.01%	0.09%
A	0.04%	3.53%	86.12%	8.63%	1.00%	0.43%	0.06%	0.20%
BBB	0.01%	0.40%	6.95%	84.32%	5.62%	1.42%	0.35%	0.93%
BB	0.00%	0.04%	0.76%	9.65%	74.34%	9.87%	1.25%	4.09%
B	0.01%	0.01%	0.32%	1.13%	9.71%	72.69%	4.92%	11.20%
CCC/C	0.00%	0.00%	0.31%	0.88%	2.26%	18.10%	50.71%	27.94%
D	0.00%	0.00%	0.00%	0.00%	0.00%	0.00%	0.00%	100.00%

Three-year transitions

	AAA	AA	A	BBB	BB	B	CCC/C	D
AAA	77.58%	17.50%	3.28%	0.52%	0.84%	0.05%	0.03%	0.19%
AA	1.38%	76.93%	18.19%	2.74%	0.35%	0.20%	0.02%	0.18%
A	0.06%	4.84%	80.31%	12.00%	1.62%	0.66%	0.12%	0.39%
BBB	0.02%	0.60%	9.66%	78.04%	7.29%	2.22%	0.46%	1.70%
BB	0.00%	0.06%	1.26%	13.08%	64.34%	12.17%	1.61%	7.48%
B	0.02%	0.02%	0.46%	1.90%	12.66%	61.17%	4.88%	18.88%
CCC/C	0.00%	0.00%	0.35%	0.98%	3.32%	18.86%	43.12%	33.35%
D	0.00%	0.00%	0.00%	0.00%	0.00%	0.00%	0.00%	100.00%

Four-year transitions

	AAA	AA	A	BBB	BB	B	CCC/C	D
AAA	70.60%	22.33%	4.62%	0.77%	1.26%	0.08%	0.04%	0.29%
AA	1.73%	70.01%	23.32%	3.81%	0.51%	0.30%	0.03%	0.28%
A	0.09%	6.15%	74.50%	15.37%	2.24%	0.90%	0.17%	0.56%
BBB	0.00%	0.81%	12.38%	71.75%	8.96%	3.01%	0.57%	2.48%
BB	0.01%	0.09%	1.75%	16.50%	54.33%	14.48%	1.97%	10.87%
B	0.02%	0.03%	0.61%	2.67%	15.66%	49.64%	4.83%	26.55%
CCC/C	0.00%	0.00%	0.40%	1.30%	4.36%	19.61%	32.54%	38.77%
D	0.00%	0.00%	0.00%	0.00%	0.00%	0.00%	0.00%	100.00%

Five-year transitions

	AAA	AA	A	BBB	BB	B	CCC/C	D
AAA	63.63%	27.15%	5.97%	1.02%	1.68%	0.11%	0.05%	0.39%
AA	2.08%	63.10%	28.46%	4.88%	0.68%	0.40%	0.04%	0.37%
A	0.12%	7.46%	68.69%	18.76%	2.85%	1.13%	0.22%	0.77%
BBB	0.04%	1.02%	15.10%	65.47%	10.63%	3.81%	0.68%	3.26%
BB	0.01%	0.12%	2.25%	19.93%	44.33%	16.79%	2.33%	14.25%
B	0.03%	0.04%	0.75%	3.44%	18.62%	38.11%	4.79%	34.23%
CCC/C	0.00%	0.00%	0.44%	1.61%	5.45%	20.36%	27.96%	44.18%
D	0.00%	0.00%	0.00%	0.00%	0.00%	0.00%	0.00%	100.00%

Table 12.6 Transition matrices from one month to five years for letter rating categories from triple-A to single-B

	1M	3M	6M	9M	1Y	2Y	3Y	4Y	5Y
AAA	99.26%	97.80%	95.66%	93.57%	91.53%	84.55%	77.58%	70.60%	63.63%
AA	0.71%	2.11%	4.11%	6.03%	7.86%	12.68%	17.50%	22.33%	27.15%
A	0.02%	0.09%	0.22%	0.39%	0.59%	1.93%	3.28%	4.62%	5.97%
BBB	0.00%	0.00%	0.01%	0.01%	0.03%	0.28%	0.52%	0.77%	1.02%
BB	0.00%	0.00%	0.00%	0.00%	0.00%	0.42%	0.84%	1.26%	1.68%
B	0.00%	0.00%	0.00%	0.00%	0.00%	0.03%	0.06%	0.08%	0.11%
CCC/C	0.00%	0.00%	0.00%	0.00%	0.00%	0.01%	0.03%	0.04%	0.05%
D	0.00%	0.00%	0.00%	0.00%	0.00%	0.10%	0.19%	0.29%	0.39%

	1M	3M	6M	9M	1Y	2Y	3Y	4Y	5Y
AAA	0.06%	0.18%	0.36%	0.52%	0.68%	1.03%	1.38%	1.73%	2.08%
AA	99.18%	97.58%	95.23%	92.96%	90.76%	83.84%	76.93%	70.01%	63.10%
A	0.72%	2.12%	4.15%	6.09%	7.93%	13.06%	18.19%	23.32%	28.45%
BBB	0.04%	0.12%	0.25%	0.42%	0.60%	1.67%	2.74%	3.81%	4.88%
BB	0.00%	0.00%	0.00%	0.01%	0.02%	0.19%	0.35%	0.51%	0.68%
B	0.00%	0.00%	0.00%	0.00%	0.01%	0.11%	0.20%	0.30%	1.40%
CCC/C	0.00%	0.00%	0.00%	0.00%	0.00%	0.01%	0.02%	0.03%	0.04%
D	0.00%	0.00%	0.00%	0.00%	0.00%	0.09%	0.18%	0.28%	0.37%

	1M	3M	6M	9M	1Y	2Y	3Y	4Y	5Y
AAA	0.00%	0.00%	0.00%	0.00%	0.01%	0.04%	0.06%	0.09%	0.12%
AA	0.20%	0.59%	1.16%	1.70%	2.22%	3.53%	4.84%	6.15%	7.46%
A	99.29%	97.87%	95.82%	93.84%	91.92%	86.12%	80.31%	74.50%	68.69%
BBB	0.48%	1.40%	2.75%	4.03%	5.25%	8.63%	12.00%	15.39%	18.75%
BB	0.03%	0.08%	0.17%	0.27%	0.38%	1.00%	1.62%	2.24%	2.85%
B	0.02%	0.05%	0.10%	0.14%	0.19%	0.43%	0.66%	0.90%	1.13%
CCC/C	0.00%	0.00%	0.00%	0.01%	0.01%	0.06%	0.12%	0.17%	0.22%
D	0.00%	0.00%	0.00%	0.00%	0.01%	0.20%	0.39%	0.58%	0.77%

	1M	3M	6M	9M	1Y	2Y	3Y	4Y	5Y
AAA	0.00%	0.00%	0.00%	0.00%	0.00%	0.01%	0.02%	0.03%	0.04%
AA	0.01%	0.04%	0.09%	0.14%	0.19%	0.40%	0.60%	0.81%	1.02%
A	0.38%	1.13%	2.21%	3.24%	4.23%	6.95%	9.66%	12.38%	15.10%
BBB	99.16%	97.51%	95.12%	92.82%	90.61%	84.32%	78.04%	71.75%	65.47%
BB	0.37%	1.09%	2.11%	3.06%	3.95%	4.62%	7.29%	8.96%	10.63%
B	0.04%	0.13%	0.28%	0.45%	0.62%	1.42%	2.22%	3.01%	3.81%
CCC/C	0.02%	0.07%	0.13%	0.18%	0.23%	0.35%	0.46%	0.57%	0.68%
D	0.01%	0.03%	0.07%	0.11%	0.16%	0.93%	1.70%	2.48%	3.25%

Table 12.6 (Continued)

	1M	3M	6M	9M	1Y	2Y	3Y	4Y	5Y
AAA	0.00%	0.00%	0.00%	0.00%	0.00%	0.00%	0.00%	0.01%	0.01%
AA	0.00%	0.00%	0.00%	0.00%	0.01%	0.04%	0.06%	0.09%	0.12%
A	0.01%	0.04%	0.10%	0.17%	0.26%	0.76%	1.25%	1.75%	2.25%
BBB	0.59%	1.72%	3.33%	4.83%	6.23%	9.65%	13.08%	16.50%	19.93%
BB	98.55%	95.74%	91.72%	87.93%	84.35%	74.34%	64.34%	54.33%	44.33%
B	0.73%	2.13%	4.09%	5.90%	7.56%	9.87%	12.17%	14.48%	16.79%
CCC/C	0.08%	0.23%	0.45%	0.67%	0.89%	1.25%	1.61%	1.97%	2.33%
D	0.04%	0.14%	0.30%	0.49%	0.71%	4.09%	7.48%	10.87%	14.25%

	1M	3M	6M	9M	1Y	2Y	3Y	4Y	5Y
AAA	0.00%	0.00%	0.00%	0.00%	0.00%	0.01%	0.02%	0.02%	0.03%
AA	0.00%	0.00%	0.00%	0.00%	0.00%	0.01%	0.02%	0.03%	0.04%
A	0.01%	0.04%	0.09%	0.13%	0.18%	0.32%	0.46%	0.61%	0.75%
BBB	0.01%	0.05%	0.12%	0.23%	0.36%	1.13%	1.90%	2.67%	3.44%
BB	0.66%	1.92%	3.67%	5.27%	6.74%	9.71%	12.68%	15.65%	18.62%
B	98.49%	85.60%	91.53%	87.74%	84.22%	72.69%	61.17%	49.64%	38.11%
CCC/C	0.57%	1.61%	2.95%	4.06%	4.97%	4.92%	4.88%	4.83%	4.79%
D	0.25%	0.78%	1.64%	2.56%	3.53%	11.20%	18.88%	26.55%	34.23%

Ratings transitions and credit spreads

One potentially useful property of accurate ratings transitions matrices is that they can be combined with market spreads to estimate the distributions of potential gains and losses on risky assets. Several noteworthy attempts at this have been made (Jarrow, Lando and Turnbull, 1997; McNulty and Levin, 2000), and these have proved useful for some valuation and risk management problems.[6] A critical feature of those previous approaches is that they use credit spreads and risk-neutral default probabilities to determine the ratings transition matrices. In fact, we have used this technique in our model for pricing corporate loans (see Benzschawel and Lee, 2012).

Despite the demonstrated usefulness of risk-neutral transition matrices, the use of risk-neutral default transitions matrices has several limitations. Consider the top panel of Figure 12.3, which shows that estimates of physical (actual) default probabilities are below those for risk-neutral default probabilities for April 2009, and this general pattern is nearly always the case. That is, risk-neutral transition matrices will overestimate expectations of transitions to default states, and those extra probabilities of transitions to default must be removed from transitions among non-default states.[7] There is also the problem, illustrated in the lower portion of Figure 12.3, that the procedure for removing transitions from among the non-default states is not clear. One attractive feature of the Jarrow–Lando–Turnbull method is that it manages to preserve well the shape of the transitions among non-default states, which becomes even more important for multi-period transitions. However, this does not solve the problem of the overestimation of default transitions at the expense of non-default ones. This imposes limitations on the usefulness of risk-neutral transition matrices for computing VaR, valuing spread options and other credit assets that depend on accurate non-default state transitions, thereby providing the motivation for the present method.

Figure 12.3 Top: estimated physical default probabilities (from Sobehart and Keenan's HPD model) and risk-neutral default probabilities (April 27, 2009); bottom: hypothetical physical (historical) ratings transitions from initial triple-B rating (blck line) and two potential risk-neutral ratings transitions that both predict risk-neutral default probabilities

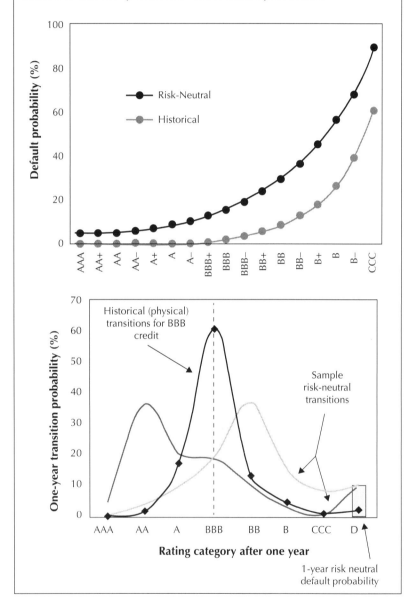

Unlike the approaches mentioned above which adjust the transition matrix to current market spreads, the method presented herein takes as input a ratings transition matrix adjusted as described in previous sections upon which we superimpose corresponding credit spreads by rating and maturity. In fact, one of the objectives is to determine if, by weighting term structures of market spreads by the probabilities in the adjusted ratings transitions matrices, one could generate credit spreads by rating category that match average spreads from bonds in that category. That is, can one derive current credit spreads for firms' bonds of various ratings and maturities from knowledge of their current credit state and the overall term structure of credit spreads? If so, this could prove useful for estimating VaR for various criteria, and for valuation of bonds with embedded call or put options.

The first step in assigning spread values to the nodes in credit cycle-adjusted transition matrices is to obtain spread values for each rating category and asset maturity. For example, each day we bucket median bond spreads by rating category into half-year intervals, which are then fit using a modified Nelson–Siegel method (Nelson and Siegel, 1987) to generate spread curves for each un-notched rating category from triple-A to triple-C. The top panel of Figure 12.4 displays an example of resulting spread curves by rating and maturity along with corresponding tabled values at 0.5 years, and annual values from one to five years in the lower panel.

Given daily data on average credit spreads versus maturity from similarly rated bonds, the objective is, for an obligor whose credit state is known, to generate a transition-inferred bond spread (TIS). Although from the term structures of credit spreads one can estimate total spread values for non-default states by rating and tenor, it is not clear how much spread should be assigned to the default state. After examining several alternatives, including a constant spread value, we devised a method based on the spread value of physical default as described in the next section.

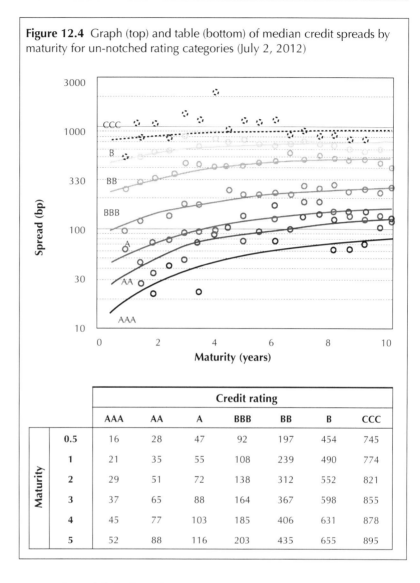

Figure 12.4 Graph (top) and table (bottom) of median credit spreads by maturity for un-notched rating categories (July 2, 2012)

		Credit rating						
		AAA	AA	A	BBB	BB	B	CCC
	0.5	16	28	47	92	197	454	745
	1	21	35	55	108	239	490	774
Maturity	**2**	29	51	72	138	312	552	821
	3	37	65	88	164	367	598	855
	4	45	77	103	185	406	631	878
	5	52	88	116	203	435	655	895

Separation of default and non-default spread

From the discussion of the credit risk premium in Chapter 5, recall that a bond's spread can be decomposed into compensation for default and a spread value related to its level of volatility. Then, as above, we let $\mathbf{P}_t$ denote the physical measure representing the transition matrix at time t, let nd denote the condition of non-default and d denote the condition of default. Now, consider the expected value of triple-A credit spreads (ie, $i = $ AAA in the notation above) under measure **P** (note, since the expressions below will hold for any time t, we omit the subscript t for clarity). Since the default state D is an absorbing one, we assume that migration only takes place among the non-default states. Then, as shown in detail in Appendix 12.1, the expected spread value for triple-A bonds can be approximated as:

$$\hat{S}^{AAA} = \sum_{j \neq D} \frac{P^{AAA \to j}}{\sum_{j \neq D} P^{AAA \to j}} * \left(\bar{S}^j - \bar{S}_d^j\right) + \bar{S}_d^{AAA}$$

(12.5)

where:

$\hat{S}^{AAA}$	:	*Estimated spread for AAA bond*
j	:	*Credit state at time t*
$P^{AAA \to j}$	:	*Probability of transition from AAA to j*
$\bar{S}^j$	:	*Market spread for state j at time t*
$\bar{S}_d^j$	:	*Spread spread of default for state j at time t*
$\bar{S}_d^{AAA}$	:	*Spread spread of default for state AAA at time t*

A critical feature of this method is the generation of daily spread values to assign to non-default states AAA, AA,…, B and CCC in the series of transition matrixes from three months to five years. For these applications, we use estimates of default probabilities from the market-implied PD (MKI) model (Benzschawel and Lee, 2011; Benzschawel and Assing, 2012). For example, the top row of data in Table 12.7 displays geometric averages of one-year spread values of expected defaults by rating category. The spread values of default at one year were calculated for individual bonds using the following:

$$s_d = -\frac{1}{t}\ln[1 - (PD_t * LGD)]$$

(12.6)

where t is the transition period in years, PD_t is the cumulative default probability for the issuer up to time t from the market-implied model, LGD is the loss given default (one minus the recovery value).[8] For the values in Table 12.7, $t = 1$ and LGD is assumed to be 60% for all credits.

Table 12.7 Top: spread values of geometric means of one-year default rates by rating category from the market-implied default model; bottom: default spread to full spread ratios (July 2, 2012)

	Agency rating						
	AAA	AA	A	BBB	BB	B	CCC
$\hat{S}_d$	2.6	1.5	4.2	14	64	136	503
k^j	7.7%	6.6%	9.8%	15.7%	26.8%	34.4%	50.5%

Note that the one-year PDs in Table 12.7 are geometric means rather than arithmetic ones. The choice of geometric averaging reflects the fact that distributions of credit spreads are more nearly Gaussian on a geometric scale. Still, the geometric average within a rating category can be influenced greatly by outlying values. An example of this is that the geometric average default spread for triple-A credits in Table 12.7 is greater than that for the lower-rated double-A bonds. In fact, on July 2, 2012, some triple-A bonds were facing downgrade pressure and, given the relatively few triple-A-rated bonds, their spread widening resulted in a greater average than that for double-A bonds. To limit this type of potential bias on transition inferred spreads, we chose an alternative method for specifying the spread value of default. That is, for each rating category, we generate a ratio of average one-year default spreads to average one-year spreads as:

$$k^j = \frac{\overline{S}_{d_1}^j}{\overline{S}_1^j}$$

(12.7)

and apply this ratio to the spreads' curve fit to that rating category for all maturities (ie, $t > 0$). The values of k^j for July 2, 2012, appear in the bottom row of Table 12.7. Those values are used to calculate a new set of average default spreads by rating and maturity, and these appear in Table 12.8. Note that the default spreads for all rating categories are calculated assuming a constant ratio of default spread to full spread over different tenors.[9]

Table 12.8 Average default spreads as calculated assuming a constant ratio of default spread to full spread for all maturities at each rating category

		Rating						
		AAA	AA	A	BBB	BB	B	CCC
	0.5	1.2	1.8	4.6	14	53	156	373
	1	1.6	2.4	5.4	17	64	168	387
Maturity	2	2.2	3.4	7.1	22	84	190	411
	3	2.9	4.3	8.7	26	98	206	428
	4	3.5	5.1	10.1	29	109	217	439
	5	4.0	5.9	11.2	32	117	225	448

Inferring spreads from probability-weighted transitions

Having adjusted ratings transition matrices (Table 12.6) and spread curves and default spreads by credit rating (Figure 12.4 and Table 12.8, respectively), one can calculate, for a given rating category and tenor, transition-inferred spreads. These TIS can be compared with actual spreads to determine the consistency of the transition adjustments. For example, the left portion of Table 12.9 displays probability-weighted spread values for each element in the one-year transition matrix. That is, each element in the matrix is the probability of being in that state after one year times the spread value of that state minus the estimated spread cost of default. Thus, for a credit transitioning from state i to state j, $j \neq D$, the element in the matrix, $s(i \rightarrow j)$ is calculated as:

$$s^{i \rightarrow j} = \frac{p^{i \rightarrow j}}{\sum_{jAD} p^{i \rightarrow j}} * \left(\bar{S}^{j} - \bar{S}_{d}^{j} \right)$$

(12.8)

where the symbols are as defined above. For example, for a triple-A credit the average one-year spread is 21bp, the probability of remaining triple-A is 91.6% and the spread value of default is 1.57bp. Thus, according to equation 12.8:

$$s^{AAA \rightarrow AAA} = \frac{91.5\% * (20.5 - 1.6)}{99.9\%} = 17.3$$

Table 12.9 Left: one-year credit spreads weighted by one-year transition probabilities for each credit state; right: TIS by rating, actual average spreads by rating, and factor and spread adjustments to reconcile the two

	To								TIS	Average spread	Adjustment	
	AAA	AA	A	BBB	BB	B	CCC	D			Factor	Spread
AAA	17	3	0.3	0	0	0	0	2	22	21	94%	1
AA	0.1	30	4	0.6	0	0	0	2	37	35	95%	2
A	0	0.7	46	5	0.7	0.6	0.0	5	58	55	95%	3
BBB	0	0.1	2	82	7	2	0.9	17	111	108	97%	4
BB	0	0	0.1	6	148	25	4	64	246	239	97%	8
B	0	0	0.1	0.3	12	280	20	168	482	490	102%	(8)
CCC	0	0	0.2	0.4	3	70	293	387	754	774	103%	(20)

The other elements in the matrix in Table 12.9 were calculated similarly. Then, the values in each row, the probability weighted value of being in each state given initial state i (ie, the TIS), is calculated as the sum of the values of $s(i,j)$ for all for all rating categories plus the spread value of its default probability as:

$$\widehat{S}^i = \sum_j s^{i \to j}$$

(12.9)

in accordance with Equation 12.5.

Values of $\widehat{S}^i$ calculated using Equation 12.9 for the one-year transition matrix in the left portion of Table 12.9 appear in the column labelled TIS in the right portion of the table. The actual average spread values by rating category for one-year in Figure 12.4 are reproduced next to the TIS values in Table 12.9, followed by the adjustment factors (ie, percentage error) and differences in basis points between the TIS and the average spreads. For all rating categories, the summed transition probability-weighted spread values obtained are within +/–4% of the market spreads, with differences ranging from 1bp greater for triple-A corporates to 20bp less for triple-C credits. The agreement between the probability-weighted spreads and the average rating-category spreads is remarkable in that the adjustments to the transition matrix are not dependent on the spread curves that are superimposed on the transition probabilities.

Although TIS for one-year transitions match average spreads well, errors become larger for transition-inferred spreads over longer time periods. For example, Table 12.10 displays five-year transition-weighted spreads along with TIS, actual spreads and error measures analogous to those shown at one year in Table 12.9. Absolute errors in spreads are larger at five years than one year and, at least for higher-quality credits, percentage errors are also larger. In fact, for triple-A credits the transitions overestimate spreads by 27% (or 19bp), reflecting the very steep credit curve at that time.[10] Still, the pattern of errors at five years, with overestimation of spreads for high ratings and slight underestimates for riskier categories, mimics that at one year.

Table 12.10 Left: five-year credit spreads weighed by five-year transition probabilities for each credit state; right: TIS by rating, actual average spreads by rating and factor and spread adjustments to reconcile the two

		To										Adjustment	
		AAA	AA	A	BBB	BB	B	CCC	D	TIS	Average spread	Spread	Factor
From	AAA	31	23	6.3	2	5	0	0	4	71	52	73%	19
	AA	1.0	52	30	8.4	2	2	0	6	101	88	87%	13
	A	0	6.2	72	32	9.2	4.9	1.0	11	137	116	84%	22
	BBB	0	0.9	16	116	35	17	3.2	32	220	203	92%	17
	BB	0	0	2.7	40	164	85	12	117	420	435	103%	(14)
	B	0	0	1.2	8.9	89	250	33	225	608	655	108%	(48)
	CCC	0	0	0.8	4.8	30	152	230	448	866	895	103%	(28)

Adjusting transitions to match credit spreads

A useful property of a transition matrix is to have those transitions consistent with credit spreads. That is, one would wish to have ratings transitions matrices whose TIS match those of ratings categories (and specific firms itself). Notable precedents in that regard are Jarrow, Lando and Turnbull (1997) and Israel, Rosenthal and Wei (2001), but those transitions have been developed under a risk-neutral measure. The transitions herein are under a physical measure. In this section, we derive a "market-implied" ratings transition matrix whereby errors between TIS and average spreads are minimised through adjustments to the ratings transition matrix.

Although several methods for adjusting the matrix might be deployed, for present purposes we chose a constrained optimisation that attempts to minimise the magnitudes of adjustments to the transition probabilities while simultaneously minimising the differences among inferred and actual spreads. From the relations developed in Equations 12.1–12.9, we have, for a given tenor, a credit cycle-adjusted transition matrix $\mathbf{P}$, from which we can compute expected spreads, $\hat{S} = \hat{S}(\mathbf{P})$, where for each rating i we have:

$$\hat{S}^i = \sum_{j \neq D} \frac{P^{i \to j}}{\sum_{j \neq D} P^{i \to j}} * \left(\bar{S}^j - \bar{S}_d^j\right) + \bar{S}_d^i \qquad (12.10)$$

Ideally, the expected spreads and average market spreads should be as close as possible. This can be achieved by solving for the market-implied rating transition matrix $\hat{\mathbf{P}}$ that minimises the difference between $\hat{S}(\hat{\mathbf{P}})$ and $\bar{S}$ while keeping $\hat{\mathbf{P}}$ close to $\mathbf{P}$. To do so, we apply a constrained optimisation where we minimise the following objective function with respective to $\hat{\mathbf{P}}$:

$$f(\hat{\mathbf{P}}) = \left\| \hat{\mathbf{P}} - \mathbf{P} \right\|_F + \lambda \left\| \hat{S}(\hat{\mathbf{P}}) - \bar{S} \right\|_\infty \qquad (12.11)$$

subject to the constraints that:

$$\sum_j \hat{P}^{i \to j} = 1 \text{ for all } i$$

and

$$\hat{P}^{i \to j} \geq 0 \text{ for all } i \text{ and } j.$$

In the objective function, $\|\mathbf{M}\|_F = \sqrt{\sum_i \sum_j M_{ij}^2}$ is the Frobenius matrix norm, $\|\mathbf{v}\|_B = \max(|v_1|, |v_2|, ..., |v_n|)$ is the vector-infinity norm and λ is a positive parameter to tune the weight between the two error terms. The value of λ was set to 100 based on a trade-off between the two error terms in Equation 12.11. The constraints in Equation 12.11 serve to ensure that $\hat{\mathbf{P}}$ is a valid transition matrix.

Applying the constrained optimisation in Equation 12.11 to the transition matrices for July 2, 2012 in Table 12.5 with the spreads in Figure 12.4 superimposed gave rise to the adjusted physical transition matrices in Table 12.11. The TIS for each rating category are shown, and these match the actual average spreads by rating for one- and five-year bonds shown in Tables 12.10 and 12.11, respectively.

Table 12.11 One-year (top) and five-year (bottom) matrices of spread values of transitions among credit states, where TIS are sums of transitions from each credit rating to all other states for a given tenor

	To								
	AAA	AA	A	BBB	BB	B	CCC	D	TIS
AAA	19	0	0	0	0	0	0	2	21
AA	1	30	2	0.0	0	0	0	2	35
A	0	1	46	3	0	0	0	5	55
BBB	0	0	2	82	6	0	0	17	108
BB	0	0	0	6	148	20	0	64	239
B	0	0	0	0	6	284	31	168	490
CCC	0	0	0	0	0	0	387	387	774

	To								
	AAA	AA	A	BBB	BB	B	CCC	D	TIS
AAA	48	0	0	0	0	0	0	4	52
AA	7	53	23	0.0	0	0	0	6	88
A	4	9	73	18	0	0	0	11	116
BB	0	0	0	36	165	94	23	117	435
CCC	0	0	0	0	0	0	447	448	895

Lines of constant VaR

Having developed physical transition matrices whose average spreads by rating match those of inferred credit curves, we can use those matrices to generate VaR for credits of various credit qualities over arbitrary timeframes. For example, each curve in Figure 12.5 displays average spreads over time for a various VaR criteria for double-B rated credits. Each panel plots the same data for VaR criteria of 1%, 5%, 10%, 50%, 90%, 95% and 99%, with spreads in the left graph plotted on a linear axis, whereas the logarithms of spreads are plotted on the right. The data appear more uniform on the logarithmic plot, and illustrate the advantage to viewing spreads in proportional, rather than arithmetic, terms (see Appendix 12.2 for similar plots of constant VaR curves for all rating categories).

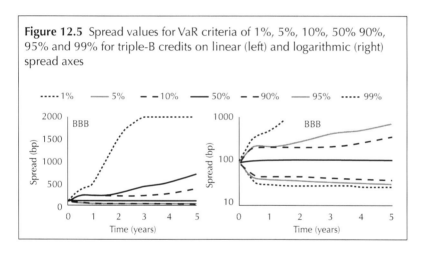

Figure 12.5 Spread values for VaR criteria of 1%, 5%, 10%, 50% 90%, 95% and 99% for triple-B credits on linear (left) and logarithmic (right) spread axes

The analytics that underlie the iso-VaR lines in Figure 12.5 and Figure A.12.2.1 (of Appendix 12.2) are of interest for several reasons. First, they allow one to infer, for credits of assumed rating categories, the likelihoods of expected spread moves of their bonds (and potentially credit default swaps) over various tenors. This, when combined with probabilities of transitioning to default, can be useful for estimating expected losses on portfolios of risky assets. In addition, accurate specification of the probabilities of transitioning among credit states can be useful for valuing assets whose value is dependent on credit-state transitions such as corporate loans. Finally, the ability to model the probability-weighted evolution of credit spreads can be useful for valuing options that depend on the future values of credit spreads.

STOCHASTIC DEFAULT RATES, TRANSITION MATRICES AND CREDIT SPREADS

So far, a framework has been presented for generating expected ratings transitions and credit spreads. However, market participants are also interested in likelihoods of unexpected losses. Calculating unexpected losses requires generation of stochastic credit-state transitions upon which stochastic credit spreads are superimposed.

Figure 12.6 illustrates the stages of the simulation. The top portion of the figure describes the process for generating expected losses as described in the previous section. The lower part of the diagram shows the stages of generating unexpected losses as described in the following sections. The simulator starts by applying an Ornstein-Uhlenbeck (O-U) process for default rates as described in the next section, with the second row representing the inputs to the simulation. The historical transition matrix (TM) is input along with the current term structure of credit spreads by agency ratings from the market. In addition, a starting one-year default rate is supplied as the output of Citi's HT 2.0 model (Benzschawel and Su, 2014). The simulator then generates 10 one-year probabilities of default, with each of those default probabilities being used to generate a one-year ratings TM from time 0 to one year. Then, the ratings TM is adjusted based on the expected upgrade-to-downgrade ratio for the given default rate. The adjusted spreads are also applied at this stage.

The remaining stages in Figure 12.6 represent the generation of unexpected losses. At this stage the stochastic credit transition matrices are generated for years from one to five.. Also, stochastic spread distributions are applied to each TM, and that process is also described below. Finally, we apply the optimisation procedure described above on each combination of TM and credit spreads starting from year five and working backward to year one. To summarise, in the simulation each year from one to five the O–U process of PDs has 10 branches. Thus, there are 111,110 PDs and resulting transition matrices, and the same number of adjusted spreads. On each transition matrix and associated adjusted spreads, we impose 10 stochastic spread variations.

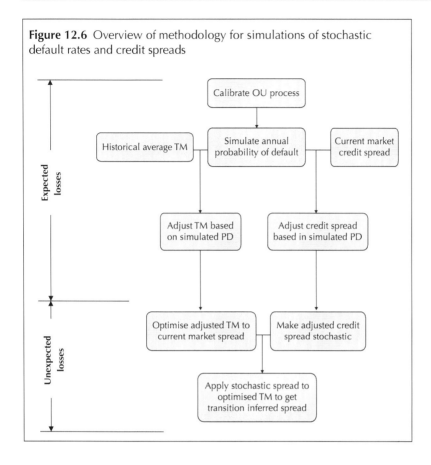

Figure 12.6 Overview of methodology for simulations of stochastic default rates and credit spreads

Generating stochastic default rates and adjusted ratings transitions

Benzschawel and Wu (2011) generated time series of credit cycle-corrected PDs. They then used those default rates along with the relations shown above in Figure 12.2 and Equation 12.4 to derive the corresponding ratings transitions. Stochastic default rates were generated using an O–U process such that:

$$dp_t = \eta(\mu - p_t)dt + \sigma dz \qquad (12.12)$$

where η is the speed of mean reversion, μ is the term average default rate, p_t is the logarithm of the default rate generated at time t and σ is the standard deviation. The parameters in Equation 12.12 as estimated by Benzschawel and Wu are $\eta = 0.43$ and $\sigma = 0.67$. Subsequently, a long-run mean parameter was added to the model to minimise the squared difference between the average simulated annual PDs for different credit ratings and their historical averages. A sample of the resulting paths starting from the 2012 default rate of 2.3% appear on linear and logarithmic PD axes in the top and bottom panels of Figure 12.7, respectively.

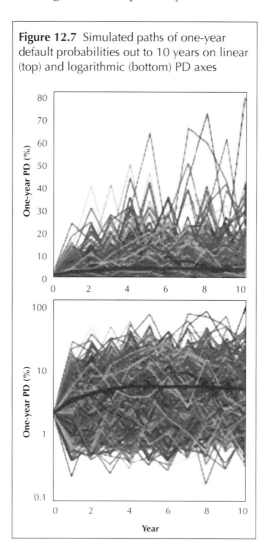

Figure 12.7 Simulated paths of one-year default probabilities out to 10 years on linear (top) and logarithmic (bottom) PD axes

Given the assumption that relative ratios of historical defaults by agency rating category are constant with changes in overall default rates, Figure 12.8 presents a comparison of default rates from the model with historical average PDs across rating categories. The lighter bars represent averages of 1,000 simulated default rates generated from the default rate simulator plotted along with historical averages. The figure reveals good agreement between simulated and historical average PDs.

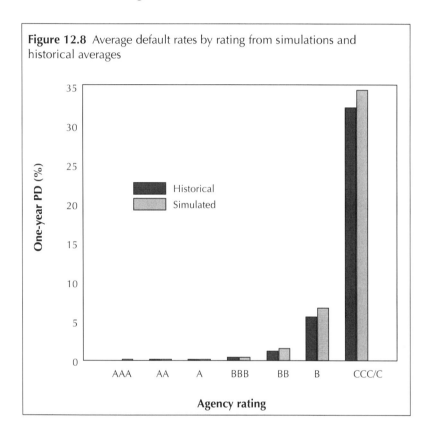

Figure 12.8 Average default rates by rating from simulations and historical averages

Figure 12.9 presents an example of simulated paths of one-year PDs for each year from one to four. The figure shows that the simulator generates 10 default paths from the current year to year one, with each default rate giving rise to 10 one-year paths over the next year using that PD as input to the PD simulator, and so on out to five years. Each of the simulated PDs is used to generate an adjusted TM using the method described above.

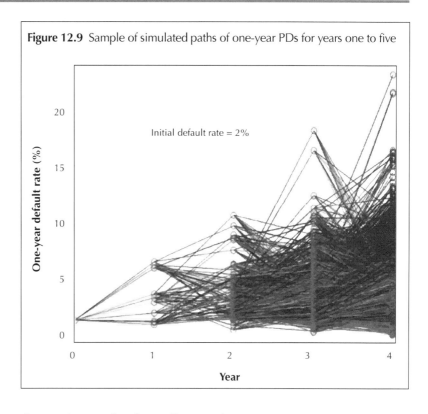

Figure 12.9 Sample of simulated paths of one-year PDs for years one to five

Generating stochastic credit spreads

To illustrate the generation of stochastic credit spreads, recall the term structure of yield spreads to US Treasuries by rating category and tenor presented in Figure 12.4. For each year from one to five, the one-year forward yields by rating are superimposed on the adjusted transition matrices generated from the stochastic default rates. To begin, we regressed the logarithms of average high-yield spreads to Treasuries against logarithms of historical default rates as shown in the left panel of Figure 12.10. On average, the levels of credit spreads, s_t, are related to annual default rates, PD_t, according to:

$$log(s_t) = 3.47 + [0.51 * log(PD_t)] \qquad (12.13)$$

Then, with the random draw on the PD path, we adjust the logarithms of credit spreads by rating to match the simulated PD in accordance with Equation 12.13. Also, as there is a good deal of variation in the relationship between spreads and default rates (shown in the lower-right panel of Table 12.10), and other factors might affect spreads, a lognormal volatility variable was added to simulate stochastic spread moves such that Equation 12.13 becomes:

$$log(s_t) = 3.47 + [0.51 * log(PD_t)] + 0.11\varepsilon_t \qquad (12.14)$$

where $\varepsilon_t \sim N(0,1)$. For each simulated PD-generated TM, 100 stochastic spread components were added in accordance with Equation 12.14. Then, as a final step, the adjusted transition matrices from year five back to year one were adjusted to minimise the error between the credit-state dependent TIS spreads and the actual spreads in accordance with the method described above.

Figure 12.10 Relationship between log default rates and credit spreads (left) and the volatility of the relationship (right)

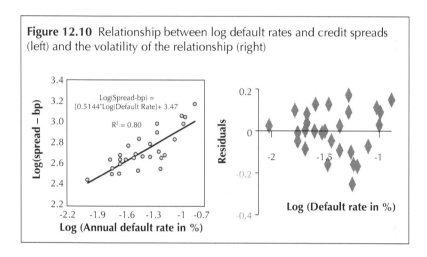

Lines of constant VaR

Having developed physical transition matrices whose average spreads by rating match those of inferred credit curves, we can use those matrices to generate VaR for credits of various credit qualities over arbitrary timeframes out to five years. Each curve in Figure 12.11 displays average spreads over time for various VaR criteria of 1%, 5%, 10%, 50%, 90%, 95% and 99%. Spreads in the left graphs for each rating category show results with a stochastic spread component, with those on the right having been generated using only a single spread curve. The iso-probability curves with stochastic credit spread components are consistently wider than those without, illustrating the need to incorporate stochastic spreads when estimating VaR.

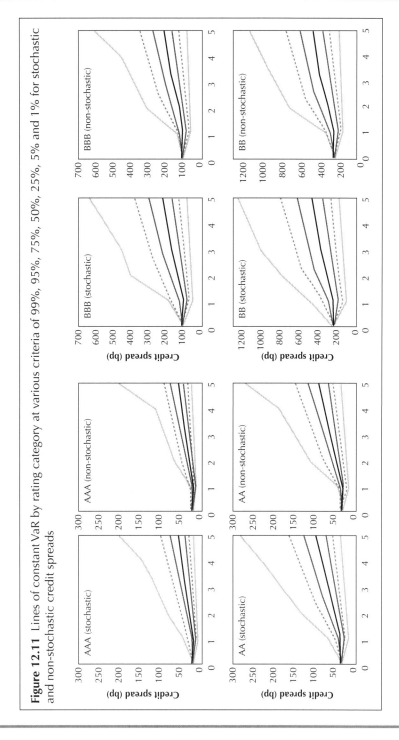

Figure 12.11 Lines of constant VaR by rating category at various criteria of 99%, 95%, 75%, 50%, 25%, 5% and 1% for stochastic and non-stochastic credit spreads

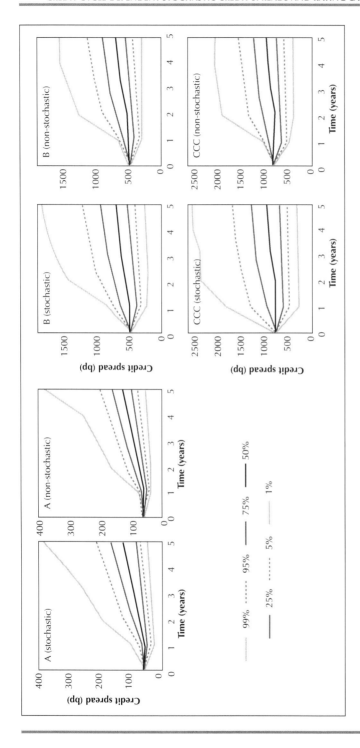

In addition to the VaR analysis, one can plot distributions of adjusted spreads and stochastic spreads for each rating category. For example, Figure 12.12 shows the distribution of credit spreads that result from the 10 simulated transitions matrices in the first year by rating category for non-stochastic and stochastic spread distributions. The difference between those two distributions reveals the additional VaR produced by adding the more realistic stochastic credit spreads to the stochastic transition matrices. Since we only have 10 simulated paths of defaults and transitions in the first year, the histograms are relatively sparse. Nevertheless, it can be seen that the stochastic TIS has a fatter tail and thus a lower peak. The stochastic TIS also has an extra right skew relative to adjusted TIS. As credit quality decreases, peaks move to higher spreads, and distributions become wider for both adjusted and stochastic spread distributions. Also, differences between adjusted and stochastic spread distributions increase with decreasing credit quality.

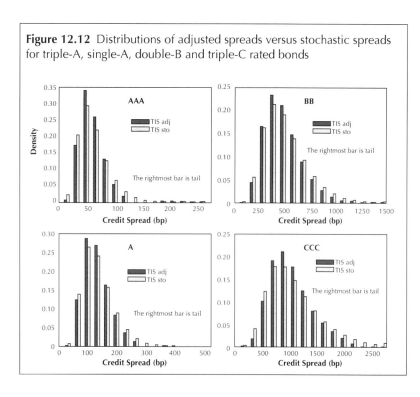

Figure 12.12 Distributions of adjusted spreads versus stochastic spreads for triple-A, single-A, double-B and triple-C rated bonds

Finally, Figure 12.13 shows distributions of stochastic spreads by tenor for triple-B-rated bonds. Distributions are shown for each year from one to five. The figure shows that at tenor increases, the peak of the spread distributions shift to higher spreads, but with decreasing density. The decrease in density of the average spreads reflects the fact that spreads at longer tenors have increased density in their high spread tails. The pattern of results shown in Figure 12.13 for triple-B rated bonds is similar for the other rating categories.

Figure 12.13 Distributions of stochastic spreads at one to five years for triple-B rated bonds

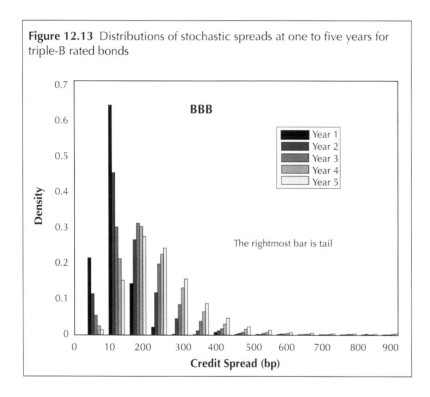

CONCLUSION

This chapter described methods for estimating VaR for corporate bonds. Those estimates involve generating stochastic credit cycle-dependent ratings transition matrices and stochastic credit spreads for credits of given agency ratings for arbitrary times out to five years.

The first part of the chapter described the calculation of expected losses. The credit cycle-adjusted ratings transition matrices were constructed by altering the historical transition matrix based on credit cycle-dependent changes in default rates and the ratios of agency ratings upgrades to downgrades. The adjustments were determined from model-based average physical default probabilities and ratings upgrade–downgrade ratios. It was shown how those credit-state adjusted matrices can be used to infer likelihoods of transitioning among various credit states given current market conditions. In addition, one-year credit spreads, as derived from market spread curves by rating category, were superimposed on each node in the transition matrix at each tenor. The resulting matrices were used to calculate TIS for bonds by rating category for tenors out to five years. TIS calculated for the spectrum of credit ratings and tenors agreed well with average market spreads, but slight deviations remained. Accordingly, we used optimisation methods to make slight adjustments to transition probabilities from model-derived values to bring TIS to near coincidence with market values.

The latter portion of the chapter described estimation of unexpected losses by generating stochastic credit-state transition matrices with stochastic credit spreads applied to each matrix. Both stochastic default rates and stochastic credit spread processes were calibrated to historical data. Finally, the transition matrices and associated spread values were used to generate iso-probability (constant VaR) spread curves by credit rating for tenors out to five years from the set of matrices whose probabilities were optimised at each tenor to match market spreads. These curves can be used in risk management for estimating likelihoods of expected spread moves and/or losses from default.

APPENDIX 12.1 ESTIMATING CREDIT SPREADS FROM THE TRANSITION MATRIX

This appendix will provide details of the derivation of the method for assigning credit spreads to elements in the ratings transition matrices. As in the main text, let $\mathbf{P}_t$ denote the physical measure representing the transition matrix at time t, let nd denote the condition of non-default and d denote the condition of default. Now, consider the expected value of triple-A credit spreads (ie, $i = \text{AAA}$ in the above notation) under measure $\mathbf{P}$ for a given time t (note, since the expressions below will hold for any time t, we omit the subscript t for clarity). Observing that we use E to denote the expectation, this can be expressed as:

$$E_P S^{AAA} = E_P(S_{nd}^{AAA} + S_d^{AAA})$$

$$= E_P S_{nd}^{AAA} + E\{E_P S_d^{AAA} \mid d\} \text{ (tower property)}$$

$$= E_P S_{nd}^{AAA} + ES_d^{AAA} \text{ (since the default state is absorbing)}$$

$$= E\{E_Q S_{nd}^{AAA}\} + ES_d^{AAA} \text{ (Q is the non-default conditional transition measure)}$$

$$= E(\sum_{j \neq D} P_{(Q)}^{AAA \to j} \cdot S_{nd}^j) + ES_d^{AAA}$$

$$= \sum_{j \neq D} P_{(Q)}^{AAA \to j} \cdot ES_{nd}^j + ES_d^{AAA}$$

$$= \sum_{j \neq D} \frac{P^{AAA \to j}}{\sum_{j \neq D} P^{AAA \to j}} \cdot (ES^j - ES_d^j\} + ES_d^{AAA}$$

where $P^{AAA \to j}$ is the original transition probability from state AAA to state j. The MLE under the assumption of normality of the above formula is then:

$$\sum_{j \neq D} \frac{P^{AAA \to j}}{\sum_{j \neq D} P^{AAA \to j}} * (\bar{S}^j - \bar{S}_d^j) + \bar{S}_d^{AAA}$$

which is the expression in Equation 12.5 of the main text. Similar analyses can be applied to obtain expressions for spread values of transitions for credits of other ratings. Note that we often observe fat-tailed distributions of spreads instead of normal distributions. Hence, the use of the population average as an estimate may be biased, and further improvements can be made with a more realistic modelling of the distribution of spreads. However, the goal of this chapter is to compare the expected values of spreads against observed average spreads, so we chose to use this straightforward estimator.

APPENDIX 12.2 CONSTANT VAR LINES BY RATING

Figure 12.2.1 displays lines of constant VaR by rating category for July 2, 2012, derived using the methods and relationships described in the main body of the text.

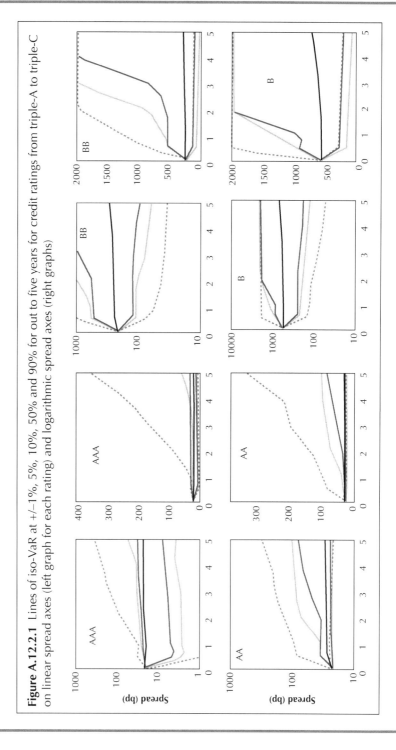

Figure A.12.2.1 Lines of iso-VaR at +/−1%, 5%, 10%, 50% and 90% for out to five years for credit ratings from triple-A to triple-C on linear spread axes (left graph for each rating) and logarithmic spread axes (right graphs)

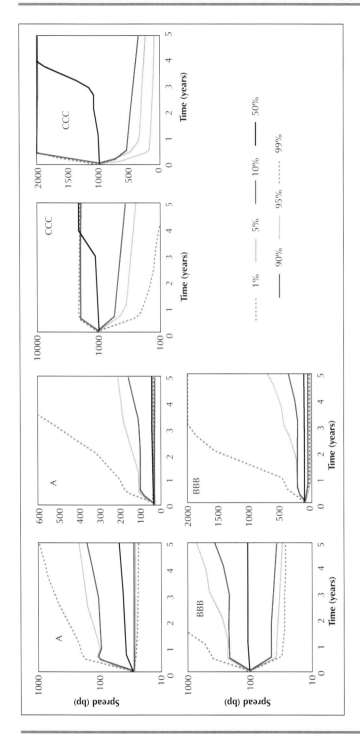

1   The rating agencies publish these tables for a number of investment horizons, at least out to five years and also including notched (plus and minus) rating categories.

2   However, it ignores changes in default rates, credit-state transitions and spread moves that evolve over time. These are considered later in the chapter when stochastic defaults and credit spreads are incorporated into the method.

3   Theorem 3 in Israel *et al* (2001) specifies three conditions under which an exact generator for a given matrix $\mathbf{P}$ does not exist. These are: (i) det $\mathbf{P} \leq 0$; (ii) det $P > \prod_i p_{ii}$; or (iii) there are states i and j such that j is accessible from i, but $p_{i,j} = 0$. The matrix $\mathbf{P}$ in Figure 12.1 satisfies condition (iii).

4   Although the one-month transitions to default from all credit states in Table 12.3 appear as zero to two decimal places, they are actually non-zero; their values are all less than one basis point.

5   That is, one cannot derive the five-year transitions by applying the one-year matrix five times.

6   A useful discussion of the literature on quantifying and modelling ratings transitions can be found in Das, Fan and Geng (2002).

7   This is because transitions from a credit state, expressed as probabilities, at time t to those at time $t+1$ must add up to 1.0.

8   See Appendix 5.1 for a derivation of Equation 12.6.

9   We make this same assumption in the market-implied default model for tenors that differ from one year.

10 In fact, the historically steep credit curve has been attributed to technical factors resulting from the Fed's quantitative easing programme, which has seen US Treasury investors moving to high-quality corporate credit in the search for yield unavailable from low Treasury yields.

13

Managing Systemic Liquidity Risk: Systems and Early Warning Signals

A defining feature of the financial crisis of 2007–08 was the inability of many financial institutions to roll over existing debt or to obtain short-term financing. Importantly, the inability to obtain financing negatively impacted global financial stability and macroeconomic performance. Many banks had exposure to common asset classes, and there was heavy reliance on the short-term funding of assets. Banks' attempts to deal with these exposures under crisis spilled over to other markets and institutions, thereby creating a vicious cycle of losses and financial stress. Ultimately, central banks in major economies found it necessary to assume the role of the money market in providing liquidity amid mutual mistrust among financial institutions. The extent of the necessary governmental intervention is evidence of the underpricing of liquidity risk by both the private and public sectors.

The government injection of taxpayer funds into financial institutions to prevent a collapse of the US banking system has proven politically unpopular. This is reflected in the spate of legislation, exemplified by the Dodd–Frank Act (Congress of the United States of America, 2010) and the Volcker Rule (Department of the Treasury, 2014), designed to prevent a recurrence of the support from the public sector. In addition, the Group of 20 (G20) has called for increased liquidity buffers. To that end, Basel III (Basil Committee on Banking Supervision, 2010), the international regulatory framework for banks, has issued standards and guidance for banks to lessen their exposure to liquidity risk. Although these new regulations address the financial risk of individual institutions, they do not directly address systemic liquidity risk. Thus, despite those actions, no global framework for mitigating systematic liquidity risk has been established. Accurately characterising systematic liquidity and pricing it appropriately will eliminate liquidity support from the public sector, and also enable assessment of firms' contributions to systemic liquidity risk.

This final chapter will provide perspective on the origin and dynamics of the liquidity crisis. In addition, it describes attempts to model systemic risk and liquidity conditions, and to contribute to an understanding and quantification of systemic liquidity risk. Finally, methods are described for hedging liquidity exposure with tradable assets, and for generating an early warning system for changes in market liquidity.

DEFINING SYSTEMIC LIQUIDITY AND THE ORIGINS OF LIQUIDITY RISK

Systemic liquidity risk involves a complex interaction between funding risk and its effects on asset values among different institutions. Despite its importance in financial markets, liquidity risk has proven difficult to quantify. The International Monetary Fund (IMF) defines systemic liquidity risk as "The probability of a simultaneous and widespread inability of multiple financial institutions to roll over or obtain new short-term funding or sell assets to obtain cash" (International Monetary Fund, 2011a). Financial institutions tend to collectively underprice liquidity risk in good times when funding markets function well. It is often asserted that institutions are convinced that the central bank will intervene in times of stress to maintain functioning markets, prevent the failure of financial institutions and thus limit the impact of liquidity shortfalls on financial institutions and the real economy. However, public sector support for the markets has proven unpopular and regulations designed to preclude the necessity of future taxpayer support for banks have been proposed. It is argued that regulations that impose accurately upon banks the costs of contingent liquidity support ought to eliminate liquidity support by the public sector. However, to do this presupposes an understanding of the origins and nature of systemic liquidity risk, and the existence of a reliable methodology for measuring such risk.

To understand and quantify liquidity risk, it is useful to consider first the origins and dynamics of systemic liquidity risk. Trading requires capital. When a trader (eg, dealer, hedge fund or investment bank) buys a security, they can borrow against it, using the security as collateral. However, they cannot borrow the entire price. The difference between the asset price and its value as collateral is denoted as the margin, and must be financed by the firm's capital. When total margin exceeds the firm's capital, the firm is technically insolvent. Although the failure of a financial institution may reflect solvency concerns, it invariably manifests itself via an inability to fund its positions. In a world with perfect information and complete capital markets, banks would only fail if their underlying fundamentals rendered them insolvent. In such a world, only firms' asset and liability positions would determine their health. Solvent banks would always be able to finance random liquidity demands by borrowing – for example, from other financial institutions. In reality, informational frictions and imperfections in capital markets make it difficult for firms to obtain funding if there are concerns about their solvency (regardless of whether or not those concerns are substantiated). In such funding crises, the fundamental solvency constraint no longer fully determines survival, what matters is whether banks have sufficient cash inflows, including income from asset sales and new borrowing, to cover all cash outflows. That is, it is often an entity's cashflow constraints rather than actual solvency that are critical to survival in a trading environment.

One characteristic of liquidity crises is that they turn buy-and-hold investors into forced sellers. The forced selling that results from deteriorating liquidity conditions reflects the high sensitivity of market liquidity to changes in funding conditions. Brunnermeier and Pedersen (2009) have characterised the dynamics of liquidity crises as involving two spirals, namely a liquidity spiral and a margin spiral, as represented in Figure 13.1. The trigger for the liquidity spirals is a loss on a firm's positions amid decreasing liquidity conditions. A margin spiral emerges if margins are increasing as the markets become more illiquid. Then, increasing margins provide a funding shock to speculators lowering market liquidity, leading to higher margins, which tightens speculators' funding constraints further, and so on. The spiral forces traders (and latterly investment banks) to de-lever. Also, a loss spiral arises if firms hold large initial positions that are correlated negatively with customers' demand shock. In this case, the funding shock increases market illiquidity, leading to speculators' losses on their initial position, forcing further selling, causing a further price drop, and so on. These liquidity spirals reinforce each other, implying a larger total effect than the sum of their separate effects. This self-reinforcing process can lead to downward cascades in asset prices and to further declines in a firm's net worth, morphing into a systemic crisis as more institutions are affected.

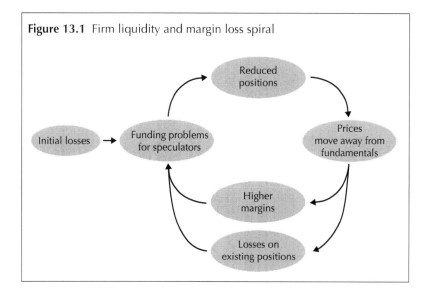

Figure 13.1 Firm liquidity and margin loss spiral

Another aspect of liquidity spirals involves market liquidity risk and funding liquidity risk. Market liquidity risk refers to firms' inability to sell assets quickly without materially affecting their prices. Brunnermeier and Pederson (2009) propose a measure of market liquidity as the difference between the transaction price and the fundamental value of a security (although this may be difficult to quantify). Funding liquidity risk refers to firms' inability to meet their expected cashflow requirements (future and current) by raising funds at short notice. The two types of liquidity risks can interact with each other and, through markets, affect multiple institutions. In periods of rising uncertainty, the interaction can give rise to systemic liquidity shortfalls. A negative spiral between market and funding liquidity can develop whereby a sudden lack of funding leads to multiple institutions attempting to sell their assets simultaneously to generate cash. This interaction between margin spiral and loss spiral underscores the difficulty of disentangling the risk of systemic insolvency from that of systemic illiquidity since the two are closely linked.

Figure 13.2 illustrates major features of the spread of systemic liquidity crises. As in Figure 13.1, the crisis begins with an initial shock, such as a downward spike in asset prices from the loss of confidence in a financial institution. As shown in Figure 13.2, the shock causes funding problems at one or more firms, and may even cause firms to fail, further decreasing confidence throughout the system. In turn, decreasing confidence motivates liquidity hording by other firms and other defensive actions, creating funding problems for firms previously dependent on those sources for funding. Funding problems then create forced selling, thereby causing further decreases in asset prices. Decreasing confidence, asset price declines and firm failures all further increase funding problems across the system and worries about counterparty credit risk increase. At this point, a full-fledged liquidity crisis has emerged.

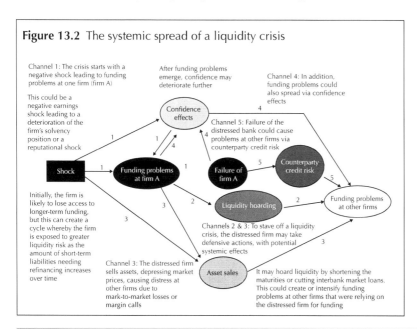

Figure 13.2 The systemic spread of a liquidity crisis

OFFICIAL LIQUIDITY MEASURES: LCR AND NSFR

In response to the credit crisis, Basel III established two liquidity standards: a liquidity coverage ratio (LCR) and a net stable funding ratio (NSFR) (Department of the Treasury, 2013). Although principles for liquidity risk management existed before the crisis, the Basel III rules represent the first time that quantitative standards for liquidity risk have been set at a global level. An observation period for each is to precede official implementation of the ratios as a minimum standard. In both cases, any revisions to the factors will be finalised one and a half years before their official implementation, which was on July 1, 2015, for the LCR and will be January 1, 2018, for the NSFR. For present purposes, the interest in in the LCR and NSFR regard their potential as measures of liquidity risk.

The LCR aims to improve banks' abilities to withstand a month-long period of liquidity stress as severe as that seen in the financial crisis of 2007–08. The LCR is defined as the "stock of high-quality liquid assets" divided by a measure of a bank's "net cash outflows over a 30-day time period". Banks' resulting ratios should be at least 100% to be in compliance. High-quality assets that qualify for the LCR are mostly government bonds and cash, while a maximum of 40% of mortgage and corporate bonds may be of a certain lower credit quality.[1] The LCR assumes a 100% drawdown of interbank deposits and other financial instruments having less than 30 days' maturity.

Thus, the requirement for the liquidity coverage ratio is defined as:

$$LCR = \frac{Stock\ of\ high\text{-}quality\ liquid\ assets}{Net\ cash\ outflows\ over\ next\ 30\ days} > 100\% \tag{13.1}$$

The LCR requires the value of the ratio be no lower than 100%. Banks are expected to meet this requirement continuously and hold a stock of liquid, high-quality assets. In addition, banks and supervisors are expected to be aware of potential mismatches within the 30-day period to ensure sufficient assets are available to meet cashflow gaps throughout the month.

The 30-day criterion for the LCR is based on the assumption that a 30-day period is sufficient for orderly resolution of the problems by banks' management and/or supervisors. The LCR builds on traditional liquidity "coverage ratio" methodologies used internally by banks to assess exposure to contingent liquidity events. The scenario proposed for the LCR standard entails a combined idiosyncratic and market-wide shock that would result in:

❑ a three-notch downgrade in the institution's public credit rating;
❑ a run-off of a significant proportion of the bank's retail deposits;
❑ loss of unsecured wholesale funding capacity and reductions of sources of secured term funding;
❑ loss of secured, short-term financing transactions for all but high-quality liquid assets;
❑ increases in market volatilities that impact values of banks' assets, thereby requiring larger collateral haircuts or additional collateral;
❑ unscheduled draws on all of the institution's committed but unused credit and liquidity facilities; and
❑ the need for the institution to fund balance-sheet growth with the goal of mitigating reputational risk.

Although lack of access to short-term funding is presumed to underlie the necessity of government intervention during the liquidity crisis of 2007-08, it is difficult to assess the impact of shortfalls in the LCR that occurred during the credit crisis. This is because information from banks on the credit quality, ratings and liquidity characteristics of the LCR's level II assets (covered bonds, rated corporate bonds and agency debt) are not publicly available. In addition, the analysis would require knowledge of the duration and composition of assets and liabilities, including off-balance-sheet exposures.

Although values of banks' LCRs during the crisis remain unknown, estimates of LCRs for major US financial institutions have been reported (Tracey, 2014). Those LCRs for 19 of the largest US financial institutions as of the first quarter of 2014 are presented in Figure 13.3. The data imply a combined shortfall of US$100 billion relative to the amount required by the regulations. Nevertheless, it is generally assumed the LCRs during the financial crisis were much lower, and previous estimates by the Federal Reserve implied a shortfall of roughly US$200 billion relative to the 100% LCR criterion. Presumably, the decrease in the estimated shortfalls reflects banks' preparations for the regulations that became effective in 2015. In particular, LCR estimates for the largest US banks were already in compliance with the required ratio.

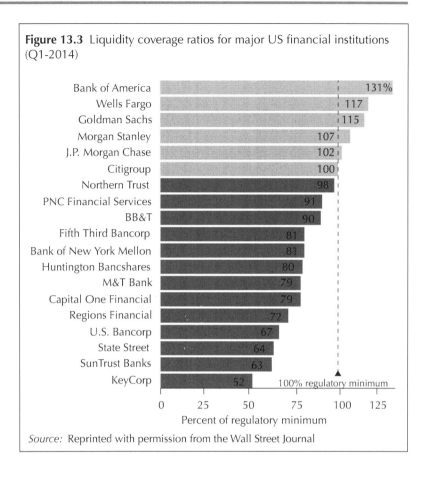

Figure 13.3 Liquidity coverage ratios for major US financial institutions (Q1-2014)

Source: Reprinted with permission from the Wall Street Journal

Fortunately, the historical information required to estimate banks' NSFRs is more readily available than for liquid assets, so it is possible to analyse banks' NSFRs during the credit crisis. As banks' liquidity problems result typically from their inability to obtain short-term funding, the NSFR is designed to encourage more medium- and long-term funding of banks' assets and activities, thereby reducing maturity mismatches. The NSFR is defined as a bank's available stable funding (ASF) divided by its required stable funding (RSF), and must be greater than 100%. The RSF includes off-balance-sheet exposures as well as capital market activities. The NSFR is intended to support the institution as a going concern for at least one year if it is subject to firm-specific funding stress. Thus, the LCR and NSFR are complementary: the LCR is intended to protect banks from short-term liquidity shortfalls, whereas the NSFR is designed to ensure that banks are able to survive longer-term liquidity crises.

SYSTEMIC LIQUIDITY RISK AND BANK EXPOSURE

The IMF has estimated NSFRs for major financial institutions to evaluate the role of shortfalls in systemic liquidity of major institutions during the crisis (International Monetary Fund, 2011b). NSFRs were calculated from publicly available data for 60 globally oriented banks in 20 countries across Europe, North America and Asia. The institutions encompassed commercial, universal and investment banks, and 13 additional banks that became insolvent during the global crisis. Assumptions were made regarding the application of Basel III weights, or factors, to components making up the ASF and RSF. The assumptions reflected broad interpretations of the liquidity and stability of banks' balance sheets.

The left panel of Figure 13.4 displays NSFRs by region from 2005 to 2009. The figure shows that, in general, maturity mismatches (ie, NSFRs) deteriorated before and during the crisis. That is, the average NSFR hovered below 100% before the crisis, worsened in 2008 and then improved slightly in 2009. In particular, NSFRs for European and US banks declined during the crisis, while Asian banks improved their ratios. NSFRs by business model appear in the right panel of Figure 13.4. Although NSFRs declined for all types of banks during the crisis, investment banks and universal banks experienced sharp declines, whereas declines for strictly commercial banks were much milder. The figure also shows that funding profiles improved in 2009 across business models, with universal banks reaching the 100% threshold. The overall average NSFR for 2009 is 96%, just below the 100% threshold, and the estimated gap between the ASF and RSF for the 60 global banks in the analysis is about US$3.1 trillion; to attain an NSFR above 100%, banks' would have needed to raise US$3.1 trillion in stable funds. Overall, the results in Figure 13.4 support the view that a 100% target for NSFRs would help to protect banks from future liquidity crises.

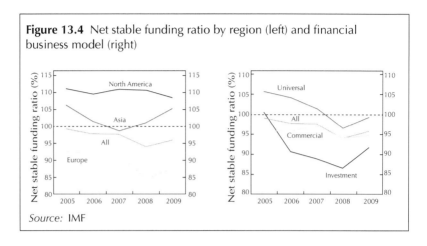

Figure 13.4 Net stable funding ratio by region (left) and financial business model (right)

Source: IMF

The challenge in evaluating the effectiveness of the NSFR in preventing bank failure is to separate liquidity from solvency problems. When a bank is perceived as insolvent, its funding options can quickly become circumscribed. In that case, having longer-term sources of financing can help prevent insolvency. Similarly, if a bank has severe liquidity problems, it may be forced to sell its assets at fire sale prices, accruing large losses with potential implications for its solvency. Nevertheless, the NSFR would be not be effective if banks' funding problems are due more to insolvency and rising counterparty concerns, rather than from liquidity problems.

The IMF has imputed NSFRs from financial statements at the end of 2006 for a sample of 60 banks, and these appear in Figure 13.5. The figure indicates that 10 of the 13 failed banks (dark grey bars) has an NSFR below 100%, with only one bank having an NSFR below 50%. Overall, banks that failed during the crisis are distributed roughly evenly across the range of NSFRs. Still, there are cases of failure during the crisis that can be attributed mainly to funding risk rather than credit-related problems. Failure in those cases resulted from overreliance on securitisation and short-term wholesale funding. Examples include Northern Rock and HBOS, two UK banks that relied considerably on wholesale funding, leaving them vulnerable to the rapidly deteriorating conditions in the wholesale funding markets. Although the evidence is not compelling, the NSFR may still be indicative of potential liquidity problems, as half of the banks below the 80% level did have such problems. Nevertheless, other indicators and tools are necessary to gauge liquidity risks.

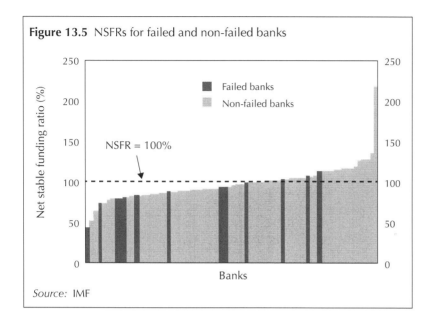

Figure 13.5 NSFRs for failed and non-failed banks

Source: IMF

ARE BASEL III LIQUIDITY REQUIREMENTS ENOUGH?

Basel III addresses basic notions of how to survive an idiosyncratic liquidity shock through requirements of the LCR and NSFR. The LCR requires banks to have more assets that can be liquidated quickly to support the remainder of the balance sheet during a stress scenario lasting one month. The NSFR is designed to promote structural changes in funding away from short-term funding, thereby ensuring ASF sufficient to cover the RSF. Both measures can help protect against a systemic liquidity shortfall.

Despite their obvious advantages, the LCR and NSFR have been criticised as being largely micro-prudential: they address risk at the individual bank level, but may not address systemic risk directly. In addition, the LCR, by requiring banks to hold liquid assets, may "tax" the liquidity of some markets during good times. For example, banks in countries with small amounts of government debt may not be able to access required assets. Also, requiring banks to hold liquid assets will remove re-hypothecatable paper from mar-

Table 13.1 Summary of pros and cons of Basel III in addressing systemic liquidity

Basel III liquidity rules - PROS	Basel III liquidity rules - CONS
❏ On balance, the new liquidity standards are a welcome addition to firm-level liquidity risk management and micro-prudential regulation	❏ Policymakers must ensure that the rules do not excessively restrict banks in their ability to undertake maturity transformation or to help institutions manage short-term liquidity
- Combined with improved supervision, these rules should strengthen liquidity management and the funding structure of individual banks	- Too-stringent rules may force banks to take similar actions to reach compliance, resulting in high correlation across certain types of assets
❏ Raising liquidity buffers reduces the chance that numerous institutions will have a simultaneous need for liquidity	❏ Restrictive rules could encourage migration of some banking activities into the less-regulated financial system including toward shadow banks
- By penalising exposures to other financial institutions they reduce the interconnectedness in the financial system and hence the likelihood of interrelated liquidity losses	- This could potentially accentuate rather than alleviate systemic risk
❏ A well-calibrated LCR and NSFR can contribute to the liquidity and funding stability of banks	❏ Uniform quantitative standards across bank types may not be suitable for all countries
- Further impact studies are needed to ensure that the factors in the construction of the NSFR are desirable from a financial stability perspective	- Countries may lack the markets to extend term funding for banks in domestic currency, so would require banks to take exchange rate risk
	❏ Policymakers have not established a macroprudential framework that mitigates system wide or systemic, liquidity risk
	- Lack of techniques to measure systemic liquidity risk and magnitude that an institution contributes

ket, thereby reducing overall liquidity. The LCR requirement may increase bank competition for the same liquid assets, actually increasing systemic risk. The NFSR may force banks to compete for deposits and long-term debt, possibly altering market dynamics such that retail deposits become more price-sensitive and volatile. By requiring investment in long-term debt, the NSFR may reduce liquidity buffers from current earnings. Thus, the Basel III liquidity requirements remain controversial among regulators and politicians, particularly over the issue of "too big to fail". A list of some pros and cons of Basel III in addressing systemic liquidity risk appears in Table 13.1.

QUANTIFYING SYSTEMIC LIQUIDITY RISK

An important aspect of managing liquidity risk is the measurement of banks' influences on systemic liquidity. This is particularly important in that proposals have been made to impose surcharges on banks in proportion to their contributions to systemic liquidity risk. Although the ability to measure contributions from individual firms to systemic liquidity risk is critical for that purpose, no generally accepted method has yet emerged. Moreover, there is no existing method for measuring the levels of systemic liquidity risk in the world economy. A successful measure of systemic liquidity risk could be used to value the liquidity assistance that an institution would receive from a central bank. Proper pricing and charging of this assistance would help lower the scale of liquidity support warranted by a central bank in times of stress.

Several attempts have been made to measure systemic liquidity risk outside of the Basel framework, and these will be discussed in this section. Those methods include:

❑ systemic liquidity risk index (SLRI) – a market-based index of systemic liquidity based on violations of common arbitrage relationships; and
❑ market liquidity index (CLX) – a market-based index of five tradable derivative contracts spanning equity, debt, interest rate and volatility markets.

In general, a successful tool for measuring and/or assessing surcharges for systemic liquidity risk would:

❏ be based on a robust measure of systemic risk;
❏ allow for extensive backtesting;
❏ be risk-adjusted – institutions that contribute more to systemic liquidity risk pay more proportionately;
❏ be countercyclical and time-varying – it should change in line with changes to an institution's risk;
❏ be relatively simple and transparent; and
❏ be not too data-intensive to compute and implement.

The methods, to be considered below, vary in the degree to which they satisfy these criteria. Importantly, both methods use publicly available information, but differ in their complexity and ease of implementation.

The systemic liquidity risk index

Kodres (2012) proposed a SLRI to characterise conditions of systemic liquidity and as a measure of banks' contributions to that risk. The SLRI exploits the fact that a breakdown of various arbitrage relationships signals a lack of market and funding liquidity. The SLRI covers 36 series of violations of arbitrage in three securities markets. That is, from daily market-based observations, the SLRI uncovers violations of arbitrage relationships that encompass identical underlying cashflows and fundamentals that trade at different prices. For example, these include:

❏ covered interest rate parity in the FX markets;
❏ firms' CDS versus cash bond basis in the non-financial corporate debt market;
❏ US Treasury on-the-run/off-the-run spreads; and
❏ the swap spread in the money market.

Under normal market conditions, similar securities that have identical cashflows are expected to have virtually no difference in price. The SLRI is constructed using a common factor approach that captures the similar characteristics of these violations in arbitrage relationships. The SLRI assumes that mispricing between similar assets should typically be exploited through arbitrage (long/short) strategies by financial investors with access to easy funding. However, in turbulent markets, arbitrage can break down due to many factors, and investors can become unable to borrow or do not have sufficient capital to take advantage of the arbitrage opportunities.

In particular, the SLRI is based on a principal components analysis (PCA) of the arbitrage violations in the 36 factors. PCA identifies a common factor across the asset classes that can explain the most variance.[2] The time series predictions of this common factor (using the underlying data) is constructed empirically and interpreted as an SLRI – a measure of the simultaneous tightening of liquidity conditions in global markets. Sharp declines in the index are associated with strong deteriorations in market liquidity. An appealing feature of the SLRI is that it is based on market measures. Previously, market-based measures have been used only to monitor market liquidity in individual markets. The approach integrates these multiple measures and incorporates the observation that they are connected to funding liquidity.

Values of the SLRI from 2004 to 2010 appear in the top panel of Figure 13.6. Sharp declines in the index, as seen in 2007 and 2008, are associated with strong deviations from the law of one price across assets, and thus suggest a global decrease in market and funding liquidity. Values of the SLRI are normalised (ie, converted to Z-scores). The normalisation subtracts from the daily SLRI the mean SLRI over the sample period, and divides it by its standard deviation. The SLRI has been examined for its ability to explain the differential effect that systemic illiquidity may have had on banks during the crisis, and for its ability to serve as a measure of banks contributions to systemic liquidity risk.

One test of the SLRI as a measure of banks' contribution to systemic liquidity risk is the strength of the relationship between changes in the SLRI and changes in banks' returns on equity. This association should reflect greater investor concern over the riskiness of an institution's prospects, including its liquidity risk. The IMF measured that relationship on a set of 53 globally oriented banks, reporting only a weak relationship between the SLRI and the banks' returns on equity. However, the middle panel of Figure 13.6 indicates that

Figure 13.6 SLRI (top); average sensitivity of volatility of banks' return on equity to SLRI (centre); and sensitivity of volatility of banks' return on equity based on NSFR to SRLI impact of decrease in SLRI (bottom)

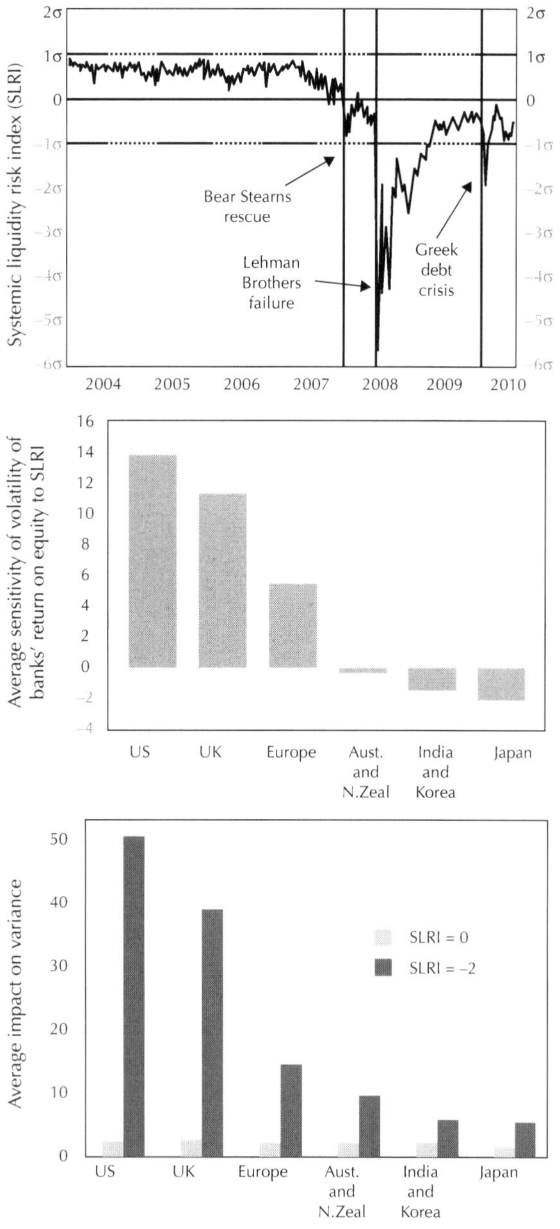

banks' equity volatility is sensitive to changes in the SLRI. Interestingly, it is the largest banks that have return volatility most sensitive to liquidity risk, suggesting size may be one possible criterion to determine the banks that should receive more supervisory attention for their liquidity management. Finally, the right panel of Figure 13.7 displays the relationship between banks' funding risk, as reflected by the NSFR, and the SLRI. Those results show that banks with the largest NSFRs have equity volatilities that are most sensitive to changes in the SLRI. This seemingly counterintuitive result can be explained by noting that the NSFR is designed to measure structural funding problems in an institution, and hence it is unlikely to proxy adequately for the same type of systemic liquidity risk in the SLRI. Thus, evidence from the IMF studies is generally supportive regarding the SLRI as a measure of banks' systemic risk. In contrast, although increasing NSFRs may lead to bank stability, the NSFR does not appear suitable as a measure of individual banks' influence on systemic risk.

Other evidence also supports the usefulness of the SLRI in predicting firm's vulnerability to liquidity shocks. The left panel of Figure 13.7 shows sensitivities of banks' equity returns based on their market capitalisation to changes in the SLRI. Consistent with the SLRI as a measure of systemic risk, equity volatilities of the largest banks are the most sensitive to changes in the SLRI. This result also supports the use of a size criterion regarding banks supervisory attention. The right-hand chart in Figure 13.7 shows sensitivities of banks' equity returns based on their NSFR to changes in the SLRI. There is a negative relationship between a bank's funding risk, as reflected by the NSFR, and the SLRI. This seemingly counterintuitive result has been explained by noting that the NSFR is a measure of structural funding problems in an institution, so is unlikely to proxy for the systemic liquidity risk.

The SLRI is easy to construct from public data, combines market and funding liquidity, and can potentially link firm-specific variables to systemic risk measure using easy-to-construct empirical relationships. Also, the SLRI holds potential to serve as the basis for a liquidity surcharge imposed on institutions for the costs associated with their systemic liquidity risks. Proceeds from the surcharges could be accumulated at the central bank or at a private sector insurer to be used as sources of financing in times of stress. The amount of an institution's charge would be determined by the institution's exposure to systemic liquidity risk, presumably based on its size. Despite these advantages, the SLRI has been criticised as being subject to market pricing (fads and panics). Also, use of the SLRI requires the assumption that the PCA is actually measuring systemic risks.[3] Furthermore, the SLRI offers no natural method to gauge the size of capital charge/insurance premium to apply, and there is no existing method for trading or hedging the SRLI.

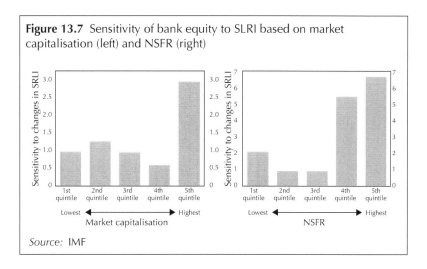

Figure 13.7 Sensitivity of bank equity to SLRI based on market capitalisation (left) and NSFR (right)

Source: IMF

To determine the potential levels of banks liquidity surcharges, Kodres (2011) proposed a method that uses the SLRI along with Merton's (1974) contingent claims approach to assess banks' contributions to systemic liquidity risk. The Merton model is schematised in the left panel of Figure 13.8, which displays the firm's assets based on the sum of the firm's equity and debt and the assumed lognormal diffusion of asset values up to some arbitrary time, T.[4] The states of the world implied by the diffusion of asset prices in which the value of the assets falls below the debt level are states in which the bank is presumed insolvent. Within this view, the bank's equity holders have a call option on bank assets, with a strike price given by the book value of its debt. Conversely, the debt holders have sold a put option to the equity holders struck at the level of the debt. As regards liquidity, banks' stock volatilities increase when liquidity conditions, as measured by the SLRI, deteriorate. As liquidity deteriorates, the value of the banks' puts increase as well. Accordingly, one should be able to use information from the distribution of a bank's equity prices (in particular, its volatility) to make inferences regarding the distribution of the market values of its assets. An important aspect of the Merton model is that, within the theory, the Black–Scholes model (Black and Scholes, 1973) can be used to estimate the value of the put option sold by the debt holders to the equity investors.

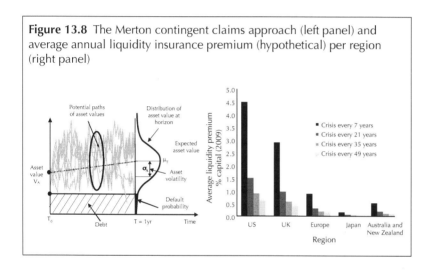

Figure 13.8 The Merton contingent claims approach (left panel) and average annual liquidity insurance premium (hypothetical) per region (right panel)

Kodres estimates volatilities of banks' equity returns from series of their trailing prices using a generalised autoregressive conditional heteroscedasticity (Garch) model (Engle, 2001). In general, estimates of each bank's volatilities would be made during both a calm pre-crisis period and a crisis period, and used to value two options associated with the underlying assets. The implied asset value and its volatility allows for the computation of the put option granted by public authorities on bank liabilities. Thus, the difference in the value of the put option pre- and during crisis can be viewed as the value of the implicit public guarantee, and can form the basis for charging banks a liquidity insurance premium.

The conditional pre- and during crisis betas of a bank's asset volatility signal how much the value of its equity will fall during bad times. It measures the loss in value of a bank due to liquidity problems, and is thus a measure of how much insurance a bank must buy to protect against liquidity stress. As for the volatilities, the assumption is that governments will rescue large banks in distress, and this is equivalent to providing banks with a put option. The price of this put, according to Black–Scholes, is determined by the equity volatility – the higher the volatility, the greater the value of the put. Thus, by controlling for the volatility in the market, one can measure the change in the put value due to liquidity risk and charge banks an amount proportional to their gammas using option pricing.

Kodres (2011) calculated hypothetical total values of losses during the 2004–10 period for different degrees of stress of the banking sector (30% worst days and 20% worst days), and different thresholds for the SLRI (when it goes below 1σ, 2σ,…, 5σ from its mean). Those values are presented as percentages of tier 1 capital for banks in various regions in the right panel of Figure 13.8. These are translated into amounts depending on what timeframe the central bank believes that the crisis will occur, and assuming the central banks want to break even over that timeframe. Note that the losses may appear high, but that these are cumulative losses spread over long time horizons.

To summarise, the SLRI holds promise as a measure of overall systemic risk. It can be constructed from public data, although it requires information on 36 arbitrage relationships. Its broad coverage of asset classes allows it to combine measures market and funding liquidity. Its underlying basis of using market measures of deviations of arbitrage relationships is attractive and the evidence, while not conclusive, is at least suggestive of its usefulness. The SLRI can also potentially link firm-specific variables to systemic risk measure using easy-to-construct empirical relationships. As mentioned, the SLRI has been criticised as being subject to market pricing that may alter arbitrage relationships in ways unrelated to systemic liquidity, and questions have been raised regarding exactly what the PCA analysis is measuring. Finally, there remains a need for consensus on how to average and/or smooth capital charges over liquidity cycles, and the method provides no natural method to gauge size of capital charge/insurance premiums – although the SLIR–Merton approach holds promise in that regard.

The market liquidity index

Another attempt to measure systemic liquidity risk is the CLX (Peng, 2005; Benzschawel, Hawker and Lee, 2012a). The CLX was developed as a tradable index intended as a hedge for liquidity risk, so is constructed from liquid derivative products – ones that require minimal risk capital. The CLX is intended to reflect liquidity conditions across financial markets and has no implications for the liquidity of individual firms. Figure 13.9 displays historical values of the index with major liquidity influencing events superimposed. The CLX captures market responses to major liquidity shocks. Although the distribution of CLX values around its average is not symmetric, the scale is a rough approximation of liquidity conditions in standard deviation units. Note that higher values of the index indicate decreasing liquidity and decreases in the CLX signal increases in liquidity. In this sense, the CLX is an illiquidity index.

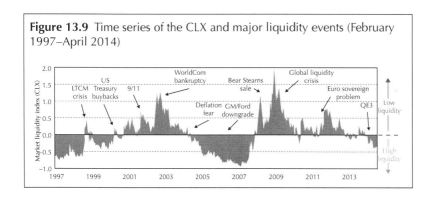

Figure 13.9 Time series of the CLX and major liquidity events (February 1997–April 2014)

The CLX is composed of a volatility-weighted combination of inputs from tradable assets in fixed income and volatility markets. These are the following.

❏ Swap spreads: The difference between the current 10-year interest rate swap yield and the yield of the current reference 10-year

Treasury bond future. These contracts (Bloomberg ticker: TY1 Comdty and USSW10 Curncy) trade on the Chicago Board of Trade, and trade in lots of US$100,000. The expiration dates fall on quarterly International Monetary Market (IMM) dates going out 15 months.

❑ Swap rate: The current 10-year interest rate swap rate (Bloomberg ticker: USSW10 Curncy) for a period ending at the maturity of the bond underlying the next-expiring 10-year bond future.

❑ VIX futures: The next-expiring Volatility Index (VIX) future as traded on the Chicago Board Options Exchange (Bloomberg ticker: UX1 Index). These contracts trade in lots of US$1,000 times the current value of the index, and mature on or around the 20th of the month.

❑ Swaption price: A one-year swaption straddle (put and call options) on a 10-year interest rate swap (Bloomberg ticker: USSP0110 Curncy), with the strike price reset to the current at-the-money swap rate at the beginning of every roll period.

❑ CDX index: The current five-year CDX.NA.IG contract (Bloomberg ticker: IBOXUMAE CMAN Curncy), rolling on March 20 and September 20 of each year.

The value of the CLX index at any time is the equally weighted average of scores from the five constituent variables, with each score being the variation (expressed as a number of standard deviations) of its current value. The means and standard deviations for the volatility-weighted scores from each component of the CLX have been fixed to their values for the period between January 1, 2005, and February 18, 2010. The CLX price can be a positive number (below average liquidity conditions) or a negative number (better than average liquidity), or can be zero (average liquidity conditions).

The means and standard deviations for the volatility-weighted scores from each asset contributing to the CLX appear at the top of Table 13.2, and the CLX index price is calculated as:

$$CLX = \frac{SP - \mu_{SP}}{\sigma_{SP}} - \frac{SR - \mu_{SR}}{\sigma_{SR}} + \frac{SS - \mu_{SS}}{\sigma_{SS}} + \frac{CDX - \mu_{CDX}}{\sigma_{CDX}} + \frac{VIXf - \mu_{VIXf}}{\sigma_{VIXf}}$$

(13.2)

When the constant means and sigma values are assigned, Equation 13.2 can be written as:

$$CLX = \frac{1}{5}\left(\frac{Swaption\ Px}{200.7} - \frac{Swap\ Rate}{0.68} + \frac{Swap\ Sprd}{22} + \frac{CDX.IG}{57.71} + \frac{VIX\ Fut\ Px}{11.30} - 1.2074\right)$$

(13.3)

Values of the CLX are determined daily from publicly available closing prices. Daily values of the CLX are also available on Bloomberg under: CMLXUS Index <GO>. Historical values of the CLX are available for download, and other Bloomberg analytical tools are available on the CLX page.

Table 13.2 Means and standard deviations of CLX inputs (top) and impact of index constituents on CLX price (bottom)

	Swaption price (US$)	Swap rate (%)	Swap spread (bp)	CDX index (bp)	VIX futures (US$)
μ	655.67	4.75	33	87.44	21.59
σ	200.70	0.68	22	57.71	11.30

Index constituent	Direction	Impact on index price
Swap spreads	Higher	Higher index price
Rate swaps	Lower	Higher index price
VIX futures	Higher	Higher index price
Swaption price	Higher	Higher index price
CDX.NA.IG	Higher	Higher index price

The impact of movements in index constituents on CLX values is summarised on the lower panel of Table 13.2. For all but interest rate swap yields, higher values result in higher index values (poorer liquidity), whereas higher swap yields signal better liquidity. The fact that swap yields rally as liquidity decreases (ie, the value of the CLX increases) is due to the US Treasury component of the swap yields, which typically are the object of a flight to quality during times of stress to market liquidity. Each of the five derivative contracts that comprise the CLX either roll or expire periodically during fixed calendar months. The CDX.NA.IG contract rolls semi-annually, in March and September of each year. The swap-related contracts roll every quarter, on a March–June–September–December cycle. The VIX futures contract rolls every month.

The CLX can be shown to relate to various aspects of the financial markets and financial assets. As shown in Figure 13.10, changes in the CLX are highly correlated with exposures that have previously been difficult to hedge in financial markets, as well as cyclical economic effects. These include:

❑ financial conditions and Federal Reserve Bank policy;
❑ financial stress;
❑ short-term financing costs;
❑ the credit risk premium;
❑ the CDS versus cash bond basis; and
❑ the economic cycle.[5]

Consider first the CLX and Citi's Financial Conditions Index (FCI) (DiClemente and Schoenholtz, 2008) in the top left panel of Figure 13.10. The FCI is a weighted-average of corporate credit spreads to Treasuries, equity values, the money stock, the trade-weighted dollar, mortgage rates and energy prices. The CLX is highly correlated with Citi's Financial Conditions Index (FCI), and the FCI has been shown to be a good indicator of Fed policy objectives. Since the CLX tracks closely financial conditions as measured by the FCI, by inference it also tracks Fed policy objectives. Not only can the CLX be used to hedge the effects of Fed policy on financial conditions, but a tradable CLX might also be useful as an instrument of Fed policy. As such, the Fed may add liquidity to the financial system by selling liquidity protection either by selling the CLX (or every using the CLX constituents) during times of financial stress. Conversely, the Fed can buy the CLX (or trade its constituents), thereby draining liquidity from financial markets.

Consider next the relationship between the CLX and the St. Louis Federal Reserve Bank's Financial Stress Index (STLFSI). The STLFSI was developed to overcome the problem of focusing on a single market indicator as a measure of financial stress (Hakkio and Keeton, 2009; Kliesen and Smith, 2010). As with the SLRI, the

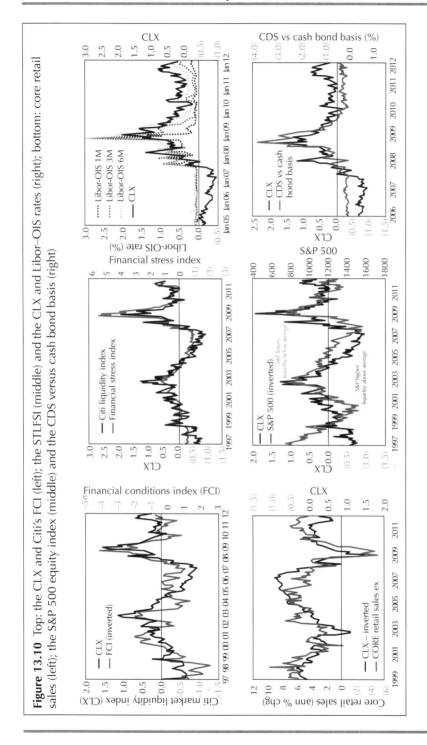

Figure 13.10 Top: the CLX and Citi's FCI (left); the STLFSI (middle) and the CLX and Libor–OIS rates (right); bottom: core retail sales (left); the S&P 500 equity index (middle) and the CDS versus cash bond basis (right)

477

STLFSI was derived using PCA but on a group of 18 weekly data series over the period 1994–2009. The variables came from three main groups: interest rates; yield spreads; and indicators related to volatility and equity markets whose asset values were correlated with periods of economic stress.

The top-middle panel of Figure 13.10 displays weekly values of the STLFSI and the CLX, revealing close agreement between the two series. The correlation between weekly values of the two series is extremely good, with the only deviations occurring during the telecom blow-up of late 2002 and the liquidity crisis of 2007–09.[6] Furthermore, those deviations are merely ones of magnitude, not direction. In fact, the agreement of the STLFSI and the CLX is sufficient that one could serve as a proxy for the other for most applications. Recall that there are 18 required inputs to the STLFSI, that the index is computed only weekly and that many of the inputs to the STLFSI are not tradable quantities. Thus, it is difficult to develop a tradable version of STLFSI to hedge risks related to financial stress. However, it is feasible for a tradable version of the five-variable CLX to serve as a hedge for exposure to financial stress.

One characteristic of liquidity crises is the diminished ability of financial institutions to secure short-term funding for their liabilities. The yield spread between Libor and the overnight indexed swap (ie, the Libor-to-OIS spread) at various tenors is assumed to measure the health of the banking system (Thorton, 2009). The OIS rate is the yield on a derivative contract on the overnight rate (effective Fed Funds rate in the US) for a fixed period of time (in the US, the overnight rate is the effective federal funds rate). There is very little default risk in the OIS market as both counterparties swap the floating rate of interest for the fixed rate of interest. However, Libor is risky in the sense that the lending bank loans cash to the borrowing bank. Thus, the spread between the two is a measure of how likely borrowing banks will default. The OIS rate is also viewed as a sign of the direction banks and investors believe the Libor rate is heading. Since the borrowing rates for all firms typically increase and decrease with changes in Libor, the Libor–OIS spread is also a proxy for the general cost of short-term financing in financial markets.

The top-right panel of Figure 13.10 presents time series of one-, three- and six-month Libor–OIS spreads, along with values of the

CLX over the same period. In general, the CLX rises when banks' funding costs increase and decreases as funding costs ease. Although the relation between the CLX and Libor–OIS spreads is far from perfect, at least in a cyclical sense the CLX is attractive for hedging exposure to rising funding costs. The figure also shows that the CLX does not always follow short-term shocks (ie, in the order of one month or so) well, which sometimes overshoot CLX values. Note also that, as the liquidity crisis of 2007–09 has receded, the CLX has not decreased to values as low as Libor–OIS levels. Presumably, this difference results from the US Federal Reserve's actions to provide liquidity to the banking system by holding overnight rates near zero.

The US Department of Commerce's retail sales report tracks the dollar value of merchandise sold within the retail trade sector (Carnes, 2002). The survey includes companies of all sizes, from large retailers such as Wal-Mart to independent, small-town businesses. Retail sales are considered a coincident indicator, in that activity reflects the current state of the economy. The retail sales report is one component used to formulate Fed policy. For analytical purposes, most economists and central bank analysts prefer the core retail sales report over the full report as core retail sales exclude the volatile contributions from car sales, petrol and building materials. The lower-left panel of Figure 13.10 plots monthly reported core retail sales since 1999, along with monthly values of the CLX. Although the relationship between spending by consumers and prices of financial market assets is not direct, the CLX appears to track the cyclical pattern of retail sales. This suggests that the CLX is a good proxy for cyclical business performance.

Values of the CLX are also related to levels of Standard & Poor's 500 equity index (S&P 500). The stocks in the S&P 500 are those of publicly held companies with large capitalisation that trade on either the New York Stock Exchange or the NASDAQ. The index is focused on US-based companies, but includes several firms incorporated in other countries. The lower-middle panel of Figure 13.10 displays daily values of the S&P 500 index from 1997 until 2012, along with those of the CLX. Although coincident values of the CLX and S&P 500 are correlated, several investigators have found an even stronger relationship between equity values and lagged values of the CLX (Montagu *et al*, 2012; Benzschawel, Hawker and Lee, 2012b). That is, changes in the CLX lead returns from both the S&P 500 and MSCI European equity indexes by nine-to-12 months, with potentially profitable trading strategies having been proposed based on those relationships.

Finally, consider the relationship between the CLX and the CDS versus cash bond basis. The CDS versus cash basis is the average difference in yield spread to Libor of corporate bonds and the premiums on their CDS. Despite their theoretical equivalence, spreads to Libor on cash bonds and their corresponding default swap spreads are rarely the same, and the difference between them is called the "basis". A variety of market factors, technical details and implementation frictions underlie the basis. The factors underlying the cash versus CDS basis and several methods for its calculations are described in detail elsewhere,[7] and so are not discussed further here. The many factors that contribute to the CDS–cash basis have made it difficult to hedge the basis with tradable assets. The lower-right panel of Figure 13.10 plots values of the CLX along with the inverted values of the CDS versus cash basis. The plot reveals substantial deviations between the series during several periods (eg, 2008 and 2011). Still, over the longer term, and particularly during periods of market stress, the ability to buy liquidity protection could mitigate exposure to changes in the CDS versus cash bond basis.

Although CLX levels appear to be only a coincident indicator of liquidity stress, changes in the CLX, and by inference changes in liquidity, appear to lead certain economic indicators. For example, consider the table of correlations of changes in various assets, economic indicators and short-term funding shown in Figure 13.11. Correlations are shown with CLX leading by –2 and –1 months, coincident at 0, as well as with the CLX trailing at +1 and +2 months. Although changes in most quantities are most correlated with coincident changes in the CLX, the CLX leads non-farm payroll reports and Institute of Supply Management (ISM) manufacturing releases by one month. In fact, employment and manufacturing releases are among those that move markets most. Furthermore, coincident changes in non-farm payrolls and ISM manufacturing releases are less strongly related to coincident changes in the CLX than when led by the CLX. Changes in the CLX also lead market values such as Citi CDS levels and repo rates (dashed circles), but less strongly than the economic releases. Of all the indicators tested, only the VIX leads the CLX, but its correlation is strongest when coincident with the CLX, as are changes in Citi's CDS premiums.

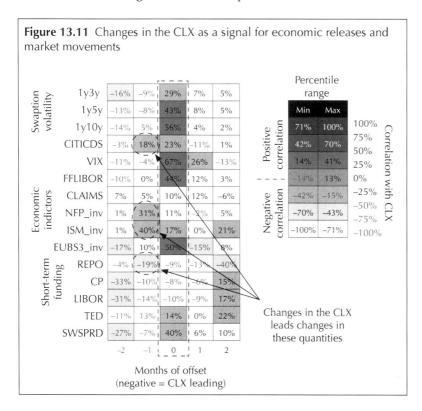

Figure 13.11 Changes in the CLX as a signal for economic releases and market movements

HEDGING SYSTEMIC LIQUIDITY RISK WITH THE CLX
The correspondence between changes in the CLX and the more traditional, but untradeable, measures of financial stress presented above suggests that the CLX might provide a suitable hedge for systemic liquidity risk. In addition to the usefulness of the CLX for mitigating changes in Libor–OIS spreads, support for the CLX as a hedge against changes in financing rates also comes from the relationship of the CLX to banks' willingness to lend to commercial and industrial firms.

The US Federal Reserve publishes a quarterly survey on banks' tightening or easing of lending standards, and whether banks are increasing or decreasing the credit spreads they charge above their costs of funds (Federal Reserve, 2011). The left panel of Figure 13.12 displays time series of the Fed survey results from January 1997 to December 2011, along with quarterly average values of the CLX. Although the CLX does not track lending standards perfectly, it captures well the major bank lending cycles. Moreover, it appears that the directional properties of the CLX track well conditions of banks' tightening and easing standards (not shown, but see Benzschawel, Hawker and Lee, 2012).

Figure 13.12 Left: the CLX and the Federal Reserve's lending survey; right: the US corporate bond risk premium

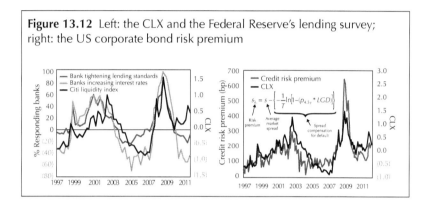

Benzschawel and Assing (2012) demonstrated that it is possible to separate a bond's yield spread to US Treasuries into a spread compensation for expected loss from default and a non-default component.[8] That is, for any given bond, if one has a good estimate of the default probability, p_T, of the issuing firm and an accurate assumption of the recovery value (RV) in default, one can decompose a spread into components, $s = s_d + s_\lambda$, where s_d is the compensation for default and s_λ is the credit risk premium. For a bond of duration, T, the spread necessary to compensate for expected default s_d can be approximated as:

$$s_d = -\frac{1}{T}\ln[1-(p_T * LGD)]$$

(13.4)

where LGD is loss given default, or 1-RV. The value of s_d can be thought of as the amount of spread necessary to break even with a similar investment in US Treasuries given expected default and recovery value in default for the risky bond. Also, since $s = s_d + s_\lambda$, if the credit spreads are used along with estimates of default probabilities, p_T, one can solve for the risk premium, s_λ, using the following relation:

$$s = s_\lambda - \left\{ \frac{1}{T} \ln[1 - (p_T * LGD)] \right\}$$

(13.5)

where all terms are as described above. Analyses have shown that nearly all of the spread for investment-grade bonds (those rated triple-B minus and above) is due to the credit risk premium rather than compensation for default (see Figure 5.1). For high yield, default plays a greater relative role, but the average risk premium can still be as large as 700bp.

The right panel of Figure 13.12 presents monthly values of the credit risk premium (left axis) versus the CLX (right axis) over the period from 1997 to January 2012. The average investment-grade risk premium is about 125bp, but the risk premium varies considerably around that value, having been below 50bp during periods of high liquidity in the mid-1990s and mid-2000s. During the latest credit/liquidity crisis, that risk premium was roughly 650bp, but returned to near-average levels by 2010. The figure reveals good agreement between the credit risk premium and the CLX, suggesting that investors who are satisfied with their current market return over default on a portfolio of corporate bonds can, to a large extent, lock in that default-adjusted spread by selling liquidity protection via a tradable CLX.[9]

As discussed above, the IMF's SRLI has the potential to serve as a measure of systemic liquidity risk. However, use of the SLRI for managing and hedging liquidity exposure has limitations. That is, the SLRI is based on 36 arbitrage relationships and the underlying assets are not easy to access, and can be expensive to acquire. In contrast, the CLX is composed of only five tradable and highly liquid derivative contracts. Thus, to the extent that the CLX and SLRI are correlated and the SLRI is an index of systemic liquidity, the CLX can be used to hedge systemic liquidity risk. The left panel of Figure 13.13 displays monthly values of the SLRI and the CLX on the same axis from 2004 to 2011. The plot reveals good agreement between the SLRI and the CLX, particularly when liquidity is deteriorating. Also, as shown in the right portion of Figure 13.13, levels of the CLX and SLRI are correlated: the R-squared between the CLX and SLRI is 0.69. Thus, the CLX (or its underlying constituents) may be a good candidate for hedging systemic risk.

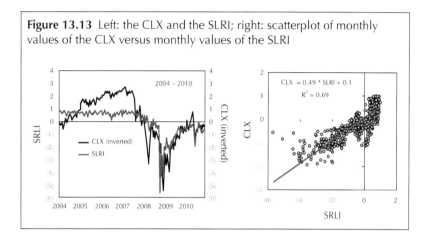

Figure 13.13 Left: the CLX and the SLRI; right: scatterplot of monthly values of the CLX versus monthly values of the SLRI

AN EARLY WARNING SYSTEM FOR LIQUIDITY RISK

One purpose of this chapter is to describe a system that we have developed for detecting changes in systemic liquidity risk based on values of the CLX. The fact that changes in the CLX are related to changes in many important macroeconomic indicators of financial stress has suggested its use as an early warning indicator of changes in systemic liquidity risk.

Recall that the CLX as defined in Equations 13.2 and 13.3 outputs Z-score values that range from $-\infty$ to $+\infty$. Although a Z-score scale for the CLX may be useful for a tradable index, its relative complexity makes it less easy to interpret as a signal of overall liquidity conditions. Instead, a CLX percentile-based scale was implemented for ease of interpretation. Accordingly, the CLX value scale was translated into a percentile scale as illustrated in the left panel of Figure 13.14. The middle and right panels of Figure 13.14 demonstrate how Z-score values of the CLX are translated to percentile values. The shaded areas in the right panel delineate 0–33, 34–66 and 67–100 percentile boundaries that correspond to regions of low, average and high liquidity, respectively.

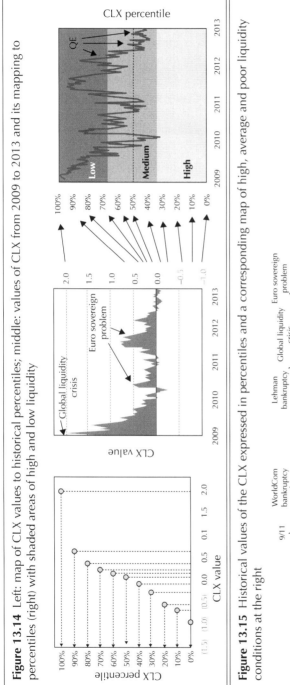

Figure 13.14 Left: map of CLX values to historical percentiles; middle: values of CLX from 2009 to 2013 and its mapping to percentiles (right) with shaded areas of high and low liquidity

Figure 13.15 Historical values of the CLX expressed in percentiles and a corresponding map of high, average and poor liquidity conditions at the right

Percentile range	**Color code**	**Liquidity signal**
67% – 100%		Poor liquidity
34% – 66%		Average liquidity
0% – 33%		Good liquidity

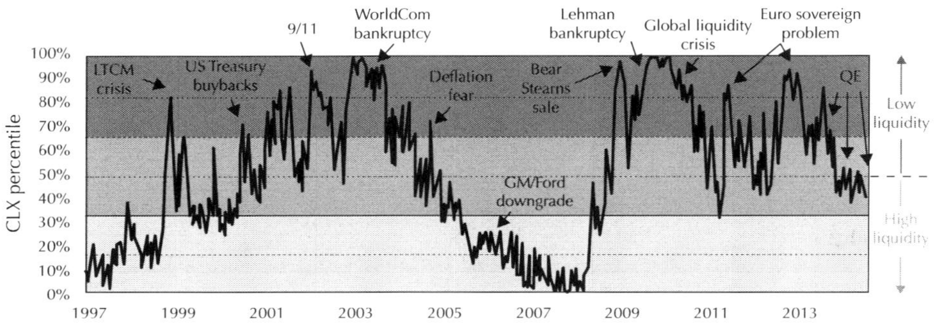

Figure 13.15 shows the historical series of the CLX from 1997 to late 2013 expressed in percentiles, with major liquidity events superimposed. Consistent with the coding in the right panel of Figure 13.14, the dark-to-light grey regions in Figure 13.15 correspond to conditions of high, medium and low liquidity, respectively.

Although CLX levels are useful as indicators of current liquidity conditions, changes in the CLX are more useful for signalling changing liquidity conditions. Accordingly, one- and three-month changes in CLX percentiles were calculated for use as indicators of changing liquidity conditions. That is, changes in the CLX were examined on two time scales: one month and three months. The one-month scale is more sensitive and may provide a very early warning signal. However, three-month changes generate fewer and more reliable signals. As for the CLX levels in Figure 13.15, we use a grey-coded scale to characterise the strength of the liquidity change:

❏ 0–33% is improving liquidity with a "light grey" signal;
❏ 34–66% is a "grey" stable liquidity signal; and
❏ 67–100% is a "dark grey" deteriorating liquidity signal.

One- and three-month changes in CLX indicators appear in the top and bottom panels of Figure 13.16, respectively. The left panels show one- and three-month changes from 2005 to 2013, while the right panels show changes from January 2012 to January 2013.

The early warning signal based on the CLX percentiles is a composite of level and change signals as illustrated in Figure 13.17. The CLX level is coded on the x-axis of the warning matrix in Figure 13.17, with momentum on the y-axis. The level signal is coded based on CLX percentiles as: "good" (0–33); "average" (34–67); and "poor" (68–100). Liquidity momentum is calculated as the sum of one-third of one-month momentum in percentile plus two-thirds of the three-month momentum in percentile. The combined momentum signal itself is then expressed in percentile as: "improving" (0–33); "stable" (34–67); and "deteriorating" (68–100). Note that the percentages displayed in each cell are frequencies of occurrence from 1997 to mid-2013. Thus, since 1997 the percentage of dark grey signals is 31% (the sum of those in the dark grey cells), light grey 16% and grey 53%. Each day, a CLX-based liquidity early warning signal is determined using the classification scheme in Figure 13.17.

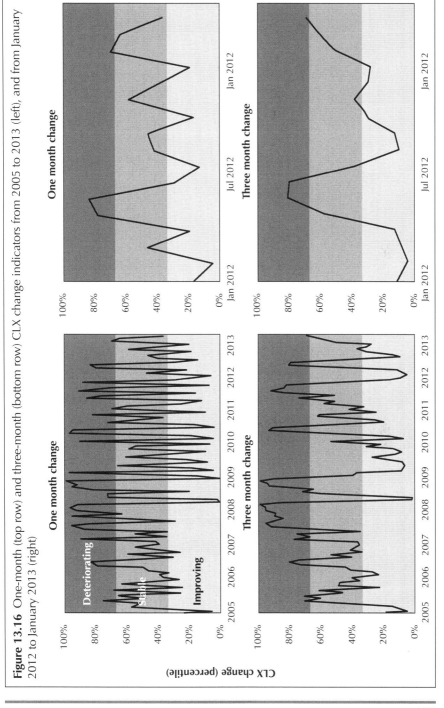

Figure 13.16 One-month (top row) and three-month (bottom row) CLX change indicators from 2005 to 2013 (left), and from January 2012 to January 2013 (right)

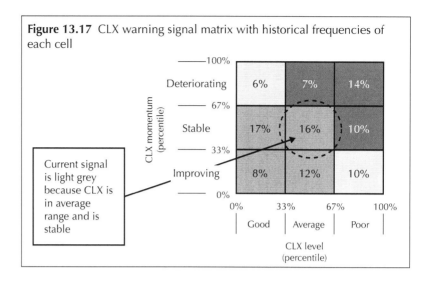

Figure 13.17 CLX warning signal matrix with historical frequencies of each cell

Figure 13.18 CLX-based warning signals from 1997 to January 2013 (top) and from January 2012 to January 2013 (bottom)

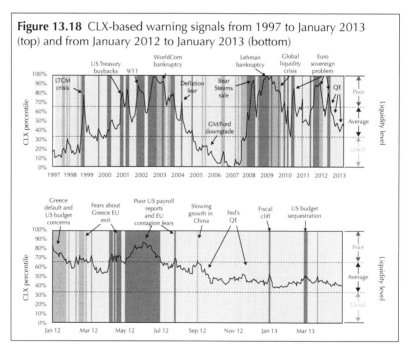

These grey-scale-coded liquidity warning signals in Figure 13.17 are mapped onto historical percentiles of the CLX in Figure 13.18. CLX values from 1997 to January 2013 appear in the top panel, with values

over the later one-year period shown in the lower panel. For perspective, major liquidity shocks are also superimposed on the historical values of CLX and warning signals. The pattern of warning signals appears consistent with major liquidity events since 1997.

CONCLUSION

This chapter has characterised systemic liquidity risk and outlined the dynamics of systemic liquidity crises. Methods proposed by the Basel Committee to circumvent the necessity of future government intervention to stem liquidity crises in financial markets are also described. In particular, the chapter considered the Basel requirements of LCR and NSFR, along with their potential relationship to bank stability and their efficacy in preventing systemic liquidity crises. Next, proposed methods for measuring banks' exposures to systemic risk and for determining their contributions to liquidity crises were introduced. These included the SLRI and the CLX. The advantages and disadvantages of the SLRI and its related contingent claims analysis were presented, as well as evidence of their ability to proxy for systemic liquidity and for banks' contributions to systemic liquidity risk. The CLX was presented as an alternative to the SLRI for assessing systemic liquidity risk, with the additional prospect of providing a hedge for systemic liquidity risk.

One attraction of the CLX is its composition of five liquid tradable derivatives. It was shown that the changes in the CLX mimic changes in a range of economic indicators and asset prices, and also its ability to mimic the SLRI. In addition, the CLX was shown as a means of forecasting equity returns, and major economic releases and changes in values of several market assets. The final section of the chapter described the development and implementation of an early warning indicator for changes in systemic liquidity, and its correlation with major historical liquidity spikes.

1   In fact, criteria specifying exactly which assets qualify for inclusion in the LCR remain a topic for debate and revision (Heisler, 2014).
2   This is more than 40% in the case of the SLRI.
3   PCA analysis is "agnostic" about interpretations of the source of the relationship it uncovers.
4   See chapter 1 for a detailed description of the Merton model.
5   A more detailed description of the relationship between the CLX and various economic indicators and asset values can be found in Benzschawel, Hawker and Lee (2012a), and so

are summarised only briefly here.

6   Although the CLX is calculated daily, only weekly values of the STLFSI are available. Also, although the fit between weekly values of the CLX and STLFSI are highly correlated, if the logarithms of STLFSI are plotted against the CLX, the R-squared is even higher at 0.84.

7   See Kumar and Mithal, 2001; Choudry, 2006; Kakodkar *et al*, 2006; King and Sandigursky. 2007; Elizalde, Doctor and Saltuk, 2009; Benzschawel and Corlu, 2011; to name but a few.

8   See Chapter 5 for a detailed description of that method.

9   Benzschawel and Su (2014) have demonstrated that the five-year CDS index (CDX.NA.IG) is an even better hedge for the credit risk premium than the CLX.

References

Altman, E., 1968, "Financial Ratios, Discriminant Analysis, and the Prediction of Corporate Bankruptcy", *Journal of Finance,* 23, pp 589–609.

Altman, E. and G. Bana, 2003, "Defaults and Returns on High Yield Bonds: The Year 2002 in Review and the Market Outlook", New York University, Salomon Center, February (available at http://pages.stern.nyu.edu/~ealtman/Q4-2002.pdf).

Altman, E., B. Brady, A. Resti and A. Sironi, 2005, "The Link between Default and Recovery Rates: Theory, Empirical Evidence and Implications", *Journal of Business,* 78(6), pp 2,203–28.

Altman, E. and A. Eberhart, 1994, "Do Seniority Provisions Protect Bondholders' Investments?", *Journal of Portfolio Management,* 20, pp 67–75.

Altman, E. and D. Kao, 1992, "The Implications of Corporate Bond Ratings Drift", *Financial Analysts Journal,* 48, pp 64–67.

Altman, E. and V. Kishore, 1996, "Almost Everything You Wanted to Know about Recoveries on Defaulted Bonds", *Financial Analysts Journal,* 66, pp 57–64.

Altman, E. and S. Nammacher, 1984, "The Default Rate Experience of High Yield Corporate Debt", *Financial Analysts Journal,* 40(4), pp 25–41.

Altman, E. and H. Rijken, 2011, "Toward a Bottom-up Approach to Assessing Sovereign Default Risk", *Journal of Applied Corporate Finance,* 23(1), pp 20–31.

Amato, J. and E. Remolona, 2003, "The Credit Spread Puzzle", *BIS Quarterly Review,* December, pp 51–63.

Ang, A., V. Bhansali and Y. Xing, 2010, "Build America Bonds", *Journal of Fixed Income,* 20(1), pp 67–73.

Asness, C., A. Frazzini and L. H. Pedersen, 2012, "Leverage Aversion and Risk Parity", *Financial Analysts Journal,* 68(1), pp 47–59.

Bader, L. and Y. Y. Ma, 1995, "The Salomon Brothers Pension Discount Curve and the Salomon Brothers Pension Liability Index", Salomon Brothers, January.

Bai, J. and P. Collin-Dufresne, 2011, "The Determinants of the CDS–Bond Basis During the Financial Crisis of 2007–2009",November 12, 2013. AFA 2013 San Diego Meetings Paper. Available at SSRN: https://ssrn.com/abstract=2024531 or http://dx.doi.org/10.2139/ssrn.2024531.

Bangia, A., F. Diebold, A. Kronimus, C. Schagen and T. Schuermann, 2002, "Ratings Migration and the Business Cycle, with Applications to Credit Portfolio Stress Testing", *Journal of Banking and Finance,* 26, pp 445–74.

Basil Committee on Banking Supervision, 2010, "Basel III: A Global Regulatory Framework for More Resilient Banks and Banking Systems", Bank for International Settlements.

Beaver, W. H., 1966, "Financial Ratios as Predictors of Failure", *Journal of Accounting Research,* 4, pp 71–111.

Belkin, B., S. Suchower and L. Forest, Jr., 1998, "A One-parameter Representation of Credit Risk and Transition Matrices", *CreditMetrics Monitor,* third quarter.

Bell, R., Y. Koren and C. Volinsky, 2008, "The BellKor 2008 Solution to the Netflix Prize", www.netflixprize.com/assets/ProgressPrize2008_BellKor.pdf, 2008.

Benzschawel, T., 2012, "Comments on Model-based Default Probabilities (PDs) for Financial Firms", Citi, July 12.

Benzschawel, T., 2012, *Credit Modelling: Facts, Theory and Applications* (London: Risk Books).

Benzschawel, T., 2013, "Citi's Hybrid Probability of Default Model: The Sobehart–Keenan HPD Model – Ten Years After", Citi, July 10.

Benzschawel, T. and D. Adler, 2002, "Empirical Analysis of Corporate Bond Spreads", *Quantitative Credit Analyst,* Citigroup, 1, pp 5–33.

Benzschawel, T. and A. Assing, 2012, "Inferring Default Probabilities from Credit Spreads", *Journal of Fixed Income,* 21(4), pp 16–24.

Benzschawel, T., A. Assing, A. Haroon and M. Lee, 2011, "Market-implied Default Probabilities for Sovereign Credits", Citi, January 31.

Benzschawel, T. and A. Corlu, 2010, "Cash Flow Analysis of Credit Default Swaps", *Journal of Fixed Income,* 20(3), pp 40–54.

Benzschawel, T., J. DaGraca and C.-Y. Lee, 2012, "Pricing Corporate Loans under Risk-neutral Measure", *Journal of Credit Risk,* 8(2), March.

Benzschawel, T., A. Haroon and T. Wu, 2011, "A Model for Recovery Value in Default", *Journal of Fixed Income,* 21(2), pp 15–29.

Benzschawel, T., B. Hawker and M. Lee, 2012a, "The CLX: Citi's Market Liquidity Index", Citigroup, February 9.

Benzschawel, T., B. Hawker and M. Lee, 2012b, "The CLX and Equity Returns", Citigroup, September 4.

Benzschawel, T. and J. Jiang, 2004, "Beat the IG.CDX Index", Citigroup Structured Credit Products Strategy, October 19.

Benzschawel, T. and J. Jiang, 2005, "Beating the IG.CDX Index in a Credit Selloff", Citigroup, May 25.

Benzschawel, T. and J. Jiang, 2006, "Beat that Index!", Citigroup Structured Credit Products Strategy, January 16.

Benzschawel, T. and M. Lee, 2011, "Market-implied Default Probabilities: Update: Inferring Credit Risk from Bond Prices", Citi, September 9.

Benzschawel, T. and M. Lee, 2012, "A Rule-Based Long/Short CDS Strategy: Beating CDX Index Returns Using the "Cut-and-Rotate" Method", Citi, April 30.

Benzschawel, T. and M. Lee, 2013, "Citi's Model for Recovery Value in Default: Validation and Testing", Citi, January 14.

Benzschawel, T., M. Lee and M. Bernstein, 2011, "Beating Credit Benchmarks: The 'Cut-and-Rotate' Strategy", Citi, November 28.

Benzschawel, T., M. Lee and J. Li, 2012, "Credit Quality Transitions, Credit Spreads, and Value-at-Risk", Citi, December 12.

Benzschawel, T., M. Lee and J. Li, 2013, "Embedded Leverage in Corporate Bond Spreads", Citi, June 5.

Benzschawel, T., M. Lee and J. Li, 2013, "Sovereign Default Risk and Relative Value", Citi, December 23.

Benzschawel, T., M. Lee, C. Lommaert and Y. Su, 2014, "Beating Global Credit Indexes: Outperforming Credit Benchmarks by Eliminating the Riskiest and Richest Credits", Citi, February 21.

Benzschawel, T., J. Li and M. Lee, 2013, "Predicting Bank Failure: An Adaptive Statistical Model for Estimating Banks' Default Risk", Citi, August 6.

Benzschawel, T., J. Li and M. Lee, 2013, "Sovereign Default Risk and Relative Value", Citi, December 24.

Benzschawel, T., C. Lommaert and J. Li, 2014, "Predicting Bank Failure II: Further Model Validation, Analysis, and Enhancements", Citi, January 10.

Benzschawel, T., L. Lorrilla and G. McDermott, 2005, "Model for Stochastic Bond Default and Recovery Value with Correlated Losses", *Journal of Structured Finance,* 11(2), pp 44–63.

Benzschawel, T. and Y. Su, 2013, "Recovery Value in Default: An Ensemble Model (E-3)", Citi, December 3.

Benzschawel, T. and Y. Su, 2014, "Hedging the Credit Risk Premium: Using CDX.IG.NA to Hedge the Cost of Spread Volatility", Citi, January 22.

Benzschawel, T. and Y. Su, 2014, "Predicting Annual Default Rates: Estimating Future Corporate Default Rates and High Yield Credit Spreads", Citi, February 7.

Benzschawel, T. and Y. Su, 2014, "Predicting Annual Default Rates: The HT-2.0 Model", Citi, February 2.

Benzschawel, T. and Y. Su, 2014, "Predicting the Credit Risk Premium", Citi, May 21.

Benzschawel, T. and Y. Su, 2015, "The Municipal Bond Risk Premium: Measuring the Risk–Reward Properties of Build America Bonds", Citi, March 19.

Benzschawel, T., Y. Su and M. Bernstein, 2014, "Managing Pension Fund Liabilities: De-Risking, Outperforming, and Predicting Changes in Pension Credit Liabilities", Citi, August 18.

Benzschawel, T., Y. Su, M. Lee and C. Lommaert, 2014, "Equity and Debt Risk Premiums and Applications", Citi, June 19.

Benzschawel, T., Y. Su and X. Xin, 2015, "The Credit Default Swap Risk Premium, λ", Citi, August 10.

Benzschawel, T., Y. Su and X. Xin, 2015, "The Credit Risk Premium: Understanding the Price of Risk in Corporate Bonds", Citi, June 25.

Benzschawel, T., G. Taksler, J. Skarabot and J. Jiang, 2003, "Beating the BIG Index using Market-based Credit Measures", Bond Market Roundup: Strategy, Citigroup, October 31, pp 9–13.

Benzschawel, T. and T. Wu, 2011, "Simulating Correlated Default Rates and Recovery Values, Bond Portfolio Analysis", Citi, May.

Benzschawel, T., X. Xin and Y. Su, 2015, "The Municipal Bond Risk Premium", Citi, July 20.

Berd, A., R. Mashal and P. Wang, 2004, "Defining, Estimating and Using Credit Term Structures: Part I: Consistent Valuation Measures", Lehman Brothers, November.

Bernstein, M., 2010, "Citi Pension Liability Index – Revised Methodology", Citi, December 30.

Bernstein, M., 2013, "The Quest for the Perfect Pension Portfolio", Citi, January 29.

Bernstein, M. and S. Li, 2013, "Expanding Our CPLI Family", Citi, January 25.

Bielecki, T. and M. Rutkowski, 2002, *Credit Risk: Modeling, Valuation and Hedging* (Berlin: Springer).

Black, F. and J. C. Cox, 1976, "Valuing Corporate Securities: Some Effects of Bond Indenture Provisions", *Journal of Finance,* 31, pp 351–67.

Black, F. and M. Scholes, 1973, "The Pricing of Options and Corporate Liabilities", *Journal of Political Economy,* 81, pp 637–59.

Bohn, J., 2000, "A Survey of Contingent-claims Approaches to Risky Debt Valuation", *Journal of Risk Finance,* 1(3), pp 53–70.

Box, G. E., 1976, "Science and Statistics", *Journal of the American Statistical Association,* 71(356), pp 791–99.

Box, G. E. and D. Cox, 1964, "An Analysis of Transformations", *Journal of the Royal Statistical Society,* Series B, 26, pp 211–52.

Bozsik, J., 2011, "Decision Tree Combined with Neural Networks for Financial Forecast", *Periodica Polytechnica Electrical Engineering,* 55(1–2), pp 95–101.

Breiman, L., 1996, "Bagging Predictors", *Machine Learning,* 24(2), pp 123–40.

Breiman, L., 2001, "Random Forests", *Machine Learning,* 45(1), pp 5–32.

Briys, E. and F. Varenne, 1997, "Valuing Risky Fixed Rate Debt: An Extension", *Journal of Financial and Quantitative Analysis,* 32(2), pp 239–48.

Brown, I., 1955, "The Historical Development of the Use of Ratios in Financial Statement Analysis to 1993", doctoral dissertation, School of Social Science, Catholic University of America.

Brunnermeier, M. and L. Pedersen, 2009, "Market Liquidity and Funding Liquidity", *Review of Financial Studies,* 22(6), pp 2,201–38.

Campbell, J., J. Hilscher and J. Szilagyi, 2008, "In Search of Distress Risk", *The Journal of Finance,* 63(6), pp 2,899–939.

Carnes, W. S. and B. Jones, 2002, "A Survival Guide to the Monthly Economic Indicators", Salomon Smith Barney, December.

Chatfield, C., 2004, *Analysis of Time Series: An Introduction (6e)* (Boca Raton, FL: Chapman & Hall/CRC).

Chava, S. and R. A. Jarrow, 2002, "Bankruptcy Prediction with Industry Effects", working paper, Johnson Graduate School of Management, Cornell University.

Choudhry, M., 2006, *The Credit Default Swap Basis* (New York, NY: Bloomberg Press).

Christensen, J., E. Hansen and D. Lando, 2004, "Confidence Sets for Continuous-time Rating Transition Probabilities", *Journal of Banking and Finance,* 28, pp 2,575–602.

Citigroup Index Group, 2011, "Citigroup Global Fixed Income Index Catalog – 2011 Edition", Citigroup, February 8.

Citigroup Index Group, 2012, "Citigroup Global Fixed-income Index Catalog – 2012 Edition", Citigroup, January 17.

Citigroup Index Group, 2013, "Index Guide – 2013 Edition", Citigroup, January.

Cleveland, W. S., 1979, "Robust Locally Weighted Regression and Smoothing Scatterplots", *Journal of the American Statistical Association,* 74(368), pp 829–36.

Cleveland, W. S. and S. J. Devlin, 1988, "Locally Weighted Regression: An Approach to Regression Analysis by Local Fitting", *Journal of the American Statistical Association,* 83, pp 596–610.

Collin-Dufresne, P. and R. Goldstein, 2001, "Do Credit Spreads Reflect Stationary Leverage Ratios?", *Journal of Finance,* 56, pp 1,929–58.

Collin-Dufresne, P., R. Goldstein and J. Martin, 2001, "The Determinants of Credit Spread Changes", *Journal of Finance,* 56(6), pp 2,177–207.

Congress of the United States of America, 2010, "Dodd–Frank Wall Street Reform and Consumer Protection Act", H.R. 4173, July 21.

Crosbie, P., 1999, "Modeling Default Risk", KMV, San Francisco, January 12.

Crosbie, P. and J. Bohn, 2001, "Modeling Default Risk", KMV.

Daniels, K., J. Dorminey, B. C. Smith and J. Vijayakumar, 2014, "Build America Bonds: An Empirical Analysis of Characteristics and Issuer Benefits", *Journal of Fixed Income,* 24(1), pp 89–103.

Das, S., R. Fan and G. Geng, 2002, "Bayesian Migration in Credit Ratings Based on Probabilities of Default", *Journal of Fixed Income,* 12, pp 17–23.

Department of the Treasury, 2013, "Regulatory Capital Rules: Regulatory Capital, Implementation of Basel III, Capital Adequacy, Transition Provisions, Prompt Corrective Action, Standardized Approach for Riskweighted Assets, Market Discipline and Disclosure Requirements, Advanced Approaches Risk-Based Capital Rule, and Market Risk Capital Rule", *Federal Register,* 78(198), October 11.

Department of the Treasury, 2014, "Prohibitions and Restrictions on Proprietary Trading and Certain Interests in, and Relationships With, Hedge Funds and Private Equity Funds", *Federal Register,* 79(21), January 31.

Dickey, D. and W. Fuller, 1979, "Distribution of the Estimators for Autoregressive Time Series with a Unit Root", *Journal of the American Statistical Association,* 74(366), pp 427–31.

Dickson, P., 1967, *The Financial Revolution in England: A Study in the Development of Public Credit. 1688–1756* (London: Macmillan).

DiClemente, R. and K. Schoenholtz, 2008, "A View of the US Subprime Crisis", EMA Special Report, Citigroup, September 26.

Dixit, R. K. and R. S. Pindyck, 1994, *Investment Under Uncertainty* (Princeton, NJ: Princeton University Press).

Driessen, J., 2003, "Is Default Event Risk Priced in Corporate Bonds?", mimeo, University of Amsterdam.

Duan, J.-C., J. Sun and T. Wang, 2012, "Multiperiod Corporate Default Prediction – A Forward Intensity Approach", *Journal of Econometrics*, 170, pp 191–209.

Duffie, D., A. Eckner, G. Horel and L. Saita, 2009, "Frailty Correlated Default", *The Journal of Finance*, 64(5), pp 2,089–123.

Duffie, D. and K. Singleton, 1999, "Modeling Term Structures of Defaultable Bonds", *Review of Financial Studies*, 12(4), pp 687–720.

Dwyer, D. and I. Korablev, 2008, "LossCalc 3.0 Methodology Document", Moody's/KMV, December 12.

Eberhart, A., C. Moore and E. Rosenfelt, 1990, "Security Pricing and Deviations from the Absolute Priority Rule in Bankruptcy Proceedings", *Journal of Finance*, 45(5), pp 1,457–79.

Egan, J., 1975, *Signal Detection Theory and ROC Analysis* (New York, NY: Academic Press).

Elizalde, A., S. Doctor and Y. Saltuk, 2009, "Bond–CDS Basis Handbook", J.P. Morgan, February.

Elton, J., M. Gruber, D. Agrawal and D. Mann, 2001, "Explaining the Rate Spread on Corporate Bonds", *Journal of Finance*, 56, pp 449–70.

Emory, K., S. Ou and J. Tennant, 2010, "Corporate Default and Recovery Rates, 1920–2009", Moody's Investors Service, February.

Emory, K., S. Ou, J. Tennant, F. Kim and R. Cantor, 2008, "Corporate Default and Recovery Rates, 1920–2007", Moody's Investors Service, February.

Engle, R., 2001, "GARCH 101: The Use of ARCH/GARCH Models in Applied Econometrics", *Journal of Economic Perspectives,* 15(4), pp 157–68.

Erasmus, D., 1500, *Collectanea Adagiorum* (Paris).

Fama, E., 1965. "The Behavior of Stock Market Prices", *Journal of Business,* 38, pp 34–105.

Fama, E. and K. R. French, 2003, "The Capital Asset Pricing Model: Theory and Evidence", CRSP Working Paper No. 550; Tuck Business School Working Paper No. 03-26 (available at http://ssrn.com/abstract=440920 or http://dx.doi.org/10.2139/ssrn.440920).

Federal Reserve, 2011, "Senior Loan Officer Opinion Survey on Bank Lending Practices", August 15 (available at http://www.federalreserve.gov/boarddocs/surveys).

Finger, C., V. Finklestein, G. Pan, J. P. Lardy and T. Ta, 2002, "CreditGrades Technical Document", RiskMetrics Group.

Fisher, L. 1959, "Determinants of Risk Premiums on Corporate Bonds", *Journal of Political Economy,* 67(3), pp 217–37.

Fons, J., 1991, "An Approach to Forecasting Default Rates", Moody's Special Report, August.

Foulke, R. A., 1961, *Practical Financial Statement Analysis (5e)* (New York, NY: McGraw-Hill).

Frazzini, A., D. Kabiller and L. H. Pedersen, 2012, "Buffet's Alpha", working paper, August 20 (available at www.econ.yale.edu/~af227).

Frazzini, A. and L. H. Pedersen, 2012, "Embedded Leverage", working paper, November 14.

Frazzini, A. and L. H. Pedersen, 2014, "Betting Against Beta", *Journal of Financial Economics,* 111, pp 1–25.

Fridson, M., 1999, "Anomaly in Intercapital Pricing? Merrill Lynch High Yield", October.

Fridson, M. and M. Garman, 1997, "Valuing Like-rated Senior and Subordinated Debt", *Journal of Fixed Income,* December, pp 83–93.

Fridson, M. and F. Wahl, 1986, "Fallen Angels Versus Original Issue High Yield Bond, High Performance", *Magazine of High Yield Bonds,* Morgan Stanley, October 2–8.

Friedman, J. H., 2001, "Approximation: A Gradient Boosting Machine", *Annals of Statistics,* 29, Greedy Function No. 5, pp 1,189–232.

Geske, R., 1979, "The Valuation of Compound Options", *Journal of Financial Economics,* 12, pp 211–35.

Gray, D. and S. Malone, 2008, *Microfinancial Risk Analysis* (Chichester, England: John Wiley).

Gray, D., R. Merton and Z. Bodie, 2007, "Contingent Claims Approach to Measuring and Managing Sovereign Credit Risk", *Journal of Investment Management,* 5(4), pp 5–28.

Green, D. and J. Swets, 1966, *Signal Detection Theory and Psychophysics* (New York, NY: Wiley).

Grömping, U., 2009, "Variable Importance Assessment in Regression: Linear Regression versus Random Forest", *The American Statistician,* 63(4), pp 308–19.

Gupton, G. and R. M. Stein, 2002, "LossCalc Model for Predicting Loss Given Default (LGD)", Moody's Investors Services, February.

Gupton, G. and R. M. Stein, 2005, "LossCalc v2: Dynamic Prediction of LGD", Moody's/KMV, January.

Hakkio, C. and W. Keeton, 2009, "Financial Stress: What Is It, How Can It Be Measured, and Why Does It Matter?", *Economic Review,* Federal Reserve Bank of Kansas City, second quarter, pp 5–55.

Hampden-Turner, M., 2009, "From Vicious to Virtuous? Corporate Default Rate Forecasting", Citi, December 3.

Hampden-Turner, M., 2010, "Will Defaults Keep Falling in 2011? Forecasting Speculative Default Rates", Citigroup, October 28.

Hastie, T., R. Tibshirani and J. Friedman, 2009, *The Elements of Statistical Learning: Data Mining, Inference, and Prediction* (2e) (New York, NY: Springer).

Heath, T. L., 1956, *The Thirteen Books of Euclid's Elements, Translation and Commentaries in Three Volumes* (Mineola, NY: Dover Publications).

Heisler, E., 2014, "Bank Treasury Newsletter", Citigroup, August 26.

Helwege, J. and P. Kleiman, 1997, "Understanding Aggregate Default Rates of High Yield Bonds", *Journal of Fixed Income,* 7(1), pp 55–61.

Hickman, W. B. 1958, *Corporate Bond Quality and Investor Experience* (Princeton, NJ: Princeton University Press).

Horrigan, J., 1968, "A Short History of Financial Ratio Analysis", *Accounting Review,* 43(2), pp 284–94.

Hsu, J., J. Saa-Requejo and P. Santa-Clara, 2010, "A Structural Model of Default Risk", *Journal of Fixed Income,* Winter, pp 77–94.

Huang, J.-Z., 2010, "The Structural Approach to Modeling Credit Risk", in C.-F. Lee, A. C. Lee and J. Lee (Eds), *Handbook of Quantitative Finance and Risk Management* (New York, NY: Springer): pp 665–73.

Huang, J.-Z. and W. Kong, 2003, "Explaining Credit Spread Changes: New Evidence from Option-bond Indexes", *Journal of Derivatives*, 11, pp 30–44.

Hull, J. and A. White, 1995, "The Impact of Default Risk on the Prices of Options and Other Derivative Securities", *Journal of Banking and Finance*, 19, pp 299–322.

International Monetary Fund, 2011a, "Durable Financial Stability: Getting There from Here", Global Financial Stability Report, April 11.

International Monetary Fund, 2011b, "How to Address the Systemic Part of Liquidity Risk", April.

Israel, R., J. Rosenthal and J. Wei, 2001, "Finding Generators for Markov Chains Via Empirical Transition Matrices, with Applications to Credit Ratings", *Mathematical Finance*, 11(2), pp 245–65.

Janossi, T., R. A. Jarrow and Y. Yildirim, 2003, "Estimating Default Probabilities Implicit in Equity Prices", *Journal of Investment Management*, first quarter, pp 1–30.

Jarrow, R., D. Lando and S. Turnbull, 1997, "A Markov Model for the Term Structure of Credit Risk Spreads", *Review of Financial Studies*, 10, pp 481–523.

Jarrow, R. and S. Turnbull, 1995, "Pricing Options on Derivatives Subject to Credit Risk", *Journal of Finance*, 50 (1),z pp 53–85.

Jenkins, G. and D. Watts, 1968, *Spectral Analysis and its Applications* (San Francisco, CA: Holden-Day).

Johnson, L. L., 1960, "The Theory of Hedging and Speculation in Commodity Futures", *Review of Economic Studies*, 27(3), pp 139–151.

Jones, E., S. Mason and E. Rosenfeld, 1984, "Contingent Claims Analysis of Corporate Capital Structures", *Journal of Finance*, 39, pp 611–25.

Jonsson, G. and M. Fridson, 1996, "Forecasting Default Rates on High Yield Bonds", *Journal of Fixed Income,* 6, June, pp 69–77.

Kakodkar, A., S. Galiani, J. G. Jonsson and A. Gallo, 2006, "Credit Derivatives Handbook 1", Merrill Lynch.

Kao, D. L., 2000, "Estimating and Pricing Credit Risk: An Overview", *Financial Analysts Journal,* 56(4), pp 50–66.

Kavvathas, D., 2001, "Estimating Credit Rating Transition Probabilities for Corporate Bonds, working paper, University of Chicago.

Kazemi, R. and A. Mosleh, 2012, "Improving Default Risk Prediction using Bayesian Model Uncertainty Techniques", *Risk Analytics,* 32(11), pp 1,888–900.

Kealhofer, S., 1999, "Credit Risk and Risk Management", AIMR Conference Proceedings, 80–94.

Kealhofer, S. and M. Kurbat, 2001, "The Default Prediction Power of the Merton Approach, Relative to Debt Ratings and Accounting Variables", KMV.

Keenan, S. C., J. Sobehart and D. T. Hamilton, 1999, "Predicting Default Rates: A Forecasting Model for Moody's Issuer-Based Default Rates", Moody's Investors Service, August.

Kiesel, R., W. Perraudin and A. Taylor, 2001, "The Structure of Credit Risk: Spread Volatility and Ratings Transitions", working paper, Bank of England.

Kim J., K. Ramaswamy and S. Sunderasan, 1993, "Does Default Risk in Coupons Affect the Valuation of Corporate Bonds? A Contingent Claims Model", *Financial Management,* pp 117–31.

King, M., 2012, "Why Good Gardeners Should Take Credit", Citigroup, November.

King, M. and M. Sandigursky, 2007, "The Added Dimensions of Credit – A Guide to Relative Value Trading", in A. Rajan, G. McDermott and R. Roy, *Structured Credit Handbook* (Hoboken, NJ: Wiley).

Kliesen, K. and D. Smith, 2010, "Measuring Financial Market Stress", *National Economic Trends,* Federal Reserve Bank of St. Louis, January.

Kodres, L., 2011, "How to Address the Systematic Part of Liquidity Risk", in IMF, "Global Financial Stability Report", April.

Kodres, L., 2012, "Measuring and Mitigating Systemic Liquidity Risk: Three Possible Techniques", IMF, December 4.

Kumar, P. and S. Mithal, 2001, "Relative Value between Cash and Default Swaps in Emerging Markets", Salomon Smith Barney.

Lando, D. and T. Skodeberg, 2002, "Analyzing Rating Transitions and Rating Drift with Continuous Observations", *Journal of Banking and Finance,* 26, pp 423–44.

Lee, M. and T. Benzschawel, 2014, "Corporate Markets Quantitative Review – January 2014", Citigroup, January 13.

Lee, M., Y. Su and T. Benzschawel, 2014, "Corporate Markets Quantitative Review", Citigroup, June 17.

Leland, H. E., 1999, "The Structural Approach to Credit Risk, Frontiers in Credit-Risk Analysis", AIMR Conference Proceedings, pp 36–46.

Levin, J. W. and D. R. van Deventer, 1997, "The Simultaneous Analysis of Interest Rate and Credit Risk", in A. G. Cornyn, R. A. Klein and J. Lederman (Eds), *Controlling and Managing Interest Rate Risk* (New York, NY: New York Institute of Finance): pp 494–506.

Li, W., 2013, "A Default Risk Model under Macroeconomic Conditions", *Journal of Fixed Income,* 23(2), pp 98–113.

Li, Z., J. Zhang and C. Crossin, 2012, "A Model-based Approach to Constructing Corporate Bond Portfolios", *Journal of Fixed Income,* Fall, pp 57–71.

Liaw, A. and M. Wiener, 2002, "Classification and Regression by Random Forest", *R News,* 2(3), pp 18–22.

Lincoln, E., 1925, *Applied Business Finance (3e)* (Chicago, IL: A. W. Shaw and Company).

Lindeman, R. H., P. F. Merenda and R. Z. Gold, 1980, *Introduction to Bivariate and Multivariate Analysis* (Glenview, IL: Scott, Foresman).

Longstaff, F. A. and E. S. Schwartz, 1995, "A Simple Approach to Valuing Risky Fixed and Floating Rate Debt", *Journal of Finance,* 50, pp 789–819.

MarkIt Group, 2009, "The CDS Big Bang: Understanding the Changes to the Global CDS Contract and North American Conventions", March 13.

Markowitz, H., 1959, *Portfolio Selection: Efficient Diversification of Investment* (New York, NY: Wiley).

Marose, R., 1990, "A Financial Neural-Network Application", *AI Expert,* 5, May.

Marose, R., D. Rothenberg and S. Sankaran, 1992, "Knowledge Based Decision Support System for Accounting Auditors", in T. Jelassi, M. Klein and W. Mayon-White (Eds), *Decision Support Systems: Experiences and Expectations* (Amsterdam: North-Holland).

McDermott, G., J. Skarabot and A. Kroujiline, 2004, "Optimizing Selection of Credit Portfolios", *Journal of Portfolio Management,* 30(3), pp 112–23.

McNulty, C. and R. Levin, 2000, "Modeling Credit Migration", J.P. Morgan, March 17.

Merton, R., 1973, "The Theory of Rational Options Pricing", *Bell Journal of Economics and Management Science,* 4, pp 141–83.

Merton, R., 1974, "On the Pricing of Corporate Debt: The Risk Structures of Interest Rates", *Journal of Finance,* 29, pp 449–70.

Montagu, C., H. Krause, M. Burgess, R. Jalan, L. Ma and D. Chew, 2012, "What Works in Equity Markets", Citigroup, March 6.

Moody's Investors Service, 2007, "The US Municipal Bond Rating Scale: Mapping to the Global Rating Scale and Assigning Global Scale Ratings to Municipal Obligations", Moody's Public Finance Credit Committee, March.

Moody's Investors Service, 2010, "Corporate Default and Recovery Rates, 1920–2009", February.

Mortimer, A., 2013, "Euromoney Country Risk", Euromoney Institutional Investor.

Murty, K. G., 1988, *Linear Complementarity, Linear and Nonlinear Programming: Sigma Series in Applied Mathematics 3* (Heldermann-Verlag: Berlin).

Neal, L., 1990, *The Rise of Financial Capitalism: International Capital Markets in the Age of Reason* (Cambridge: Cambridge University Press).

Nelson, C. R. and A. F. Siegel, 1987, "Parsimonious Modeling of Yield Curves", *Journal of Business,* 60(4), pp 473–89.

Nocedal, J. and S. Wright, 2006, *Numerical Optimization (2e)* (New York, NY: Springer).

Odom, M. D. and R. Sharda, 1990, "A Neural Network Model for Bankruptcy Prediction", in "Proceedings of the International Joint Conference on Neural Networks, Vol. II", IEEE Neural Networks Council, pp 163–71.

Office of the Comptroller of the Currency, 2012, "12 CFR Parts 1, 5, 16, 28 and 160 [Docket ID OCC–2012–0005] RIN 1557–AD36, Alternatives to the Use of External Credit Ratings in the Regulations of the OCC", *Federal Register,* 77(114), June 13.

Ou, S., D. Chiu and A. Metz, 2012, "Annual Default Study: Corporate Default and Recovery Rates, 1920–2011", Moody's Investors Service, February 29.

Ou, S., D. Chiu, B. Wen and A. Metz, 2013, "Annual Default Study: Corporate Default and Recovery Rates, 1920–2012", Moody's Investors Service, February 28.

Peng, S., 2005, "Special Topic: A Do-it-yourself Guide to Making Your Own Liquidity/Crisis Index (Some Assembly Required)", Citigroup, October 28.

Perry, C., 1995, "Implied Default Probabilities: A New Approach to Risky Debt", CS First Boston, April 26.

Puentes, R., P. Sabol and J. Kane, 2013, "Revive Build America Bonds (BABs) to Support State and Local Investments", The Brookings Institute, August.

Rai, V. and G. Friedlander, 2015, "ECB QE Will Enhance the Spillover Demand for BABs", Citigroup, February 4.

Rai, V., G. Friedlander and J. Muller, 2015, "Yield Rationalizations and Assessing BAB Refunding Possibilities", Citigroup, May 4.

Rosendale, W. H., 1908, "Credit Department Methods", *Bankers' Magazine.*

Roser, R., G. Bonne and C. Smith-Hill, 2013, "StarMine Text Mining Credit Risk Model: Overview and Performance", Thomson Reuters.

Sakia, R. M., 1992, "The Box–Cox Transformation Technique: A Review", *The Statistician,* 41, pp 169–78.

Salomon Brothers, 1994, "Introducing the Salomon Brothers Pension Discount Curve and the Salomon Brothers Pension Liability Index", March.

Salton, G. and M. J. McGill, 1983, *Introduction to Modern Information Retrieval* (New York, NY: McGraw-Hill).

Schuermann, T., 2005, "What Do We Know About Loss Given Default", in E. Altman, A. Resti and A Sironi (Eds), *Recovery Risk* (London: Risk Books).

Schwartz, E. and M. Moon, 2000, "Rational Pricing of Internet Companies", *Financial Analysts Journal,* 56(3), pp 62–75.

Schwarz, G. E., 1978, "Estimating the Dimension of a Model", *Annals of Statistics,* 6(2), pp 461–64.

Sharpe, W. F., 1964, "Capital Asset Prices: A Theory of Market Equilibrium under Conditions of Risk", *Journal of Finance,* 19(3), pp 425–42.

Sharpe, W. F., 1994, "The Sharpe Ratio", *Journal of Portfolio Management,* Fall, pp 49–58.

Sobehart, J., 2005, "Modeling Default Risk Beyond Statistical, Structural and Reduced Form Approaches, Citigroup Risk Architecture", presentation at Advanced Credit Risk Measurement and Modeling Techniques conference, New York, March 14–15.

Sobehart, J. and S. Keenan, 2002, "Hybrid Contingent Claims Models: A Practical Approach to Modeling Default Risk", in M. Ong (Ed), *Credit Ratings: Methodology, Rationale and Default Risk* (London: Risk Books).

Sobehart, J. and S. Keenan, 2003, "Hybrid Probability of Default Models: A Practical Approach to Modeling Default Risk", *Quantitative Credit Analyst,* 3, pp 5–29.

Sobehart, J., S. Keenan and R. Stein, 2000, "Benchmarking Quantitative Default Risk Models: A Validation Methodology", Moody's Risk Management Services.

Sobehart, J., R. Stein, V. Mikityanskaya and L. Li, 2000, "Moody's Public Firm Risk Model: A Hybrid Approach to Modeling Short-Term Default Risk", Moody's Investors Service.

Standard and Poor's, 2008, "Standard and Poor's Extends Recovery Ratings to Unsecured Speculative-Grade Corporate Issuers", *Ratings Direct,* March 21.

Stein, R., 2000, "Evidence on the Incompleteness of Merton-type Structural Models for Default Prediction", Moody's Risk Management Services, January 2.

Stein, R., 2007, "Benchmarking Default Prediction Models: Pitfalls and Remedies in Model Validation", *Journal of Risk Model Validation,* 1(1), pp 77–113.

Su, Y. and T. Benzschawel, 2014, "Credit Markets Quantitative Review: May 2015", Citigroup, June 8.

Sundaresan, S. M., 2000, "Continuous-time Methods in Finance: A Review and an Assessment", *Journal of Finance,* 55(4), pp 1,569–622.

Sylla, R., 2002, "A Historical Primer on the Business of Credit Rating", in R. M Levich, G. Majnoni, and C. Reinhart (Eds), *Ratings, Rating Agencies and the Global Financial System* (Boston, MA: Kluwer Academic Publishers).

Thorton, D., 2009, "What the LIBOR–OIS Spread Says", *Economic Synopses,* 24, Federal Reserve Bank of St. Louis.

Tibshirani, R., 1996, "Regression Shrinkage and Selection via the Lasso", *Journal of the Royal Statistical Society, Series B,* 58(1), pp. 267–88.

Tracy, R., 2014, "U.S. Regulators Tweak Final Liquidity Rule for Large Banks", *Wall Street Journal,* September 3.

Traynor, J. L., 1962, "Toward a Theory of Market Value of Risky Assets", unpublished manuscript, a final version was published in R. A. Korajczyk (Ed), *Asset Pricing and Portfolio Performance: Models, Strategy and Performance Metrics* (London: Risk Books), 1999.

Tudela, M., A. Mediolo, and A. Van Praagh, 2012, "U.S. Municipal Bond Defaults and Recoveries, 1970–2011", Moody's Investors Service, March 7.

Turnbull, S., 2005, "Unresolved Issues in Modeling Credit-Risky Assets", *Journal of Fixed Income,* 15(1), pp 68–87.

Uhlenbeck, G. E. and L. S. Ornstein, 1930, "On the Theory of Brownian Motion", *Physics Review,* 36, pp 823–41.

US Treasury Department, 2011, "Treasury Analysis of Build America Bonds Issuance and Savings", May 16.

Varma, P. and R. Cantor, 2004, "Determinants of Recovery Rates on Defaulted Bonds and Loans for North American Corporate Issuers: 1983–2003", Moody's Investors Service, December.

Vasicek, O., 1984, "Credit Valuation", KMV white paper.

Vasicek, O., 1995, "EDF and Corporate Bond Pricing", KMV.

Vazza, D., D. Aurora and C. Miller, 2007, "U.S. Recovery Study: Liquidity Avalanche Propels Recovery Rates into the Stratosphere", Standard & Poor's, February.

Vazza, D. and R. Khan, 2011, "2010 Annual Global Corporate Default Study and Rating Transitions", Standard & Poor's, March 30.

Vazza, D. and N. Kraemer, 2011, "Default, Transition and Recovery: 2010 Annual Global Corporate Default Study and Rating Transitions", Standard & Poor's, March 30.

Vazza, D. and N. Kraemer, 2012, "Default, Transition, and Recovery: 2011 Annual Global Corporate Default Study and Rating Transitions", Standard & Poor's, March 21.

Vazza, D. and N. Kraemer, 2013, "2012 Annual Global Corporate Default Study and Rating Transitions", Standard and Poor's, March 18.

Verde, M., 2003, "Recovery Rates Return to Historic Norms", Fitch Ratings, September.

Wall, A., 1919, "Study of Credit Biometrics", *Federal Reserve Bulletin,* March, pp 229–43.

Washburn, L., 2002, "Moody's US Municipal Bond Rating Scale", Moody's Investors Service, November.

Wei, D. G. and D. Guo, 1997, "Pricing Risky Debt: An Empirical Comparison of Longstaff and Schwartz and Merton Models", *Journal of Fixed Income,* 7, pp 8–28.-

Index

(page numbers in italics refer to figures and tables)